629.287 GEO 1990-93
Maddox, Robert (Robert
Geo Storm automotive repair

MIDDLETON PUBLIC LIBRARY

3 9078 01875 7188

AUG 0 1 1994

D1408597

Geo Storm Automotive Repair Manual

by Robert Maddox and John H Haynes
Member of the Guild of Motoring Writers

Models covered:
All Geo Storm models
1990 through 1993

ABCDE
FGHIJ
KLMNO
PQRST

Haynes Publishing Group
Sparkford Nr Yeovil
Somerset BA22 7JJ England

Haynes North America, Inc
861 Lawrence Drive
Newbury Park
California 91320 USA

Middleton Public Library
7425 Hubbard Avenue
Middleton, WI 53562

Acknowledgements

The Champion Spark Plug Company supplied the illustrations of various spark plug conditions. Wiring diagrams were provided by Mitchell International. Technical writers who contributed to this project include Larry Warren, Mike Stubblefield and Mark Ryan.

© **Haynes North America, Inc. 1993**

With permission from J.H. Haynes & Co. Ltd.

A book in the Haynes Automotive Repair Manual Series

Printed in the U.S.A.

All rights reserved. No part of this book may be reproduced or transmitted in any form or by any means, electronic or mechanical, including photocopying, recording or by any information storage or retrieval system, without permission in writing from the copyright holder.

ISBN 1 56392 039 5

Library of Congress Catalog Card Number 93-78144

While every attempt is made to ensure that the information in this manual is correct, no liability can be accepted by the authors or publishers for loss, damage or injury caused by any errors in, or omissions from, the information given.

93-264

Contents

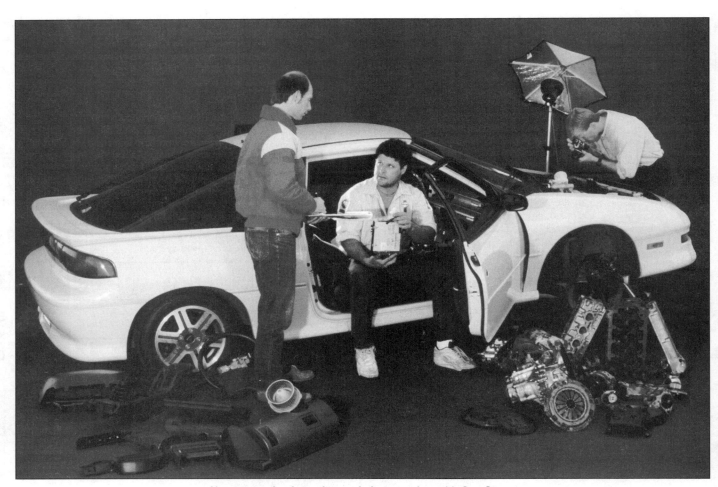

Haynes mechanic, author and photographer with Geo Storm

About this manual

Its purpose

The purpose of this manual is to help you get the best value from your vehicle. It can do so in several ways. It can help you decide what work must be done, even if you choose to have it done by a dealer service department or a repair shop; it provides information and procedures for routine maintenance and servicing; and it offers diagnostic and repair procedures to follow when trouble occurs.

We hope you use the manual to tackle the work yourself. For many simpler jobs, doing it yourself may be quicker than arranging an appointment to get the vehicle into a shop and making the trips to leave it and pick it up. More importantly, a lot of money can be saved by avoiding the expense the shop must pass on to you to cover its labor and overhead costs. An added benefit is the sense of satisfaction and accomplishment that you feel after doing the job yourself.

Using the manual

The manual is divided into Chapters. Each Chapter is divided into numbered Sections, which are headed in bold type between horizontal lines. Each Section consists of consecutively numbered paragraphs.

At the beginning of each numbered Section you will be referred to any illustrations which apply to the procedures in that Section. The reference numbers used in illustration captions pinpoint the pertinent Section and the Step within that Section. That is, illustration 3.2 means the illustration refers to Section 3 and Step (or paragraph) 2 within that Section.

Procedures, once described in the text, are not normally repeated. When it's necessary to refer to another Chapter, the reference will be given as Chapter and Section number. Cross references given without use of the word "Chapter" apply to Sections and/or paragraphs in the same Chapter. For example, "see Section 8" means in the same Chapter.

References to the left or right side of the vehicle assume you are sitting in the driver's seat, facing forward.

Even though we have prepared this manual with extreme care, neither the publisher nor the author can accept responsibility for any errors in, or omissions from, the information given.

NOTE

A **Note** provides information necessary to properly complete a procedure or information which will make the procedure easier to understand.

CAUTION

A **Caution** provides a special procedure or special steps which must be taken while completing the procedure where the Caution is found. Not heeding a Caution can result in damage to the assembly being worked on.

WARNING

A Warning provides a special procedure or special steps which must be taken while completing the procedure where the Warning is found. Not heeding a Warning can result in personal injury.

Introduction to the Geo Storm

Geo Storm models are available in two-door hatchback and lift-back body styles.

The transversely mounted inline four-cylinder engines used in these models are equipped with electronic fuel injection.

The engine drives the front wheels through either a five-speed manual or a three- or four-speed automatic transaxle via independent driveaxles.

Independent suspension, featuring coil spring/strut damper units, is used on all four wheels. The power-assisted rack and pinion steering unit is mounted behind the engine.

The brakes are disc at the front and drums at the rear, with power assist standard.

Vehicle identification numbers

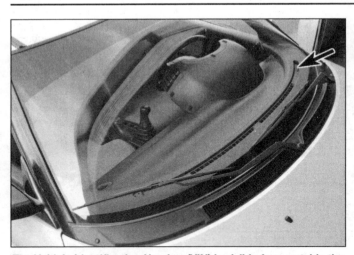

The Vehicle Identification Number (VIN) is visible from outside the vehicle through the driver's side of the windshield

The engine number plate is visible on the cylinder head (arrow)

Modifications are a continuing and unpublicized process in vehicle manufacturing. Since spare parts lists and manuals are compiled on a numerical basis, the individual vehicle numbers are necessary to correctly identify the component required.

Vehicle Identification Number (VIN)

This very important identification number is stamped on a plate attached to the dashboard inside the windshield on the driver's side of the vehicle (see illustration). The VIN also appears on the Vehicle Certificate of Title and Registration. It contains information such as where and when the vehicle was manufactured, the model year and the body style.

Vehicle Certification Label

The Vehicle Certification Label is attached to the driver's side door pillar. Information on this label includes the name of the manufacturer, the month and year of production, the Gross Vehicle Weight Rating (GVWR), the Gross Axle Weight Rating (GAWR) and the certification statement.

Engine number

The engine number is stamped onto a machined pad on the external surface of the engine block. There's also an identification label that's usually on the timing belt cover (see illustration).

Buying parts

Replacement parts are available from many sources, which generally fall into one of two categories - authorized dealer parts departments and independent retail auto parts stores. Our advice concerning these parts is as follows:

Retail auto parts stores: Good auto parts stores will stock frequently needed components which wear out relatively fast, such as clutch components, exhaust systems, brake parts, tune-up parts, etc. These stores often supply new or reconditioned parts on an exchange basis, which can save a considerable amount of money. Discount auto parts stores are often very good places to buy materials and parts needed for general vehicle maintenance such as oil, grease, filters, spark plugs, belts, touch-up paint, bulbs, etc. They also usually sell tools and general accessories, have convenient hours, charge lower prices and can often be found not far from home.

Authorized dealer parts department: This is the best source for parts which are unique to the vehicle and not generally available elsewhere (such as major engine parts, transmission parts, trim pieces, etc.).

Warranty information: If the vehicle is still covered under warranty, be sure that any replacement parts purchased - regardless of the source - do not invalidate the warranty!

To be sure of obtaining the correct parts, have engine and chassis numbers available and, if possible, take the old parts along for positive identification.

Maintenance techniques, tools and working facilities

Maintenance techniques

There are a number of techniques involved in maintenance and repair that will be referred to throughout this manual. Application of these techniques will enable the home mechanic to be more efficient, better organized and capable of performing the various tasks properly, which will ensure that the repair job is thorough and complete.

Fasteners

Fasteners are nuts, bolts, studs and screws used to hold two or more parts together. There are a few things to keep in mind when working with fasteners. Almost all of them use a locking device of some type, either a lockwasher, locknut, locking tab or thread adhesive. All threaded fasteners should be clean and straight, with undamaged threads and undamaged corners on the hex head where the wrench fits. Develop the habit of replacing all damaged nuts and bolts with new ones. Special locknuts with nylon or fiber inserts can only be used once. If they are removed, they lose their locking ability and must be replaced with new ones.

Rusted nuts and bolts should be treated with a penetrating fluid to ease removal and prevent breakage. Some mechanics use turpentine in a spout-type oil can, which works quite well. After applying the rust penetrant, let it work for a few minutes before trying to loosen the nut or bolt. Badly rusted fasteners may have to be chiseled or sawed off or removed with a special nut breaker, available at tool stores.

If a bolt or stud breaks off in an assembly, it can be drilled and removed with a special tool commonly available for this purpose. Most automotive machine shops can perform this task, as well as other repair procedures, such as the repair of threaded holes that have been stripped out.

Flat washers and lockwashers, when removed from an assembly, should always be replaced exactly as removed. Replace any damaged washers with new ones. Never use a lockwasher on any soft metal surface (such as aluminum), thin sheet metal or plastic.

Fastener sizes

For a number of reasons, automobile manufacturers are making wider and wider use of metric fasteners. Therefore, it is important to be able to tell the difference between standard (sometimes called U.S. or SAE) and metric hardware, since they cannot be interchanged.

All bolts, whether standard or metric, are sized according to diameter, thread pitch and length. For example, a standard 1/2 - 13 x 1 bolt is 1/2 inch in diameter, has 13 threads per inch and is 1 inch long. An M12 - 1.75 x 25 metric bolt is 12 mm in diameter, has a thread pitch of 1.75 mm (the distance between threads) and is 25 mm long. The two bolts are nearly identical, and easily confused, but they are not interchangeable.

In addition to the differences in diameter, thread pitch and length, metric and standard bolts can also be distinguished by examining the bolt heads. To begin with, the distance across the flats on a standard bolt head is measured in inches, while the same dimension on a metric bolt is sized in millimeters (the same is true for nuts). As a result, a standard wrench should not be used on a metric bolt and a metric wrench should not be used on a standard bolt. Also, most standard bolts have slashes radiating out from the center of the head to denote the grade or strength of the bolt, which is an indication of the amount of torque that can be applied to it. The greater the number of slashes, the greater the strength of the bolt. Grades 0 through 5 are commonly used on automobiles. Metric bolts have a property class (grade) number, rather than a slash, molded into their heads to indicate bolt strength. In this case, the higher the number, the stronger the bolt. Property class numbers 8.8, 9.8 and 10.9 are commonly used on automobiles.

Strength markings can also be used to distinguish standard hex nuts from metric hex nuts. Many standard nuts have dots stamped into one side, while metric nuts are marked with a number. The greater the number of dots, or the higher the number, the greater the strength of the nut.

Metric studs are also marked on their ends according to property class (grade). Larger studs are numbered (the same as metric bolts), while smaller studs carry a geometric code to denote grade.

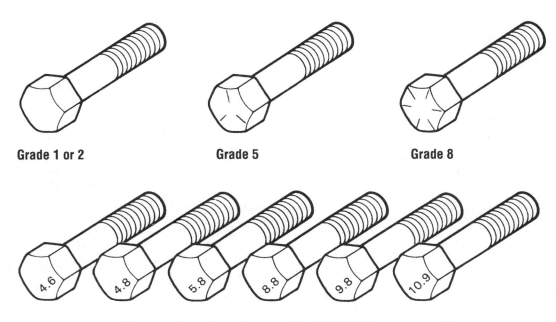

Grade 1 or 2   **Grade 5**   **Grade 8**

Bolt strength markings (top - standard/SAE/USS; bottom - metric)

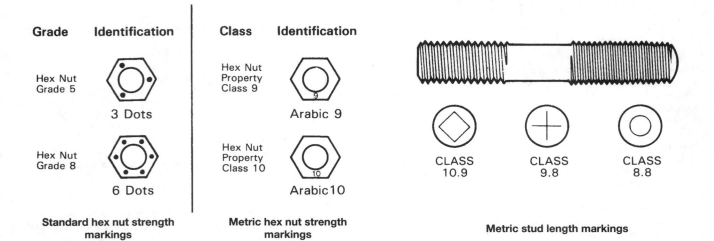

Grade	Identification
Hex Nut Grade 5	3 Dots
Hex Nut Grade 8	6 Dots

Standard hex nut strength markings

Class	Identification
Hex Nut Property Class 9	Arabic 9
Hex Nut Property Class 10	Arabic 10

Metric hex nut strength markings

CLASS 10.9   CLASS 9.8   CLASS 8.8

Metric stud length markings

It should be noted that many fasteners, especially Grades 0 through 2, have no distinguishing marks on them. When such is the case, the only way to determine whether it is standard or metric is to measure the thread pitch or compare it to a known fastener of the same size.

Standard fasteners are often referred to as SAE, as opposed to metric. However, it should be noted that SAE technically refers to a non-metric fine thread fastener only. Coarse thread non-metric fasteners are referred to as USS sizes.

Since fasteners of the same size (both standard and metric) may have different strength ratings, be sure to reinstall any bolts, studs or nuts removed from your vehicle in their original locations. Also, when replacing a fastener with a new one, make sure that the new one has a strength rating equal to or greater than the original.

Tightening sequences and procedures

Most threaded fasteners should be tightened to a specific torque value (torque is the twisting force applied to a threaded component such as a nut or bolt). Overtightening the fastener can weaken it and cause it to break, while undertightening can cause it to eventually come loose. Bolts, screws and studs, depending on the material they are made of and their thread diameters, have specific torque values, many of which are noted in the Specifications at the beginning of each Chapter. Be sure to follow the torque recommendations closely. For fasteners not assigned a specific torque, a general torque value chart is presented here as a guide. These torque values are for dry (unlubricated) fasteners threaded into steel or cast iron (not aluminum). As was previously mentioned, the size and grade of a fastener determine the amount of torque that can safely be applied to it. The figures listed

Metric thread sizes	Ft-lbs	Nm
M-6	6 to 9	9 to 12
M-8	14 to 21	19 to 28
M-10	28 to 40	38 to 54
M-12	50 to 71	68 to 96
M-14	80 to 140	109 to 154

Pipe thread sizes		
1/8	5 to 8	7 to 10
1/4	12 to 18	17 to 24
3/8	22 to 33	30 to 44
1/2	25 to 35	34 to 47

U.S. thread sizes		
1/4 - 20	6 to 9	9 to 12
5/16 - 18	12 to 18	17 to 24
5/16 - 24	14 to 20	19 to 27
3/8 - 16	22 to 32	30 to 43
3/8 - 24	27 to 38	37 to 51
7/16 - 14	40 to 55	55 to 74
7/16 - 20	40 to 60	55 to 81
1/2 - 13	55 to 80	75 to 108

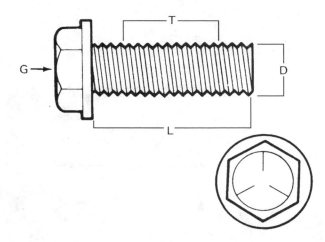

Standard (SAE and USS) bolt dimensions/grade marks

G   Grade marks (bolt length)
L   Length (in inches)
T   Thread pitch (number of threads per inch)
D   Nominal diameter (in inches)

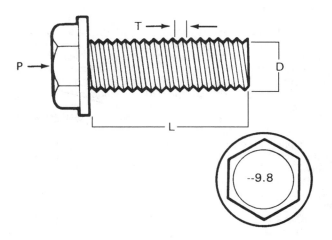

Metric bolt dimensions/grade marks

P   Property class (bolt strength)
L   Length (in millimeters)
T   Thread pitch (distance between threads in millimeters)
D   Diameter

here are approximate for Grade 2 and Grade 3 fasteners. Higher grades can tolerate higher torque values.

Fasteners laid out in a pattern, such as cylinder head bolts, oil pan bolts, differential cover bolts, etc., must be loosened or tightened in sequence to avoid warping the component. This sequence will normally be shown in the appropriate Chapter. If a specific pattern is not given, the following procedures can be used to prevent warping.

Initially, the bolts or nuts should be assembled finger-tight only. Next, they should be tightened one full turn each, in a criss-cross or diagonal pattern. After each one has been tightened one full turn, return to the first one and tighten them all one-half turn, following the same pattern. Finally, tighten each of them one-quarter turn at a time until each fastener has been tightened to the proper torque. To loosen and remove the fasteners, the procedure would be reversed.

Component disassembly

Component disassembly should be done with care and purpose to help ensure that the parts go back together properly. Always keep track of the sequence in which parts are removed. Make note of special characteristics or marks on parts that can be installed more than one way, such as a grooved thrust washer on a shaft. It is a good idea to lay the disassembled parts out on a clean surface in the order that they were removed. It may also be helpful to make sketches or take instant photos of components before removal.

When removing fasteners from a component, keep track of their locations. Sometimes threading a bolt back in a part, or putting the washers and nut back on a stud, can prevent mix-ups later. If nuts and bolts cannot be returned to their original locations, they should be kept in a compartmented box or a series of small boxes. A cupcake or muffin tin is ideal for this purpose, since each cavity can hold the bolts and nuts from a particular area (i.e. oil pan bolts, valve cover bolts, engine mount bolts, etc.). A pan of this type is especially helpful when working on assemblies with very small parts, such as the carburetor, alternator, valve train or interior dash and trim pieces. The cavities can be marked with paint or tape to identify the contents.

Whenever wiring looms, harnesses or connectors are separated, it is a good idea to identify the two halves with numbered pieces of masking tape so they can be easily reconnected.

Gasket sealing surfaces

Throughout any vehicle, gaskets are used to seal the mating surfaces between two parts and keep lubricants, fluids, vacuum or pressure contained in an assembly.

Many times these gaskets are coated with a liquid or paste-type gasket sealing compound before assembly. Age, heat and pressure can sometimes cause the two parts to stick together so tightly that they are very difficult to separate. Often, the assembly can be loosened by striking it with a soft-face hammer near the mating surfaces. A regular hammer can be used if a block of wood is placed between the hammer and the part. Do not hammer on cast parts or parts that could be easily damaged. With any particularly stubborn part, always recheck to make sure that every fastener has been removed.

Avoid using a screwdriver or bar to pry apart an assembly, as they can easily mar the gasket sealing surfaces of the parts, which must remain smooth. If prying is absolutely necessary, use an old broom handle, but keep in mind that extra clean up will be necessary if the wood splinters.

After the parts are separated, the old gasket must be carefully scraped off and the gasket surfaces cleaned. Stubborn gasket material can be soaked with rust penetrant or treated with a special chemical to soften it so it can be easily scraped off. A scraper can be fashioned from a piece of copper tubing by flattening and sharpening one end. Copper is recommended because it is usually softer than the surfaces to be scraped, which reduces the chance of gouging the part. Some gaskets can be removed with a wire brush, but regardless of the method used, the mating surfaces must be left clean and smooth. If for some reason the gasket surface is gouged, then a gasket sealer thick enough to fill scratches will have to be used during reassembly of the components. For most applications, a non-drying (or semi-drying) gasket sealer should be used.

Hose removal tips

Warning: *If the vehicle is equipped with air conditioning, do not disconnect any of the A/C hoses without first having the system depressurized by a dealer service department or a service station.*

Hose removal precautions closely parallel gasket removal precautions. Avoid scratching or gouging the surface that the hose mates against or the connection may leak. This is especially true for radiator hoses. Because of various chemical reactions, the rubber in hoses can bond itself to the metal spigot that the hose fits over. To remove a hose, first loosen the hose clamps that secure it to the spigot. Then, with slip-joint pliers, grab the hose at the clamp and rotate it around the spigot. Work it back and forth until it is completely free, then pull it off. Silicone or other lubricants will ease removal if they can be applied between the hose and the outside of the spigot. Apply the same lubricant to the inside of the hose and the outside of the spigot to simplify installation.

As a last resort (and if the hose is to be replaced with a new one anyway), the rubber can be slit with a knife and the hose peeled from the spigot. If this must be done, be careful that the metal connection is not damaged.

If a hose clamp is broken or damaged, do not reuse it. Wire-type clamps usually weaken with age, so it is a good idea to replace them with screw-type clamps whenever a hose is removed.

Tools

A selection of good tools is a basic requirement for anyone who plans to maintain and repair his or her own vehicle. For the owner who has few tools, the initial investment might seem high, but when compared to the spiraling costs of professional auto maintenance and repair, it is a wise one.

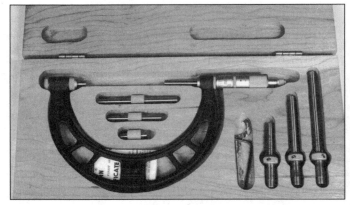

Micrometer set

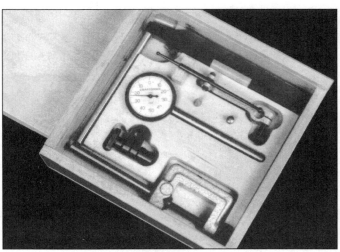

Dial indicator set

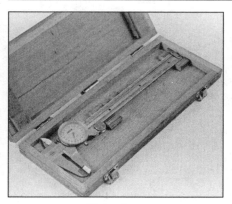

Dial caliper

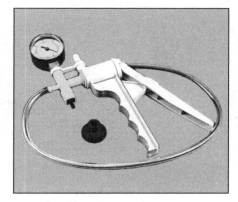

Hand-operated vacuum pump

Timing light

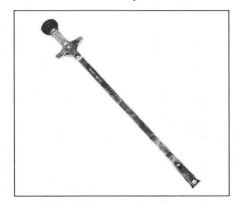

Compression gauge with spark plug
hole adapter

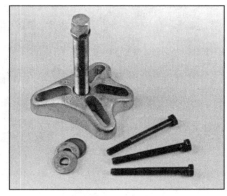

Damper/steering wheel puller

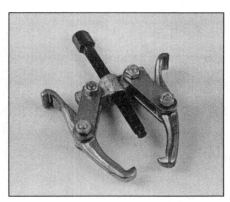

General purpose puller

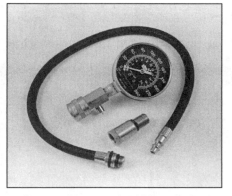

Hydraulic lifter removal tool

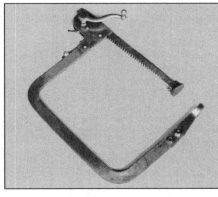

Valve spring compressor

Valve spring compressor

Ridge reamer

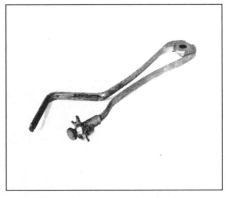

Piston ring groove cleaning tool

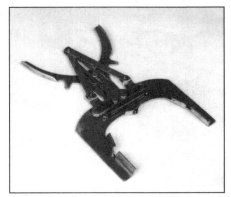

Ring removal/installation tool

Ring compressor

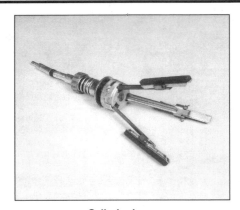

Cylinder hone

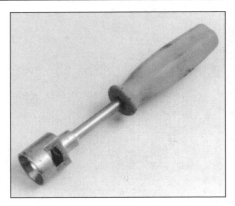

Brake hold-down spring tool

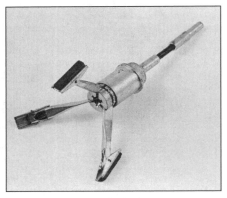

Brake cylinder hone

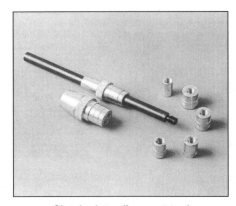

Clutch plate alignment tool

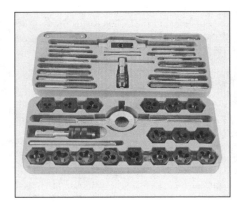

Tap and die set

To help the owner decide which tools are needed to perform the tasks detailed in this manual, the following tool lists are offered: *Maintenance and minor repair, Repair/overhaul* and *Special.*

The newcomer to practical mechanics should start off with the *maintenance and minor repair* tool kit, which is adequate for the simpler jobs performed on a vehicle. Then, as confidence and experience grow, the owner can tackle more difficult tasks, buying additional tools as they are needed. Eventually the basic kit will be expanded into the *repair and overhaul* tool set. Over a period of time, the experienced do-it-yourselfer will assemble a tool set complete enough for most repair and overhaul procedures and will add tools from the special category when it is felt that the expense is justified by the frequency of use.

Maintenance and minor repair tool kit

The tools in this list should be considered the minimum required for performance of routine maintenance, servicing and minor repair work. We recommend the purchase of combination wrenches (box-end and open-end combined in one wrench). While more expensive than open end wrenches, they offer the advantages of both types of wrench.

Combination wrench set (1/4-inch to 1 inch or 6 mm to 19 mm)
Adjustable wrench, 8 inch
Spark plug wrench with rubber insert
Spark plug gap adjusting tool
Feeler gauge set
Brake bleeder wrench
Standard screwdriver (5/16-inch x 6 inch)
Phillips screwdriver (No. 2 x 6 inch)
Combination pliers - 6 inch
Hacksaw and assortment of blades
Tire pressure gauge
Grease gun
Oil can
Fine emery cloth
Wire brush

Battery post and cable cleaning tool
Oil filter wrench
Funnel (medium size)
Safety goggles
Jackstands (2)
Drain pan

Note: *If basic tune-ups are going to be part of routine maintenance, it will be necessary to purchase a good quality stroboscopic timing light and combination tachometer/dwell meter. Although they are included in the list of special tools, it is mentioned here because they are absolutely necessary for tuning most vehicles properly.*

Repair and overhaul tool set

These tools are essential for anyone who plans to perform major repairs and are in addition to those in the maintenance and minor repair tool kit. Included is a comprehensive set of sockets which, though expensive, are invaluable because of their versatility, especially when various extensions and drives are available. We recommend the 1/2-inch drive over the 3/8-inch drive. Although the larger drive is bulky and more expensive, it has the capacity of accepting a very wide range of large sockets. Ideally, however, the mechanic should have a 3/8-inch drive set and a 1/2-inch drive set.

Socket set(s)
Reversible ratchet
Extension - 10 inch
Universal joint
Torque wrench (same size drive as sockets)
Ball peen hammer - 8 ounce
Soft-face hammer (plastic/rubber)
Standard screwdriver (1/4-inch x 6 inch)
Standard screwdriver (stubby - 5/16-inch)
Phillips screwdriver (No. 3 x 8 inch)
Phillips screwdriver (stubby - No. 2)
Pliers - vise grip
Pliers - lineman's

Pliers - needle nose
Pliers - snap-ring (internal and external)
Cold chisel - 1/2-inch
Scribe
Scraper (made from flattened copper tubing)
Centerpunch
Pin punches (1/16, 1/8, 3/16-inch)
Steel rule/straightedge - 12 inch
Allen wrench set (1/8 to 3/8-inch or 4 mm to 10 mm)
A selection of files
Wire brush (large)
Jackstands (second set)
Jack (scissor or hydraulic type)

Note: *Another tool which is often useful is an electric drill with a chuck capacity of 3/8-inch and a set of good quality drill bits*

Special tools

The tools in this list include those which are not used regularly, are expensive to buy, or which need to be used in accordance with their manufacturer's instructions. Unless these tools will be used frequently, it is not very economical to purchase many of them. A consideration would be to split the cost and use between yourself and a friend or friends. In addition, most of these tools can be obtained from a tool rental shop on a temporary basis.

This list primarily contains only those tools and instruments widely available to the public, and not those special tools produced by the vehicle manufacturer for distribution to dealer service departments. Occasionally, references to the manufacturer's special tools are included in the text of this manual. Generally, an alternative method of doing the job without the special tool is offered. However, sometimes there is no alternative to their use. Where this is the case, and the tool cannot be purchased or borrowed, the work should be turned over to the dealer service department or an automotive repair shop.

Valve spring compressor
Piston ring groove cleaning tool
Piston ring compressor
Piston ring installation tool
Cylinder compression gauge
Cylinder ridge reamer
Cylinder surfacing hone
Cylinder bore gauge
Micrometers and/or dial calipers
Hydraulic lifter removal tool
Balljoint separator
Universal-type puller
Impact screwdriver
Dial indicator set
Stroboscopic timing light (inductive pick-up)
Hand operated vacuum/pressure pump
Tachometer/dwell meter
Universal electrical multimeter
Cable hoist
Brake spring removal and installation tools
Floor jack

Buying tools

For the do-it-yourselfer who is just starting to get involved in vehicle maintenance and repair, there are a number of options available when purchasing tools. If maintenance and minor repair is the extent of the work to be done, the purchase of individual tools is satisfactory. If, on the other hand, extensive work is planned, it would be a good idea to purchase a modest tool set from one of the large retail chain stores. A set can usually be bought at a substantial savings over the individual

tool prices, and they often come with a tool box. As additional tools are needed, add-on sets, individual tools and a larger tool box can be purchased to expand the tool selection. Building a tool set gradually allows the cost of the tools to be spread over a longer period of time and gives the mechanic the freedom to choose only those tools that will actually be used.

Tool stores will often be the only source of some of the special tools that are needed, but regardless of where tools are bought, try to avoid cheap ones, especially when buying screwdrivers and sockets, because they won't last very long. The expense involved in replacing cheap tools will eventually be greater than the initial cost of quality tools.

Care and maintenance of tools

Good tools are expensive, so it makes sense to treat them with respect. Keep them clean and in usable condition and store them properly when not in use. Always wipe off any dirt, grease or metal chips before putting them away. Never leave tools lying around in the work area. Upon completion of a job, always check closely under the hood for tools that may have been left there so they won't get lost during a test drive.

Some tools, such as screwdrivers, pliers, wrenches and sockets, can be hung on a panel mounted on the garage or workshop wall, while others should be kept in a tool box or tray. Measuring instruments, gauges, meters, etc. must be carefully stored where they cannot be damaged by weather or impact from other tools.

When tools are used with care and stored properly, they will last a very long time. Even with the best of care, though, tools will wear out if used frequently. When a tool is damaged or worn out, replace it. Subsequent jobs will be safer and more enjoyable if you do.

Working facilities

Not to be overlooked when discussing tools is the workshop. If anything more than routine maintenance is to be carried out, some sort of suitable work area is essential.

It is understood, and appreciated, that many home mechanics do not have a good workshop or garage available, and end up removing an engine or doing major repairs outside. It is recommended, however, that the overhaul or repair be completed under the cover of a roof.

A clean, flat workbench or table of comfortable working height is an absolute necessity. The workbench should be equipped with a vise that has a jaw opening of at least four inches.

As mentioned previously, some clean, dry storage space is also required for tools, as well as the lubricants, fluids, cleaning solvents, etc. which soon become necessary.

Sometimes waste oil and fluids, drained from the engine or cooling system during normal maintenance or repairs, present a disposal problem. To avoid pouring them on the ground or into a sewage system, pour the used fluids into large containers, seal them with caps and take them to an authorized disposal site or recycling center. Plastic jugs, such as old antifreeze containers, are ideal for this purpose.

Always keep a supply of old newspapers and clean rags available. Old towels are excellent for mopping up spills. Many mechanics use rolls of paper towels for most work because they are readily available and disposable. To help keep the area under the vehicle clean, a large cardboard box can be cut open and flattened to protect the garage or shop floor.

Whenever working over a painted surface, such as when leaning over a fender to service something under the hood, always cover it with an old blanket or bedspread to protect the finish. Vinyl covered pads, made especially for this purpose, are available at auto parts stores.

Jacking and towing

Jacking

Warning: *The jack supplied with the vehicle should only be used for changing a tire or placing jackstands under the frame. Never work under the vehicle or start the engine while this jack is being used as the only means of support.*

The vehicle should be on level ground. Place the shift lever in Park, if you have an automatic, or Reverse if you have a manual transaxle. Block the wheel diagonally opposite the wheel being changed. Set the parking brake.

Remove the spare tire and jack from stowage. Remove the wheel cover and trim ring (if so equipped) with the tapered end of the lug nut wrench by inserting and twisting the handle and then prying against the back of the wheel cover. Loosen, but do not remove, the lug nuts (one-half turn is sufficient).

Place the scissors-type jack under the side of the vehicle and adjust the jack height until it fits between the notches in the vertical rocker panel flange nearest the wheel to be changed. There is a front and rear jacking point on each side of the vehicle **(see illustration)**.

Turn the jack handle clockwise until the tire clears the ground. Remove the lug nuts and pull the wheel off. Replace it with the spare.

Install the lug nuts with the beveled edges facing in. Tighten them snugly. Don't attempt to tighten them completely until the vehicle is lowered or it could slip off the jack. Turn the jack handle counterclockwise to lower the vehicle. Remove the jack and tighten the lug nuts in a criss-cross pattern.

Install the cover (and trim ring, if used) and be sure it's snapped into place all the way around.

Stow the tire, jack and wrench. Unblock the wheels.

Towing

As a general rule, the vehicle should be towed with the front (drive) wheels off the ground. If they can't be raised, place them on a dolly. The ignition key must be in the OFF position, since the steering lock mechanism isn't strong enough to hold the front wheels straight while towing.

Vehicles equipped with an automatic transaxle can be towed from the front only with all four wheels on the ground, provided that speeds

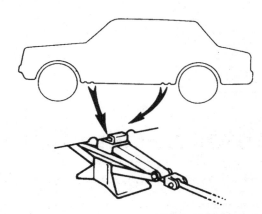

The jack fits between the notches near the wheels on each side of the vehicle

don't exceed 30 mph and the distance is not over 50 miles. Before towing, check the transmission fluid level (see Chapter 1). If the level is below the HOT line on the dipstick, add fluid or use a towing dolly. Release the parking brake, put the transaxle in Neutral and place the ignition key in the OFF position. **Caution:** *Never tow a vehicle with an automatic transaxle from the rear with the front wheels on the ground.*

When towing a vehicle equipped with a manual transaxle with all four wheels on the ground, be sure to place the shift lever in neutral and release the parking brake.

Equipment specifically designed for towing should be used. It should be attached to the main structural members of the vehicle, not the bumpers or brackets.

Safety is a major consideration when towing and all applicable state and local laws must be obeyed. A safety chain system must be used at all times. Remember that power steering and power brakes will not work with the engine off.

Booster battery (jump) starting

Observe these precautions when using a booster battery to start a vehicle:

  a) Before connecting the booster battery, make sure the ignition switch is in the Off position.
  b) Turn off the lights, heater and other electrical loads.
  c) Your eyes should be shielded. Safety goggles are a good idea.
  d) Make sure the booster battery is the same voltage as the dead one in the vehicle.
  e) The two vehicles MUST NOT TOUCH each other!
  f) Make sure the transaxle is in Neutral (manual) or Park (automatic).
  g) If the booster battery is not a maintenance-free type, remove the vent caps and lay a cloth over the vent holes.

Connect the red jumper cable to the positive (+) terminals of each battery **(see illustration)**.

Connect one end of the black jumper cable to the negative (-) terminal of the booster battery. The other end of this cable should be connected to a good ground on the vehicle to be started, such as a bolt or bracket on the body.

Start the engine using the booster battery, then, with the engine running at idle speed, disconnect the jumper cables in the reverse order of connection.

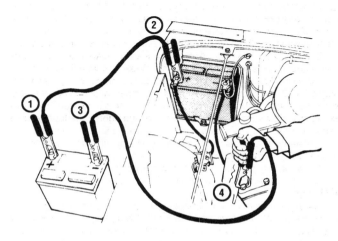

Make the booster battery cable connections in the numerical order shown (note that the negative cable of the booster battery is NOT attached to the negative terminal of the dead battery)

Automotive chemicals and lubricants

A number of automotive chemicals and lubricants are available for use during vehicle maintenance and repair. They include a wide variety of products ranging from cleaning solvents and degreasers to lubricants and protective sprays for rubber, plastic and vinyl.

Cleaners

Carburetor cleaner and choke cleaner is a strong solvent for gum, varnish and carbon. Most carburetor cleaners leave a dry-type lubricant film which will not harden or gum up. Because of this film it is not recommended for use on electrical components

Brake system cleaner is used to remove grease and brake fluid from the brake system, where clean surfaces are absolutely necessary. It leaves no residue and often eliminates brake squeal caused by contaminants.

Electrical cleaner removes oxidation, corrosion and carbon deposits from electrical contacts, restoring full current flow. It can also be used to clean spark plugs, carburetor jets, voltage regulators and other parts where an oil-free surface is desired.

Demoisturants remove water and moisture from electrical components such as alternators, voltage regulators, electrical connectors and fuse blocks. They are non-conductive, non-corrosive and non-flammable.

Degreasers are heavy-duty solvents used to remove grease from the outside of the engine and from chassis components. They can be sprayed or brushed on and, depending on the type, are rinsed off either with water or solvent.

Lubricants

Motor oil is the lubricant formulated for use in engines. It normally contains a wide variety of additives to prevent corrosion and reduce foaming and wear. Motor oil comes in various weights (viscosity ratings) from 5 to 80. The recommended weight of the oil depends on the season, temperature and the demands on the engine. Light oil is used in cold climates and under light load conditions. Heavy oil is used in hot climates and where high loads are encountered. Multi-viscosity oils are designed to have characteristics of both light and heavy oils and are available in a number of weights from 5W-20 to 20W-50.

Gear oil is designed to be used in differentials, manual transmissions and other areas where high-temperature lubrication is required.

Chassis and wheel bearing grease is a heavy grease used where increased loads and friction are encountered, such as for wheel bearings, balljoints, tie-rod ends and universal joints.

High-temperature wheel bearing grease is designed to withstand the extreme temperatures encountered by wheel bearings in disc brake equipped vehicles. It usually contains molybdenum disulfide (moly), which is a dry-type lubricant.

White grease is a heavy grease for metal-to-metal applications where water is a problem. White grease stays soft under both low and high temperatures (usually from -100 to +190-degrees F), and will not wash off or dilute in the presence of water.

Assembly lube is a special extreme pressure lubricant, usually containing moly, used to lubricate high-load parts (such as main and rod bearings and cam lobes) for initial start-up of a new engine. The assembly lube lubricates the parts without being squeezed out or washed away until the engine oiling system begins to function.

Silicone lubricants are used to protect rubber, plastic, vinyl and nylon parts.

Graphite lubricants are used where oils cannot be used due to contamination problems, such as in locks. The dry graphite will lubricate metal parts while remaining uncontaminated by dirt, water, oil or acids. It is electrically conductive and will not foul electrical contacts in locks such as the ignition switch.

Moly penetrants loosen and lubricate frozen, rusted and corroded fasteners and prevent future rusting or freezing.

Heat-sink grease is a special electrically non-conductive grease that is used for mounting electronic ignition modules where it is essential that heat is transferred away from the module.

Sealants

RTV sealant is one of the most widely used gasket compounds. Made from silicone, RTV is air curing, it seals, bonds, waterproofs, fills surface irregularities, remains flexible, doesn't shrink, is relatively easy to remove, and is used as a supplementary sealer with almost all low and medium temperature gaskets.

Anaerobic sealant is much like RTV in that it can be used either to seal gaskets or to form gaskets by itself. It remains flexible, is solvent resistant and fills surface imperfections. The difference between an anaerobic sealant and an RTV-type sealant is in the curing. RTV cures when exposed to air, while an anaerobic sealant cures only in the absence of air. This means that an anaerobic sealant cures only after the assembly of parts, sealing them together.

Thread and pipe sealant is used for sealing hydraulic and pneumatic fittings and vacuum lines. It is usually made from a Teflon compound, and comes in a spray, a paint-on liquid and as a wrap-around tape.

Chemicals

Anti-seize compound prevents seizing, galling, cold welding, rust and corrosion in fasteners. High-temperature ant-seize, usually made with copper and graphite lubricants, is used for exhaust system and exhaust manifold bolts.

Anaerobic locking compounds are used to keep fasteners from vibrating or working loose and cure only after installation, in the absence of air. Medium strength locking compound is used for small nuts, bolts and screws that may be removed later. High-strength locking compound is for large nuts, bolts and studs which aren't removed on a regular basis.

Oil additives range from viscosity index improvers to chemical treatments that claim to reduce internal engine friction. It should be noted that most oil manufacturers caution against using additives with their oils.

Gas additives perform several functions, depending on their chemical makeup. They usually contain solvents that help dissolve gum and varnish that build up on carburetor, fuel injection and intake parts. They also serve to break down carbon deposits that form on the inside surfaces of the combustion chambers. Some additives contain upper cylinder lubricants for valves and piston rings, and others contain chemicals to remove condensation from the gas tank.

Miscellaneous

Brake fluid is specially formulated hydraulic fluid that can withstand the heat and pressure encountered in brake systems. Care must be taken so this fluid does not come in contact with painted surfaces or plastics. An opened container should always be resealed to prevent contamination by water or dirt.

Weatherstrip adhesive is used to bond weatherstripping around doors, windows and trunk lids. It is sometimes used to attach trim pieces.

Undercoating is a petroleum-based, tar-like substance that is designed to protect metal surfaces on the underside of the vehicle from corrosion. It also acts as a sound-deadening agent by insulating the bottom of the vehicle.

Waxes and polishes are used to help protect painted and plated surfaces from the weather. Different types of paint may require the use of different types of wax and polish. Some polishes utilize a chemical or abrasive cleaner to help remove the top layer of oxidized (dull) paint on older vehicles. In recent years many non-wax polishes that contain a wide variety of chemicals such as polymers and silicones have been introduced. These non-wax polishes are usually easier to apply and last longer than conventional waxes and polishes.

Safety first

Regardless of how enthusiastic you may be about getting on with the job at hand, take the time to ensure that your safety is not jeopardized. A moment's lack of attention can result in an accident, as can failure to observe certain simple safety precautions. The possibility of an accident will always exist, and the following points should not be considered a comprehensive list of all dangers. Rather, they are intended to make you aware of the risks and to encourage a safety conscious approach to all work you carry out on your vehicle.

Essential DOs and DON'Ts

DON'T rely on a jack when working under the vehicle. Always use approved jackstands to support the weight of the vehicle and place them under the recommended lift or support points.

DON'T attempt to loosen extremely tight fasteners (i.e. wheel lug nuts) while the vehicle is on a jack - it may fall.

DON'T start the engine without first making sure that the transmission is in Neutral (or Park where applicable) and the parking brake is set.

DON'T remove the radiator cap from a hot cooling system - let it cool or cover it with a cloth and release the pressure gradually.

DON'T attempt to drain the engine oil until you are sure it has cooled to the point that it will not burn you.

DON'T touch any part of the engine or exhaust system until it has cooled sufficiently to avoid burns.

DON'T siphon toxic liquids such as gasoline, antifreeze and brake fluid by mouth, or allow them to remain on your skin.

DON'T inhale brake lining dust - it is potentially hazardous (see *Asbestos* below)

DON'T allow spilled oil or grease to remain on the floor - wipe it up before someone slips on it.

DON'T use loose fitting wrenches or other tools which may slip and cause injury.

DON'T push on wrenches when loosening or tightening nuts or bolts. Always try to pull the wrench toward you. If the situation calls for pushing the wrench away, push with an open hand to avoid scraped knuckles if the wrench should slip.

DON'T attempt to lift a heavy component alone - get someone to help you.

DON'T rush or take unsafe shortcuts to finish a job.

DON'T allow children or animals in or around the vehicle while you are working on it.

DO wear eye protection when using power tools such as a drill, sander, bench grinder, etc. and when working under a vehicle.

DO keep loose clothing and long hair well out of the way of moving parts.

DO make sure that any hoist used has a safe working load rating adequate for the job.

DO get someone to check on you periodically when working alone on a vehicle.

DO carry out work in a logical sequence and make sure that everything is correctly assembled and tightened.

DO keep chemicals and fluids tightly capped and out of the reach of children and pets.

DO remember that your vehicle's safety affects that of yourself and others. If in doubt on any point, get professional advice.

Asbestos

Certain friction, insulating, sealing, and other products - such as brake linings, brake bands, clutch linings, torque converters, gaskets, etc. - contain asbestos. Extreme care must be taken to avoid inhalation of dust from such products, since it is hazardous to health. If in doubt, assume that they do contain asbestos.

Fire

Remember at all times that gasoline is highly flammable. Never smoke or have any kind of open flame around when working on a vehicle. But the risk does not end there. A spark caused by an electrical short circuit, by two metal surfaces contacting each other, or even by static electricity built up in your body under certain conditions, can ignite gasoline vapors, which in a confined space are highly explosive. Do not, under any circumstances, use gasoline for cleaning parts. Use an approved safety solvent.

Always disconnect the battery ground (-) cable at the battery before working on any part of the fuel system or electrical system. Never risk spilling fuel on a hot engine or exhaust component. It is strongly recommended that a fire extinguisher suitable for use on fuel and electrical fires be kept handy in the garage or workshop at all times. Never try to extinguish a fuel or electrical fire with water.

Fumes

Certain fumes are highly toxic and can quickly cause unconsciousness and even death if inhaled to any extent. Gasoline vapor falls into this category, as do the vapors from some cleaning solvents. Any draining or pouring of such volatile fluids should be done in a well ventilated area.

When using cleaning fluids and solvents, read the instructions on the container carefully. Never use materials from unmarked containers.

Never run the engine in an enclosed space, such as a garage. Exhaust fumes contain carbon monoxide, which is extremely poisonous. If you need to run the engine, always do so in the open air, or at least have the rear of the vehicle outside the work area.

If you are fortunate enough to have the use of an inspection pit, never drain or pour gasoline and never run the engine while the vehicle is over the pit. The fumes, being heavier than air, will concentrate in the pit with possibly lethal results.

The battery

Never create a spark or allow a bare light bulb near a battery. They normally give off a certain amount of hydrogen gas, which is highly explosive.

Always disconnect the battery ground (-) cable at the battery before working on the fuel or electrical systems.

If possible, loosen the filler caps or cover when charging the battery from an external source (this does not apply to sealed or maintenance-free batteries). Do not charge at an excessive rate or the battery may burst.

Take care when adding water to a non maintenance-free battery and when carrying a battery. The electrolyte, even when diluted, is very corrosive and should not be allowed to contact clothing or skin.

Always wear eye protection when cleaning the battery to prevent the caustic deposits from entering your eyes.

Household current

When using an electric power tool, inspection light, etc., which operates on household current, always make sure that the tool is correctly connected to its plug and that, where necessary, it is properly grounded. Do not use such items in damp conditions and, again, do not create a spark or apply excessive heat in the vicinity of fuel or fuel vapor.

Secondary ignition system voltage

A severe electric shock can result from touching certain parts of the ignition system (such as the spark plug wires) when the engine is running or being cranked, particularly if components are damp or the insulation is defective. In the case of an electronic ignition system, the secondary system voltage is much higher and could prove fatal.

Conversion factors

Length (distance)

Inches (in)	X	25.4	= Millimetres (mm)	X 0.0394	= Inches (in)
Feet (ft)	X	0.305	= Metres (m)	X 3.281	= Feet (ft)
Miles	X	1.609	= Kilometres (km)	X 0.621	= Miles

Volume (capacity)

Cubic inches (cu in; in³)	X	16.387	= Cubic centimetres (cc; cm³)	X 0.061	= Cubic inches (cu in; in³)
Imperial pints (Imp pt)	X	0.568	= Litres (l)	X 1.76	= Imperial pints (Imp pt)
Imperial quarts (Imp qt)	X	1.137	= Litres (l)	X 0.88	= Imperial quarts (Imp qt)
Imperial quarts (Imp qt)	X	1.201	= US quarts (US qt)	X 0.833	= Imperial quarts (Imp qt)
US quarts (US qt)	X	0.946	= Litres (l)	X 1.057	= US quarts (US qt)
Imperial gallons (Imp gal)	X	4.546	= Litres (l)	X 0.22	= Imperial gallons (Imp gal)
Imperial gallons (Imp gal)	X	1.201	= US gallons (US gal)	X 0.833	= Imperial gallons (Imp gal)
US gallons (US gal)	X	3.785	= Litres (l)	X 0.264	= US gallons (US gal)

Mass (weight)

Ounces (oz)	X	28.35	= Grams (g)	X 0.035	Ounces (oz)
Pounds (lb)	X	0.454	= Kilograms (kg)	X 2.205	= Pounds (lb)

Force

Ounces-force (ozf; oz)	X	0.278	= Newtons (N)	X 3.6	= Ounces-force (ozf; oz)
Pounds-force (lbf; lb)	X	4.448	= Newtons (N)	X 0.225	= Pounds-force (lbf; lb)
Newtons (N)	X	0.1	= Kilograms-force (kgf; kg)	X 9.81	= Newtons (N)

Pressure

Pounds-force per square inch (psi; lbf/in²; lb/in²)	X	0.070	= Kilograms-force per square centimetre (kgf/cm²; kg/cm²)	X 14.223	= Pounds-force per square inch (psi; lbf/in²; lb/in²)
Pounds-force per square inch (psi; lbf/in²; lb/in²)	X	0.068	= Atmospheres (atm)	X 14.696	= Pounds-force per square inch (psi; lbf/in²; lb/in²)
Pounds-force per square inch (psi; lbf/in²; lb/in²)	X	0.069	= Bars	X 14.5	= Pounds-force per square inch (psi; lbf/in²; lb/in²)
Pounds-force per square inch (psi; lbf/in²; lb/in²)	X	6.895	= Kilopascals (kPa)	X 0.145	= Pounds-force per square inch (psi; lbf/in²; lb/in²)
Kilopascals (kPa)	X	0.01	= Kilograms-force per square centimetre (kgf/cm²; kg/cm²)	X 98.1	= Kilopascals (kPa)

Torque (moment of force)

Pounds-force inches (lbf in; lb in)	X	1.152	= Kilograms-force centimetre (kgf cm; kg cm)	X 0.868	= Pounds-force inches (lbf in; lb in)
Pounds-force inches (lbf in; lb in)	X	0.113	= Newton metres (Nm)	X 8.85	= Pounds-force inches (lbf in; lb in)
Pounds-force inches (lbf in; lb in)	X	0.083	= Pounds-force feet (lbf ft; lb ft)	X 12	= Pounds-force inches (lbf in; lb in)
Pounds-force feet (lbf ft; lb ft)	X	0.138	= Kilograms-force metres (kgf m; kg m)	X 7.233	= Pounds-force feet (lbf ft; lb ft)
Pounds-force feet (lbf ft; lb ft)	X	1.356	= Newton metres (Nm)	X 0.738	= Pounds-force feet (lbf ft; lb ft)
Newton metres (Nm)	X	0.102	= Kilograms-force metres (kgf m; kg m)	X 9.804	= Newton metres (Nm)

Power

Horsepower (hp)	X	745.7	= Watts (W)	X 0.0013	= Horsepower (hp)

Velocity (speed)

Miles per hour (miles/hr; mph)	X	1.609	= Kilometres per hour (km/hr; kph)	X 0.621	= Miles per hour (miles/hr; mph)

Fuel consumption*

Miles per gallon, Imperial (mpg)	X	0.354	= Kilometres per litre (km/l)	X 2.825	= Miles per gallon, Imperial (mpg)
Miles per gallon, US (mpg)	X	0.425	= Kilometres per litre (km/l)	X 2.352	= Miles per gallon, US (mpg)

Temperature

Degrees Fahrenheit = ($°C \times 1.8$) + 32   Degrees Celsius (Degrees Centigrade; °C) = ($°F - 32$) x 0.56

It is common practice to convert from miles per gallon (mpg) to litres/100 kilometres (l/100km), where mpg (Imperial) x l/100 km = 282 and mpg (US) x l/100 km = 235

Troubleshooting

Contents

This section provides an easy reference guide to the more common problems which may occur during the operation of your vehicle. These problems and their possible causes are grouped under headings denoting various components or systems, such as Engine, Cooling system, etc. They also refer you to the chapter and/or section which deals with the problem.

Remember that successful troubleshooting is not a mysterious black art practiced only by professional mechanics. It is simply the result of the right knowledge combined with an intelligent, systematic approach to the problem. Always work by a process of elimination, starting with the simplest solution and working through to the most complex - and never overlook the obvious. Anyone can run the gas tank dry or leave the lights on overnight, so don't assume that you are exempt from such oversights.

Finally, always establish a clear idea of why a problem has occurred and take steps to ensure that it doesn't happen again. If the electrical system fails because of a poor connection, check the other connections in the system to make sure that they don't fail as well. If a particular fuse continues to blow, find out why - don't just replace one fuse after another. Remember, failure of a small component can often be indicative of potential failure or incorrect functioning of a more important component or system.

Engine

1   Engine will not rotate when attempting to start

1   Battery terminal connections loose or corroded (Chapter 1).
2   Battery discharged or faulty (Chapter 1).
3   Automatic transmission not completely engaged in Park (Chapter 7) or clutch not completely depressed (Chapter 8).
4   Broken, loose or disconnected wiring in the starting circuit (Chapters 5 and 12).
5   Starter motor pinion jammed in flywheel ring gear (Chapter 5).
6   Starter solenoid faulty (Chapter 5).
7   Starter motor faulty (Chapter 5).
8   Ignition switch faulty (Chapter 12).
9   Starter pinion or flywheel teeth worn or broken (Chapter 5).

2   Engine rotates but will not start

1   Fuel tank empty.
2   Battery discharged (engine rotates slowly) (Chapter 5).
3   Battery terminal connections loose or corroded (Chapter 1).
4   Leaking fuel injector(s), faulty fuel pump, pressure regulator, etc. (Chapter 4).
5   Fuel not reaching fuel rail (Chapter 4).
6   Ignition components damp or damaged (Chapter 5).
7   Worn, faulty or incorrectly gapped spark plugs (Chapter 1).
8   Broken, loose or disconnected wiring in the starting circuit (Chapter 5).
9   Loose distributor is changing ignition timing (Chapter 5).
10   Broken, loose or disconnected wires at the ignition coil or faulty coil (Chapter 5).

3   Engine hard to start when cold

1   Battery discharged or low (Chapter 1).
2   Malfunctioning fuel system (Chapter 4).
3   Injector(s) leaking (Chapter 4).
4   Distributor rotor carbon tracked (Chapter 5).

4   Engine hard to start when hot

1   Air filter clogged (Chapter 1).

2   Fuel not reaching the fuel injection system (Chapter 4).
3   Corroded battery connections, especially ground (Chapter 1).

5   Starter motor noisy or excessively rough in engagement

1   Pinion or flywheel gear teeth worn or broken (Chapter 5).
2   Starter motor mounting bolts loose or missing (Chapter 5).

6   Engine starts but stops immediately

1   Loose or faulty electrical connections at distributor, coil or alternator (Chapter 5).
2   Insufficient fuel reaching the fuel injector(s) (Chapters 1 and 4).
3   Vacuum leak at the gasket between the intake manifold and throttle body (Chapters 1 and 4).

7   Oil puddle under engine

1   Oil pan gasket and/or oil pan drain bolt washer leaking (Chapter 2).
2   Oil pressure sending unit leaking (Chapter 2).
3   Cylinder head covers leaking (Chapter 2).
4   Engine oil seals leaking (Chapter 2).

8   Engine lopes while idling or idles erratically

1   Vacuum leakage (Chapters 2 and 4).
2   Leaking EGR valve (Chapter 6).
3   Air filter clogged (Chapter 1).
4   Fuel pump not delivering sufficient fuel to the fuel injection system (Chapter 4).
5   Leaking head gasket (Chapter 2).
6   Timing belt and/or pulleys worn (Chapter 2).
7   Camshaft lobes worn (Chapter 2).

9   Engine misses at idle speed

1   Spark plugs worn or not gapped properly (Chapter 1).
2   Faulty spark plug wires (Chapter 1).
3   Vacuum leaks (Chapter 1).
4   Incorrect ignition timing (Chapter 1).
5   Uneven or low compression (Chapter 2).

10   Engine misses throughout driving speed range

1   Fuel filter clogged and/or impurities in the fuel system (Chapter 1).
2   Low fuel output at the injector(s) (Chapter 4).
3   Faulty or incorrectly gapped spark plugs (Chapter 1).
4   Incorrect ignition timing (Chapter 5).
5   Cracked distributor cap, disconnected distributor wires or damaged distributor components (Chapters 1 and 5).
6   Leaking spark plug wires (Chapters 1 or 5).
7   Faulty emission system components (Chapter 6).
8   Low or uneven cylinder compression pressures (Chapter 2).
9   Weak or faulty ignition system (Chapter 5).
10   Vacuum leak in fuel injection system, intake manifold, air control valve or vacuum hoses (Chapter 4).

11 Engine stumbles on acceleration

1 Spark plugs fouled (Chapter 1).
2 Fuel injection system needs faulty (Chapter 4).
3 Fuel filter clogged (Chapters 1 and 4).
4 Incorrect ignition timing (Chapter 5).
5 Intake manifold air leak (Chapters 2 and 4).

12 Engine surges while holding accelerator steady

1 Intake air leak (Chapter 4).
2 Fuel pump faulty (Chapter 4).
3 Loose fuel injector wire harness connectors (Chapter 4).
4 Defective ECU or information sensor (Chapter 6).

13 Engine stalls

1 Idle speed incorrect (Chapter 1).
2 Fuel filter clogged and/or water and impurities in the fuel system (Chapters 1 and 4).
3 Distributor components damp or damaged (Chapter 5).
4 Faulty emissions system components (Chapter 6).
5 Faulty or incorrectly gapped spark plugs (Chapter 1).
6 Faulty spark plug wires (Chapter 1).
7 Vacuum leak in the fuel injection system, intake manifold or vacuum hoses (Chapters 2 and 4).
8 Valve clearances incorrectly set (Chapter 1).

14 Engine lacks power

1 Incorrect ignition timing (Chapter 5).
2 Excessive play in distributor shaft (Chapter 5).
3 Worn rotor, distributor cap or wires (Chapters 1 and 5).
4 Faulty or incorrectly gapped spark plugs (Chapter 1).
5 Fuel injection system out of adjustment or excessively worn (Chapter 4).
6 Faulty coil (Chapter 5).
7 Brakes binding (Chapter 9).
8 Automatic transaxle fluid level incorrect (Chapter 1).
9 Clutch slipping (Chapter 8).
10 Fuel filter clogged and/or impurities in the fuel system (Chapters 1 and 4).
11 Emission control system not functioning properly (Chapter 6).
12 Low or uneven cylinder compression pressures (Chapter 2).
13 Obstructed exhaust system (Chapter 4).

15 Engine backfires

1 Emission control system not functioning properly (Chapter 6).
2 Ignition timing incorrect (Chapter 5).
3 Faulty secondary ignition system (cracked spark plug insulator, faulty plug wires, distributor cap and/or rotor) (Chapters 1 and 5).
4 Fuel injection system in need of adjustment or worn excessively (Chapter 4).
5 Vacuum leak at fuel injector(s), intake manifold, air control valve or vacuum hoses (Chapters 2 and 4).
6 Valve clearances incorrectly set and/or valves sticking (Chapter 1).

16 Pinging or knocking engine sounds during acceleration or uphill

1 Incorrect grade of fuel.

2 Ignition timing incorrect (Chapter 5).
3 Fuel injection system faulty (Chapter 4).
4 Improper or damaged spark plugs or wires (Chapter 1).
5 Worn or damaged distributor components (Chapter 5).
6 EGR valve not functioning (Chapter 6).
7 Vacuum leak (Chapters 2 and 4).

17 Engine runs with oil pressure light on

1 Low oil level (Chapter 1).
2 Short in wiring circuit (Chapter 12).
3 Faulty oil pressure sender (Chapter 2).
4 Worn engine bearings and/or oil pump (Chapter 2).

18 Engine diesels (continues to run) after switching off

1 Idle speed too high (Chapter 5)
2 Excessive engine operating temperature (Chapter 3).
3 Ignition timing in need of adjustment (Chapter 5).

Engine electrical system

19 Battery will not hold a charge

1 Alternator drivebelt defective or not adjusted properly (Chapter 1).
2 Battery electrolyte level low (Chapter 1).
3 Battery terminals loose or corroded (Chapter 1).
4 Alternator not charging properly (Chapter 5).
5 Loose, broken or faulty wiring in the charging circuit (Chapter 5).
6 Short in vehicle wiring (Chapter 12).
7 Internally defective battery (Chapters 1 and 5).

20 Alternator light fails to go out

1 Faulty alternator or charging circuit (Chapter 5).
2 Alternator drivebelt defective or out of adjustment (Chapter 1).
3 Alternator voltage regulator inoperative (Chapter 5).

21 Alternator light fails to come on when key is turned on

1 Warning light bulb defective (Chapter 12).
2 Fault in the printed circuit, dash wiring or bulb holder (Chapter 12).

Fuel system

22 Excessive fuel consumption

1 Dirty or clogged air filter element (Chapter 1).
2 Incorrectly set ignition timing (Chapter 5).
3 Emissions system not functioning properly (Chapter 6).
4 Fuel injection internal parts excessively worn or damaged (Chapter 4).
5 Low tire pressure or incorrect tire size (Chapter 1).

23 Fuel leakage and/or fuel odor

1 Leaking fuel feed or return line (Chapters 1 and 4).
2 Tank overfilled.

3   Evaporative canister filter clogged (Chapters 1 and 6).
4   Fuel injector internal parts excessively worn (Chapter 4).

Cooling system

24   Overheating

1   Insufficient coolant in system (Chapter 1).
2   Water pump drivebelt defective or out of adjustment (Chapter 1).
3   Radiator core blocked or grille restricted (Chapter 3).
4   Thermostat faulty (Chapter 3).
5   Electric coolant fan blades broken or cracked (Chapter 3).
6   Radiator cap not maintaining proper pressure (Chapter 3).
7   Ignition timing incorrect (Chapter 5).

25   Overcooling

1   Faulty thermostat (Chapter 3).
2   Inaccurate temperature gauge sending unit (Chapter 3)

26   External coolant leakage

1   Deteriorated/damaged hoses; loose clamps (Chapters 1 and 3).
2   Water pump defective (Chapter 3).
3   Leakage from radiator core or coolant reservoir bottle (Chapter 3).
4   Engine drain or water jacket core plugs leaking (Chapter 2).

27   Internal coolant leakage

1   Leaking cylinder head gasket (Chapter 2).
2   Cracked cylinder bore or cylinder head (Chapter 2).

28   Coolant loss

1   Too much coolant in system (Chapter 1).
2   Coolant boiling away because of overheating (Chapter 3).
3   Internal or external leakage (Chapter 3).
4   Faulty radiator cap (Chapter 3).

29   Poor coolant circulation

1   Inoperative water pump (Chapter 3).
2   Restriction in cooling system (Chapters 1 and 3).
3   Water pump drivebelt defective/out of adjustment (Chapter 1).
4   Thermostat sticking (Chapter 3).

Clutch

30   Pedal travels to floor - no pressure or very little resistance

1   Damaged cable or pedal mechanism (Chapter 8).
2   Broken release bearing or fork (Chapter 8).

31   Unable to select gears

1   Faulty transaxle (Chapter 7).
2   Faulty clutch disc (Chapter 8).

3   Release lever and bearing not assembled properly (Chapter 8).
4   Faulty pressure plate (Chapter 8).
5   Pressure plate-to-flywheel bolts loose (Chapter 8).

32   Clutch slips (engine speed increases with no increase in vehicle speed)

1   Clutch plate worn (Chapter 8).
2   Clutch plate is oil soaked by leaking rear main seal (Chapter 8).
3   Clutch plate not seated. It may take 30 or 40 normal starts for a new one to seat.
4   Warped pressure plate or flywheel (Chapter 8).
5   Weak diaphragm spring (Chapter 8).
6   Clutch plate overheated. Allow to cool.

33   Grabbing (chattering) as clutch is engaged

1   Oil on clutch plate lining, burned or glazed facings (Chapter 8).
2   Worn or loose engine or transaxle mounts (Chapters 2 and 7).
3   Worn splines on clutch plate hub (Chapter 8).
4   Warped pressure plate or flywheel (Chapter 8).
5   Burned or smeared resin on flywheel or pressure plate (Chapter 8).

34   Transaxle rattling (clicking)

1   Release lever loose (Chapter 8).
2   Clutch plate damper spring failure (Chapter 8).
3   Low engine idle speed (Chapter 1).

35   Noise in clutch area

1   Fork shaft improperly installed (Chapter 8).
2   Faulty bearing (Chapter 8).

36   Clutch pedal stays on floor

1   Broken or damaged clutch cable (Chapter 8).
2   Broken release bearing or fork (Chapter 8).

37   High pedal effort

1   Clutch cable or pedal mechanism binding in bore (Chapter 8).
2   Pressure plate faulty (Chapter 8).
3   Incorrect size master or release cylinder (Chapter 8).

Manual transaxle

38   Knocking noise at low speeds

1   Worn driveaxle constant velocity (CV) joints (Chapter 8).
2   Worn side gear shaft counterbore in differential case (Chapter 7A).*

39   Noise most pronounced when turning

Differential gear noise (Chapter 7A).*

40 Clunk on acceleration or deceleration

1 Loose engine or transaxle mounts (Chapters 2 and 7A).
2 Worn differential pinion shaft in case.*
3 Worn side gear shaft counterbore in differential case (Chapter 7A).*
4 Worn or damaged driveaxle inboard CV joints (Chapter 8).

41 Clicking noise in turns

Worn or damaged outboard CV joint (Chapter 8).

42 Vibration

1 Rough wheel bearing (Chapters 1 and 10).
2 Damaged driveaxle (Chapter 8).
3 Out of round tires (Chapter 1).
4 Tire out of balance (Chapters 1 and 10).
5 Worn CV joint (Chapter 8).

43 Noisy in neutral with engine running

1 Damaged input gear bearing (Chapter 7A).*
2 Damaged clutch release bearing (Chapter 8).

44 Noisy in one particular gear

1 Damaged or worn constant mesh gears (Chapter 7A).*
2 Damaged or worn synchronizers (Chapter 7A).*
3 Bent reverse fork (Chapter 7A).*
4 Damaged fourth speed gear or output gear (Chapter 7A).*
5 Worn or damaged reverse idler gear or idler bushing (Chapter 7A).*

45 Noisy in all gears

1 Insufficient lubricant (Chapter 7A).
2 Damaged or worn bearings (Chapter 7A).*
3 Worn or damaged input gear shaft and/or output gear shaft (Chapter 7A).*

46 Slips out of gear

1 Worn or improperly adjusted linkage (Chapter 7A).
2 Transaxle loose on engine (Chapter 7A).
3 Shift linkage does not work freely, binds (Chapter 7A).
4 Input gear bearing retainer broken or loose (Chapter 7A).*
5 Dirt between clutch cover and engine housing (Chapter 7A).
6 Worn shift fork (Chapter 7A).*

47 Leaks lubricant

1 Side gear shaft seals worn (Chapter 7).
2 Excessive amount of lubricant in transaxle (Chapters 1 and 7A).
3 Loose or broken input gear shaft bearing retainer (Chapter 7A).*
4 Input gear bearing retainer O-ring and/or lip seal damaged (Chapter 7A).*

48 Locked in gear

Lock pin or interlock pin missing (Chapter 7A).*
* Although the corrective action necessary to remedy the symptoms described is beyond the scope of the home mechanic, the above information should be helpful in isolating the cause of the condition so that the owner can communicate clearly with a professional mechanic.

Automatic transaxle

Note: Due to the complexity of the automatic transaxle, it is difficult for the home mechanic to properly diagnose and service this component. For problems other than the following, the vehicle should be taken to a dealer or transmission shop.

49 Fluid leakage

1 Automatic transmission fluid is a deep red color. Fluid leaks should not be confused with engine oil, which can easily be blown onto the transaxle by air flow.
2 To pinpoint a leak, first remove all built-up dirt and grime from the transaxle housing with degreasing agents and/or steam cleaning. Then drive the vehicle at low speeds so air flow will not blow the leak far from its source. Raise the vehicle and determine where the leak is coming from. Common areas of leakage are:
   a) Pan (Chapters 1 and 7)
   b) Dipstick tube (Chapters 1 and 7)
   c) Transaxle oil lines (Chapter 7)
   d) Speed sensor (Chapter 7)

50 Transaxle fluid brown or has a burned smell

Transaxle fluid burned (Chapter 1).

51 General shift mechanism problems

1 Chapter 7, Part B, deals with checking and adjusting the shift linkage on automatic transaxles. Common problems which may be attributed to poorly adjusted linkage are:
   a) Engine starting in gears other than Park or Neutral.
   b) Indicator on shifter pointing to a gear other than the one actually being used.
   c) Vehicle moves when in Park.
2 Refer to Chapter 7B for the shift linkage adjustment procedure.

52 Transaxle will not downshift with accelerator pedal pressed to the floor

Throttle valve cable out of adjustment (Chapter 7B).

53 Engine will start in gears other than Park or Neutral

Neutral start switch malfunctioning (Chapter 7B).

54 Transaxle slips, shifts roughly, is noisy or has no drive in forward or reverse gears

There are many probable causes for the above problems, but the home mechanic should be concerned with only one possibility - fluid level. Before taking the vehicle to a repair shop, check the level and condition of the fluid as described in Chapter 1. Correct the fluid level as necessary or change the fluid and filter if needed. If the problem persists, have a professional diagnose the cause.

Driveaxles

55   Clicking noise in turns

Worn or damaged outboard CV joint (Chapter 8).

56   Shudder or vibration during acceleration

1   Excessive toe-in (Chapter 10).
2   Incorrect spring heights (Chapter 10).
3   Worn or damaged inboard or outboard CV joints (Chapter 8).
4   Sticking inboard CV joint assembly (Chapter 8).

57   Vibration at highway speeds

1   Out of balance front wheels and/or tires (Chapters 1 and 10).
2   Out of round front tires (Chapters 1 and 10).
3   Worn CV joint(s) (Chapter 8).

Brakes

Note: *Before assuming that a brake problem exists, make sure that:*
a)   The tires are in good condition and properly inflated (Chapter 1).
b)   The front end alignment is correct (Chapter 10).
c)   The vehicle is not loaded with weight in an unequal manner.

58   Vehicle pulls to one side during braking

1   Incorrect tire pressures (Chapter 1).
2   Front end out of line (have the front end aligned).
3   Front, or rear, tires not matched to one another.
4   Restricted brake lines or hoses (Chapter 9).
5   Malfunctioning drum brake or caliper assembly (Chapter 9).
6   Loose suspension parts (Chapter 10).
7   Loose calipers (Chapter 9).
8   Excessive wear of brake shoe or pad material or disc/drum on one side.

59   Noise (high-pitched squeal when the brakes are applied)

Front disc brake pads worn out. The noise comes from the wear sensor rubbing against the disc (does not apply to all vehicles). Replace pads with new ones immediately (Chapter 9).

60   Brake roughness or chatter (pedal pulsates)

1   Excessive lateral runout (Chapter 9).
2   Uneven pad wear (Chapter 9).
3   Defective disc (Chapter 9).

61   Excessive brake pedal effort required to stop vehicle

1   Malfunctioning power brake booster (Chapter 9).
2   Partial system failure (Chapter 9).
3   Excessively worn pads or shoes (Chapter 9).
4   Piston in caliper or wheel cylinder stuck or sluggish (Chapter 9).
5   Brake pads or shoes contaminated with oil or grease (Chapter 9).
6   New pads or shoes installed and not yet seated. It will take a while for the new material to seat against the disc or drum.

62   Excessive brake pedal travel

1   Partial brake system failure (Chapter 9).
2   Insufficient fluid in master cylinder (Chapters 1 and 9).
3   Air trapped in system (Chapters 1 and 9).

63   Dragging brakes

1   Incorrect adjustment of brake light switch (Chapter 9).
2   Master cylinder pistons not returning correctly (Chapter 9).
3   Restricted brakes lines or hoses (Chapters 1 and 9).
4   Incorrect parking brake adjustment (Chapter 9).

64   Grabbing or uneven braking action

1   Malfunction of proportioning valve (Chapter 9).
2   Malfunction of power brake booster unit (Chapter 9).
3   Binding brake pedal mechanism (Chapter 9).

65   Brake pedal feels spongy when depressed

1   Air in hydraulic lines (Chapter 9).
2   Master cylinder mounting bolts loose (Chapter 9).
3   Master cylinder defective (Chapter 9).

66   Brake pedal travels to the floor with little resistance

1   Little or no fluid in the master cylinder reservoir caused by leaking caliper piston(s) (Chapter 9).
2   Loose, damaged or disconnected brake lines (Chapter 9).

67   Parking brake does not hold

Parking brake linkage improperly adjusted (Chapters 1 and 9).

Suspension and steering systems

Note: *Before attempting to diagnose the suspension and steering systems, perform the following preliminary checks:*
a)   Tires for wrong pressure and uneven wear.
b)   Steering universal joints from the column to the rack-and-pinion for loose connectors or wear.
c)   Front and rear suspension and the rack and pinion assembly for loose or damaged parts.
d)   Out-of-round or out-of-balance tires, bent rims and loose and/or rough wheel bearings.

68 Vehicle pulls to one side

1   Mismatched or uneven tires (Chapter 10).
2   Broken or sagging springs (Chapter 10).
3   Wheel alignment (Chapter 10).
4   Front brake dragging (Chapter 9).

69 Abnormal or excessive tire wear

1   Wheel alignment (Chapter 10).
2   Sagging or broken springs (Chapter 10).
3   Tire out of balance (Chapter 10).
4   Worn strut damper (Chapter 10).
5   Overloaded vehicle.
6   Tires not rotated regularly.

70 Wheel makes a thumping noise

1   Blister or bump on tire (Chapter 10).
2   Improper strut damper action (Chapter 10).

71 Shimmy, shake or vibration

1   Tire or wheel out-of-balance or out-of-round (Chapter 10).
2   Loose or worn front hub or wheel bearings (Chapters 1, 8 and 10).
3   Worn tie-rod ends (Chapter 10).
4   Worn lower balljoints (Chapters 1 and 10).
5   Excessive wheel runout (Chapter 10).
6   Blister or bump on tire (Chapter 10).

72 Hard steering

1   Lack of lubrication at balljoints, tie-rod ends and rack and pinion assembly (Chapter 10).
2   Front wheel alignment (Chapter 10).
3   Low tire pressure(s) (Chapters 1 and 10).

73 Poor returnability of steering to center

1   Lack of lubrication at balljoints and tie-rod ends (Chapter 10).
2   Binding in balljoints (Chapter 10).
3   Binding in steering column (Chapter 10).
4   Lack of lubricant in steering gear assembly (Chapter 10).
5   Front wheel alignment (Chapter 10).

74 Abnormal noise at the front end

1   Lack of lubrication at balljoints and tie-rod ends (Chapters 1 and 10).
2   Damaged strut mounting (Chapter 10).
3   Worn control arm bushings or tie-rod ends (Chapter 10).
4   Loose stabilizer bar (Chapter 10).
5   Loose wheel nuts (Chapters 1 and 10).
6   Loose suspension bolts (Chapter 10)

75 Wander or poor steering stability

1   Mismatched or uneven tires (Chapter 10).

2   Lack of lubrication at balljoints and tie-rod ends (Chapters 1 and 10).
3   Worn strut assemblies (Chapter 10).
4   Loose stabilizer bar (Chapter 10).
5   Broken or sagging springs (Chapter 10).
6   Wheels out of alignment (Chapter 10).

76 Erratic steering when braking

1   Front hub bearings worn (Chapter 10).
2   Broken or sagging springs (Chapter 10).
3   Leaking wheel cylinder or caliper (Chapter 10).
4   Warped rotors or drums (Chapter 10).

77 Excessive pitching and/or rolling around corners or during braking

1   Loose stabilizer bar (Chapter 10).
2   Worn strut dampers or mountings (Chapter 10).
3   Broken or sagging springs (Chapter 10).
4   Overloaded vehicle.

78 Suspension bottoms

1   Overloaded vehicle.
2   Worn strut dampers (Chapter 10).
3   Incorrect, broken or sagging springs (Chapter 10).

79 Cupped tires

1   Front wheel or rear wheel alignment (Chapter 10).
2   Worn strut dampers (Chapter 10).
3   Wheel bearings worn (Chapter 10).
4   Excessive tire or wheel runout (Chapter 10).
5   Worn balljoints (Chapter 10).

80 Excessive tire wear on outside edge

1   Inflation pressures incorrect (Chapter 1).
2   Excessive speed in turns.
3   Front end alignment incorrect (excessive toe-in). Have professionally aligned.
4   Suspension arm bent or twisted (Chapter 10).

81 Excessive tire wear on inside edge

1   Inflation pressures incorrect (Chapter 1).
2   Front end alignment incorrect (toe-out). Have professionally aligned.
3   Loose or damaged steering or suspension components (Chapter 10).

82 Tire tread worn in one place

1   Tires out of balance.
2   Damaged or buckled wheel. Inspect and replace if necessary.
3   Defective tire (Chapter 1).

83   Excessive play or looseness in steering system

1   Front hub bearing(s) worn (Chapter 10).
2   Tie-rod end loose (Chapter 10).
3   Steering gear loose (Chapter 10).
4   Worn or loose steering intermediate shaft (Chapter 10).

84   Rattling or clicking noise in steering gear

1   Steering gear loose (Chapter 10).
2   Steering gear defective.

Chapter 1 Tune-up and routine maintenance

Contents

Specifications

Recommended lubricants and fluids

Engine oil type	API grade SG or SG/CD multigrade and fuel efficient oil
Viscosity	See accompanying chart

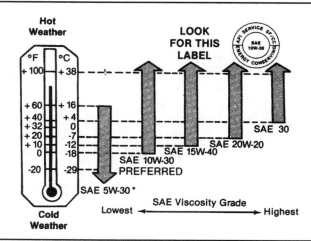

Engine oil viscosity chart - for best fuel economy and cold starting, select the lowest SAE viscosity grade for the expected temperature range

Recommended lubricants and fluids (continued)

Fuel	Unleaded gasoline, 87 octane or higher
Automatic transaxle fluid type	DEXRON II automatic transmission fluid
Manual transaxle lubricant type	GM transmission lubricant # 12345349 or equivalent
Brake fluid type	DOT 3 brake fluid
Power steering system fluid	GM power steering fluid # 10552884 or equivalent

Capacities*

Engine oil (including filter)	
SOHC engine	3.6 qts
DOHC engine	4.6 qts
Coolant	7 qts
Transaxle	
Automatic (drain and refill)	3.2 qts
Manual	2 qts

* All capacities approximate. Add as necessary to bring to appropriate level.

Ignition system

Spark plug type and gap	
SOHC engine	
Type	Champion R42XLS or equivalent
Gap	0.041 inch
DOHC engine	
Type	NGK BKR6E-11 or equivalent
Gap	0.041 inch
Spark plug wire resistance	10,000 to 22,000 ohms
Engine firing order	1-3-4-2

Valve clearances (engine cold)

SOHC engine	
Intake valve	0.006 inch
Exhaust valve	0.010 inch
1.6L DOHC engine	
Intake valve	0.004 to 0.008 inch
Exhaust valve	0.008 to 0.012 inch
1.8L DOHC engine	Hydraulic (non-adjustable)

Cooling system

Thermostat rating	
Starts to open	190-degrees F
Fully open	212-degrees F

Clutch

Clutch pedal freeplay	5/8 inch

Brakes

Disc brake pad lining thickness (minimum)	1/16 inch
Drum brake shoe lining thickness (minimum)	1/16 inch
Parking brake adjustment	6 to 7 clicks

Suspension and steering

Steering wheel freeplay limit	1-3/16 inch
Balljoint allowable movement	0 inch

Torque specifications

	Ft-lbs (unless otherwise indicated)
Automatic transaxle	
Pan bolts	71 in-lbs
Filter bolt	71 in-lbs
Manual transaxle drain and filler plugs	20
Spark plugs	13
Wheel lug nuts	90

Engine compartment components (1990 DOHC engine model shown, others similar)

1   Brake fluid reservoir
2   Fuse box
3   Battery
4   Radiator hose
5   Distributor cap and wires
6   Radiator cap

7   Engine oil dipstick
8   Engine oil filler cap
9   Coolant reservoir
10 Windshield washer fluid reservoir
11 Power steering fluid reservoir
12 Relay box

Engine compartment underside components (1990 model shown, others similar)

1   Engine drivebelt
2   Transaxle
3   Manual transaxle drain plug
4   Balljoint

5   Exhaust system
6   Engine oil drain plug
7   Driveaxle boot
8   Front disc brake

Typical rear underside components (1993 model shown, others similar)

1   *Exhaust system*
2   *Rear assembly strut*
3   *Rear suspension trailing arm*
4   *Fuel tank*
5   *Fuel tank inlet hose*

1   Introduction

This chapter is designed to help the home mechanic maintain the Geo Storm for peak performance, economy, safety and long life.

On the following pages is a master maintenance schedule, followed by sections dealing specifically with each item on the schedule. Visual checks, adjustments, component replacement and other helpful items are included. Refer to the accompanying illustrations of the engine compartment and the underside of the vehicle for the location of various components.

Servicing your Storm in accordance with the mileage/time maintenance schedule and the following Sections will provide it with a planned maintenance program that should result in a long and reliable service life. This is a comprehensive plan, so maintaining some items but not others at the specified service intervals will not produce the same results.

As you service your Storm, you will discover that many of the procedures can - and should - be grouped together because of the nature of the particular procedure you're performing or because of the close proximity of two otherwise unrelated components to one another.

For example, if the vehicle is raised for any reason, you should inspect the exhaust, suspension, steering and fuel systems while you're under the vehicle. When you're rotating the tires, it makes good sense to check the brakes and wheel bearings since the wheels are already removed.

Finally, let's suppose you have to borrow or rent a torque wrench. Even if you only need to tighten the spark plugs, you might as well check the torque of as many critical fasteners as time allows.

The first step of this maintenance program is to prepare yourself before the actual work begins. Read through all sections pertinent to the procedures you're planning to do, then make a list of and gather together all the parts and tools you will need to do the job. If it looks as if you might run into problems during a particular segment of some procedure, seek advice from your local parts man or dealer service department.

2 Geo Storm maintenance schedule

The maintenance intervals in this manual are provided with the assumption that you, not the dealer, will be doing the work. These are the minimum maintenance intervals recommended by the factory for Storms that are driven daily. If you wish to keep your vehicle in peak condition at all times, you may wish to perform some of these procedures even more often. Because frequent maintenance enhances the efficiency, performance and resale value of your car, we encourage you to do so. If you drive in dusty areas, tow a trailer, idle or drive at low speeds for extended periods or drive for short distances (less than four miles) in below freezing temperatures, shorter intervals are also recommended.

When your vehicle is new, it should be serviced by a factory authorized dealer service department to protect the factory warranty. In many cases, the initial maintenance check is done at no cost to the owner.

Every 250 miles or weekly, whichever comes first

Check the engine oil level (Section 4)
Check the engine coolant level (Section 4)
Check the windshield washer fluid level (Section 4)
Check the brake fluid level (Section 4)
Check the tires and tire pressures (Section 5)

Every 3000 miles or 3 months, whichever comes first

All items listed above plus:
Check the power steering fluid level (Section 6)
Check the automatic transaxle fluid level (Section 7)
Change the engine oil and oil filter (Section 8)

Every 6000 miles or 6 months, whichever comes first

Inspect and replace if necessary the windshield
    wiper blades (Section 9)
Check the clutch pedal for proper freeplay (Section 10)
Check and service the battery (Section 11)
Check and adjust if necessary the engine
    drivebelts (Section 12)
Inspect and replace if necessary all underhood
    hoses (Section 13)
Check the cooling system (Section 14)
Rotate the tires (Section 15)

Every 15,000 miles or 12 months, whichever comes first

All items listed above plus:
Inspect the brake system (Section 16)*

Replace the air filter (Section 17)
Inspect the fuel system (Section 18)
Check and adjust if necessary, the valve clearances
    (SOHC engine) (Section 19)
Check the manual transaxle lubricant level (Section 20)*
Inspect the suspension and steering components
    (Section 21)*
Check the driveaxle boots (Section 22)
Change the power steering fluid (Section 23)

Every 30,000 miles or 24 months, whichever comes first

All items listed above plus:
Replace the fuel filter (Section 24)
Check and replace if necessary the spark
    plugs (Section 25)
Inspect and replace if necessary the spark plug
    wires, distributor cap and rotor (Section 26)
Service the cooling system (drain, flush and
    refill) (Section 27)
Inspect the evaporative emissions control system
    (Section 28)
Inspect the exhaust system (Section 29)
Change the automatic transaxle fluid and filter and
    differential oil (Section 30) **
Change the manual transaxle lubricant (Section 31)
Check and replace if necessary, the PCV valve (Section 32)

Every 60,000 miles or 48 months, whichever comes first

Inspect and if necessary adjust the valve clearance
    (DOHC models) (Section 33)
Replace the timing belt (Chapter 2A)
* This item is affected by "severe" operating conditions as
    described below. If your vehicle is operated under "se-
    vere" conditions, perform all maintenance indicated with
    an asterisk (*) at 3000 mile/3 month intervals. Severe
    conditions are indicated if you mainly operate your vehi-
    cle under one or more of the following conditions:
Operating in dusty areas
Towing a trailer
Idling for extended periods and/or low speed operation
Operating when outside temperatures remain below
    freezing and when most trips are less than 4 miles
** If operated under one or more of the following conditions,
    change the automatic transaxle fluid and differential lu-
    bricant every 15,000 miles:
In heavy city traffic where the outside temperature regularly
    reaches 90-degrees F (32-degrees C) or higher
In hilly or mountainous terrain
Frequent trailer pulling

4.2 The engine oil dipstick (arrow) is located on the front side of the engine, behind the radiator

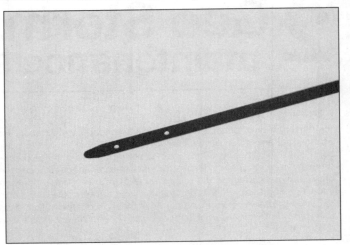

4.4 The oil level should be at or near the upper hole or mark on the dipstick - if it isn't, add enough oil to bring the level to near the upper hole or mark (it takes one quart of oil to raise the level from the lower to upper mark)

3   Tune-up general information

The term tune-up is used in this manual to represent a combination of individual operations rather than one specific procedure.

If, from the time the vehicle is new, the routine maintenance schedule is followed closely and frequent checks are made of fluid levels and high wear items, as suggested throughout this manual, the engine will be kept in relatively good running condition and the need for additional work will be minimized.

More likely than not, however, there will be times when the engine is running poorly due to lack of regular maintenance. This is even more likely if a used vehicle, which has not received regular and frequent maintenance checks, is purchased. In such cases, an engine tune-up will be needed outside of the regular routine maintenance intervals.

The first step in any tune-up or engine diagnosis to help correct a poor running engine would be a cylinder compression check. A check of the engine compression (Chapter 2 Part B) will give valuable information regarding the overall performance of many internal components and should be used as a basis for tune-up and repair procedures. If, for instance, a compression check indicates serious internal engine wear, a conventional tune-up will not help the running condition of the engine and would be a waste of time and money.

The following series of operations are those most often needed to bring a generally poor running engine back into a proper state of tune.

Minor tune-up
Clean, inspect and test the battery (Section 11)
Check all engine related fluids (Section 4)
Check and adjust the drivebelts (Section 12)
Replace the spark plugs (Section 25)
Inspect the distributor cap and rotor (Section 26)
Inspect the spark plug and coil wires (Section 26)
Check the air filter (Section 17)
Check the cooling system (Section 14)
Check all underhood hoses (Section 13)

Major tune-up
All items listed under Minor tune-up, plus . . .
Check the charging system (Chapter 5)
Check the fuel system (Section 18)
Replace the air filter (Section 17)
Replace the distributor cap and rotor (Section 26)
Replace the spark plug wires (Section 26)

4   Fluid level checks (every 250 miles or weekly)

1   Fluids are an essential part of the lubrication, cooling, brake, clutch and other systems. Because these fluids gradually become de-

pleted and/or contaminated during normal operation of the vehicle, they must be periodically replenished. See *Recommended lubricants and fluids* and *capacities* at the beginning of this Chapter before adding fluid to any of the following components. **Note:** *The vehicle must be on level ground before fluid levels can be checked.*

Engine oil
Refer to illustrations 4.2, 4.4 and 4.6
2   The engine oil level is checked with a dipstick located at the front side of the engine **(see illustration)**. The dipstick extends through a metal tube from which it protrudes down into the engine oil pan.
3   The oil level should be checked before the vehicle has been driven, or about 15 minutes after the engine has been shut off. If the oil is checked immediately after driving the vehicle, some of the oil will remain in the upper engine components, producing an inaccurate reading on the dipstick.
4   Pull the dipstick from the tube and wipe all the oil from the end with a clean rag or paper towel. Insert the clean dipstick all the way back into its metal tube and pull it out again. Observe the oil at the end of the dipstick. At its highest point, the level should be between the L and F marks **(see illustration)**.
5   It takes one quart of oil to raise the level from the L mark to the F mark on the dipstick. Do not allow the level to drop below the L mark or oil starvation may cause engine damage. Conversely, overfilling the engine (adding oil above the F mark) may cause oil fouled spark plugs, oil leaks or oil seal failures.
6   Remove the threaded cap from the valve cover to add oil **(see illustration)**. Use a funnel to prevent spills. After adding the oil, install the filler cap hand tight. Start the engine and look carefully for any small leaks around the oil filter or drain plug. Stop the engine and check the oil level again after it has had sufficient time to drain from the upper block and cylinder head galleys.
7   Checking the oil level is an important preventive maintenance step. A continually dropping oil level indicates oil leakage through damaged seals, from loose connections, or past worn rings or valve guides. If the oil looks milky in color or has water droplets in it, a cylinder head gasket may be blown. The engine should be checked immediately. The condition of the oil should also be checked. Each time you check the oil level, slide your thumb and index finger up the dipstick before wiping off the oil. If you see small dirt or metal particles clinging to the dipstick, the oil should be changed (see Section 8).

Engine coolant
Refer to illustration 4.8
Warning: *Do not allow antifreeze to come in contact with your skin or painted surfaces of the vehicle. Flush contaminated areas immediately*

4.6 The threaded oil filler cap is located on the valve cover - always make sure the area around the opening is clean before unscrewing the cap to prevent dirt from contaminating the engine

4.8 The coolant reservoir is located in the right front corner of the engine compartment - keep the level between the MAX and MIN lines

1

4.14a The windshield washer fluid reservoir is located in the right front corner of the engine compartment - fluid can be added after flipping up the cap

with plenty of water. Don't store new coolant or leave old coolant lying around where it's accessible to children or pets – they're attracted by its sweet smell. Ingestion of even a small amount of coolant can be fatal! Wipe up garage floor and drip pan spills immediately. Keep antifreeze containers covered and repair cooling system leaks as soon as they're noticed.

8   All vehicles covered by this manual are equipped with a pressurized coolant recovery system. A white coolant reservoir located in the front corner of the engine compartment is connected by a hose to the base of the coolant filler cap **(see illustration)**. If the coolant heats up during engine operation, coolant can escape through a pressurized filler cap, then through a connecting hose into the reservoir. As the engine cools, the coolant is automatically drawn back into the cooling system to maintain the correct level.

9   The coolant level should be checked regularly. It must be between the MAX and MIN lines on the tank. The level will vary with the temperature of the engine. When the engine is cold, the coolant level should be at or slightly above the MIN mark on the tank. Once the engine has warmed up, the level should be at or near the MAX mark. If it isn't, allow the fluid in the tank to cool, then remove the cap from the reservoir and add coolant to bring the level up to the Full line. Use only ethylene/glycol type coolant and water in the mixture ratio recommended by your owner's manual. Do not use supplemental inhibitors or additives. If only a small amount of coolant is required to bring the system up to the proper level, water can be used. However, repeated additions of water will dilute the recommended antifreeze and water solution. In order to maintain the proper ratio of antifreeze and water, it is advisable to top up the coolant level with the correct mixture. Refer to your owner's manual for the recommended ratio.

10   If the coolant level drops within a short time after replenishment, there may be a leak in the system. Inspect the radiator, hoses, engine coolant filler cap, drain plugs, air bleeder plugs and water pump. If no leak is evident, have the radiator cap pressure tested by your dealer. **Warning:** *Never remove the radiator cap or the coolant recovery reservoir cap when the engine is running or has just been shut down, because the cooling system is hot. Escaping steam and scalding liquid could cause serious injury.*

11   If it is necessary to open the radiator cap, wait until the system has cooled completely, then wrap a thick cloth around the cap and turn it to the first stop. If any steam escapes, wait until the system has cooled further, then remove the cap.

12   When checking the coolant level, always note its condition. It should be relatively clear. If it is brown or rust colored, the system should be drained, flushed and refilled. Even if the coolant appears to be normal, the corrosion inhibitors wear out with use, so it must be replaced at the specified intervals.

13   Do not allow antifreeze to come in contact with your skin or painted surfaces of the vehicle. Flush contacted areas immediately with plenty of water.

Washer fluid

Refer to illustrations 4.14a and 4.14b

14   Fluid for the windshield washer system is stored in a plastic reservoir which is located at the right front corner of the engine compartment **(see illustration)**. The rear window wiper washer is located under a cover in the rear compartment **(see illustration).** In milder climates, plain water can be used to top up the reservoir, but the reservoir should be kept no more than two-thirds full to allow for expansion should the water freeze. In colder climates, the use of a specially designed windshield washer fluid, available at your dealer and any auto parts store, will help lower the freezing point of the fluid. Mix the solution with water in accordance with the manufacturer's directions on the container. Do not use regular antifreeze. It will damage the vehicle's paint.

Battery electrolyte

Refer to illustration 4.15

15   On models not equipped with a sealed battery, check the electrolyte level of all six battery cells. Remove the filler caps and check the

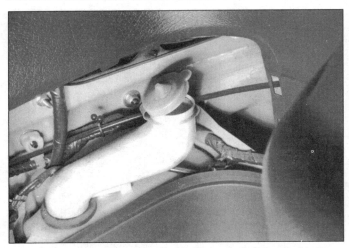

4.14b The rear window washer fluid reservoir is located in the
rear compartment on the right side, under a cover

4.15 Remove the cell caps to check the electrolyte level in the
battery - if the level is low, add distilled water only

4.17 The brake fluid level should be kept between the MIN and
MAX marks on the translucent plastic reservoir - unscrew
the cap to add fluid

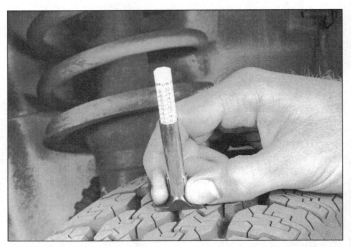

5.2 Use a tire tread depth indicator to monitor tire wear - they are
available at auto parts stores and service stations and cost
very little

level **(see illustration)** - it must be at or near the split ring. If the level is low, add distilled water. Install and securely retighten the cap. **Caution:** *Overfilling the cells may cause electrolyte to spill over during periods of heavy charging, causing corrosion or damage.*

Brake fluid

Refer to illustration 4.17

16   The brake master cylinder is mounted on the front of the power booster unit in the engine compartment.

17   To check the fluid level of the brake master cylinder reservoir, simply look at the MAX and MIN marks on the reservoir **(see illustration)**. To check the fluid level of the clutch master cylinder reservoir, note whether the fluid level is even with the maximum level line. The level should be within the specified distance from the maximum fill line for both reservoirs.

18   If the level is low for either reservoir, wipe the top of the reservoir cover with a clean rag to prevent contamination of the brake or clutch system before lifting the cover.

19   Add only the specified brake fluid to the brake or clutch reservoir (refer to *Recommended lubricants and fluids* at the front of this chapter or to your owner's manual). Mixing different types of brake fluid can damage the system. Fill the brake master cylinder reservoir only to the dotted line - this brings the fluid to the correct level when you put the cover back on. **Warning:** *Use caution when filling either reservoir-brake fluid can harm your eyes and damage painted surfaces. Do not*

use brake fluid that has been opened for more than one year or has been left open. Brake fluid absorbs moisture from the air. Excess moisture can cause a dangerous loss of braking.

20   While the reservoir cap is removed, inspect the master cylinder reservoir for contamination. If deposits, dirt particles or water droplets are present, the system should be drained and refilled (see Chapter 9).

21   After filling the reservoir to the proper level, make sure the lid is properly seated to prevent fluid leakage and/or system pressure loss.

22   The brake fluid in the master cylinder will drop slightly as the brake pads at each wheel wear down during normal operation. If the master cylinder requires repeated replenishing to keep it at the proper level, this is an indication of leakage in the brake system, which should be corrected immediately. Check all brake lines and connections, along with the wheel cylinders and booster (see Section 16 for more information).

23   If, upon checking the master cylinder fluid level, you discover one or both reservoirs empty or nearly empty, the brake system should be bled (see Chapter 9).

---

5   Tire and tire pressure checks (every 250 miles or weekly)

Refer to illustrations 5.2, 5.3, 5.4a, 5.4b and 5.8

1   Periodic inspection of the tires may spare you from the inconvenience of being stranded with a flat tire. It can also provide you with vi-

Condition	Probable cause	Corrective action	Condition	Probable cause	Corrective action
Shoulder wear	• Underinflation (both sides wear) • Incorrect wheel camber (one side wear) • Hard cornering • Lack of rotation	• Measure and adjust pressure. • Repair or replace axle and suspension parts. • Reduce speed. • Rotate tires.	Feathered edge **Toe wear**	• Incorrect toe	• Adjust toe-in.
Center wear	• Overinflation • Lack of rotation	• Measure and adjust pressure. • Rotate tires.	**Uneven wear**	• Incorrect camber or caster • Malfunctioning suspension • Unbalanced wheel • Out-of-round brake drum • Lack of rotation	• Repair or replace axle and suspension parts. • Repair or replace suspension parts. • Balance or replace. • Turn or replace. • Rotate tires.

5.3 This chart will help you determine the condition of the tires, the probable cause(s) of abnormal wear and the corrective action necessary

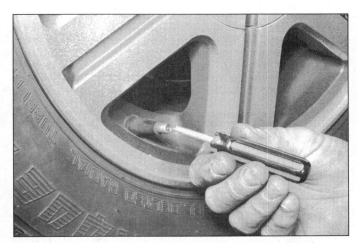

5.4a If a tire loses air on a steady basis, check the valve stem core first to make sure it's snug (special inexpensive wrenches are commonly available at auto parts stores)

5.4b If the valve stem core is tight, raise the corner of the vehicle with the low tire and spray a soapy water solution onto the tread as the tire is turned slowly - leaks will cause small bubbles to appear

tal information regarding possible problems in the steering and suspension systems before major damage occurs.

2   Normal tread wear can be monitored with a simple, inexpensive device known as a tread depth indicator **(see illustration)**. When the tread depth reaches the specified minimum, replace the tire(s).

3   Note any abnormal tread wear **(see illustration)**. Tread pattern irregularities such as cupping, flat spots and more wear on one side than the other are indications of front end alignment and/or balance problems. If any of these conditions are noted, take the vehicle to a tire shop or service station to correct the problem.

4   Look closely for cuts, punctures and embedded nails or tacks. Sometimes a tire will hold its air pressure for a short time or leak down very slowly even after a nail has embedded itself into the tread. If a slow leak persists, check the valve stem core to make sure it is tight **(see illustration)**. Examine the tread for an object that may have embedded itself into the tire or for a "plug" that may have begun to leak (radial tire punctures are repaired with a plug that is installed in a punc-

ture). If a puncture is suspected, it can be easily verified by spraying a solution of soapy water onto the puncture area **(see illustration)**. The soapy solution will bubble if there is a leak. Unless the puncture is inordinately large, a tire shop or gas station can usually repair the punctured tire.

5   Carefully inspect the inner sidewall of each tire for evidence of brake fluid leakage. If you see any, inspect the brakes immediately.

6   Correct tire air pressure adds miles to the lifespan of the tires, improves mileage and enhances overall ride quality. Tire pressure cannot be accurately estimated by looking at a tire, particularly if it is a radial. A tire pressure gauge is therefore essential. Keep an accurate gauge in the glovebox. The pressure gauges fitted to the nozzles of air hoses at gas stations are often inaccurate.

7   Always check tire pressure when the tires are cold. "Cold," in this case, means the vehicle has not been driven over a mile in the three hours preceding a tire pressure check. A pressure rise of four to eight

5.8 To extend the life of the tires, check the air pressure at least once a week with an accurate gauge (don't forget the spare!)

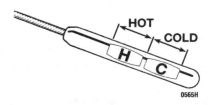

7.4 Check the fluid with the transaxle at normal operating temperature - the level should be kept in the HOT range

pounds is not uncommon once the tires are warm.

8   Unscrew the valve stem cap protruding from the wheel or hubcap and push the gauge firmly onto the valve **(see illustration)**. Note the reading on the gauge and compare this figure to the recommended tire pressure shown on the tire placard on the left door. Be sure to reinstall the valve cap to keep dirt and moisture out of the valve stem mechanism. Check all four tires and, if necessary, add enough air to bring them up to the recommended pressure levels.

9   Don't forget to keep the spare tire inflated to the specified pressure (consult your owner's manual). Note that the air pressure specified for the compact spare is significantly higher than the pressure of the regular tires.

6   Power steering fluid level check (every 3000 miles or 3 months)

Refer to illustration 6.3

1   Unlike manual steering, the power steering system relies on fluid which may, over a period of time, require replenishing.

2   The fluid reservoir for the power steering pump is located on the inner fender panel near the front of the engine on the right (passenger) side of the engine compartment.

3   On these models the reservoir is translucent plastic and the fluid level can be checked visually **(see illustration)**.

4   The fluid level should be kept between the MIN and MAX marks on the reservoir.

5   If additional fluid is required, pour the specified type directly into the reservoir, using a funnel to prevent spills.

6   If the reservoir requires frequent fluid additions, all power steering hoses, hose connections, the power steering pump and the rack and pinion assembly should be carefully checked for leaks.

6.3 The power steering fluid reservoir is translucent so the fluid level can be checked without removing the cap - unscrew the cap to add fluid

7   Automatic transaxle fluid level check (every 3000 miles or 3 months)

Refer to illustration 7.4

1   The level of the automatic transaxle fluid should be carefully maintained. Low fluid level can lead to slipping or loss of drive, while overfilling can cause foaming, loss of fluid and transaxle damage.

2   The transaxle fluid level should only be checked when the transaxle is hot (at its normal operating temperature). If the vehicle has just been driven over 10 miles (15 miles in a frigid climate), and the fluid temperature is 160 to 175-degrees F, the transaxle is hot. **Caution:** *If the vehicle has just been driven for a long time at high speed or in city traffic in hot weather, or if it has been pulling a trailer, an accurate fluid level reading cannot be obtained. Allow the fluid to cool down for about 30 minutes.*

3   If the vehicle has not just been driven, park the vehicle on level ground, set the parking brake and start the engine. While the engine is idling, depress the brake pedal and move the selector lever through all the gear ranges, beginning and ending in Park.

4   With the engine still idling, remove the dipstick from its tube, located at the left (drivers) side of the engine compartment, below the distributor. Check the level of the fluid on the dipstick **(see illustration)** and note its condition.

5   Wipe the fluid from the dipstick with a clean rag and reinsert it back into the filler tube until the cap seats.

6   Pull the dipstick out again and note the fluid level. If the transaxle is cold, the level should be in the COLD or COOL range on the dipstick. If it is hot, the fluid level should be in the HOT range. If the level is at the low side of either range, add the specified automatic transmission fluid through the dipstick tube with a funnel.

7   Add just enough of the recommended fluid to fill the transaxle to the proper level. It takes about one pint to raise the level from the low mark to the high mark when the fluid is hot, so add the fluid a little at a time and keep checking the level until it is correct.

8   The condition of the fluid should also be checked along with the level. If the fluid at the end of the dipstick is black or a dark reddish brown color, or if it emits a burned smell, the fluid should be changed (see Section 30). If you are in doubt about the condition of the fluid, purchase some new fluid and compare the two for color and smell.

8   Engine oil and oil filter change (every 3000 miles or 3 months)

Refer to illustrations 8.2, 8.7, 8.13 and 8.15

1   Frequent oil changes are the best preventive maintenance the

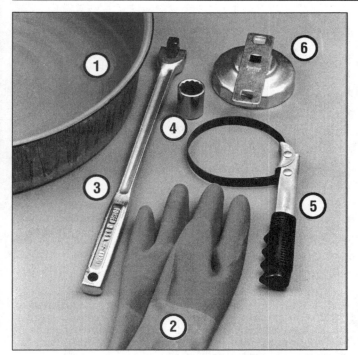

8.2 These tools are required when changing the engine oil and filter

1   **Drain pan** - *It should be fairly shallow in depth, but wide to prevent spills*
2   **Rubber gloves** - *When removing the drain plug and filter, you will get oil on your hands (the gloves will prevent burns)*
3   **Breaker bar** - *Sometimes the oil drain plug is tight, and a long breaker bar is needed to loosen it*
4   **Socket** – *To be used with the breaker bar or a ratchet (must be the correct size to fit the drain plug - six-point preferred)*
5   **Filter wrench** - *This is a metal band-type wrench, which requires clearance around the filter to be effective*
6   **Filter wrench** - *This type fits on the bottom of the filter and can be turned with a ratchet or breaker bar (different-size wrenches are available for different types of filters)*

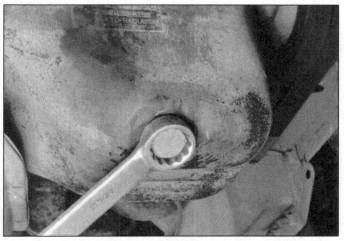

8.7 Use a proper size box-end wrench or socket to remove the oil drain plug and avoid rounding it off

8.13 Since the oil filter (accessible from below) is on very tight, you'll need a special wrench for removal - DO NOT use the wrench to tighten the new filter

home mechanic can give the engine, because aging oil becomes diluted and contaminated, which leads to premature engine wear.

2   Make sure that you have all the necessary tools before you begin this procedure **(see illustration)**. You should also have plenty of rags or newspapers handy for mopping up any spills.

3   Access to the underside of the vehicle is greatly improved if the vehicle can be lifted on a hoist, driven onto ramps or supported by jackstands. **Warning:** *Do not work under a vehicle which is supported only by a bumper, hydraulic or scissors-type jack.*

4   If this is your first oil change, get under the vehicle and familiarize yourself with the location of the oil drain plug. The engine and exhaust components will be warm during the actual work, so try to anticipate any potential problems before the engine and accessories are hot.

5   Park the vehicle on a level spot. Start the engine and allow it to reach its normal operating temperature (the needle on the temperature gauge should be at least above the bottom mark). Warm oil and sludge will flow out more easily. Turn off the engine when it's warmed up. Remove the filler cap in the rear cam cover.

6   Raise the vehicle and support it on jackstands. **Warning:** *To avoid personal injury, never get beneath the vehicle when it is supported by only by a jack. The jack provided with your vehicle is designed solely for raising the vehicle to remove and replace the wheels. Always use jackstands to support the vehicle when it becomes necessary to place your body underneath the vehicle.*

7   Being careful not to touch the hot exhaust components, place the drain pan under the drain plug in the bottom of the pan and remove the

plug **(see illustration)**. You may want to wear gloves while unscrewing the plug the final few turns if the engine is really hot.

8   Allow the old oil to drain into the pan. It may be necessary to move the pan farther under the engine as the oil flow slows to a trickle. Inspect the old oil for the presence of metal shavings and chips.

9   After all the oil has drained, wipe off the drain plug with a clean rag. Even minute metal particles clinging to the plug would immediately contaminate the new oil.

10   Clean the area around the drain plug opening, reinstall the plug and tighten it securely, but do not strip the threads.

11   Move the drain pan into position under the oil filter.

12   Remove all tools, rags, etc. from under the vehicle, being careful not to spill the oil in the drain pan, then lower the vehicle.

13   Loosen the oil filter **(see illustration)** by turning it counterclockwise with the filter wrench. Any standard filter wrench will work. Sometimes the oil filter is screwed on so tightly that it cannot be loosened. If this situation occurs, punch a metal bar or long screwdriver directly through the side of the canister and use it as a T-bar to turn the filter. Be prepared for oil to spurt out of the canister as it is punctured. Once the filter is loose, use your hands to unscrew it from the block. Just as the filter is detached from the block, immediately tilt the open end up to prevent the oil inside the filter from spilling out. **Warning:** *The engine exhaust manifold may still be hot, so be careful.*

14   With a clean rag, wipe off the mounting surface on the block. If a

8.15 Lubricate the oil filter gasket with clean engine oil before installing the filter on the engine

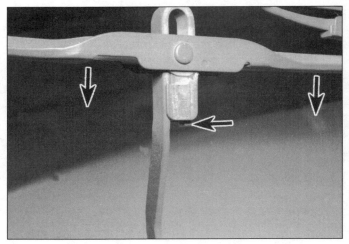

9.6 Press the tab and push the wiper down out of the hook in the end of arm

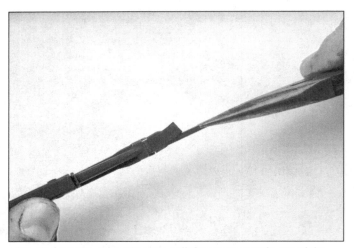

9.7 Use needle-nose pliers to pull the support rods out of the wiper element

residue of old oil is allowed to remain, it will smoke when the block is heated up. It will also prevent the new filter from seating properly. Also make sure that the none of the old gasket remains stuck to the mounting surface. It can be removed with a scraper if necessary.

15   Compare the old filter with the new one to make sure they are the same type. Smear some engine oil on the rubber gasket of the new filter and screw it into place **(see illustration)**. Because overtightening the filter will damage the gasket, do not use a filter wrench to tighten the filter. Tighten it by hand until the gasket contacts the seating surface. Then seat the filter by giving it an additional 3/4-turn.

16   Add new oil to the engine through the oil filler cap in the valve cover. Use a spout or funnel to prevent oil from spilling onto the top of the engine. Pour three quarts of fresh oil into the engine. Wait a few minutes to allow the oil to drain into the pan, then check the level on the oil dipstick (see Section 4 if necessary). If the oil level is at or near the F mark, install the filler cap hand tight, start the engine and allow the new oil to circulate.

17   Allow the engine to run for about a minute. While the engine is running, look under the vehicle and check for leaks at the oil pan drain plug and around the oil filter. If either is leaking, stop the engine and tighten the plug or filter slightly.

18   Wait a few minutes to allow the oil to trickle down into the pan, then recheck the level on the dipstick and, if necessary, add enough oil to bring the level to the F mark.

19   During the first few trips after an oil change, make it a point to

check frequently for leaks and proper oil level.

20   The old oil drained from the engine cannot be reused in its present state and should be discarded. Oil reclamation centers, auto repair shops and gas stations will normally accept the oil, which can be refined and used again. After the oil has cooled, it can be drained into a suitable container (capped plastic jugs, topped bottles, milk cartons, etc.) for transport to one of these disposal sites.

9   Windshield wiper blade inspection and replacement (every 6000 miles or 6 months)

Refer to illustrations 9.6 and 9.7

1   The wiper and blade assembly should be inspected periodically for damage, loose components and cracked or worn blade elements.

2   Road film can build up on the wiper blades and affect their efficiency, so they should be washed regularly with a mild detergent solution.

3   The action of the wiping mechanism can loosen bolts, nuts and fasteners, so they should be checked and tightened, as necessary, at the same time the wiper blades are checked.

4   If the wiper blade elements are cracked, worn or warped, or no longer clean adequately, they should be replaced with new ones.

5   Lift the arm assembly away from the glass for clearance.

6   Depress the retaining tab and slide the blade assembly down, out of the hook in the end of the wiper arm **(see illustration)**.

7   Bend the end of the wiper element out of the way and use needle-nose pliers to pull the two support rods out of the element **(see illustration)**.

8   With the support rods removed, slide the element out of the blade assembly.

9   Slide the new element into place and insert the support rods.

10   Clutch pedal freeplay check and adjustment (every 6000 miles or 6 months)

Refer to illustrations 10.1 and 10.2

1   Press down lightly on the clutch pedal and, with a small steel ruler, measure the distance that it moves freely before the clutch resistance is felt **(see illustration)**. The freeplay should be within the specified limits. If it isn't, it must be adjusted.

2   In the engine compartment, pull up on the clutch cable until the adjusting nut turns freely. Turn the adjusting nut clockwise or counterclockwise to achieve the specified freeplay at the pedal **(see illustration)**.

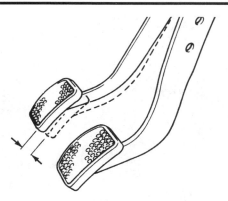

10.1 To determine the clutch pedal freeplay, depress the pedal, stop the moment clutch resistance is felt, then measure the distance

10.2 Pull up on the cable until the adjusting nut (arrow) turns freely, then turn the nut to adjust the clutch pedal freeplay

11 Battery check, maintenance and charging (every 6000 miles or 6 months)

Refer to illustrations 11.1, 11.6a, 11.6b, 11.7a, 11.7b and 11.8

Warning: *Certain precautions must be followed when checking and servicing the battery. Hydrogen gas, which is highly flammable, is always present in the battery cells, so keep lighted tobacco and all other open flames and sparks away from the battery. The electrolyte inside the battery is actually dilute sulfuric acid, which will cause injury if splashed on your skin or in your eyes. It will also ruin clothes and painted surfaces. When removing the battery cables, always detach the negative cable first and hook it up last!*

1   A routine preventive maintenance program for the battery in your vehicle is the only way to ensure quick and reliable starts. But before performing any battery maintenance, make sure that you have the proper equipment necessary to work safely around the battery **(see illustration)**.

2   There are also several precautions that should be taken whenever battery maintenance is performed. Before servicing the battery, always turn the engine and all accessories off and disconnect the cable from the negative terminal of the battery.

3   The battery produces hydrogen gas, which is both flammable and explosive. Never create a spark, smoke or light a match around the battery. Always charge the battery in a ventilated area.

4   Electrolyte contains poisonous and corrosive sulfuric acid. Do not allow it to get in your eyes, on your skin on your clothes. Never ingest it. Wear protective safety glasses when working near the battery. Keep children away from the battery.

5   Note the external condition of the battery. If the positive terminal and cable clamp on your vehicle's battery is equipped with a rubber protector, make sure that it's not torn or damaged. It should completely cover the terminal. Look for any corroded or loose connections, cracks in the case or cover or loose hold-down clamps. Also check the entire length of each cable for cracks and frayed conductors.

6   If corrosion, which looks like white, fluffy deposits **(see illustration)** is evident, particularly around the terminals, the battery should be removed for cleaning. Loosen the cable clamp bolts with a wrench, being careful to remove the ground cable first, and slide them off the terminals **(see illustration)**. Then disconnect the hold-down clamp bolt and nut, remove the clamp and lift the battery from the engine compartment.

7   Clean the cable clamps thoroughly with a battery brush or a terminal cleaner and a solution of warm water and baking soda **(see illustration)**. Wash the terminals and the top of the battery case with the same solution but make sure that the solution doesn't get into the battery When cleaning the cables, terminals and battery top, wear safety

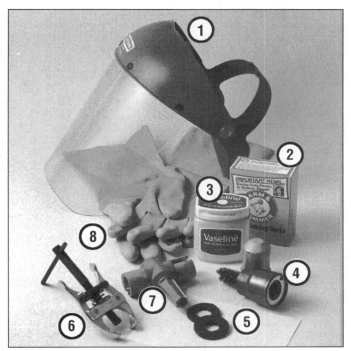

11.1 Tools and materials required for battery maintenance

1   ***Face shield/safety goggles*** - *When removing corrosion with a brush, the acidic particles can easily fly up into your eyes*

2   ***Baking soda*** - *A solution of baking soda and water can be used to neutralize corrosion*

3   ***Petroleum jelly*** - *A layer of this on the battery posts will help prevent corrosion*

4   ***Battery post/cable cleaner*** - *This wire brush cleaning tool will remove all traces of corrosion from the battery posts and cable clamps*

5   ***Treated felt washers*** - *Placing one of these on each post, directly under the cable clamps, will help prevent corrosion*

6   ***Puller*** - *Sometimes the cable clamps are very difficult to pull off the posts, even after the nut/bolt has been completely loosened. This tool pulls the clamp straight up and off the post without damage*

7   ***Battery post/cable cleaner*** - *Here is another cleaning tool which is a slightly different version of Number 4 above, but it does the same thing*

8   ***Rubber gloves*** - *Another safety item to consider when servicing the battery; remember that's acid inside the battery!*

11.6a Battery terminal corrosion usually appears as light, fluffy powder

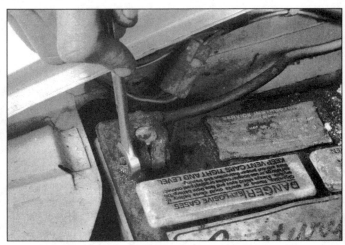

11.6b Removing the cable from a battery post with a wrench - sometimes special battery pliers are required for this procedure if corrosion has caused deterioration of the nut hex (always remove the ground cable first and hook it up last!)

11.7a When cleaning the cable clamps, all corrosion must be removed (the inside of the clamp is tapered to match the taper on the post, so don't remove too much material)

11.7b Regardless of the type of tool used on the battery posts, a clean, shiny surface should be the result

11.8 Make sure the battery hold-down nut (arrow) is tight

goggles and rubber gloves to prevent any solution from coming in contact with your eyes or hands. Wear old clothes too - even diluted, sulfuric acid splashed onto clothes will burn holes in them. If the terminals have been extensively corroded, clean them up with a terminal cleaner **(see illustration)**. Thoroughly wash all cleaned areas with plain water.

8   Make sure that the battery tray is in good condition and the hold-down clamp bolt or nut is tight **(see illustration)**. If the battery is removed from the tray, make sure no parts remain in the bottom of the tray when the battery is reinstalled. When reinstalling the hold-down clamp bolt or nut, do not overtighten it.

9   Information on removing and installing the battery can be found in Chapter 5. Information on jump starting can be found at the front of this manual. For more detailed battery checking procedures, refer to the *Haynes Automotive Electrical Manual*.

Cleaning

10   Corrosion on the hold-down components, battery case and surrounding areas can be removed with a solution of water and baking soda. Thoroughly rinse all cleaned areas with plain water.

11   Any metal parts of the vehicle damaged by corrosion should be covered with a zinc-based primer, then painted.

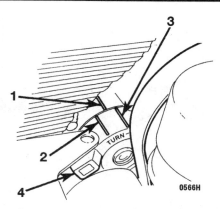

12.2 The serpentine drivebelt tensioner automatically keeps proper tension on the drivebelt, but it does have limits - the indicator mark (1) must remain between the minimum (2) and maximum (3) stretch lines on the tensioner (4)

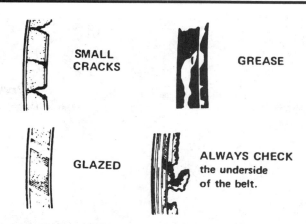

12.3 Here are some of the more common problems associated with drivebelts (check the belts very carefully to prevent an untimely breakdown)

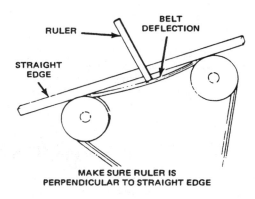

12.4   Measuring drivebelt deflection with a straightedge and ruler

Charging

Warning: *When batteries are being charged, hydrogen gas, which is very explosive and flammable, is produced. Do not smoke or allow open flames near a charging or a recently charged battery. Wear eye protection when near the battery during charging. Also, make sure the charger is unplugged before connecting or disconnecting the battery from the charger.*

12   Slow-rate charging is the best way to restore a battery that's discharged to the point where it will not start the engine. It's also a good way to maintain the battery charge in a vehicle that's only driven a few miles between starts. Maintaining the battery charge is particularly important in the winter when the battery must work harder to start the engine and electrical accessories that drain the battery are in greater use.

13   It's best to use a one or two-amp battery charger (sometimes called a "trickle" charger). They are the safest and put the least strain on the battery. They are also the least expensive. For a faster charge, you can use a higher amperage charger, but don't use one rated more than 1/10th the amp/hour rating of the battery. Rapid boost charges that claim to restore the power of the battery in one to two hours are hardest on the battery and can damage batteries not in good condition. This type of charging should only be used in emergency situations.

14   The average time necessary to charge a battery should be listed in the instructions that come with the charger. As a general rule, a trickle charger will charge a battery in 12 to 16 hours.

12   Drivebelt check, adjustment and replacement (every 6000 miles or 6 months)

Refer to illustrations 12.2, 12.3, 12.4, 12.5, 12.6 and 12.9

Check

1   The alternator and air conditioning compressor drivebelts, also referred to as V-ribbed belts or simply "fan" belts, are located at the right end of the engine. The good condition and proper adjustment of the alternator belt is critical to the operation of the engine. Because of their composition and the high stresses to which they are subjected, drivebelts stretch and deteriorate as they get older. They must therefore be periodically inspected.

2   The number of belts used on a particular vehicle depends on the accessories installed. One belt transmits power from the crankshaft to the power steering and air conditioning. The alternator is driven by its own belt. On some later models a single serpentine drivebelt driving the alternator, power steering pump and air conditioning compressor is used. The tension of the serpentine belt is checked visually **(see illustration)**

3   With the engine off, open the hood and locate the drivebelts at the left end of the engine. With a flashlight, check each belt for separation of the adhesive rubber on both sides of the core, core separation from the belt side, a severed core, separation of the ribs from the adhesive rubber, cracking or separation of the ribs, and torn or worn ribs or cracks in the inner ridges of the ribs . Also check for fraying and glazing, which gives the belt a shiny appearance. Both sides of the belt should be inspected, which means you will have to twist the belt to check the underside **(see illustration)**. Use your fingers to feel the belt where you can't see it. If any of the above conditions are evident, replace the belt (go to Step 9 or 10).

4   To check the tension on conventional drivebelts, push firmly on the belt with your thumb at a distance halfway between the pulleys and note how far the belt can be pushed (deflected). Measure this deflection with a ruler **(see illustration)**. The belt should deflect 1/4-inch if the distance from pulley center to pulley center is between 7 and 11 inches; the belt should deflect 1/2-inch if the distance from pulley center to pulley center is between 12 and 16 inches.

5   Adjust the power steering pump/air conditioner compressor or alternator belts by loosening the pivot and adjustment bolts and pivot the component (away from the engine to tighten the belt, toward it to loosen it) **(see illustration)**. Repeat the procedure until the drivebelt tension is correct and tighten the bolts.

Replacement
Serpentine drivebelt

6   Use a 3/8 inch drive socket wrench to rotate the tensioner clockwise and release the tension on the belt **(see illustration)**. The ten-

12.5 Loosen the adjustment bolt (arrow) and move the alternator in-or-out to adjust the drivebelt tension

CORRECT   WRONG

12.9 When installing a V-ribbed belt, make sure that it is centered - it must not overlap either edge of the pulley

sioner will swing down out of the way once the tension of the belt is released. Remove the belt and carefully release the tensioner. Route the new belt over the pulleys, again rotating the tensioner to allow the belt to be installed,then release the belt tensioner.

Conventional drivebelt

7   To replace a belt, follow the above procedures for drivebelt adjustment but slip the belt off the crankshaft pulley and remove it. If you are replacing the power steering pump belt, you will have to remove the air conditioning compressor belt first because of the way they are arranged on the crankshaft pulley. Because of this and because belts tend to wear out more or less together, it is a good idea to replace both belts at the same time. Mark each belt and its appropriate pulley groove so the replacement belts can be installed in their proper positions.

All belts

8   Take the old belts to the parts store in order to make a direct comparison for length, width and design.
9   After replacing the drivebelt, make sure that it fits properly in the pulley or ribbed grooves in the pulleys **(see illustration)**. It is essential that the belt be properly centered.
10   Adjust the belt(s) in accordance with the procedure outlined above.

---

13   Underhood hose check and replacement (every 6000 miles or 6 months)

Warning: *Replacement of air conditioning hoses must be left to a dealer service department or air conditioning shop that has the equipment to depressurize the system safely. Never remove air conditioning components or hoses until the system has been depressurized.*

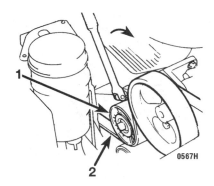

12.6 Use a 3/8-inch breaker bar to lift the tensioner (1) in the direction shown to release the tension from the belt (2)

General

1   High temperatures in the engine compartment can cause the deterioration of the rubber and plastic hoses used for engine, accessory and emission systems operation. Periodic inspection should be made for cracks, loose clamps, material hardening and leaks.
2   Information specific to the cooling system hoses can be found in Section 14.
3   Some, but not all, hoses are secured to the fittings with clamps. Where clamps are used, check to be sure they haven't lost their tension, allowing the hose to leak. If clamps aren't used, make sure the hose has not expanded and/or hardened where it slips over the fitting, allowing it to leak.

Vacuum hoses

4   It's quite common for vacuum hoses, especially those in the emissions system, to be color coded or identified by colored stripes molded into them. Various systems require hoses with different wall thicknesses, collapse resistance and temperature resistance. When replacing hoses, be sure the new ones are made of the same material.
5   Often the only effective way to check a hose is to remove it completely from the vehicle. If more than one hose is removed, be sure to label the hoses and fittings to ensure correct installation.
6   When checking vacuum hoses, be sure to include any plastic T-fittings in the check. Inspect the fittings for cracks and the hose where it fits over the fitting for distortion, which could cause leakage.
7   A small piece of vacuum hose (1/4-inch inside diameter) can be used as a stethoscope to detect vacuum leaks. Hold one end of the hose to your ear and probe around vacuum hoses and fittings, listening for the "hissing" sound characteristic of a vacuum leak. **Warning:** *When probing with the vacuum hose stethoscope, be very careful not to come into contact with moving engine components such as the drivebelts, cooling fan, etc.*

Fuel hose

Warning: *There are certain precautions which must be taken when inspecting or servicing fuel system components. Work in a well ventilated area and do not allow open flames (cigarettes, appliance pilot lights, etc.) or bare light bulbs near the work area. Mop up any spills immediately and do not store fuel soaked rags where they could ignite.*
8   Check all rubber fuel lines for deterioration and chafing. Check especially for cracks in areas where the hose bends and just before fittings, such as where a hose attaches to the fuel filter.
9   High quality fuel line, usually identified by the word *Fluroelastomer* printed on the hose, should be used for fuel line replacement. Never, under any circumstances, use unreinforced vacuum line, clear plastic tubing or water hose for fuel lines.
10   Spring-type clamps are commonly used on fuel lines. These clamps often lose their tension over a period of time, and can be "sprung" during removal. Replace all spring-type clamps with screw clamps whenever a hose is replaced.

ALWAYS CHECK hose for
chafed or burned areas that
may cause an untimely
and costly failure.

SOFT hose indicates inside
deterioration. This deterioration can
contaminate the cooling system and
cause particles to clog the radiator.

HARDENED hose can fail at any
time. Tightening hose clamps will
not seal the connection or stop leaks.

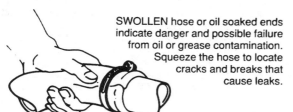

SWOLLEN hose or oil soaked ends
indicate danger and possible failure
from oil or grease contamination.
Squeeze the hose to locate
cracks and breaks that
cause leaks.

**14.4 Hoses, like drivebelts, have a habit of failing at the worst
possible time - to prevent the inconvenience of a blown radiator
or heater hose, inspect them carefully as shown here**

Metal lines

11   Sections of metal line are often used for fuel line between the fuel
pump and fuel injection unit. Check carefully to be sure the line has not
been bent or crimped and that cracks have not started in the line.
12   If a section of metal fuel line must be replaced, only seamless
steel tubing should be used, since copper and aluminum tubing don't
have the strength necessary to withstand normal engine vibration.
13   Check the metal brake lines where they enter the master cylinder
and brake proportioning unit (if used) for cracks in the lines or loose fittings. Any sign of brake fluid leakage calls for an immediate thorough
inspection of the brake system.

14   Cooling system check (every 6000 miles or 6 months)

Refer to illustration 14.4

1   Many major engine failures can be attributed to a faulty cooling
system. If the vehicle is equipped with an automatic transaxle, the
cooling system also cools the transaxle fluid and thus plays an important role in prolonging transaxle life.
2   The cooling system should be checked with the engine cold. Do
this before the vehicle is driven for the day or after the engine has been
shut off for at least three hours.
3   Remove the radiator cap by turning it to the left until it reaches a
stop. If you hear a hissing sound (indicating there is still pressure in the
system), wait until it stops. Now press down on the cap with the palm
of your hand and continue turning to the left until the cap can be removed. Thoroughly clean the cap, inside and out, with clean water.
Also clean the filler neck on the radiator. All traces of corrosion should
be removed. The coolant inside the radiator should be relatively trans-
parent. If it's rust colored, the system should be drained and refilled
(see Section 27). If the coolant level isn't up to the top, add additional

15.2 The recommended tire rotation pattern for these vehicles

antifreeze/coolant mixture (see Section 4).
4   Carefully check the large upper and lower radiator hoses along
with the smaller diameter heater hoses which run from the engine to
the firewall. Inspect each hose along its entire length, replacing any
hose which is cracked, swollen or shows signs of deterioration. Cracks
may become more apparent if the hose is squeezed **(see illustration)**.
Regardless of condition, it's a good idea to replace hoses with new
ones every two years.
5   Make sure that all hose connections are tight. A leak in the cooling system will usually show up as white or rust colored deposits on
the areas adjoining the leak. If wire-type clamps are used at the ends
of the hoses, it may be a good idea to replace them with more secure
screw-type clamps.
6   Use compressed air or a soft brush to remove bugs, leaves, etc.
from the front of the radiator or air conditioning condenser. Be careful
not to damage the delicate cooling fins or cut yourself on them.
7   Every other inspection, or at the first indication of cooling system
problems, have the cap and system pressure tested. If you don't have
a pressure tester, most gas stations and repair shops will do this for a
minimal charge.

15   Tire rotation (every 6000 miles or 6 months)

Refer to illustration 15.2

1   The tires should be rotated at the specified intervals and whenever uneven wear is noticed. Since the vehicle will be raised and the
tires removed anyway, check the brakes (see Section 16) at this time.
2   Radial tires must be rotated in a specific pattern **(see illustration)**.
3   Refer to the information in *Jacking and towing* at the front of this
manual for the proper procedures to follow when raising the vehicle
and changing a tire. If the brakes are to be checked, do not apply the
parking brake as stated. Make sure the tires are blocked to prevent the
vehicle from rolling.
4   Preferably, the entire vehicle should be raised at the same time.
This can be done on a hoist or by jacking up each corner and then lowering the vehicle onto jackstands placed under the frame rails. Always
use four jackstands and make sure the vehicle is firmly supported.
5   After rotation, check and adjust the tire pressures as necessary
and be sure to check the lug nut tightness.
6   For further information on the wheels and tires, refer to Chapter 10.

16   Brake check (every 15,000 miles or 12 months)

Note: *For detailed photographs of the brake system, refer to Chapter 9.*
1   In addition to the specified intervals, the brakes should be inspected every time the wheels are removed or whenever a defect is
suspected. Any of the following symptoms could indicate a potential

16.6 You will find an inspection hole like this in each caliper - placing a ruler across the hole should enable you to determine the thickness of remaining pad material for both inner and outer pads

16.16 Carefully peel back the wheel cylinder boot and check for leaking fluid indicating that the cylinder must be replaced or rebuilt

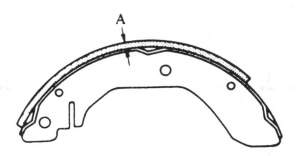

16.14 If the lining is bonded to the brake shoe, measure the lining thickness from the outer surface to the metal shoe, as shown here; if the lining is riveted to the shoe, measure from the lining outer surface to the rivet head

in this measurement.

8   If it is difficult to determine the exact thickness of the remaining pad material by the above method, or if you are at all concerned about the condition of the pads, remove the caliper(s), then remove the pads from the calipers for further inspection (refer to Chapter 9).

9   Once the pads are removed from the calipers, clean them with brake cleaner and remeasure them with a small steel pocket ruler or a vernier caliper.

10   Measure the disc thickness with a micrometer to make sure that it still has service life remaining. If any disc is thinner than the specified minimum thickness, replace it (refer to Chapter 9). Even if the disc has service life remaining, check its condition. Look for scoring, gouging and burned spots. If these conditions exist, remove the disc and have it resurfaced (see Chapter 9).

11   Before installing the wheels, check all brake lines and hoses for damage, wear, deformation, cracks, corrosion, leakage, bends and twists, particularly in the vicinity of the rubber hoses at the calipers. Check the clamps for tightness and the connections for leakage. Make sure that all hoses and lines are clear of sharp edges, moving parts and the exhaust system. If any of the above conditions are noted, repair, reroute or replace the lines and/or fittings as necessary (see Chapter 9).

Rear drum brakes

Refer to illustrations 16.14 and 16.16

12   Refer to Chapter 9 and remove the rear brake drums.

13   **Warning:** *Brake dust produced by lining wear and deposited on brake components may contain asbestos, which is hazardous to your health. DO NOT blow it out with compressed air and DO NOT inhale it! DO NOT use gasoline or solvents to remove the dust. Brake system cleaner should be used to flush the dust into a drain pan. After the brake components are wiped clean with a damp rag, dispose of the contaminated rag(s) and solvent in a covered and labeled container. Try to use non-asbestos replacement parts whenever possible.*

14   Note the thickness of the lining material on the rear brake shoes **(see illustration)** and look for signs of contamination by brake fluid and grease. If the lining material is within 1/16-inch of the recessed rivets or metal shoes, replace the brake shoes with new ones. The shoes should also be replaced if they are cracked, glazed (shiny lining surfaces) or contaminated with brake fluid or grease. See Chapter 9 for the replacement procedure.

15   Check the shoe return and hold-down springs and the adjusting mechanism to make sure they're installed correctly and in good condition. Deteriorated or distorted springs, if not replaced, could allow the linings to drag and wear prematurely.

16   Check the wheel cylinders for leakage by carefully peeling back the rubber boots **(see illustration)**. If brake fluid is noted behind the boots, the wheel cylinders must be replaced (see Chapter 9).

17   Check the drums for cracks, score marks, deep scratches and hard spots, which will appear as small discolored areas. If imperfections cannot be removed with emery cloth, the drums must be resur-

brake system defect: The vehicle pulls to one side when the brake pedal is depressed; the brakes make squealing or dragging noises when applied; brake travel is excessive; the pedal pulsates; brake fluid leaks, usually onto the inside of the tire or wheel.

2   The disc brake pads have built-in wear indicators which should make a high pitched squealing or scraping noise when they are worn to the replacement point. When you hear this noise, replace the pads immediately or expensive damage to the discs can result.

3   Loosen the wheel lug nuts.

4   Raise the vehicle and place it securely on jackstands.

5   Remove the wheels (see *Jacking and towing* at the front of this book, or your owner's manual, if necessary).

Disc brakes

Refer to illustration 16.6

6   There are two pads - an outer and an inner - in each caliper. The pads are visible through small inspection holes in each caliper **(see illustration)** .

7   Check the pad thickness by looking at each end of the caliper and through the inspection hole in the caliper body. If the lining material is less than the thickness listed in this Chapter's Specifications, replace the pads. **Note:** *Keep in mind that the lining material is riveted or bonded to a metal backing plate and the metal portion is not included*

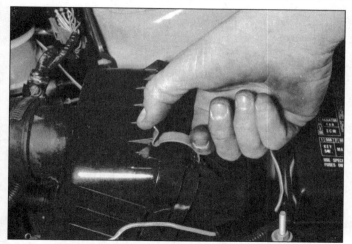

17.1a Press down on the center of the clip while lifting up on the end to detach the clips

17.1b Loosen the screw (arrow), detach the hose and remove the air cleaner housing cover

17.2 Lift the filter out of the housing

faced by an automotive machine shop (see Chapter 9 for more detailed information).

18   Refer to Chapter 9 and install the brake drums.

19   Install the wheels and snug the wheel lug nuts finger tight.

20   Remove the jackstands and lower the vehicle.

21   Tighten the wheel lug nuts to the torque listed.

Brake booster check

22   Sit in the driver's seat and perform the following sequence of tests.

23   With the engine stopped, depress the brake pedal several times-the travel distance should not change.

24   With the brake fully depressed, start the engine - the pedal should move down a little when the engine starts.

25   Depress the brake, stop the engine and hold the pedal in for about 30 seconds - the pedal should neither sink nor rise.

26   Restart the engine, run it for about a minute and turn it off. Then firmly depress the brake several times - the pedal travel should decrease with each application.

27   If your brakes do not operate as described above when the preceding tests are performed, the brake booster is either in need of repair or has failed. Refer to Chapter 9 for the removal procedure.

Parking brake

28   Slowly pull up on the parking brake and count the number of clicks you hear until the handle is up as far as it will go. The adjustment

is correct if you hear the number of clicks listed in this Chapter's Specifications. If you hear more or fewer clicks, it's time to adjust the parking brake (refer to Chapter 9).

29   An alternative method of checking the parking brake is to park the vehicle on a steep hill with the parking brake set and the transmission in Neutral. If the parking brake cannot prevent the vehicle from rolling, it is in need of adjustment (see Chapter 9).

17   Air filter replacement (every 15,000 miles or 12 months)

Refer to illustrations 17.1a, 17.1b and 17.2

1   The air filter is located inside a housing at the left (drivers) side of the engine compartment. To remove the air filter, loosen the air hose screw and release the four spring clips that keep the two halves of the air cleaner housing together **(see illustrations)**.

2   Lift the cover up and remove the air filter element **(see illustration)**.

3   Inspect the outer surface of the filter element. If it is dirty, replace it. If it is only moderately dusty, it can be reused by blowing it clean from the back to the front surface with compressed air. Because it is a pleated paper type filter, it cannot be washed or oiled. If it cannot be cleaned satisfactorily with compressed air, discard and replace it.

Caution: *Never drive the vehicle with the air cleaner removed. Excessive engine wear could result and backfiring could even cause a fire under the hood.*

4   Installation is the reverse of removal.

18   Fuel system check (every 15,000 miles or 12 months)

Warning: *Certain precautions should be observed when inspecting or servicing the fuel system components. Work in a well ventilated area and do not allow open flames (cigarettes, appliance pilot lights, etc.) near the work area. Mop up spills immediately and do not store fuel soaked rags where they could ignite. It is a good idea to keep a dry chemical (Class B) fire extinguisher near the work area any time the fuel system is being serviced.*

1   If you smell gasoline while driving or after the vehicle has been sitting in the sun, inspect the fuel system immediately.

2   Remove the gas filler cap and inspect if for damage and corrosion. The gasket should have an unbroken sealing imprint. If the gasket is damaged or corroded, remove it and install a new one.

3   Inspect the fuel feed and return lines for cracks. Make sure that the threaded flare nut type connectors which secure the metal fuel lines to the fuel injection system and the banjo bolts which secure the banjo fittings to the in-line fuel filter are tight.

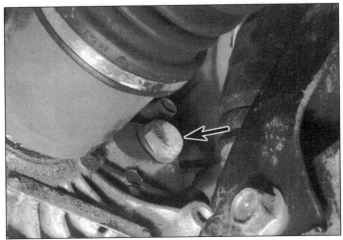

20.1 Remove the fill plug (arrow) from the transaxle and use your finger to make sure the lubricant level is even with the bottom of the plug hole

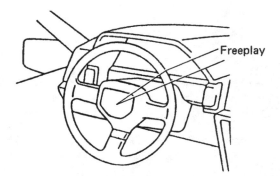

21.1 The steering wheel freeplay is the amount of travel between an initial steering input and the point at which the front wheels begin to turn (indicated by a slight resistance)

4   Since some components of the fuel system - the fuel tank and part of the fuel feed and return lines, for example - are underneath the vehicle, they can be inspected more easily with the vehicle raised on a hoist. If that's not possible, raise the vehicle and support it securely on jackstands.
5   With the vehicle raised and safely supported, inspect the gas tank and filler neck for punctures, cracks and other damage. The connection between the filler neck and the tank is particularly critical. Sometimes a rubber filler neck will leak because of loose clamps or deteriorated rubber. These are problems a home mechanic can usually rectify. **Warning:** *Do not, under any circumstances, try to repair a fuel tank (except rubber components). A welding torch or any open flame can easily cause fuel vapors inside the tank to explode.*
6   Carefully check all rubber hoses and metal lines leading away from the fuel tank. Check for loose connections, deteriorated hoses, crimped lines and other damage. Carefully inspect the lines from the tank to the fuel injection system. Repair or replace damaged sections as necessary (see Chapter 4).

19   Valve clearance check and adjustment (SOHC engine) (every 15,000 miles or 12 months)

SOHC engines
1   The valve clearances are checked and adjusted with the engine cold.
2   Remove the valve cover (Chapter 2A).
3   Place the number one piston at Top Dead Center (TDC) on the compression stroke (see Chapter 2A). The number one cylinder rocker arms (closest to the timing belt end of the engine) should be loose (able to move up-and-down slightly) and the number four cylinder rocker arms are tight.
4   With the crankshaft in this position, the following valves can be checked and adjusted:
   a) Intake and exhaust valves on the number one cylinder
   b) Intake valves on number two cylinder
   c) Exhaust valve on number three cylinder
5   Loosen the locknut, turn the the adjusting screw counterclockwise and insert the appropriate size feeler gauge between the valve stem and adjusting screw. Compare these measurements to the ones in the Specifications Section at the beginning of this Chapter. Carefully tighten the adjusting screw until you can feel a slight drag as you withdraw it from between the stem and adjusting screw.
6   After adjustment, hold the adjusting screw with a screwdriver (to keep it from turning) and tighten the locknut. Recheck the clearance to make sure it hasn't changed.

7   Rotate the crankshaft one full revolution (360-degrees) until the number four piston is at TDC on the compression stroke. The number four cylinder rockers arms (closest to the transaxle end of the engine) should be loose.
8   With the crankshaft in this position, the following valves can be checked and adjusted:
   a) Intake and exhaust valves on the number four cylinder
   b) Intake valves on number three cylinder
   c) Exhaust valve on number two cylinder
9   Install the valve cover.

20   Manual transaxle lubricant level check (every 15,000 miles or 12 months)

Refer to illustration 20.1
1   The manual transaxle does not have a dipstick. To check the fluid level, raise the vehicle and support it securely on jackstands. On the lower front side of the transaxle housing, you will see a plug **(see illustration)**. Remove it. If the lubricant level is correct, it should be up to the lower edge of the hole.
2   If the transaxle needs more lubricant (if the level is not up to the hole), use a syringe or a gear oil pump to add more. Stop filling the transaxle when the lubricant begins to run out the hole.
3   Install the plug and tighten it securely. Drive the vehicle a short distance, then check for leaks.

21   Steering and suspension check (every 15,000 miles or 12 months)

Refer to illustrations 21.1and 21.8
Note: *For detailed illustrations of the steering and suspension components, refer to Chapter 10.*

With the wheels on the ground
1   With the vehicle stopped and the front wheels pointed straight ahead, rock the steering wheel gently back and forth. If freeplay **(see illustration)** is excessive , a front wheel bearing, intermediate shaft U-joint, control arm balljoint or tie-rod end is worn or the steering gear is out of adjustment or broken. Refer to Chapter 10 for the appropriate repair procedure.
2   Other symptoms, such as excessive vehicle body movement over rough roads, swaying (leaning) around corners and binding as the steering wheel is turned, may indicate faulty steering and/or suspension components.
3   Check the shock absorbers by pushing down and releasing the vehicle several times at each corner. If the vehicle does not come back to a level position within one or two bounces, the shocks/struts are worn and must be replaced. When bouncing the vehicle up and down,

21.8 Inspect the balljoint boots (arrow) for damage

22.2 Flex the driveaxle boots by hand to check for cracks and/or leaking grease

23.4 Remove the clamp (arrow) and detach the power steering hose and allow the fluid to drain from the hose and the pump

listen for squeaks and noises from the suspension components. Additional information on suspension components can be found in Chapter 10.

Under the vehicle

4   Raise the vehicle with a floor jack and support it securely on jackstands. See *Jacking and towing* at the front of this book for the proper jacking points.
5   Check the tires for irregular wear patterns and proper inflation. See Section 5 in this Chapter for information regarding tire wear and Chapter 10 for the wheel bearing replacement procedures.
6   Inspect the universal joint between the steering shaft and the steering gear housing. Check the steering gear housing for grease leakage or oozing. Make sure that the dust seals and boots are not damaged and that the boot clamps are not loose. Check the steering linkage for looseness or damage. Check the tie-rod ends for excessive play. Look for loose bolts, broken or disconnected parts and deteriorated rubber bushings on all suspension and steering components. While an assistant turns the steering wheel from side to side, check the steering components for free movement, chafing and binding. If the steering components do not seem to be reacting with the movement of the steering wheel, try to determine where the slack is located.
7   Check the balljoint for wear by grasping each front wheel securely and moving it in-and-out to ensure that the balljoint has no play. If any

balljoint does have play, replace it. See Chapter 10 for the front balljoint replacement procedure.
8   Inspect the balljoint boots for damage and leaking grease **(see illustration)**. Replace the balljoints with new ones if they are damaged (see Chapter 10).

---

22   Driveaxle boot check (every 15,000 miles or 12 months)

Refer to illustration 22.2
1   The driveaxle boots are very important because they prevent dirt, water and foreign material from entering and damaging the constant velocity (CV) joints. Oil and grease can cause the boot material to deteriorate prematurely, so it's a good idea to wash the boots with soap and water.
2   Inspect the boots for tears and cracks as well as loose clamps **(see illustration)**. If there is any evidence of cracks or leaking lubricant, they must be replaced as described in Chapter 8.

---

23   Power steering fluid replacement (every 15,000 miles or 12 months)

Refer to illustration 23.4
1   At the specified intervals the power steering fluid must be drained and replaced.
2   Place a suitable container under the engine compartment to catch the fluid as it drains.
3   Remove the fluid reservoir cap.
4   Remove the clamp, detach the hose and allow the fluid to drain into the container **(see illustration)**.
5   Once the fluid has drained, connect the hose and install the clamp.
6   Fill the reservoir with the specified fluid. Start the engine and bleed the air from the power steering system as described in Chapter 10.

---

24   Fuel filter replacement (every 30,000 miles or 24 months)

Refer to illustration 24.3
Warning: *Certain precautions should be observed when inspecting or servicing the fuel system components. Work in a well ventilated area and do not allow open flames (cigarettes, appliance pilot lights, etc.) near the work area. Mop up spills immediately and do not store fuel soaked rags where they could ignite. It is a good idea to keep a dry chemical (Class B) fire extinguisher near the work area any time the fuel system is being serviced.*

24.3 Using a backup wrench on the filter, unscrew the fuel line fittings (arrows)

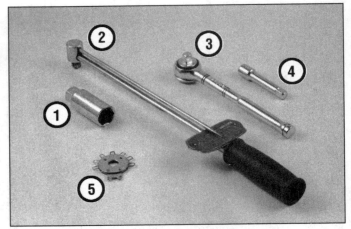

25.1 Tools required for changing spark plugs

1   **Spark plug socket** - *This will have special padding inside to protect the spark plug's porcelain insulator*
2   **Torque wrench** - *Although not mandatory, using this tool is the best way to ensure the plugs are tightened properly*
3   **Ratchet** - *Standard hand tool to fit the spark plug socket*
4   **Extension** - *Depending on model and accessories, you may need special extensions and universal joints to reach one or more of the plugs*
5   **Spark plug gap gauge** - *This gauge for checking the gap comes in a variety of styles. Make sure the gap for your engine is included*

25.4a Spark plug manufacturers recommend using a wire-type gauge when checking the gap - if the wire does not slide between the electrodes with a slight drag, adjustment is required

1   Relieve the fuel system pressure (see Chapter 4).
2   Raise the vehicle and support it securely on jackstands.
3   Using a backup wrench to steady the filter, unscrew the threaded fittings at each end of the fuel filter (use a flare nut wrench if possible), then remove the clamp bolt and detach the filter from the bracket (**see illustration**).
4   Install the new filter in the bracket, making sure the flanged end of the filter faces up. Tighten the bracket bolt securely.
5   Reattach the fuel lines to the filter, then tighten them securely.

---

25   Spark plug check and replacement (every 30,000 miles or 24 months)

Refer to illustrations 25.1, 25.4a, 25.4b, 25.6a, 25.6b, 25.6c, 25.8, 25.10a, 25.10b and 24.10c

1   Spark plug replacement requires a spark plug socket which fits onto a ratchet wrench. This socket is lined with a rubber grommet to protect the porcelain insulator of the spark plug and to hold the plug while you insert it into the spark plug hole. You will also need a wire-type feeler gauge to check and adjust the spark plug gap and a torque wrench to tighten the new plugs to the specified torque (**see illustration**).
2   If you are replacing the plugs, purchase the new plugs, adjust them to the proper gap and then replace each plug one at a time. **Note:** *When buying new spark plugs, it's essential that you obtain the*

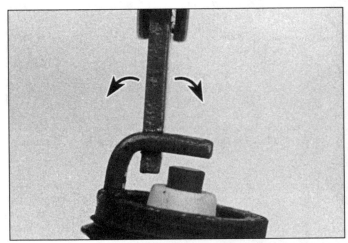

25.4b To change the gap, bend the side electrode only, as indicated by the arrows, and be very careful not to crack or chip the porcelain insulator surrounding the center electrode

correct plugs for your specific vehicle. This information can be found in the Specifications Section at the beginning of this Chapter, on the Vehicle Emissions Control Information (VECI) label located on the underside of the hood or in the owner's manual. If these sources specify different plugs, purchase the spark plug type specified on the VECI label because that information is provided specifically for your engine.
3   Inspect each of the new plugs for defects. If there are any signs of cracks in the porcelain insulator of a plug, don't use it.
4   Check the electrode gaps of the new plugs. Check the gap by inserting the wire gauge of the proper thickness between the electrodes at the tip of the plug (**see illustration**). The gap between the electrodes should be identical to that listed in this Chapter's Specifications or on the VECI label. If the gap is incorrect, use the notched adjuster on the feeler gauge body to bend the curved side electrode slightly (**see illustration**).

CARBON DEPOSITS

Symptoms: Dry sooty deposits indicate a rich mixture or weak ignition. Causes misfiring, hard starting and hesitation.

Recommendation: Check for a clogged air cleaner, high float level, sticky choke and worn ignition points. Use a spark plug with a longer core nose for greater anti-fouling protection.

OIL DEPOSITS

Symptoms: Oily coating caused by poor oil control. Oil is leaking past worn valve guides or piston rings into the combustion chamber. Causes hard starting, misfiring and hesition.

Recommendation: Correct the mechanical condition with necessary repairs and install new plugs.

TOO HOT

Symptoms: Blistered, white insulator, eroded electrode and absence of deposits. Results in shortened plug life.

Recommendation: Check for the correct plug heat range, over-advanced ignition timing, lean fuel mixture, intake manifold vacuum leaks and sticking valves. Check the coolant level and make sure the radiator is not clogged.

PREIGNITION

Symptoms: Melted electrodes. Insulators are white, but may be dirty due to misfiring or flying debris in the combustion chamber. Can lead to engine damage.

Recommendation: Check for the correct plug heat range, over-advanced ignition timing, lean fuel mixture, clogged cooling system and lack of lubrication.

HIGH SPEED GLAZING

Symptoms: Insulator has yellowish, glazed appearance. Indicates that combustion chamber temperatures have risen suddenly during hard acceleration. Normal deposits melt to form a conductive coating. Causes misfiring at high speeds.

Recommendation: Install new plugs. Consider using a colder plug if driving habits warrant.

GAP BRIDGING

Symptoms: Combustion deposits lodge between the electrodes. Heavy deposits accumulate and bridge the electrode gap. The plug ceases to fire, resulting in a dead cylinder.

Recommendation: Locate the faulty plug and remove the deposits from between the electrodes.

NORMAL

Symptoms: Brown to grayish-tan color and slight electrode wear. Correct heat range for engine and operating conditions.

Recommendation: When new spark plugs are installed, replace with plugs of the same heat range.

ASH DEPOSITS

Symptoms: Light brown deposits encrusted on the side or center electrodes or both. Derived from oil and/or fuel additives. Excessive amounts may mask the spark, causing misfiring and hesitation during acceleration.

Recommendation: If excessive deposits accumulate over a short time or low mileage, install new valve guide seals to prevent seepage of oil into the combustion chambers. Also try changing gasoline brands.

1

WORN

Symptoms: Rounded electrodes with a small amount of deposits on the firing end. Normal color. Causes hard starting in damp or cold weather and poor fuel economy.

Recommendation: Replace with new plugs of the same heat range.

DETONATION

Symptoms: Insulators may be cracked or chipped. Improper gap setting techniques can also result in a fractured insulator tip. Can lead to piston damage.

Recommendation: Make sure the fuel anti-knock values meet engine requirements. Use care when setting the gaps on new plugs. Avoid lugging the engine.

SPLASHED DEPOSITS

Symptoms: After long periods of misfiring, deposits can loosen when normal combustion temperature is restored by an overdue tune-up. At high speeds, deposits flake off the piston and are thrown against the hot insulator, causing misfiring.

Recommendation: Replace the plugs with new ones or clean and reinstall the originals.

MECHANICAL DAMAGE

Symptoms: May be caused by a foreign object in the combustion chamber or the piston striking an incorrect reach (too long) plug. Causes a dead cylinder and could result in piston damage.

Recommendation: Remove the foreign object from the engine and/or install the correct reach plug.

25.6a On DOHC engines, us an allen wrench to remove the spark plug cover screws . . .

25.6b . . . then lift off the cover

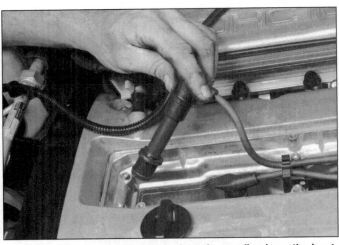

25.6c When removing the spark plug wires, pull only on the boot and twist it back-and-forth

25.8 Use a socket wrench with a long extension to unscrew the spark plug

5   If the side electrode is not exactly over the center electrode, use the notched adjuster to align them. **Caution:** *If the gap of a new plug must be adjusted, bend only the base of the ground electrode – do not touch the tip.*

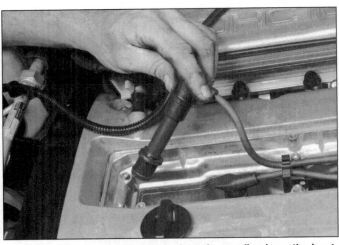

25.10a Apply a coat of anti-seize compound to the spark plug threads

Removal

6   On DOHC models, use an allen wrench to remove the spark plug cover **(see illustrations)**. To prevent the possibility of mixing up spark plug wires, work on one spark plug at a time. Remove the wire and boot from one spark plug. Grasp the boot - not the cable - as shown, give it a half twisting motion and pull straight up **(see illustration)**.
7   If compressed air is available, blow any dirt or foreign material away from the spark plug area before proceeding (a common bicycle pump will also work).
8   Remove the spark plug **(see illustration)**.
9   Whether you are replacing the plugs at this time or intend to reuse the old plugs, compare each old spark plug with those shown in the accompanying color photos to determine the overall running condition of the engine.

Installation

10   Prior to installation, apply a coat of anti-seize compound to the spark plug threads **(see illustration)**. It's often difficult to insert spark plugs into their holes without cross-threading them. To avoid this possibility, fit a short piece of 3/16-inch ID rubber hose over the end of the spark plug **(see illustrations)**. The flexible hose acts as a universal joint to help align the plug with the plug hole. Should the plug begin to cross-thread, the hose will slip on the spark plug, preventing thread damage. Tighten the plug to the torque listed in this Chapter's Specifications.

25.10b A length of 3/8-inch ID rubber hose will save time and
prevent damaged threads when installing the spark plugs

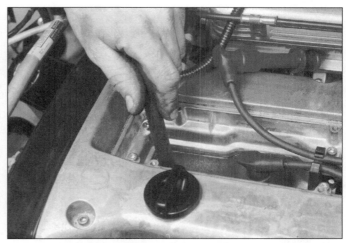

25.10c Start the spark plug into the hole with the rubber hose
and as soon as it starts to slip, finish tightening with the
socket wrench

26.11a Use a screwdriver to loosen the distributor cap screws

26.11b Inspect the inside of the distributor cap

11   Attach the plug wire to the new spark plug, again using a twisting motion on the boot until it is firmly seated on the end of the spark plug.
12   Follow the above procedure for the remaining spark plugs, replacing them one at a time to prevent mixing up the spark plug wires.

---

26   Spark plug wire, distributor cap and rotor check and replacement (every 30,000 miles or 24 months)

Refer to illustrations 26.11a, 26.11b, 26.11c, 26.12a and 26.12b

1   The spark plug wires should be checked whenever new spark plugs are installed.
2   Begin this procedure by making a visual check of the spark plug wires while the engine is running. In a darkened garage (make sure there is ventilation) start the engine and observe each plug wire. Be careful not to come into contact with any moving engine parts. If there is a break in the wire, you will see arcing or a small spark at the damaged area. If arcing is noticed, make a note to obtain new wires, then allow the engine to cool and check the distributor cap and rotor.
3   The spark plug wires should be inspected one at a time to prevent mixing up the order, which is essential for proper engine operation. Each original plug wire should be numbered to help identify its location. If the number is illegible, a piece of tape can be marked with the correct number and wrapped around the plug wire.

4   Disconnect the plug wire from the spark plug. A removal tool can be used for this purpose or you can grasp the rubber boot, twist the boot half a turn and pull the boot free. Do not pull on the wire itself.
5   Check inside the boot for corrosion, which will look like a white crusty powder.
6   Push the wire and boot back onto the end of the spark plug. It should fit tightly onto the end of the plug. If it doesn't, remove the wire and use pliers to carefully crimp the metal connector inside the wire boot until the fit is snug.
7   Using a clean rag, wipe the entire length of the wire to remove built-up dirt and grease. Once the wire is clean, check for burns, cracks and other damage. Do not bend the wire sharply, because the conductor might break.
8   Disconnect the wire from the distributor. Again, pull only on the rubber boot. Check for corrosion and a tight fit. Replace the wire in the distributor.
9   Inspect the remaining spark plug wires, making sure that each one is securely fastened at the distributor and spark plug when the check is complete.
10   If new spark plug wires are required, purchase a set for your specific engine model. Pre-cut wire sets with the boots already installed are available. Remove and replace the wires one at a time to avoid mix-ups in the firing order.
11   Detach the distributor cap by removing the two cap retaining

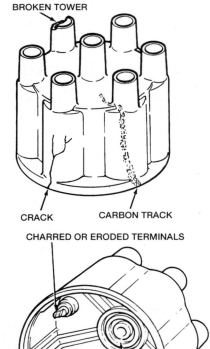

26.12a Pull the ignition rotor off the distributor shaft

26.11c Shown here are some of the common defects to look for when inspecting the distributor cap (if in doubt about its condition, install a new one)

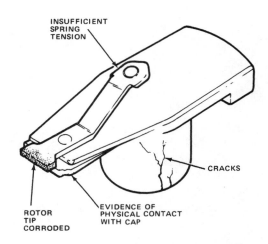

26.12b The ignition rotor should be checked for wear and corrosion as indicated here (if in doubt about its condition, buy a new one)

screws **(see illustration)**. Look inside it for cracks, carbon tracks and worn, burned or loose contacts **(see illustrations)**.

12   Pull the rotor off the distributor shaft and examine it for cracks and carbon tracks **(see illustrations)**. Replace the cap and rotor if any damage or defects are noted.

13   It is common practice to install a new cap and rotor whenever new spark plug wires are installed, but if you wish to continue using the old cap, check the resistance between the spark plug wires and the cap first. If the indicated resistance is more than the maximum value listed in this Chapter's Specifications, replace the cap and/or wires.

14   When installing a new cap, remove the wires from the old cap one at a time and attach them to the new cap in the exact same location – do not simultaneously remove all the wires from the old cap or firing order mix-ups may occur.

27   Cooling system servicing (draining, flushing and refilling) (every 30,000 miles or 24 months)

Warning: *Do not allow engine coolant (antifreeze) to come in contact with your skin or painted surfaces of the vehicle. Rinse off spills immediately with plenty of water. Antifreeze is highly toxic if ingested. Never leave antifreeze laying around in an open container or in puddles on the floor; children and pets are attracted by it's sweet smell and may drink it. Check with local authorities about disposing of used antifreeze. Many communities have collection centers which will see that an-*

tifreeze is disposed of safely.

1   Periodically, the cooling system should be drained, flushed and refilled to replenish the antifreeze mixture and prevent formation of rust and corrosion, which can impair the performance of the cooling system and cause engine damage. When the cooling system is serviced, all hoses and the radiator cap should be checked and replaced if necessary.

Draining

Refer to illustrations 27.4 and 27.5

2   Apply the parking brake and block the wheels. If the vehicle has just been driven, wait several hours to allow the engine to cool down before beginning this procedure.

3   Once the engine is completely cool, remove the radiator cap.

4   Move a large container under the radiator drain to catch the coolant. Open the drain fitting (a pair of pliers may be required to turn it) **(see illustration)**.

5   After the coolant stops flowing out of the radiator, move the container under the engine block drain plug **(see illustration)**. Loosen the plug and allow the coolant in the block to drain.

6   While the coolant is draining, check the condition of the radiator hoses, heater hoses and clamps (refer to Section 13 if necessary).

7   Replace any damaged clamps or hoses (see Chapter 3).

27.4 On most models you will have to remove a cover for access to the radiator drain fitting (arrow)

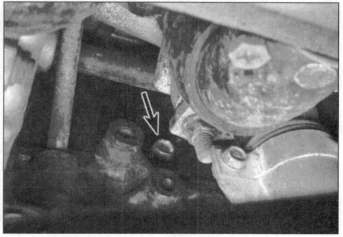

27.5 The block drain plug (arrow) is located on the side of the engine block, near the dipstick tube

15   Turn the engine off and let it cool. Add more coolant mixture to bring the level back up to the lip on the radiator filler neck.
16   Squeeze the upper radiator hose to expel air, then add more coolant mixture if necessary. Replace the radiator cap.
17   Start the engine, allow it to reach normal operating temperature and check for leaks.

28   Evaporative emissions control system check (every 30,000 miles or 24 months)

Refer to illustration 28.2
1   The function of the evaporative emissions control system is to draw fuel vapors from the gas tank and fuel system, store them in a charcoal canister and then burn them during normal engine operation.
2   The most common symptom of a fault in the evaporative emissions system is a strong fuel odor in the engine compartment. If a fuel odor is detected, inspect the charcoal canister, located at the front of the engine compartment. Check the canister and all hoses for damage and deterioration **(see illustration)**.
3   The evaporative emissions control system is explained in more detail in Chapter 6.

29   Exhaust system check (every 30,000 miles or 24 months)

1   With the engine cold (at least three hours after the vehicle has been driven), check the complete exhaust system from its starting point at the engine to the end of the tailpipe. This should be done on a hoist where unrestricted access is available.
2   Check the pipes and connections for evidence of leaks, severe corrosion or damage. Make sure that all brackets and hangers are in good condition and tight.
3   At the same time, inspect the underside of the body for holes, corrosion, open seams, etc. which may allow exhaust gases to enter the passenger compartment. Seal all body openings with silicone or body putty.
4   Rattles and other noises can often be traced to the exhaust system, especially the mounts and hangers. Try to move the pipes, muffler and catalytic converter. If the components can come in contact with the body or suspension parts, secure the exhaust system with new mounts.
5   Check the running condition of the engine by inspecting inside the end of the tailpipe. The exhaust deposits here are an indication of engine state-of-tune. If the pipe is black and sooty or coated with white deposits, the engine is in need of a tune-up, including a thorough fuel system inspection.

28.2 Check the charcoal canister for damage and the hose connections (arrows) for cracks and damage

Flushing

8   Once the system is completely drained, flush the radiator with fresh water from a garden hose until water runs clear at the drain. The flushing action of the water will remove sediments from the radiator but will not remove rust and scale from the engine and cooling tube surfaces.
9   These deposits can be removed by the chemical action of a cleaner. Follow the procedure outlined in the manufacturer's instructions. If the radiator is severely corroded, damaged or leaking, it should be removed (see Chapter 3) and taken to a radiator repair shop.
10   Remove the overflow hose from the coolant recovery reservoir. Drain the reservoir and flush it with clean water, then reconnect the hose.

Refilling

11   Close and tighten the radiator drain. Install and tighten the block drain plug.
12   Place the heater temperature control in the maximum heat position.
13   Slowly add new coolant (a 50/50 mixture of water and antifreeze) to the radiator until it's full. Add coolant to the reservoir up to the lower mark.
14   Leave the radiator cap off and run the engine in a well-ventilated area until the thermostat opens (coolant will begin flowing through the radiator and the upper radiator hose will become hot).

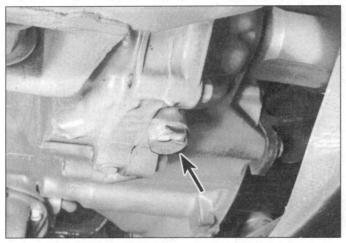

30.7 Remove the drain plug to drain the automatic transmission fluid

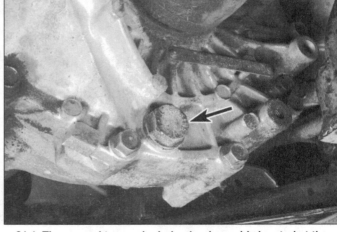

31.1 The manual transaxle drain plug (arrow) is located at the lower edge of the case

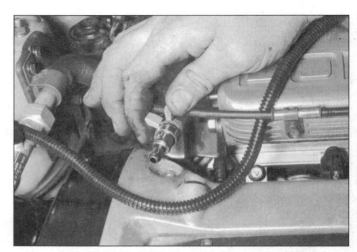

32.3 Shake the PCV valve to make sure it rattles

30 Automatic transaxle fluid and filter change (every 30,000 miles or 24 months)

Refer to illustration 30.7

1 At the specified time intervals, the automatic transaxle fluid should be drained and replaced.

2 Before beginning work, purchase the specified transmission fluid (see *Recommended fluids and lubricants* at the front of this Chapter).

3 Other tools necessary for this job include jackstands to support the vehicle in a raised position, a wrench, a drain pan capable of holding at least eight pints, newspapers and clean rags.

4 The fluid should be drained immediately after the vehicle has been driven. Hot fluid is more effective than cold fluid at removing built up sediment. **Warning:** *Fluid temperature can exceed 350-degrees F in a hot transaxle. Wear protective gloves.*

5 After the vehicle has been driven to warm up the fluid, raise it and place it on jackstands for access to the transaxle and differential drain plugs.

6 Move the necessary equipment under the vehicle, being careful not to touch any of the hot exhaust components.

7 With the drain pan in place, remove the drain plug and allow the fluid to drain. Once the fluid has drained, remove the bolts and lower the pan **(see illustration).**

8 Remove the filter retaining bolts and lower the filter from the transaxle. Be careful when lowering the filter as it contains residual fluid.

9 Place the new filter in position and install the bolts. Tighten the bolts to the torque listed in the Specifications Section at the beginning of this Chapter.

10 Carefully clean the gasket surfaces of the fluid pan, removing all traces of old gasket material. Noting the location, remove the magnet, wash the pan in clean solvent and dry it with compressed air. Be sure to clean and reinstall the magnet.

11 Install a new gasket, place the fluid pan in position and install the bolts in their original positions. Tighten the bolts to the torque listed in the Specifications Section at the beginning of this Chapter.

12 Lower the vehicle.

13 With the engine off, add new fluid to the transaxle through the dipstick tube (see *Recommended fluids and lubricants* for the recommended fluid type and capacity). Use a funnel to prevent spills. It is best to add a little fluid at a time, continually checking the level with the dipstick (see Section 7). Allow the fluid time to drain into the pan.

14 Start the engine and shift the selector into all positions from P through L, then shift into P and apply the parking brake.

15 With the engine idling, check the fluid level. Add fluid up to the Cold level on the dipstick.

31 Manual transaxle lubricant change (every 30,000 miles or 24 months)

Refer to illustration 31.1

1 Remove the drain plug(s) and drain the fluid. **(see illustration).**

2 Reinstall the drain plug(s) securely.

3 Add new fluid until it begins to run out of the filler hole (Section 20). See *Recommended lubricants and fluids* for the specified lubricant type.

32 Positive Crankcase Ventilation (PCV) valve and hose check and replacement (every 30,000 miles or 24 months)

Refer to illustration 32.3

1 The PCV valve and hose is located in the valve cover.

2 With the engine idling at normal operating temperature, place your finger over the valve opening. If there's no vacuum at the valve, check for a plugged hose or valve. Replace any plugged or deteriorated hoses.

3 Turn off the engine and shake the PCV valve, listening for a rattle. If the valve doesn't rattle, replace it with a new one **(see illustration).**

4 When purchasing a replacement PCV valve, make sure it's for your particular vehicle and engine size. Compare the old valve with the new one to make sure they're the same.

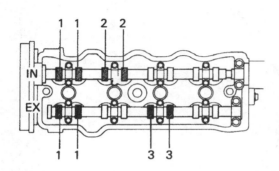

33.6a When the no. 1 piston is at TDC on the compression stroke, the valve clearances for the no. 1 and no. 3 cylinder exhaust valves and the no. 1 and no. 2 cylinder intake valves can be measured

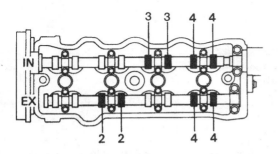

33.7 When the no. 4 piston is at TDC on the compression stroke, the valve clearances for the no. 2 and no. 4 exhaust valves and the no. 3 and no. 4 intake valves can be measured

33.6b Measure the clearance for each valve with a feeler gauge of the specified thickness - if the clearance is correct, you should feel a slight drag on the gauge as you pull it out

33.9a Install the valve lifter tool as shown and squeeze the handles together to lower the valve lifter so the shim can be removed

33.9b Remove the shim with a small screwdriver, a pair of tweezers or a magnet

---

33   Valve clearance check and adjustment (1.6L DOHC engines) (every 60,000 miles or 48 months)

Refer to illustrations 33.6a, 33.6b, 33.7, 33.9a, 33.9b, 33.10 and 33.13
Note: *The following procedure requires the use of a special valve lifter tool.*

1   Disconnect the negative battery cable.
2   Disconnect the air cleaner duct or other components which will interfere with valve cover removal.
3   Blow out the recessed area between the camshafts with compressed air, if available, to remove any debris that might fall into the cylinders, then remove the spark plugs (see Section 25).
4   Remove the valve cover (see Chapter 2A).
5   Refer to Chapter 2A and position the number 1 piston at TDC on the compression stroke.
6   Measure the clearances of the indicated valves with a feeler gauge of the specified thickness **(see illustrations)**. Record the measurements which are out of specification. They will be used later to determine the required replacement shims.
7   Turn the crankshaft one complete revolution and realign the timing marks. Measure the remaining valves **(see illustration)**.
8   After all the valve clearances have been measured, turn the crankshaft pulley until the camshaft lobe above the first valve which you intend to adjust is pointing up, away from the shim.
9   Position the notch in the valve lifter toward the spark plug. Then press down the valve lifter with the special valve lifter tool **(see illustration)**. Place the special valve lifter tool in position as shown, with the longer jaw of the tool gripping the lower edge of the cast lifter boss and the upper, shorter jaw gripping the upper edge of the lifter itself. Press down the valve lifter by squeezing the handles of the valve lifter tool together and remove the adjusting shim with a small screwdriver or a pair of tweezers **(see illustration)**. Note that the wire hook on the end of one valve lifter tool handle can be used to clamp both handles together to keep the lifter depressed while the shim is removed.
10   Measure the thickness of the shim with a micrometer **(see illus-**

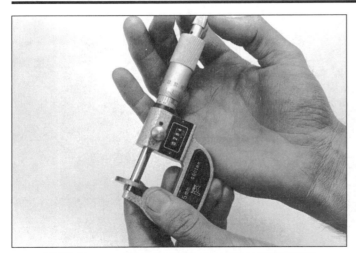

33.10 Measure the shim thickness with a micrometer

33.13 Remove the indicated camshaft bearing caps (arrows) for access to the shims for the cylinder number 4 valves

tration). To calculate the correct thickness of a replacement shim that will place the valve clearance within the specified value, use the following formula:

Intake side: N = T + (A − 0.008-inch)
Exhaust side: N = T + (A − 0.012-inch)
    T = thickness of the old shim
    A = valve clearance measured
    N = thickness of the new shim

11   Select a shim with a thickness as close as possible to the valve clearance calculated. Shims, which are available in 19 sizes in increments of 0.0020-inch (0.050 mm), range in size from 0.1005-inch (2.55 mm) to 0.1359-inch (3.45 mm). **Note:** *Through careful analysis of the shim sizes needed to bring all the out-of-specification valve clearances within specification, it is often possible to simply move a shim that has to come out anyway to another valve lifter requiring a shim of that particular size, thereby reducing the number of new shims that*

must be purchased.
12   Place the special valve lifter tool in position as shown in **illustration 33.9a,** with the longer jaw of the tool gripping the lower edge of the cast lifter boss and the upper, shorter jaw gripping the upper edge of the lifter itself, press down the valve lifter by squeezing the handles of the valve lifter tool together and install the new adjusting shim (note that the wire hook on the end of one valve lifter tool handle can be used to clamp the handles together to keep the lifter depressed while the shim is inserted). Measure the clearance with a feeler gauge to make sure that your calculations are correct.
13   Repeat this procedure until all the valves which are out of clearance have been corrected. **Note:** *To replace the selective shims for the cylinder number four valves, the camshaft bearing caps on the left end of the cylinder head must be removed* **(see illustration).**
14   Installation of the spark plugs, valve cover, spark plug wires and boots, accelerator cable bracket, etc. is the reverse of removal.

Chapter 2 Part A   Engines

Contents

Specifications

General

Firing order	1-3-4-2
Cylinder numbers (timing belt end-to-transaxle end)	1-2-3-4

Engine identification (8th character of the Vehicle Identification Number)

VIN code 6	1.6L Single overhead camshaft (SOHC)
VIN code 5	1.6L Double overhead camshaft (DOHC)
VIN code 8	1.8L Double overhead camshaft (DOHC)

Camshaft

1.6L SOHC
Lobe height
    1990 thru 1992.. 1.426 inches minimum
    1993
        Intake.. 1.399 inches minimum
        Exhaust.. 1.413 inches minimum
Journal diameter .... 1.0157 inches minimum
Runout.. 0.00394 inch maximum
Journal oil clearance .... 0.0059 inch maximum
Endplay .... 0.008 inch maximum
Distributor slot width .... 0.196 inch maximum
1.6L DOHC
Lobe height .... 1.503 inches minimum
Journal diameter .... 1.0157 inches minimum
Runout.. 0.0039 inch maximum
Journal oil clearance .... 0.0059 inch maximum
Endplay .... 0.008 inch maximum
Distributor slot width .... 0.196 inch maximum
1.8L DOHC
Lobe height .... 1.531 inches minimum
Journal diameter .... 1.0157 inches minimum
Runout.. 0.0039 inch maximum
Journal oil clearance .... 0.0059 inch maximum
Endplay .... 0.008 inch maximum
Distributor slot width .... 0.196 inch maximum

Warpage limits

Cylinder head warpage.. 0.0078 inch maximum
Exhaust manifold warpage .... 0.0157 inch maximum

Oil pump clearances

Driven gear-to-pump housing .... 0.0078 inch maximum
Drive gear-to-oil pump driven gear .... 0.012 inch maximum
Gear set-to-oil pump housing (endplay).......................... 0.004 inch maximum

Rocker arm shaft (1.6L SOHC)

Outside diameter .... 0.6299 inch minimum
Oil clearance.. 0.000197 to 0.00177 inch
Shaft runout - 1990 thru 1993 .... 0.01575 inch maximum

Valve clearances (engine cold)

1.6L SOHC
Intake .... 0.006 inch
Exhaust .... 0.010 inch
1.6L DOHC
Intake .... 0.004 to 0.008 inch
Exhaust .... 0.008 to 0.012 inch
1.8L DOHC .... Hydraulic (non-adjustable)

Valve lifter/tappet diameter

1.6L DOHC (solid lifter).. 1.218 inches minimum
1.8L DOHC (hydraulic lifter)... 1.219 inches minimum

Torque specifications   **Ft-lbs** (unless otherwise indicated)

Camshaft bearing cap bolts (1.8L DOHC only) .... 89 in-lbs
Camshaft sprocket retaining bolt(s)
SOHC
    1990 43
    1991 through 1993... 106 in-lbs
DOHC.. 43
Crankshaft pulley side bolts (1.6L SOHC)
1990 .... 89 in-lbs
1991 through 1993... 17
Crankshaft pulley center bolt
SOHC 87
DOHC
    1.6L.. 87
    1.8L.. 108

Cylinder head bolts (in sequence - **see illustrations 11.25a and 11.25b**)
    Step 1 29
    Step 2 58
Exhaust manifold nuts and bolts 30
Flywheel/driveplate
    1990
        Manual transaxle.. 58
        Automatic transaxle 47
    1991 through 1993
        Step 1 22
        Step 2 .... turn an additional 45 to 60-degrees
Idler pulley bolts 22
Intake manifold nuts and bolts 17
Oil pan nuts and bolts .... 89 in-lbs
Oil pump bolts .... 89 in-lbs
Oil pump cover screws... 89 in-lbs
Oil pump relief valve plug 27
Rear main oil seal retainer bolts .... 89 in-lbs
Rear mount center bolts 76
Rear mount-to-transaxle case bolts... 37
Rocker arm bracket bolts (1.6L SOHC only) 16
Timing belt cover bolts .... 89 in-lbs
Timing belt tensioner (all engines) 31
Valve cover bolts
    1.6L SOHC .... 89 in-lbs
    1.6L DOHC .... 26 in-lbs
    1.8L DOHC... 53 in-lbs

2A

1   General information

This Part of Chapter 2 is devoted to in-vehicle repair procedures for all engines. All information concerning engine removal and installation and engine block and cylinder head overhaul can be found in Part B of this Chapter.

The following repair procedures are based on the assumption that the engine is installed in the vehicle. If the engine has been removed from the vehicle and mounted on a stand, many of the steps outlined in this Part of Chapter 2 will not apply.

The Specifications included in this Part of Chapter 2 apply only to the procedures contained in this Part. Part B of Chapter 2 contains the Specifications necessary for cylinder head and engine block rebuilding.

2   Repair operations possible with the engine in the vehicle

Many major repair operations can be accomplished without removing the engine from the vehicle.

Clean the engine compartment and the exterior of the engine with some type of degreaser before any work is done. It will make the job easier and help keep dirt out of the internal areas of the engine.

Depending on the components involved, it may be helpful to remove the hood to improve access to the engine as repairs are performed (refer to Chapter 11 if necessary). Cover the fenders to prevent damage to the paint. Special pads are available, but an old bedspread or blanket will also work.

If vacuum, exhaust, oil or coolant leaks develop, indicating a need for gasket or seal replacement, the repairs can generally be made with the engine in the vehicle. The intake and exhaust manifold gaskets, oil pan gasket, crankshaft oil seals and cylinder head gasket are all accessible with the engine in place.

Exterior engine components, such as the intake and exhaust manifolds, the oil pan, the oil pump, the water pump, the starter motor, the alternator, the distributor and the fuel system components can be removed for repair with the engine in place.

Since the cylinder head can be removed without pulling the engine, camshaft and valve component servicing can also be accomplished with the engine in the vehicle. Replacement of the timing belt and sprockets is also possible with the engine in the vehicle.

In extreme cases caused by a lack of necessary equipment, repair or replacement of piston rings, pistons, connecting rods and rod bearings is possible with the engine in the vehicle. However, this practice is not recommended because of the cleaning and preparation work that must be done to the components involved.

3   Top Dead Center (TDC) for number one piston - locating

Refer to illustration 3.8
Note: *The following procedure is based on the assumption that the distributor is correctly installed. If you are trying to locate TDC to install the distributor correctly, piston position must be determined by feeling for compression at the number one spark plug hole, then aligning the ignition timing marks as described in Step 8.*

1   Top Dead Center (TDC) is the highest point in the cylinder that each piston reaches as it travels up-and-down when the crankshaft turns. Each piston reaches TDC on the compression stroke and again on the exhaust stroke, but TDC generally refers to piston position on the compression stroke.

2   Positioning the piston(s) at TDC is an essential part of many procedures such as camshaft and timing belt/sprocket removal and distributor removal.

3   Before beginning this procedure, be sure to place the transmission in Neutral and apply the parking brake or block the rear wheels. Also, disable the ignition system by detaching the primary (low voltage) wires from the coil (see Chapter 5). Remove the spark plugs (see Chapter 1).

4   In order to bring any piston to TDC, the crankshaft must be turned using one of the methods outlined below. When looking at the front of the engine, normal crankshaft rotation is clockwise.

  a) The preferred method is to turn the crankshaft with a socket and ratchet attached to the bolt threaded into the front of the crankshaft.

  b) A remote starter switch, which may save some time, can also be used. Follow the instructions included with the switch. Once the piston is close to TDC, use a socket and ratchet as described in the previous paragraph.

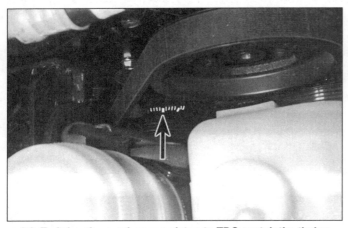

3.8 To bring the number one piston to TDC, watch the timing notch on the edge of the crankshaft pulley and align it with the 0-degree mark on the timing cover

c) If an assistant is available to turn the ignition switch to the Start position in short bursts, you can get the piston close to TDC without a remote starter switch. Make sure your assistant is out of the vehicle, away from the ignition switch, then use a socket and ratchet as described in Paragraph a) to complete the procedure.

5   Note the position of the terminal for the number one spark plug wire on the distributor cap. If the terminal isn't marked, follow the plug wire from the number one cylinder spark plug to the cap.

6   Use a felt-tip pen or chalk to make a mark on the distributor body directly under the terminal.

7   Detach the cap from the distributor and set it aside (see Chapter 1 if necessary).

8   Turn the crankshaft (see Paragraph 3 above) until the notch in the crankshaft sprocket is aligned with the 0 on the timing plate (located at the front of the engine) **(see illustration)**.

9   Look at the distributor rotor - it should be pointing directly at the mark you made on the distributor body.

10   If the rotor is 180-degrees off, the number one piston is at TDC on the exhaust stroke.

11   To get the piston to TDC on the compression stroke, turn the crankshaft one complete turn (360-degrees) clockwise. The rotor should now be pointing at the mark on the distributor. When the rotor is pointing at the number one spark plug wire terminal in the distributor cap and the ignition timing marks are aligned, the number one piston is at TDC on the compression stroke. **Note:** *If it's impossible to align the ignition timing marks when the rotor is pointing at the mark on the distributor body, the timing belt may have jumped the teeth on the sprockets or may have been installed incorrectly.*

4.4 Remove the timing belt cover bolts (arrows) - SOHC engine

12   After the number one piston has been positioned at TDC on the compression stroke, TDC for any of the remaining pistons can be located by turning the crankshaft and following the firing order. Mark the remaining spark plug wire terminal locations on the distributor body just like you did for the number one terminal, then number the marks to correspond with the cylinder numbers. As you turn the crankshaft, the rotor will also turn. When it's pointing directly at one of the marks on the distributor, the piston for that particular cylinder is at TDC on the compression stroke.

4   Valve cover - removal and installation

Refer to illustrations 4.4, 4.5, 4.7, 4.10, 4.11 and 4.13

Removal

1   Disconnect the negative cable from the battery.

2   Detach the PCV valve and breather hose from the valve cover.

SOHC engine

3   Disconnect the spark plug wires from the clips.

4   Remove the two upper bolts from the timing belt cover and loosen, but don't remove, the lower timing belt cover bolts **(see illustration)**.

5   Remove the valve cover bolts **(see illustration)**.

6   Pull the timing belt cover away from the valve cover, then lift the valve cover from the cylinder head. If it sticks, knock it loose with a rubber mallet or a hammer and a block of wood. Don't pry between the sealing surfaces.

4.5 Remove the two valve cover bolts (SOHC engine)

4.7 Remove the six Allen bolts that secure the spark plug cover, then remove the cover

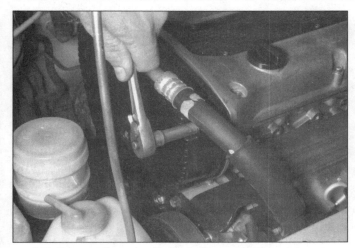

4.10 Remove the upper timing belt cover bolts and remove the cover

4.11 Remove the twelve Allen bolts (arrows) that hold the valve cover to the cylinder head

DOHC engines

7   Remove the spark plug cover from the center of the valve cover **(see illustration)**.
8   Disconnect the spark plug wires from the spark plugs.
9   Remove the bolt holding the wiring harness in place and reposition the harness in front of the timing belt cover.
10   Remove the bolts attaching the upper timing belt cover **(see illustration)**, then remove the cover.
11   Remove the twelve bolts holding the valve cover in place and remove the cover **(see illustration)**. If it sticks, knock it loose with a rubber mallet or a hammer and a block of wood. Don't pry between the sealing surfaces.

Installation

12   The mating surfaces of the housing or cylinder head and cover must be clean when the cover is installed. Use a gasket scraper to remove all traces of sealant and old gasket material, then clean the mating surfaces with lacquer thinner or acetone. If there's residue or oil on the mating surfaces when the cover is installed, oil leaks may develop.
13   Apply a light coating of silicone sealant to the arched areas of the camshaft bearing caps **(see illustration)**.
14   Reinstall the valve cover.
15   Tighten the bolts in several steps to the torque listed in this Chapter's Specifications.
16   Reinstall the remaining parts, run the engine and check for oil leaks.

4.13 Apply RTV sealant to the camshaft bearing caps (arrows)

5   Intake manifold - removal and installation

1   Disconnect the negative cable from the battery.
2   Drain the cooling system (see Chapter 1).
3   Remove the EGR pipe.
4   Remove the air intake plenum (see Chapter 4).
5   Remove the fuel rail (see Chapter 4).
6   Label and detach all wire harnesses, control cables and hoses still connected to the intake manifold.
7   Raise the vehicle and support it securely on jackstands.
8   Disconnect the oil cooler pipe and move it out of the way.
9   Remove the intake manifold braces.
10   Remove the lower mounting bolts.
11   Lower the vehicle.
12   Remove three upper mounting bolts and nuts.
13   Remove the intake manifold.

Installation

14   Use a scraper to remove all traces of old gasket material and sealant from the manifold and cylinder head, then clean the mating surfaces with lacquer thinner or acetone. Be careful not to gouge the soft aluminum. If the gasket was leaking, have the manifold checked for warpage at an automotive machine shop and resurfaced if necessary.
15   Install a new gasket, then position the manifold on the head and install the nuts/bolts.
16   Tighten the nuts/bolts in three or four equal steps to the torque listed in this Chapter's Specifications. Work from the center outwards to the ends to avoid warping the manifold.
17   Install the remaining parts in the reverse order of removal.
18   Before starting the engine, check the throttle linkage for smooth operation.
19   Run the engine and check for coolant and vacuum leaks.
20   Road test the vehicle and check for proper operation of all accessories, including the cruise control system (if equipped).

6   Exhaust manifold - removal and installation

Refer to illustrations 6.3 and 6.9
Warning: *The engine must be completely cool before beginning this procedure.*

Removal

1   Disconnect the negative cable from the battery.
2   Unplug the oxygen sensor electrical connector. If you're installing a new manifold, remove the sensor (see Chapter 6).

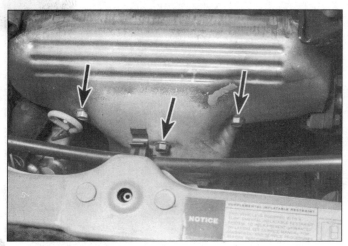

6.3 Remove the exhaust manifold heat shield bolts (arrows) and remove the shield (the two lower bolts aren't visible in this photo)

6.9 Disconnect the EGR pipe from the exhaust manifold by removing the two bolts (arrows)

3   Remove the heat shield from the manifold **(see illustration)**.
4   Apply penetrating oil to the exhaust manifold mounting nuts/bolts.
5   Raise the vehicle and support it securely on jackstands (see Chapter 1).
6   Remove the exhaust manifold brace.
7   Remove the exhaust pipe bracket.
8   Disconnect the exhaust pipe from the exhaust manifold. Lower the vehicle.
9   Disconnect the EGR pipe from the end of the manifold **(see illustration)**.
10   Remove the nuts/bolts and detach the manifold from the cylinder head.

Installation

11   Use a scraper to remove all traces of old gasket material and carbon deposits from the manifold and cylinder head mating surfaces. If the gasket was leaking, have the manifold checked for warpage at an automotive machine shop and resurfaced if necessary. **Caution:** *When scraping, be very careful not to gouge or scratch the delicate aluminum cylinder head.*
12   Position a new exhaust manifold gasket over the studs on the cylinder head.
13   Install the manifold and thread the mounting nuts/bolts into place.
14   Working from the center out, tighten the nuts/bolts to the torque listed in this Chapter's Specifications in several equal steps.
15   Reinstall the remaining parts in the reverse order of removal.
16   Run the engine and check for exhaust leaks.

7   Timing belt and sprockets - removal, inspection and installation

Removal

Refer to illustrations 7.6, 7.7a, 7.7b, 7.8, 7.9, 7.11, 7.16 and 7.17
1   Disconnect the negative cable from the battery.
2   Block the rear wheels and set the parking brake.
3   Position the engine at TDC compression for the number one cylinder (see Section 3).
4   Remove the drivebelts on SOHC engines or the serpentine belt and idler pulley on DOHC engines (see Chapter 1).
5   Support the engine with a hoist from above or with a floor jack and a block of wood positioned under the oil pan. **Caution:** *If a floor jack and a block of wood are used, be very careful not to damage the oil pan.*
6   Remove the right engine mount **(see illustration)**.
7   Remove the right and left side splash shields **(see illustrations)**.
8   Remove the crankshaft pulley center bolt **(see illustration)**. **Note:** *On DOHC engines it may be necessary to lower the engine slightly to gain access to the pulley bolt.* **Note:** *On DOHC engines it may be necessary to lower the engine slightly to gain access to the pulley bolt.* To prevent the crankshaft from turning, remove the flywheel/driveplate access cover and wedge a screwdriver between the ring gear teeth and the engine block.
9   Remove the crankshaft pulley **(see illustration)**. **Note:** *On SOHC engines remove the four additional crankshaft pulley bolts.*
10   On DOHC engines unbolt and reposition the wiring harness that

7.6 Unbolt the right engine mount from the bridge (which is attached to the chassis), then remove the support bracket (arrow)

7.7a From underneath the car remove the screws on both the left . . .

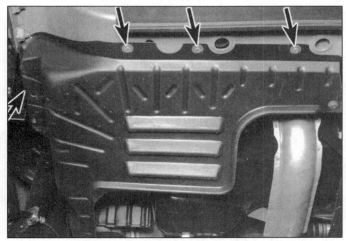

7.7b . . . and right splash shields and remove the shields

7.8 Remove the center bolt from the crankshaft pulley using a large socket and ratchet or breaker bar (four additional bolts will have to be removed on the SOHC engine to remove this pulley)

7.9 Use two prybars to carefully slide the pulley off the crankshaft

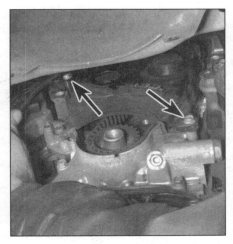

7.11 Remove the two bolts (arrows) and remove the lower timing belt cover

7.16 Once the timing belt cover(s) are removed the timing belt can be removed by working the belt off the sprockets and tensioner, removing the belt from the crankshaft sprocket last (shown here)

runs across the upper timing belt cover.

11   Remove either the single timing belt cover on the SOHC engine **(see illustration 4.4)** or the upper and lower covers on the DOHC engines **(see accompanying illustration and illustration 4.10)**.

12   If you plan to reuse the timing belt, paint match marks on the pulley and belt and an arrow indicating direction of travel on the belt.

13   If you're working on a DOHC model, remove the exhaust manifold heat shield **(see illustration 6.3)**.

14   Also, if you're working on a DOHC model, remove the power steering pump (don't disconnect the lines) and move it forward out of the way to gain access to the serpentine belt tensioner. Remove the tensioner.

15   Loosen the timing belt tensioner by turning the bolt clockwise. Do not remove the tensioner. **Note**: *The timing belt tensioner can be turned with the use of an Allen wrench placed in the hole in the tensioner.*

16   Remove the timing belt **(see illustration)**.

17   If it's necessary to remove the camshaft sprocket(s) (to replace the seal(s), for example), remove the valve cover (see Section 4). Remove the camshaft sprocket bolt(s) and remove the sprocket(s) from the camshaft(s) **(see illustration)**. Prevent the camshaft from turning by placing a wrench on the hex surface on the shaft. If it's necessary to remove the crankshaft sprocket, carefully pry it off with two prybars.

7.17 Prevent the camshaft from turning by holding it with a wrench (arrow), then remove the sprocket bolt

7.20 Check the timing belt for cracked and missing teeth

7.21 If the belt is cracked or worn, check the pulleys for nicks and burrs

7.22 Wear on one side of the belt indicates pulley misalignment problems

Inspection

Refer to illustrations 7.20, 7.21, 7.22, 7.27a, 7.26b and 7.27c

Caution: *Do not bend, twist or turn the timing belt inside out. Do not allow it to come in contact with oil, coolant or fuel. Do not utilize timing belt tension to keep the camshaft or crankshaft from turning when installing the sprocket bolt(s). Do not turn the crankshaft or camshaft more than a few degrees (necessary for tooth alignment) while the timing belt is removed.*

18   Remove the idler pulleys and check the bearings for smooth operation and excessive play. Inspect the spring for damage.

19   If the timing belt broke during engine operation, the belt may have been contaminated so check for belt material in the teeth of the sprockets. This must be cleaned out of all the sprockets before installing the new belt or the belt won't mesh properly when installed.

20   If the belt teeth are cracked or pulled off **(see illustration)**, the distributor, water pump, oil pump or camshaft(s) may have seized.

21   If there is noticeable wear or cracks in the belt **(see illustration)**, check to see if there are nicks or burrs on the sprockets.

22   If there is wear or damage on only one side of the belt **(see illustration)**, check the belt guide and the alignment of all sprockets. Also check the oil seals at the front of the engine and replace them if they are leaking.

23   Replace the timing belt with a new one if obvious wear or damage is noted or if it is the least bit questionable. Correct any problems which contributed to belt failure prior to belt installation. **Note**: *We recommend replacing the belt whenever it is removed, since belt failure can lead to expensive engine damage.*

Installation

24   Remove all dirt and oil from the timing belt area at the front of the engine.

25   If they were removed, install the idler pulleys and tensioner. The upper idler should be pulled back against spring tension as far as possible and the bolt temporarily tightened.

26   If they were removed, install the camshaft(s) and crankshaft sprocket(s). Tighten the sprocket bolt(s) to the torque listed in this Chapter's Specifications, using the method shown in illustration 7.17.

27   Recheck the camshaft and crankshaft timing marks to be sure they are properly aligned **(see illustrations)**. On DOHC engines, the marks on the camshaft sprockets should be pointing towards each other, in alignment with the machined surface of the top of the cylinder head. On SOHC engines, the mark on the camshaft sprocket should also be in alignment with the machined surface of the cylinder head, but the mark should be pointing towards the firewall. **Note**: *If necessary, rotate the camshaft slightly to achieve proper alignment.*

28   Install the timing belt on the crankshaft sprocket, water pump, tensioner and idler pulleys. If the original belt is being reinstalled, align the marks made during removal.

29   Slip the timing belt over the camshaft sprocket(s). On DOHC engines, keep tension on the side nearest the front of the vehicle. On SOHC models, keep tension on the side nearest the firewall.

30   Loosen the tensioner bolt to allow the tensioner to apply pressure to the belt, then tighten the bolt to the torque listed in this Chapter's Specifications..

31   Slowly turn the crankshaft clockwise two complete revolutions by hand. **Caution**: *If you feel resistance while rotating the engine by hand, do not continue. The valves may be contacting the pistons due to incorrect valve timing. Recheck the camshaft and crankshaft sprockets to be sure they are correctly aligned with their marks.*

32   If the marks are not aligned exactly as they should be, repeat the belt installation procedure. **Caution**: *DO NOT start the engine until you're absolutely certain that the timing belt is installed correctly. Serious and costly engine damage could occur if the belt is installed wrong.*

33   Reinstall the remaining parts in the reverse order of removal.

34   Run the engine and check for proper operation.

7.27a On DOHC engines, align the marks on each camshaft sprocket with the machined surface of the top of the cylinder head and pointing towards each other

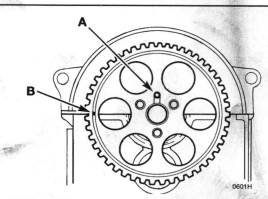

7.27b On SOHC engines, the dowel pin on the camshaft (A) should be in the 12-o'clock position and the mark on the camshaft should be in the 9-o'clock position (in alignment with the machined surface of the top of the cylinder head

7.27c The crankshaft sprocket alignment is the same for either the SOHC or DOHC engines - the triangular mark on the front cover should align with the small mark on the sprocket

8   Camshaft oil seal - replacement

Refer to illustration 8.8

Removal

1   Disconnect the cable from the negative battery terminal.
2   Block the rear wheels and set the parking brake.
3   Position cylinder number one on TDC compression (see Section 3).
4   Remove the valve cover (see Section 4).
5   Remove the distributor (see Chapter 5).
6   Remove the timing belt and camshaft sprocket(s) (see Section 7).
7   Before removing the seal(s) note how far into the bearing cap the old seal is placed and use this as a guide for installation depth.
8   Carefully pry the oil seal out using a thin screwdriver **(see illustration)** or using a small screw, turn the screw into the camshaft oil seal one or two threads and use the screw to pull the seal from the bearing cap.
9   On DOHC engines repeat this procedure for the second camshaft.
10   Clean the bearing caps and the camshaft journals with lacquer thinner or acetone.

Installation

11   Apply a light coating of clean engine oil or a film of a multi-purpose grease to the lip and outer edge of the seal, then place the seal squarely in the bore of the bearing cap.

8.8 Carefully pry the camshaft seal out of the bore - DO NOT nick or scratch the camshaft or seal bore

12   Using a seal driver or a socket of slightly smaller diameter than the outside diameter of the seal, drive the new seal into place.
13   The remainder of installation is the reverse of the removal procedure.

9   Camshafts, lifters and rocker arms - removal, inspection and installation

Removal

Refer to illustrations 9.4, 9.6 and 9.8

1   Remove the valve cover (see Section 4).
2   Remove the distributor (see Chapter 5).
3   Remove the timing belt and camshaft sprocket(s) (see Section 7).
4   Measure the thrust clearance (endplay) of the camshaft(s) with a dial indicator **(see illustration)**. If the clearance is greater than the value listed in this Chapter's Specifications, replace the camshaft and/or the cylinder head.

SOHC engine

Note: *The 1.6L SOHC engine uses a rocker shaft and rocker arm with an adjustable lash system for valve adjustment. See Chapter 1 for valve adjustment.*

5   Number or mark the components before removal to be sure that the parts will be reinstalled in the same location when reassembled.
6   Loosen the camshaft bearing cap bolts in the sequence shown 1/4-turn at a time working from the center out to the ends of the camshaft **(see illustration)**.

2A

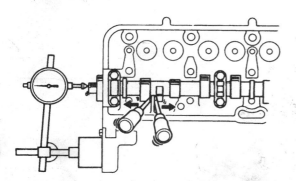

9.4 Pry the camshaft back-and-forth to check the endplay (thrust clearance)

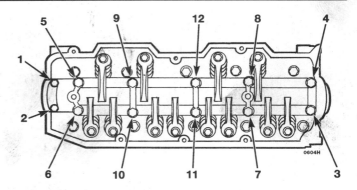

9.6 Loosen the camshaft bearing cap bolts, a little at a time, in the sequence shown (SOHC engine)

9.8 On DOHC engines the camshaft bearing caps are numbered from front to rear, and marked I for the intake side and E for the exhaust side (arrows)

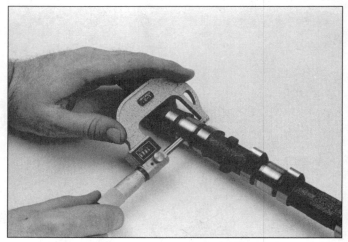

9.14a Measure each journal diameter with a micrometer (if any journal measures less than the specified limit, replace the camshaft)

7   When removing the bearing caps, along with them will come the rocker shaft assemblies and the camshaft oil seal.

DOHC engines

Note: *The 1.6L DOHC engine used in 1990 and 1991 used a solid valve lifter and an adjustable shim method of adjustment. 1.8L DOHC engines use a hydraulic lifter, which eliminates the need for an adjusting shim. The removal procedure is the same for both engines. The need to properly label parts for proper reassembly is very important (see Chapter 1 for valve adjustment).*

8   The bearing caps are numbered from front to rear, on both the intake and exhaust camshafts, to ensure they are reinstalled in the same locations when reassembled **(see illustration)**.

9   Loosen the bearing cap bolts 1/4-turn at a time on the exhaust camshaft starting from the center and moving toward each end of the camshaft.

10   Remove the caps and lift the exhaust camshaft off the cylinder head. Remove the oil seal from the camshaft.

11   Using a magnet if necessary, lift out each valve lifter and set them in numbered boxes, plastic sandwich bags or other containers so they can be reinstalled in the same position during reassembly.

12   Repeat this procedure for the intake camshaft.

Inspection

Refer to illustrations 9.14a, 9.14b, 9.16, 9.17, 9.22a and 9.22b

SOHC engine

13   Examine all parts, looking for signs of pitting, scoring or scuffing.

14   Measure the rocker arm shafts, camshaft journals and camshaft lobes and compare your measurements to the values listed in this Chapter's Specifications **(see illustrations)**.

15   Replace any parts that are worn beyond these limits.

DOHC engines

16   Inspect each hydraulic lifter or solid lifter and shim, depending which your engine uses, for scuffing and score marks **(see illustration)**.

17   Measure the outside diameter of each lifter and compare your measurements with the values listed in this Chapter's Specifications **(see illustration)**. Replace any lifter that is worn excessively.

18   There are shims used with the solid lifters - make sure the shims stay with the correct lifters (don't mix them up).

19   Visually examine the cam lobes and bearing journals for score marks, pitting, galling and evidence of overheating (blue, discolored areas). Look for flaking away of the hardened surface of each lobe.

20   Using a micrometer, measure the diameter of each camshaft journal **(see illustration 9.14a)**. If the diameter of any one journal is less

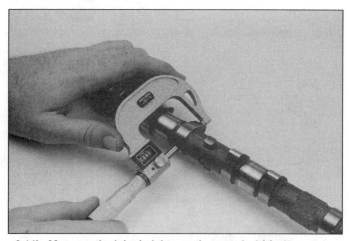

9.14b Measure the lobe heights on the camshaft(s) - if any lobe height is less than the minimum listed in this Chapter's specifications, replace the camshaft

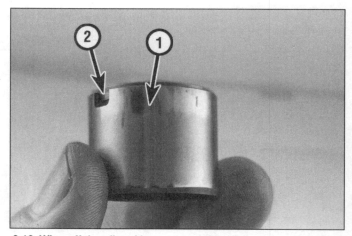

9.16 Wipe off the oil and inspect each lifter for wear and scuffing

    1   Lifter   *2   Shim*

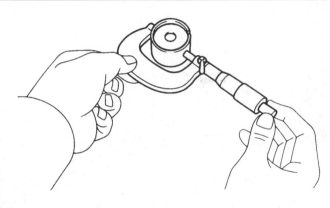

9.17 Use a micrometer to measure lifter diameter

9.22a Lay a strip of Plastigage on each camshaft journal

than specified, replace the camshaft.

21   Using a micrometer, measure the height of each lobe **(see illustration 9.14b)**. If the height for any one lobe is less than the specified minimum, replace the camshaft.

All engines

22   Check the oil clearance for each camshaft journal as follows:
  a) Clean the bearing caps and the camshaft journals with lacquer thinner or acetone.
  b) Carefully lay the camshaft(s) in place in the head. Don't install the lifters and don't use any lubrication.
  c) Lay a strip of Plastigage on each journal **(see illustration)**.
  d) Install the bearing caps with the arrows pointing toward the front (timing belt end) of the engine.
  e) If you're working on an SOHC engine, tighten the bolts IN SEQUENCE (use the reverse of the sequence shown in illustration 9.6) to the torque listed in this Chapter's Specifications in 1/4-turn increments. If you're working on a DOHC engine, tighten the bearing cap bolts, a little at a time, to the torque listed in this Chapter's Specifications. **Note**: *Don't turn the camshaft while the Plastigage is in place.*
  f) Remove the bolts and detach the caps.
  g) Compare the width of the crushed Plastigage (at its widest point) to the scale on the Plastigage envelope **(see illustration)**.
  h) If the clearance is greater than specified, replace the camshaft and/or cylinder head.
  i) Scrape off the Plastigage with your fingernail or the edge of a credit card - don't scratch or nick the journals or bearing caps.

Installation

Refer to illustration 9.23

SOHC engine

23   Apply moly-base grease or camshaft installation lube to the camshaft lobes and bearing journals **(see illustration)**.
24   Install the camshaft in the cylinder head, making sure that the dowel pin is in the up (12-o'clock) position.
25   Install the rocker arm assembly and tighten the bearing cap bolts, OPPOSITE the sequence shown in illustration 9.6, to the torque listed in this Chapter's Specifications.
26   Install a new camshaft oil seal (see Section 8).
27   Install the camshaft sprocket (see Section 7) and tighten the bolts to the torque listed in this Chapter's Specifications.
28   Install the timing belt (see Section 7).
29   The remainder of installation is the reverse of the removal procedure.

DOHC engines

30   Apply moly-base grease or camshaft installation lube to the lifters **(see illustration 9.23)**, then install them in their original locations. Make sure the valve adjustment shims are in place in the lifters.
31   The crankshaft sprocket should still be aligned at TDC. If it has moved slightly, move it back into alignment.
32   Apply moly-base grease or engine assembly lube to the camshaft lobes and bearing journals. Install each camshaft with the dowel pin in the 12-o'clock position. Make sure the camshafts are installed in their

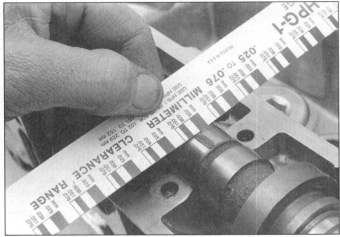

9.22b Compare the width of the crushed Plastigage to the scale on the envelope to determine the oil clearance

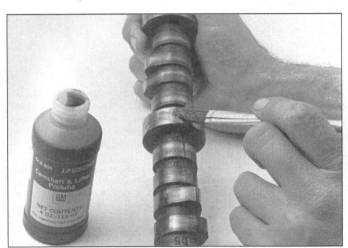

9.23 Coat the lobes and journals with cam lube

2A

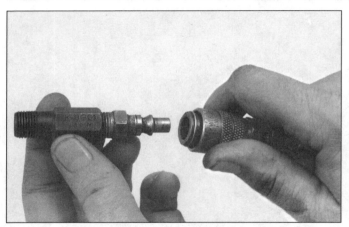

10.4 This is what the air hose adapter that threads into the spark plug hole looks like - they're commonly available from auto parts stores

10.9 Use a valve spring compressor to compress the springs, then remove the keepers from the valve stem with a magnet or small needle-nose pliers

correct positions.

33   Install the camshaft bearing caps in numerical order with the arrows pointing toward the timing belt end of the engine, then tighten the bolts, a little at a time, to the torque listed in this Chapter's Specifications. Start with the center bolts and work towards the outer bolts. Install the camshaft oil seals (see Section 8).

34   Install the camshaft sprockets on their correct camshafts. Make sure the alignment marks on the sprockets point towards each other **(see illustration 7.27a)**. Install the sprocket bolts and tighten them to the torque listed in this Chapter's Specifications. Be sure to prevent the camshafts from turning using the technique shown in illustration 7.17.

35   Install the timing belt (see Section 7).

36   The remainder of installation is the reverse of the removal procedure.

10   Valve springs, retainers and seals - disassembly, inspection and reassembly

Refer to illustrations 10.4, 10.9, 10.10, 10.15 and 10.17
Note: *Broken valve springs and defective valve stem seals can be replaced without removing the cylinder head. Two special tools and a compressed air source are normally required to perform this operation, so read through this Section carefully and rent or buy the tools before beginning the job. If compressed air isn't available, a length of nylon rope can be used to keep the valves from falling into the cylinder during this procedure.*

Disassembly

1   Refer to Section 9 and remove the camshaft(s).

2   Remove the spark plug from the cylinder which has the defective component. If all of the valve stem seals are being replaced, all of the spark plugs should be removed.

3   Turn the crankshaft until the piston in the affected cylinder is at Top Dead Center (TDC) on the compression stroke (refer to Section 3 for instructions). If you're replacing all of the valve stem seals, begin with cylinder number one and work on the valves for one cylinder at a time. Move from cylinder-to-cylinder following the firing order sequence (see this Chapter's Specifications).

4   Thread an adapter into the spark plug hole **(see illustration)** and connect an air hose from a compressed air source to it. Most auto parts stores can supply the air hose adapter. **Note:** *Many cylinder compression gauges utilize a screw-in fitting that may work with your air hose quick-disconnect fitting.*

5   Apply compressed air to the cylinder. **Warning:** *The piston may be forced down by compressed air, causing the crankshaft to turn suddenly. If the wrench used when positioning the number one piston at TDC is still attached to the bolt in the crankshaft nose, it could cause*

damage or injury when the crankshaft moves.

6   The valves should be held in place by the air pressure. If the valve faces or seats are in poor condition, leaks may prevent air pressure from retaining the valves - refer to the alternative procedure below.

7   If you don't have access to compressed air, an alternative method can be used. Position the piston at a point approximately 45-degrees before TDC on the compression stroke, then feed a long piece of nylon rope through the spark plug hole until it fills the combustion chamber. Be sure to leave the end of the rope hanging out of the engine so it can be removed easily.

8   Use a large ratchet and socket to rotate the crankshaft in the normal direction of rotation (clockwise, viewed from the front) until slight resistance is felt.

9   Stuff shop rags into the cylinder head holes above and below the valves to prevent parts and tools from falling into the engine, then use a valve spring compressor to compress the spring. Remove the keepers with small needle-nose pliers or a magnet **(see illustration)**. **Note:** *A couple of different types of tools are available for compressing the valve springs with the head in place. One type grips the lower spring coils and presses on the retainer as the knob is turned, while the other type utilizes a bolt or stud and nut for leverage. Both types work very well, although the lever type is usually less expensive.*

10   Remove the spring retainer and valve spring, then remove the stem oil seal **(see illustration)**. **Note:** *If air pressure fails to hold the valve in the closed position during this operation, the valve face and/or seat is probably damaged. If so, the cylinder head will have to be removed for additional repair operations.*

11   Wrap a rubber band or tape around the top of the valve stem so the valve won't fall into the combustion chamber, then release the air pressure. **Note:** *If a rope was used instead of air pressure, turn the crankshaft slightly in the direction opposite normal rotation.*

12   Inspect the valve stem for damage. Rotate the valve in the guide and check the end for eccentric movement, which would indicate that the valve is bent.

13   Move the valve up-and-down in the guide and make sure it doesn't bind. If the valve stem binds, either the valve is bent or the guide is damaged. In either case, the head will have to be removed for repair.

Reassembly

14   Reapply air pressure to the cylinder to retain the valve in the closed position, then remove the tape or rubber band from the valve stem. If a rope was used instead of air pressure, rotate the crankshaft in the normal direction of rotation until slight resistance is felt.

15   Lubricate the valve stem with engine oil and install a new oil seal **(see illustration)**.

16   Install the spring in position over the valve. Be sure the closely wound coils are next to the head.

10.10 Remove the valve guide seal with a pair of pliers

10.15 Gently tap the seal into place with a hammer and a deep socket

10.17 Apply a small dab of grease to each keeper as shown here before installation - it'll hold them in place on the valve stem as the spring is released

17   Install the valve spring retainer. Compress the valve spring and carefully position the keepers in the groove. Apply a small dab of grease to the inside of each keeper to hold it in place if necessary **(see illustration)**.

18   Remove the pressure from the spring tool and make sure the keepers are seated.

19   Disconnect the air hose and remove the adapter from the spark plug hole. If a rope was used in place of air pressure, pull it out of the cylinder.

20   Refer to Section 9 and install the camshaft(s).

21   Install the rest of the parts in the reverse order of the removal procedure.

22   Start and run the engine, then check for oil leaks and unusual sounds coming from the valve cover area

---

11   Cylinder head - removal and installation

Refer to illustrations 11.19, 11.25a and 11.25b
Caution: *The engine must be completely cool before beginning this procedure.*

Removal

1   Disconnect the negative cable from the battery.

2   Drain the coolant from the engine block and radiator (see Chapter 1).

3   Drain the engine oil and remove the oil filter (see Chapter 1).

4   Remove the air intake plenum and the fuel rail (see Chapter 4).

5   Remove the intake manifold (see Section 5).

6   Remove the exhaust manifold (see Section 6).

7   Remove the valve cover (see Section 4).

8   Remove the timing belt (see Section 7).

9   Remove the alternator (see Chapter 5).

10   Remove the distributor (see Chapter 5).

11   Unbolt the power steering pump and set it aside without disconnecting the hoses (see Chapter 10).

12   Check the cylinder head. Label and detach any remaining wiring or hoses that would interfere with head removal.

13   Using a breaker bar and the appropriate Allen-head driver or 12-point socket, loosen the cylinder head bolts in 1/4-turn increments until they can be removed by hand. Use the opposite of the tightening sequence **(see illustrations 11.25a and 11.25b)** to avoid warping or cracking the head.

14   Lift the cylinder head off the engine block. If it's stuck, very carefully pry up at the transaxle end, beyond the gasket surface.

15   Remove all external components from the head to allow for thorough cleaning and inspection. See Chapter 2, Part B, for cylinder head servicing procedures.

Installation

16   The mating surfaces of the cylinder head and block must be perfectly clean when the head is installed.

17   Use a gasket scraper to remove all traces of carbon and old gasket material, then clean the mating surfaces with lacquer thinner or acetone. If there's oil on the mating surfaces when the head is installed, the gasket may not seal correctly and leaks could develop. When working on the block, stuff the cylinders with clean shop rags to keep out debris. Use a vacuum cleaner to remove material that falls into the cylinders. **Caution:** *Be careful not to gouge the soft aluminum of the cylinder head.*

18   Check the block and head mating surfaces for nicks, deep scratches and other damage. If damage is slight, it can be removed with a file; if it's excessive, machining may be the only alternative.

19   Use a tap of the correct size to chase the threads in the head bolt holes **(see illustration)**, then clean the holes with compressed air - make sure that nothing remains in the holes. **Warning:** *Wear eye protection when using compressed air!*

20   Mount each bolt in a vise and run a die down the threads to remove corrosion and restore the threads. Dirt, corrosion, sealant and damaged threads will affect torque readings.

21   Install the components that were removed from the head.

22   Position the new gasket over the dowel pins in the block.

23   Carefully set the head on the block without disturbing the gasket.

24   Before installing the head bolts, apply a small amount of clean engine oil to the threads.

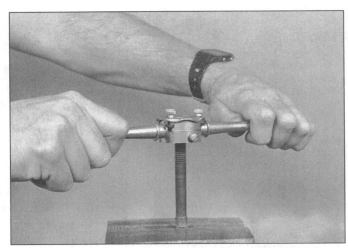

11.19 A die should be used to remove corrosion from the head bolt threads prior to installation

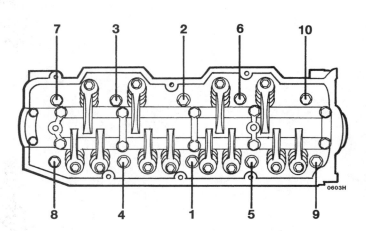

11.25a Cylinder head bolt TIGHTENING sequence (SOHC engine)

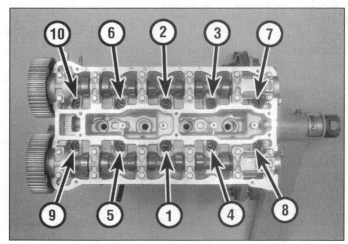

11.25b Cylinder head bolt TIGHTENING sequence (DOHC engine)

25   Install the bolts and tighten them finger tight. Following the recommended sequence **(see illustrations)**, tighten the bolts to the initial torque listed in this Chapter's Specifications.
26   Tighten the bolts, in sequence, to the final torque listed in this Chapter's Specifications.
27   The remaining installation steps are the reverse of removal.
28   Refill the cooling system, install a new oil filter and add oil to the engine (see Chapter 1).
29   Run the engine and check for leaks. Set the ignition timing (see Chapter 5) and road test the vehicle.

12   Oil pan - removal and installation

Refer to illustrations 12.11 and 12.15
1   Disconnect the negative cable from the battery.
2   Set the parking brake and block the rear wheels. Raise the front of the vehicle and support it securely on jackstands.
3   Remove the splash shields under the engine.
4   Support the engine from above using an engine hoist. If a hoist isn't available, support the engine/transaxle assembly with a floor jack, placed under the transaxle. Position a block of wood on the jack head to serve as a pad.
5   Drain the engine oil and remove the oil filter (see Chapter 1).
6   Disconnect the exhaust pipe from the exhaust manifold.

7   Unbolt the torque rod from the crossmember and the engine. Also unbolt the rear engine/transaxle mount from the crossmember.
8   Check to be sure the engine/transaxle assembly is still securely supported, then unbolt and remove the crossmember.
9   Remove the engine block-to-transaxle braces.
10   Remove the flywheel access cover.
11   Remove the bolts/nuts and detach the oil pan. If it's stuck, pry it loose very carefully with a small screwdriver or putty knife **(see illustration)**. Don't damage the mating surfaces of the pan and block or oil leaks could develop.
12   Use a scraper to remove all traces of old gasket material and sealant from the block and oil pan. Clean the mating surfaces with lacquer thinner or acetone.
13   Make sure the threaded bolt holes in the block are clean.
14   Check the oil pan flange for distortion, particularly around the bolt holes. If necessary, place the pan on a block of wood and use a hammer to flatten and restore the gasket surface.
15   Apply a bead of sealant to the oil pan flange **(see illustration)**.
Note: *The oil pan must be installed within 3 minutes once the sealant has been applied.*
16   Carefully position the oil pan on the engine block and install the bolts/nuts. Working from the center out, tighten them to the torque listed in this Chapter's Specifications in three or four steps.
17   The remainder of installation is the reverse of removal. Be sure to add oil and install a new oil filter.
18   Run the engine and check for oil leaks.

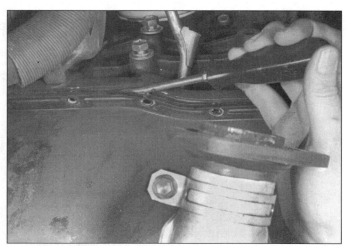

12.11 Carefully pry the oil pan away from the block - if the mating surfaces are damaged, oil leaks could develop

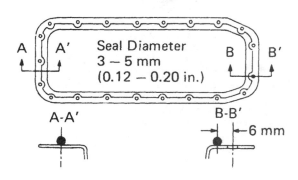

12.15 Apply a bead of sealant to the oil pan flange, to the inside of the inside of the bolt holes

13.5 Remove the bolts from the front cover (arrows) and remove the cover from the block

14.5a Measure the clearance between the oil pump driven gear and the pump housing . .

13 Front cover - removal and installation

Refer to illustration 13.5

Removal

1   Disconnect the negative battery cable.
2   Remove the timing belt (see Section 7).
3   Remove the crankshaft sprocket using two prybars or screwdrivers placed behind the gear to apply even pressure on the gear to slide it off the crankshaft.
4   Remove the nuts that attach the oil pan to the front cover.
5   Remove the front cover bolts from the engine block **(see illustration)** and separate the front cover from the engine block. You may have to pry carefully between the front main bearing cap and the pump housing with a screwdriver.

Installation

6   Use a scraper to remove all traces of sealant from the cover and engine block, then clean the mating surfaces with lacquer thinner or acetone.
7   Install new O-rings in the two grooves in the front cover. Apply a thin coat of RTV sealant to the front cover gasket surface and reinstall the front cover to the engine block. **Note:** *Be sure the sealant doesn't plug or cover any oil passages.*
8   Install the bolts and nuts, tightening them to the torque listed in this Chapter's Specifications.
9   The remainder of installation is the reverse of the removal procedure.

14 Oil pump - removal, inspection and installation

Refer to illustrations 14.5a, 14.5b and 14.5c

Removal

1   Remove the front cover, which is also the housing for the oil pump assembly (see Section 13).
2   Remove the relief valve from the housing. Turn the front cover over and place it on a bench and remove the screws that hold the oil pump cover to the oil pump housing.
3   Remove the oil pump gears from the housing and set them aside.
4   Note how far the seal is seated in the bore, then carefully pry it out of the oil pump housing with a screwdriver or seal removal tool. Don't scratch the housing bore or damage the crankshaft in the process (if the crankshaft is damaged, the new seal will end up leaking).

Inspection and reassembly

5   Reinstall the gears into the oil pump housing **(see illustrations)** and measure the clearances of:
   a) The driven gear-to-pump housing.
   b) The drive gear-to-oil pump driven gear.
   c) The gear set-to-oil pump housing clearance.
Compare your measurements to the ones listed in this Chapter's Specifications.
6   Be sure the surfaces of the pump housing are clean and dry before reassembly.
7   Lightly coat the outer edge of a new oil seal with engine oil or moly based grease. Using a socket with an outside diameter slightly

2A

14.5b . . .then measure the clearance between the drive and driven gear . .

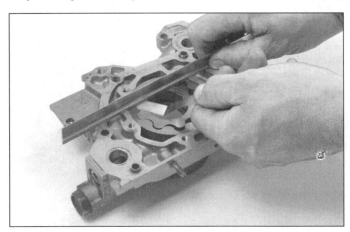

14.5c . . .and finally, use a straightedge and measure the endplay between the gears and the pump housing

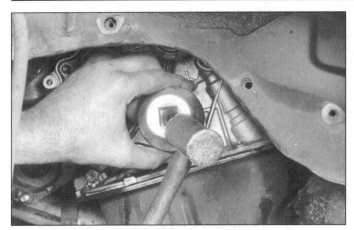

15.4 Gently tap the new seal into place with the spring side toward the engine

smaller than the outside diameter of the seal, carefully drive the new seal into place with a hammer. Make sure it's installed squarely and driven in to the same depth as the original. If a socket isn't available, a short section of large diameter pipe will also work. Check the seal after installation to make sure the garter spring didn't pop out of place. Apply multi-purpose grease to the seal lip surface that contacts the crankshaft.

8   Lubricate the oil pressure relief valve piston with clean engine oil and reinstall the valve components into the pump case. Tighten the plug to the torque listed in this Chapter's Specifications.

9   Lubricate the gear set with clean engine oil. Reinstall the gears.

10   Pack the pump cavities with petroleum jelly (this will prime the pump and ensure good suction when the engine is started).

11   Install the cover and tighten the screws to the torque listed in this Chapter's Specifications.

12   It's a good idea to remove the oil pan and inspect the screen at the end of the oil pick-up tube for any debris that might be plugging it. Either clean the tube and screen completely or replace it with a new one at this time.

Installation

13   Install the front cover (see Section 13).

14   Reinstall the remaining parts in the reverse order of removal.

15   Add oil (see Chapter 1), start the engine and check for oil pressure and leaks.

---

15   Crankshaft front oil seal - replacement

Refer to illustration 15.4

1   Remove the timing belt and crankshaft pulley (see Section 7).

2   Note how far the seal is seated in the bore, then carefully pry it out of the oil pump housing with a screwdriver or seal removal tool. Don't scratch the housing bore or damage the crankshaft in the process (if the crankshaft is damaged, the new seal will end up leaking).

3   Clean the bore in the housing and coat the outer edge of the new seal with engine oil or multi-purpose grease. Apply multi-purpose grease to the seal lip.

4   Using a seal driver or a socket with an outside diameter slightly smaller than the outside diameter of the seal, carefully drive the new seal into place with a hammer **(see illustration)**. Make sure it's installed squarely and driven in to the same depth as the original. Check the seal after installation to make sure the garter spring didn't pop out of place.

5   Reinstall the crankshaft timing gear and timing belt (see Section 7).

6   The rest of the installation is the reverse of the removal procedure.

7   Run the engine and check for oil leaks at the front seal.

16.3 Mark the flywheel/driveplate and the crankshaft so they can be reassembled in the same relative position

---

16   Flywheel/driveplate - removal, inspection and installation

Refer to illustration 16.3

Removal

1   Raise the vehicle and support it securely on jackstands, then refer to Chapter 7 and remove the transaxle.

2   If you're working on a model with a manual transaxle, remove the pressure plate and clutch disc (see Chapter 8). Now is a good time to check/replace the clutch components and pilot bearing.

3   Use a center-punch or paint to make alignment marks on the flywheel/driveplate and crankshaft to ensure correct alignment during installation **(see illustration)**.

4   Remove the bolts that secure the flywheel/driveplate to the crankshaft. If the crankshaft turns, wedge a screwdriver in the ring gear teeth to jam the flywheel.

5   Remove the flywheel/driveplate from the crankshaft. Since the flywheel is fairly heavy, be sure to support it while removing the last bolt. Automatic transaxle equipped vehicles have spacers on both sides of the driveplate.

Inspection

6   Clean the flywheel to remove grease and oil. Inspect the surface for cracks, rivet grooves, burned areas and score marks. Light scoring can be removed with emery cloth. Check for cracked and broken ring gear teeth. Lay the flywheel on a flat surface and use a straightedge to check for warpage. If necessary, take the flywheel to an automotive machine shop to have it resurfaced.

7   Clean and inspect the mating surfaces of the flywheel/driveplate and the crankshaft. If the crankshaft rear seal is leaking, replace it before reinstalling the flywheel/driveplate.

Installation

8   Position the flywheel/driveplate against the crankshaft. Be sure to align the marks made during removal. Note that some engines have an alignment dowel or staggered bolt holes to ensure correct installation. Before installing the bolts, apply thread locking compound to the threads.

9   Wedge a screwdriver in the ring gear teeth to keep the flywheel/driveplate from turning as you tighten the bolts to the torque listed in this Chapter's Specifications. Follow a criss-cross pattern and work up to the final torque in three or four steps.

10   The remainder of installation is the reverse of the removal procedure.

17.2a The quick way to replace the rear main oil seal is to simply pry the old one out . . .

17.2b . . . then lubricate the crankshaft journal and the lip of the new seal with engine oil and tap the new seal into place - the seal lip is stiff and can be easily damaged during installation if you're not careful

17 Rear main oil seal - replacement

Refer to illustrations 17.2a, 17.2b, 17.5 and 17.6

1   The transaxle must be removed from the vehicle for this procedure (see Chapter 7).
2   The seal can be replaced without dropping the oil pan or removing the seal retainer. However, this method can be more difficult because the lip of the seal is quite stiff and it's possible to cock the seal in the retainer bore or damage it during installation. If you want to take the chance, pry out the old seal with a screwdriver or seal removal tool **(see illustration)**. Apply engine oil to the crankshaft seal journal and the lip of the new seal and carefully push the new seal into place. The lip is stiff so carefully work it onto the seal journal of the crankshaft with a smooth object like the end of a socket extension as you tap the seal into place **(see illustration)**.
3   The following method is recommended but requires removal of the oil pan (see Section 12) and the seal retainer.
4   After the oil pan has been removed, remove the bolts, detach the seal retainer and peel off all the old gasket material.
5   Position the seal and retainer assembly on a couple of wood blocks and drive the old seal out from the back side with a punch **(see illustration)**.
6   Drive the new seal into the retainer with a block of wood **(see illustration)** or a section of pipe slightly smaller in diameter than the

outside diameter of the seal.
7   Lubricate the crankshaft seal journal and the lip of the new seal with engine oil. Position a new gasket on the engine block.
8   Slowly and carefully push the seal onto the crankshaft. The seal lip is stiff, so work it onto the crankshaft with a smooth object such as the end of a socket extension as you push the retainer against the block.
9   Install and tighten the retainer bolts to the torque listed in this Chapter's Specifications. The bottom sealing flange of the retainer must not extend below the bottom sealing flange (oil pan rail) of the block.
10   The remaining steps are the reverse of removal.

18 Engine mounts - check and replacement

Refer to illustrations 18.8a, 18.8b and 18.10

1   Engine mounts seldom require attention, but broken or deteriorated mounts should be replaced immediately or the added strain placed on the driveline components may cause damage or wear.

Check

2   During the check, the engine must be raised slightly to remove

2A

17.5 After removing the retainer from the engine, support it on wood blocks and drive out the old seal with a punch and hammer

17.6 Drive the new seal into the retainer with a wood block or a section of pipe, if you have one large enough - make sure you don't cock the seal in the retainer bore

18.8a Remove the through-bolt (arrow)

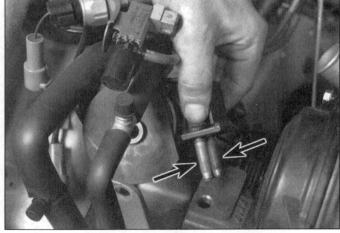

18.8b The mount is attached to the engine with studs (arrows) - remove the nuts and lift the mount up to remove it

the weight from the mounts.

3   Raise the vehicle and support it securely on jackstands, then position a jack under the engine oil pan. Place a block of wood between the jack head and the oil pan, then carefully raise the engine just enough to take the weight off the mounts. **Warning:** *DO NOT place any part of your body under the engine when it's supported only by a jack!*

4   Check the mounts to see if the rubber is cracked, hardened or separated from the metal portion. Sometimes the rubber will split right down the center.

5   Check for relative movement between the mounts and the engine or frame (use a large screwdriver or prybar to attempt to move the mounts). If movement is noted, lower the engine and tighten the mount fasteners.

6   Rubber preservative should be applied to the mounts to slow deterioration.

Replacement

7   Disconnect the negative battery cable from the battery, then raise the vehicle and support it securely on jackstands (if not already done). Support the engine as described in Step 3.

8   To remove the right engine mount, remove the nut and withdraw the through-bolt from the frame bracket **(see illustrations)**.

9   Remove the mount-to-bracket nuts and detach the mount.

10   To remove the rear engine mount, detach the crossmember as described in Section 12, Steps 7 and 8, then remove the nuts from the side of the mount **(see illustration)** and lower the mount from the bracket. **Warning:** *Do not remove the crossmember if the upper mounts are disconnected!*

18.10 Remove the nuts from the side of the mount and lower the mount from the bracket

11   Installation is the reverse of removal. Use thread locking compound on the mount bolts/nuts and be sure to tighten them securely.

12   See Chapter 7A, **illustrations 6.15 and 6.16** for the torque rod replacement procedure.

Chapter 2 Part B
General engine overhaul procedures

Contents

Specifications

General

Cylinder compression pressure (at 300 rpm)
   SOHC engine .... 159 psi
   DOHC engines .... 170 psi
Oil pressure at 3000 rpm (engine warm)
   SOHC engine .... 43 to 73 psi
   DOHC engine .... 51 to 80 psi

Engine block

Deck surface warpage... 0.008 inch maximum
Bore
   1.6L engines... 3.1496 to 3.1512 inches
   1.8L engine... 3.1496 to 3.1508 inches
   Taper (all engines)
      Less than 0.005 inch... Hone cylinder
      More than 0.005 inch... Bore cylinder
Note: *If the bore diameter is larger than 3.1575 inches, bore the cylinders to the next oversize*

Crankshaft and connecting rods

Crankshaft runout.. 0.0039 inch maximum
Endplay
    Standard.. 0.0024 to 0.0095 inch
    Maximum... 0.0118 inch
Main bearing journal
    Diameter
        Standard .... 2.0440 to 2.0448 inches
        Minimum .... 2.0436 inches
    Taper .... 0.0002 inch
    Out-of-round .... 0.0002 inch
Main bearing oil clearance
    Standard.. 0.00079 to 0.00199 inch
    Maximum... 0.0047 inch
Connecting rod journal
    Diameter
        SOHC engine
            Standard .... 1.5722 to 1.5728 inches
            Minimum .... 1.5718 inches
        DOHC engines
            Standard .... 1.8083 to 1.8089 inches
            Minimum .... 1.8081 inches
    Taper .... 0.0002 inch
    Out-of-round .... 0.0002 inch
Connecting rod side clearance (endplay)
    Standard.. 0.0079 to 0.0138 inch
    Maximum... 0.0158 inch
Connecting rod bearings (standard sizes)
    All SOHC engines and 1990 and 1991 DOHC engines
        I .... 0.0594 to 0.0595 inch
        II .... 0.0593 to 0.0594 inch
        III .... 0.0591 to 0.0593 inch
    1992 and 1993 DOHC engines
        I .... 0.0592 to 0.0593 inch
        II .... 0.0590 to 0.0592 inch
        III .... 0.0589 to 0.0590 inch
Connecting rod bearing oil clearance
    SOHC engine .... 0.00079 to 0.00185 inch
    DOHC engines .... 0.00098 to 0.00229 inch

Piston and rings

Piston diameter
    Standard (all years and all engines)
        A .... 3.1473 to 3.1477 inches
        B .... 3.1477 to 3.1481 inches
        C .... 3.1481 to 3.1485 inches
    Oversize -Two available
        0.0197 inch .... 3.1671 to 3.1679 inches
        0.0394 inch .... 3.1868 to 3.1875 inches
Piston-to-bore clearance
    SOHC engine
        1990 .... 0.0024 to 0.0031 inch
        1991 and 1992 .... 0.0011 to 0.0019 inch
        1993 .... 0.0012 to 0.0017 inch
    DOHC engines
        1990 .... 0.0024 to 0.0031 inch
        1991 on .... 0.0019 to 0.0027 inch
Piston rings
    End gap
        No. 1 (top ring)
            Standard .... 0.0110 to 0.0157 inch
            Maximum .... 0.059 inch
        No. 2 (middle ring)
            Standard .... 0.0177 to 0.0236 inch
            Maximum .... 0.059 inch
        Oil ring
            Standard .... 0.039 to 0.0236 inch
            Maximum .... 0.059 inch

Piston ring side clearance
    No. 1 (top ring)
        Standard .... 0.00177 to 0.00315 inch
        Maximum .... 0.0059 inch
    No. 2 (middle ring)
        Standard .... 0.00078 to 0.00236 inch
        Maximum .... 0.0059 inch

Valves and related components

Valve lash .... See Chapter 1
Valve spring free length
    SOHC engine
        Intake .... 1.73 inches
        Exhaust .... 1.67 inches
    DOHC engines .... Not available
Valve margin (all engines) .... 0.0315 inch minimum
Valve face contact width (all engines)
    Intake .... 0.087 inch minimum
    Exhaust .... 0.079 inch minimum
Valve stem diameter
    1.6L engines (SOHC and DOHC) .... 0.2335 inch minimum
    1.8L engine .... 0.2320 inch minimum
Valve stem-to-guide clearance
    1.6L engines (SOHC and DOHC) .... 0.00787 inch maximum
    1.8L engine .... 0.008 inch maximum

Torque specifications*

Ft-lbs (unless otherwise indicated)

Main bearing cap bolts
    1.6L engines (SOHC and DOHC) 44
    1.8L engine
        Step 1 22
        Step 2 44
        Step 3 65
Connecting rod cap nuts
    SOHC engine 44
    1.6L DOHC engine
        1990 36
        1991
            Step 1 11
            Step 2 .... Turn an additional 45 to 60-degrees
    1.8L DOHC
        1992 and 1993
            Step 1 18
            Step 2 .... Turn an additional 100-degrees

* **Note:** *Refer to Part A for additional torque specifications.*

---

1 General information

    Included in this portion of Chapter 2 are the general overhaul procedures for the cylinder head and internal engine components.

    The information ranges from advice concerning preparation for an overhaul and the purchase of replacement parts to detailed, step-by-step procedures covering removal and installation of internal engine components and the inspection of parts.

    The following Sections have been written based on the assumption that the engine has been removed from the vehicle. For information concerning in-vehicle engine repair, as well as removal and installation of the external components necessary for the overhaul, see Part A of this Chapter and Section 7 of this Part.

    The Specifications included in this Part are only those necessary for the inspection and overhaul procedures which follow. Refer to Part A for additional Specifications.

2 Engine overhaul - general information

    It's not always easy to determine when, or if, an engine should be completely overhauled, as a number of factors must be considered.

    High mileage is not necessarily an indication that an overhaul is needed, while low mileage doesn't preclude the need for an overhaul. Frequency of servicing is probably the most important consideration. An engine that's had regular and frequent oil and filter changes, as well as other required maintenance, will most likely give many thousands of miles of reliable service. Conversely, a neglected engine may require an overhaul very early in its life.

    Excessive oil consumption is an indication that piston rings, valve seals and/or valve guides are in need of attention. Make sure that oil leaks aren't responsible before deciding that the rings and/or guides are bad. Perform a cylinder compression check to determine the extent of the work required (see Section 3).

Check the oil pressure with a gauge installed in place of the oil pressure sending unit and compare it to the Specifications. If it's extremely low, the bearings and/or oil pump are probably worn out.

Loss of power, rough running, knocking or metallic engine noises, excessive valve train noise and high fuel consumption rates may also point to the need for an overhaul, especially if they're all present at the same time. If a complete tune-up doesn't remedy the situation, major mechanical work is the only solution.

An engine overhaul involves restoring the internal parts to the specifications of a new engine. During an overhaul, the piston rings are replaced and the cylinder walls are reconditioned (rebored and/or honed). If a rebore is done by an automotive machine shop, new oversize pistons will also be installed. The main bearings, connecting rod bearings and camshaft bearings are generally replaced with new ones and, if necessary, the crankshaft may be reground to restore the journals. Generally, the valves are serviced as well, since they're usually in less-than-perfect condition at this point. While the engine is being overhauled, other components, such as the distributor, starter and alternator, can be rebuilt as well. The end result should be a like-new engine that will give many trouble free miles. **Note:** *Critical cooling system components such as the hoses, drivebelts, thermostat and water pump MUST be replaced with new parts when an engine is overhauled. The radiator should be checked carefully to ensure that it isn't clogged or leaking (see Chapter 3).*

Before beginning the engine overhaul, read through the entire procedure to familiarize yourself with the scope and requirements of the job. Overhauling an engine isn't difficult, but it is time consuming. Plan on the vehicle being tied up for a minimum of two weeks, especially if parts must be taken to an automotive machine shop for repair or reconditioning. Check on availability of parts and make sure that any necessary special tools and equipment are obtained in advance. Most work can be done with typical hand tools, although a number of precision measuring tools are required for inspecting parts to determine if they must be replaced. Often an automotive machine shop will handle the inspection of parts and offer advice concerning reconditioning and replacement. **Note:** *Always wait until the engine has been completely disassembled and all components, especially the engine block, have been inspected before deciding what service and repair operations must be performed by an automotive machine shop. Since the block's condition will be the major factor to consider when determining whether to overhaul the original engine or buy a rebuilt one, never purchase parts or have machine work done on other components until the block has been thoroughly inspected. As a general rule, time is the primary cost of an overhaul, so it doesn't pay to install worn or substandard parts.*

As a final note, to ensure maximum life and minimum trouble from a rebuilt engine, everything must be assembled with care in a spotlessly clean environment.

3   Cylinder compression check

Refer to illustration 3.6

1   A compression check will tell you what mechanical condition the upper end (pistons, rings, valves, head gasket[s]) of your engine is in. Specifically, it can tell you if the compression is down due to leakage caused by worn piston rings, defective valves and seats or a blown head gasket. **Note:** *The engine must be at normal operating temperature and the battery must be fully charged for this check.*

2   Begin by cleaning the area around the spark plugs before you remove them (compressed air should be used, if available, otherwise a small brush or even a bicycle tire pump will work). The idea is to prevent dirt from getting into the cylinders as the compression check is being done.

3   Remove all of the spark plugs from the engine (see Chapter 1).

4   Block the throttle wide open.

5   Detach the primary (low voltage) wiring from the coil (see Chapter 5). The fuel pump circuit should also be disabled (see Chapter 4).

6   Install the compression gauge in the spark plug hole **(see illustration)**.

7   Crank the engine over at least seven compression strokes and

3.6 A compression gauge with a threaded fitting for the spark plug hole is preferred over the type that requires hand pressure to maintain the seal - be sure to open the throttle valve as far as possible during the compression check

watch the gauge. The compression should build up quickly in a healthy engine. Low compression on the first stroke, followed by gradually increasing pressure on successive strokes, indicates worn piston rings. A low compression reading on the first stroke, which doesn't build up during successive strokes, indicates leaking valves or a blown head gasket (a cracked head could also be the cause). Deposits on the undersides of the valve heads can also cause low compression. Record the highest gauge reading obtained.

8   Repeat the procedure for the remaining cylinders and compare the results to the Specifications.

9   Add some engine oil (about three squirts from a plunger-type oil can) to each cylinder, through the spark plug holes, and repeat the test.

10   If the compression increases after the oil is added, the piston rings are definitely worn. If the compression doesn't increase significantly, the leakage is occurring at the valves or head gasket. Leakage past the valves may be caused by burned valve seats and/or faces or warped, cracked or bent valves.

11   If two adjacent cylinders have equally low compression, there's a strong possibility that the head gasket between them is blown. The appearance of coolant in the combustion chambers or the crankcase would verify this condition.

12   If one cylinder is 20-percent lower than the others, and the engine has a slightly rough idle, a worn exhaust lobe on the camshaft could be the cause.

13   If the compression is unusually high, the combustion chambers are probably coated with carbon deposits. If that's the case, the cylinder head(s) should be removed and decarbonized.

14   If compression is way down or varies greatly between cylinders, it would be a good idea to have a leak-down test performed by an automotive repair shop. This test will pinpoint exactly where the leakage is occurring and how severe it is.

4   Engine removal - methods and precautions

If you've decided that an engine must be removed for overhaul or major repair work, several preliminary steps should be taken.

Locating a suitable place to work is extremely important. Adequate work space, along with storage space for the vehicle, will be needed. If a shop or garage isn't available, at the very least a flat, level, clean work surface made of concrete or asphalt is required.

Cleaning the engine compartment and engine before beginning the removal procedure will help keep tools clean and organized.

An engine hoist or A-frame will also be necessary. Make sure the equipment is rated in excess of the combined weight of the engine and

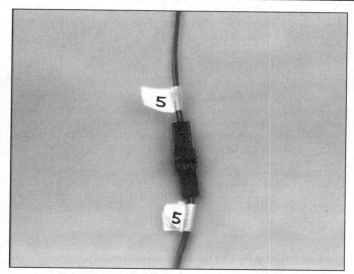

5.6 Label each wire before unplugging the connector

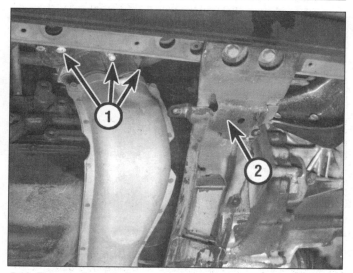

5.13 Remove the nuts (arrows) and detach the exhaust pipe from the manifold

1   *Exhaust pipe nuts*   2   *Center crossmember*

transaxle. Safety is of primary importance, considering the potential hazards involved in lifting the engine out of the vehicle.

If the engine is being removed by a novice, a helper should be available. Advice and aid from someone more experienced would also be helpful. There are many instances when one person cannot simultaneously perform all of the operations required when lifting the engine out of the vehicle.

Plan the operation ahead of time. Arrange for or obtain all of the tools and equipment you'll need prior to beginning the job. Some of the equipment necessary to perform engine removal and installation safely and with relative ease are (in addition to an engine hoist) a heavy duty floor jack, complete sets of wrenches and sockets as described in the front of this manual, wooden blocks and plenty of rags and cleaning solvent for mopping up spilled oil, coolant and gasoline. If the hoist must be rented, make sure that you arrange for it in advance and perform all of the operations possible without it beforehand. This will save you money and time.

Plan for the vehicle to be out of use for quite a while. A machine shop will be required to perform some of the work which the do-it-yourselfer can't accomplish without special equipment. These shops often have a busy schedule, so it would be a good idea to consult them before removing the engine in order to accurately estimate the amount of time required to rebuild or repair components that may need work.

Always be extremely careful when removing and installing the engine. Serious injury can result from careless actions. Plan ahead, take your time and a job of this nature, although major, can be accomplished successfully.

---

5   Engine - removal and installation

Refer to illustrations 5.6, 5.13, 5.19a, 5.19b, 5.21 and 5.23
Warning: *Gasoline is extremely flammable, so take extra precautions when disconnecting any part of the fuel system. Don't smoke or allow open flames or bare light bulbs in or near the work area and don't work in a garage where a natural gas appliance (such as a clothes dryer or water heater) is installed. If you spill gasoline on your skin, rinse it off immediately. Have a fire extinguisher rated for gasoline fires handy and know how to use it.*
Note: *Read through the entire Section before beginning this procedure. The engine and transaxle are removed as a unit and then separated outside the vehicle.*

Removal

1   Relieve the fuel system pressure (see Chapter 4).

2   Place protective covers on the fenders and cowl and remove the hood (see Chapter 11).
3   Remove the battery and battery tray (see Chapter 5).
4   Remove the air cleaner assembly (see Chapter 4).
5   Remove the cruise control actuator and bracket, if equipped.
6   Clearly label and disconnect all vacuum lines, coolant and emissions hoses, electrical connectors, ground straps and fuel lines. Masking tape and/or a touch up paint applicator work well for marking items **(see illustration)**. Take instant photos or sketch the locations of components and brackets.
7   Remove the cooling fan(s), shroud(s) and radiator (see Chapter 3).
8   Release the residual fuel pressure in the tank by removing the gas cap, then disconnect the fuel lines between the engine and chassis (see Chapter 4). Plug or cap all open fittings.
9   Disconnect the throttle linkage (and transaxle shift control cable, if equipped) from the throttle body (see Chapter 4).
10   On power steering equipped vehicles, unbolt the power steering pump. If clearance allows, tie the pump aside without disconnecting the hoses. If necessary, remove the pump (see Chapter 10).
11   Raise the vehicle and support it securely on jackstands. Drain the cooling system and engine oil and remove the drivebelts (see Chapter 1). **Note:** *Don't raise the vehicle any higher than necessary.*
12   On air conditioned models, unbolt the compressor and set it aside (see Chapter 3). **Warning:** *Do not disconnect the refrigerant hoses.*
13   Unbolt the exhaust pipe from the exhaust manifold **(see illustration)**.
14   Remove the driveaxles (see Chapter 8), wire harness, shift cable(s) and speedometer cable from the transaxle (see Chapter 7A or 7B).
15   Attach a lifting sling or chain to the brackets on the engine. Position a hoist and connect the sling or chain to it. Take up the slack until there is slight tension on the hoist. **Warning:** *Do not place any part of your body under the engine/transaxle when it's supported only by a hoist or other lifting device.*
16   Unbolt the torque rod and rear engine/transaxle mount from the center crossmember (see Chapter 7A), then remove the center crossmember **(see illustration 5.13)**.
17   Recheck to be sure nothing except the mounts are still connecting the engine/transaxle to the vehicle. Disconnect anything still remaining.
18   Remove the through-bolt from the right engine mount, then unbolt the mount bracket from the engine (see Chapter 2A). Remove the left transaxle mount (see Chapter 7A).

5.19a Slowly raise the engine from the vehicle - keep checking for anything still attached to the engine assembly

5.19b Rotate the engine/transaxle assembly to clear the components in the engine compartment

5.21 Remove the engine-to-transaxle brace (arrow)

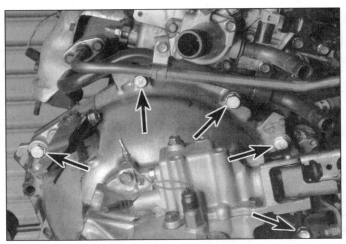

5.23 Support the engine and transaxle with wood blocks, then remove the bolts connecting the engine and transmission together

19   Slowly lift the engine/transaxle out of the vehicle **(see illustrations)**. It may be necessary to pry the mounts away from the frame brackets.

20   Move the engine/transaxle away from the vehicle and carefully lower the hoist until the transaxle is supported in a level position.

21   Remove the engine block-to-transaxle brace **(see illustration)**.

22   On automatic transaxle equipped models, detach the torque converter dust shield from the lower bellhousing. Remove the torque converter-to-driveplate fasteners (see Chapter 7A) and push the converter back slightly into the bellhousing.

23   Support the engine and transaxle with wood blocks, then remove the engine-to-transaxle bolts and separate the engine from the transaxle **(see illustration)**. The torque converter should remain in the transaxle.

24   Place the engine on the floor or remove the flywheel or driveplate and mount the engine on an engine stand.

Installation

25   Check the engine/transaxle mounts. If they're worn or damaged, replace them.

26   On manual transaxle equipped models, inspect the clutch components (see Chapter 8) and, on automatic transaxle models, inspect the converter seal and bushing.

27   On automatic transaxle equipped models, apply a dab of grease to the nose of the torque converter and to the seal lips.

28   Carefully guide the transaxle into place, following the procedure outlined in Chapter 7A or 7B. **Caution:** *Do not use the bolts to force the engine and transaxle into alignment. It may crack or damage major components.* If you're working on a model equipped with an automatic transaxle, install the torque converter-to-driveplate fasteners and tighten them to the torque listed in the Chapter 7B Specifications.

29   Install the engine-to-transaxle bolts and tighten them securely.

30   Attach the hoist to the engine and carefully lower the engine/transaxle assembly into the engine compartment.

31   Install the mount bolts and tighten them securely.

32   Reinstall the remaining components and fasteners in the reverse order of removal.

33   Add coolant, oil, power steering and transmission fluids as needed (see Chapter 1).

34   Run the engine and check for proper operation and leaks. Shut off the engine and recheck the fluid levels.

6   Engine rebuilding alternatives

The do-it-yourselfer is faced with a number of options when performing an engine overhaul. The decision to replace the engine block, piston/connecting rod assemblies and crankshaft depends on a number of factors, with the number one consideration being the condition of the block. Other considerations are cost, access to machine shop facilities, parts availability, time required to complete the project and the extent of prior mechanical experience on the part of the do-it-your-selfer.

Some of the rebuilding alternatives include:

Individual parts - If the inspection procedures reveal that the engine block and most engine components are in reusable condition, purchasing individual parts may be the most economical alternative. The block, crankshaft and piston/connecting rod assemblies should all be inspected carefully. Even if the block shows little wear, the cylinder bores should be surface honed.

Short block - A short block consists of an engine block with a crankshaft and piston/connecting rod assemblies already installed. All new bearings are incorporated and all clearances will be correct. The existing camshaft, valve train components, cylinder head(s) and external parts can be bolted to the short block with little or no machine shop work necessary.

Long block - A long block consists of a short block plus an oil pump, oil pan, cylinder head, camshaft and valve train components, timing pulleys and belt. All components are installed with new bearings, seals and gaskets incorporated throughout. The installation of manifolds and external parts is all that's necessary.

Give careful thought to which alternative is best for you and discuss the situation with local automotive machine shops, auto parts dealers and experienced rebuilders before ordering or purchasing replacement parts.

---

7 Engine overhaul - disassembly sequence

1   It's much easier to disassemble and work on the engine if it's mounted on a portable engine stand. A stand can often be rented quite cheaply from an equipment rental yard. Before the engine is mounted on a stand, the flywheel/driveplate and rear oil seal retainer should be removed from the engine.

2   If a stand isn't available, it's possible to disassemble the engine with it blocked up on the floor. Be extra careful not to tip or drop the engine when working without a stand.

3   If you're going to obtain a rebuilt engine, all external components must come off first, to be transferred to the replacement engine, just as they will if you're doing a complete engine overhaul yourself. These include:

Alternator and brackets
Emissions control components
Distributor, spark plug wires and spark plugs
Thermostat and housing
Water pump
EFI components
Intake/exhaust manifolds
Oil filter
Engine mounts
Clutch and flywheel/driveplate
Engine rear plate

Note: *When removing the external components from the engine, pay close attention to details that may be helpful or important during installation. Note the installed position of gaskets, seals, spacers, pins, brackets, washers, bolts and other small items.*

4   If you're obtaining a short block, which consists of the engine block, crankshaft, pistons and connecting rods all assembled, then the cylinder head, oil pan and oil pump will have to be removed as well. See *Engine rebuilding alternatives* for additional information regarding the different possibilities to be considered.

5   If you're planning a complete overhaul, the engine must be disassembled and the internal components removed in the following order:

Valve cover
Timing belt covers
Timing belt and sprockets
Camshaft and rocker arms
Camshafts and lifters
Cylinder head
Oil pan

8.2 A small plastic bag, with an appropriate label, can be used to store the valve train components so they can be kept together and reinstalled in the original position

Oil pump
Piston/connecting rod assemblies
Crankshaft rear oil seal retainer
Crankshaft and main bearings

6   Before beginning the disassembly and overhaul procedures, make sure the following items are available. Also, refer to *Engine overhaul - reassembly sequence* for a list of tools and materials needed for engine reassembly.

Common hand tools
Small cardboard boxes or plastic bags for storing parts
Gasket scraper
Ridge reamer
Vibration damper puller
Micrometers
Telescoping gauges
Dial indicator set
Valve spring compressor
Cylinder surfacing hone
Piston ring groove cleaning tool
Electric drill motor
Tap and die set
Wire brushes
Oil gallery brushes
Cleaning solvent

---

8 Cylinder head - disassembly

Refer to illustrations 8.2, 8.3 and 8.4

Note: *New and rebuilt cylinder heads are commonly available for most engines at dealerships and auto parts stores. Due to the fact that some specialized tools are necessary for the disassembly and inspection procedures, and replacement parts may not be readily available, it may be more practical and economical for the home mechanic to purchase a replacement head rather than taking the time to disassemble, inspect and recondition the original.*

1   Cylinder head disassembly involves removal of the intake and exhaust valves and related components. It's assumed that the lifters or rocker arms and camshaft(s) have already been removed (see Part A as needed).

2   Before the valves are removed, arrange to label and store them, along with their related components, so they can be kept separate and reinstalled in the same valve guides they are removed from **(see illustration)**.

3   Compress the springs on the first valve with a spring compressor

8.3 Use a valve spring compressor to compress the spring, then remove the keepers from the valve stem

8.4 If the valve won't pull through the guide, deburr the edge of the stem end and the area around the top of the keeper groove with a file or whetstone

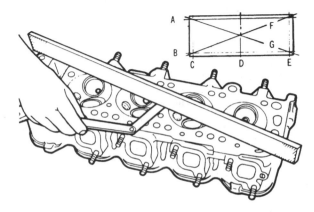

9.12 Check the cylinder head gasket surface for warpage by trying to slip a feeler gauge under the straightedge (see this Chapter's Specifications for the maximum warpage allowed and use a feeler gauge of that thickness)

and remove the keepers **(see illustration)**. Carefully release the valve spring compressor and remove the retainer, the spring and the spring seat (if used).

4   Pull the valve out of the head, then remove the oil seal from the guide. If the valve binds in the guide (won't pull through), push it back into the head and deburr the area around the keeper groove with a fine file or whetstone **(see illustration)**

5   Repeat the procedure for the remaining valves. Remember to keep all the parts for each valve together so they can be reinstalled in the same locations.

6   Once the valves and related components have been removed and stored in an organized manner, the head should be thoroughly cleaned and inspected. If a complete engine overhaul is being done, finish the engine disassembly procedures before beginning the cylinder head cleaning and inspection process.

9   Cylinder head - cleaning and inspection

Refer to illustrations 9.12, 9.14, 9.15, 9.16, 9.17 and 9.18

1   Thorough cleaning of the cylinder head and related valve train components, followed by a detailed inspection, will enable you to decide how much valve service work must be done during the engine overhaul. **Note:** *If the engine was severely overheated, the cylinder head is probably warped (see Step 12).*

Cleaning

2   Scrape all traces of old gasket material and sealing compound off the head gasket, intake manifold and exhaust manifold sealing surfaces. Be very careful not to gouge the cylinder head. Special gasket removal solvents that soften gaskets and make removal much easier are available at auto parts stores.

3   Remove all built-up scale from the coolant passages.

4   Run a stiff wire brush through the various holes to remove deposits that may have formed in them.

5   Run an appropriate size tap into each of the threaded holes to remove corrosion and thread sealant that may be present. If compressed air is available, use it to clear the holes of debris produced by this operation. **Warning:** *Wear eye protection when using compressed air!*

6   Clean the exhaust and intake manifold stud threads with a wire brush.

7   Clean the cylinder head with solvent and dry it thoroughly. Compressed air will speed the drying process and ensure that all holes and recessed areas are clean. **Note:** *Decarbonizing chemicals are available and may prove very useful when cleaning cylinder heads and valve train components. They are very caustic and should be used with caution. Be sure to follow the instructions on the container.*

8   Clean the lifters and rocker arms (if used) with solvent and dry them thoroughly (don't mix them up during the cleaning process). Compressed air will speed the drying process and can be used to clean out the oil passages.

9   Clean all the valve springs, spring seats, keepers and retainers with solvent and dry them thoroughly. Do the components from one valve at a time to avoid mixing up the parts.

10   Scrape off any heavy deposits that may have formed on the valves, then use a motorized wire brush to remove deposits from the valve heads and stems. Again, make sure the valves don't get mixed up.

Inspection

Note: *Be sure to perform all of the following inspection procedures before concluding that machine shop work is required. Make a list of the items that need attention. The inspection procedures for the lifters and rocker arms, as well as the camshaft(s), can be found in Part A.*

Cylinder head

11   Inspect the head very carefully for cracks, evidence of coolant leakage and other damage. If cracks are found, check with an automotive machine shop concerning repair. If repair isn't possible, a new cylinder head should be obtained.

12   Using a straightedge and feeler gauge, check the head gasket mating surface for warpage **(see illustration)**. If the warpage exceeds the specified limit, it can be resurfaced at an automotive machine shop.

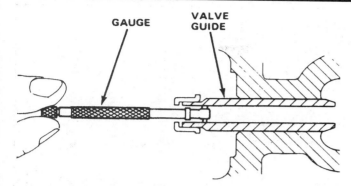

9.14 Use a small hole gauge to determine the inside diameter of the valve guides (the gauge is then measured with a micrometer)

13 Examine the valve seats in each of the combustion chambers. If they're pitted, cracked or burned, the head will require valve service that's beyond the scope of the home mechanic.

14 Measure the valve guide inside diameter with a small hole gauge and micrometer **(see illustration)**, then measure the valve stem diameter and subtract it from the valve guide diameter to obtain the stem-to-guide clearance. Also, check the valve stem deflection crosswise (parallel to the rocker arm) with a dial indicator attached securely to the head. The valve must be in the guide and approximately 1/16-inch off the seat. The total valve stem movement indicated by the gauge needle must be noted. If it exceeds the specified stem-to-guide clearance limit, the valve guides should be replaced. After this is done, if there's still some doubt regarding the condition of the valve guides they should be checked by an automotive machine shop (the cost should be minimal).

Valves

15 Carefully inspect each valve face for uneven wear, deformation, cracks, pits and burned areas. Check the valve stem for scuffing and galling and the neck for cracks. Rotate the valve and check for any obvious indication that it's bent. Look for pits and excessive wear on the end of the stem **(see illustration)**. The presence of any of these conditions indicates the need for valve service by an automotive machine shop.

16 Measure the margin width on each valve **(see illustration)**. Any valve with a margin narrower than specified will have to be replaced with a new one.

Valve components

Note: *As of the time of writing, no valve spring specifications were available for the DOHC engines.*

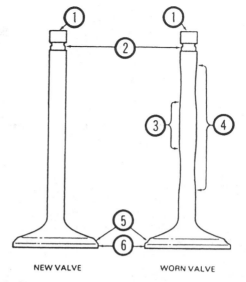

9.15 Check for valve wear at the points shown here

1	Valve tip	4	Stem (most worn area)
2	Keeper groove	5	Valve face
3	Stem (least worn area)	6	Margin

17 Check each valve spring for wear (on the ends) and pits. Measure the free height and compare it to the Specifications **(see illustration)**. Any springs that are shorter than specified have sagged and should not be reused. The tension of all springs should be checked with a special fixture before deciding that they're suitable for use in a rebuilt engine (take the springs to an automotive machine shop for this check).

18 Stand each spring on a flat surface and check it for squareness **(see illustration)**. If any of the springs are distorted or sagged, replace all of them with new parts.

19 Check the spring retainers and keepers for obvious wear and cracks. Any questionable parts should be replaced with new ones, as extensive damage will occur if they fail during engine operation.

20 Any damaged or excessively worn parts must be replaced with new ones.

21 If the inspection process indicates that the valve components are in generally poor condition and worn beyond the limits specified, which is usually the case in an engine that's being overhauled, reassemble the valves in the cylinder head and refer to valve servicing recommendations (see Section 10).

2B

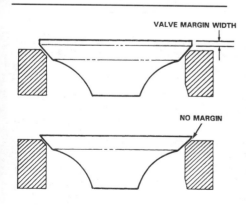

9.16 The margin width on each valve must be as specified (if no margin exists, the valve cannot be reused)

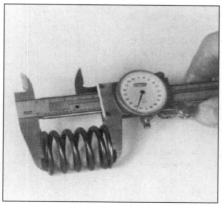

9.17 Measure the free length of each valve spring with a dial or vernier caliper

9.18 Check each valve spring for squareness

11.3 Using either the special tool made for installation of valve seals or a small deep socket, lightly tap the seal into place until it's seated

12.1 A ridge reamer is required to remove the ridge from the top of each cylinder - do this before removing the pistons!

12.3 Check the connecting rod side clearance (endplay) with a feeler gauge as shown here

10   Valves - servicing

1   Because of the complex nature of the job and the special tools and equipment needed, servicing of the valves, the valve seats and the valve guides, commonly known as a valve job, should be done by a professional.

2   The home mechanic can remove and disassemble the head, do the initial cleaning and inspection, then reassemble and deliver it to a dealer service department or an automotive machine shop for the actual service work. Doing the inspection will enable you to see what condition the head and valvetrain components are in and will ensure that you know what work and new parts are required when dealing with an automotive machine shop.

3   The dealer service department, or automotive machine shop, will remove the valves and springs, recondition or replace the valves and valve seats, recondition the valve guides, check and replace the valve springs, spring retainers and keepers (as necessary), replace the valve seals with new ones, reassemble the valve components and make sure the installed spring height is correct. The cylinder head gasket surface will also be resurfaced if it's warped.

4   After the valve job has been performed by a professional, the head will be in like-new condition. When the head is returned, be sure to clean it again before installation on the engine to remove any metal particles and abrasive grit that may still be present from the valve service or head resurfacing operations. Use compressed air, if available, to blow out all the oil holes and passages.

11   Cylinder head - reassembly

Refer to illustration 11.3

1   Regardless of whether or not the head was sent to an automotive repair shop for valve servicing, make sure it's clean before beginning reassembly.

2   If the head was sent out for valve servicing, the valves and related components will already be in place.

3   Install new seals on each of the valve guides. **Note:** *Intake and exhaust valves require different seals - DO NOT mix them up!* Gently tap each intake valve seal into place until it's seated on the guide **(see illustration). Caution:** *Don't hammer on the valve seals once they're seated or you may damage them. Don't twist or cock the seals during installation or they won't seat properly on the valve stems.*

4   Beginning at one end of the head, lubricate and install the first valve. Apply moly-base grease or clean engine oil to the valve stem.

5   Drop the spring seat or shim(s) (if equipped) over the valve guide and set the valve spring and retainer in place.

6   Compress the springs with a valve spring compressor and carefully install the keepers in the upper groove, then slowly release the compressor and make sure the keepers seat properly. Apply a small dab of grease to each keeper to hold it in place if necessary.

7   Repeat the procedure for the remaining valves. Be sure to return the components to their original locations - don't mix them up!

12   Pistons/connecting rods - removal

Refer to illustrations 12.1, 12.3, 12.4 and 12.6
Note: *Prior to removing the piston/connecting rod assemblies, remove the cylinder head, the oil pan and the oil pump pick-up tube by referring to the appropriate Sections in Part A.*

1   Use your fingernail to feel if a ridge has formed at the upper limit of ring travel (about 1/4-inch down from the top of each cylinder). If carbon deposits or cylinder wear have produced ridges, they must be completely removed with a special tool **(see illustration)**. Follow the manufacturer's instructions provided with the tool. Failure to remove the ridges before attempting to remove the piston/connecting rod assemblies may result in piston breakage.

2   After the cylinder ridges have been removed, turn the engine upside-down so the crankshaft is facing up.

3   Before the connecting rods are removed, check the endplay (side clearance) with feeler gauges. Slide them between the first connecting rod and the crankshaft throw until the play is removed **(see illustration)**. The endplay is equal to the thickness of the feeler gauge(s). If the endplay exceeds the service limit, new connecting rods will be required. If new rods (or a new crankshaft) are installed, the endplay may

12.4 Mark the rod bearing caps in order from the front of the engine to the rear (one mark for the front cap, two for the second one and so on)

12.6 To prevent damage to the crankshaft journals and cylinder walls, slip sections of hose over the rod bolts before removing the piston/rod assemblies

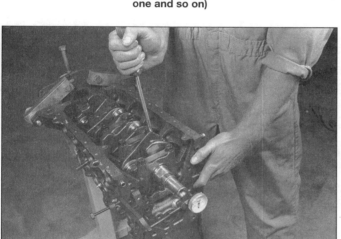

13.1 Checking crankshaft endplay with a dial indicator

13.3 Checking crankshaft endplay with a feeler gauge

fall under the specified minimum (if it does, the rods will have to be machined to restore it - consult an automotive machine shop for advice if necessary). Repeat the procedure for the remaining connecting rods.

4   Check the connecting rods and caps for identification marks. If they aren't plainly marked, use a small center-punch to make the appropriate number of indentations on each rod and cap (1, 2, 3, etc., depending on the engine type and cylinder they're associated with) **(see illustration)**.

5   Loosen each of the connecting rod cap nuts 1/2-turn at a time until they can be removed by hand. Remove the number one connecting rod cap and bearing insert. Don't drop the bearing insert out of the cap.

6   Slip a short length of plastic or rubber hose over each connecting rod cap bolt to protect the crankshaft journal and cylinder wall as the piston is removed **(see illustration)**.

7   Remove the bearing insert and push the connecting rod/piston assembly out through the top of the engine. Use a wooden hammer handle to push on the upper bearing surface in the connecting rod. If resistance is felt, double-check to make sure that all of the ridge was removed from the cylinder.

8   Repeat the procedure for the remaining cylinders.

9   After removal, reassemble the connecting rod caps and bearing inserts in their respective connecting rods and install the cap nuts finger tight. Leaving the old bearing inserts in place until reassembly will help prevent the connecting rod bearing surfaces from being accidentally nicked or gouged.

10   Don't separate the pistons from the connecting rods (see Section 17).

---

13   Crankshaft - removal

Refer to illustrations 13.1, 13.3 and 13.5

Note: *The crankshaft can be removed only after the engine has been removed from the vehicle. It's assumed that the flywheel or driveplate, vibration damper, timing belt, oil pan, oil pick-up tube, oil pump and piston/connecting rod assemblies have already been removed. The rear main oil seal retainer must be unbolted and separated from the block before proceeding with crankshaft removal.*

1   Before the crankshaft is removed, check the endplay. Mount a dial indicator with the stem in line with the crankshaft and touching the crankshaft end **(see illustration)**.

2   Pry the crankshaft all the way to the rear and zero the dial indicator. Next, pry the crankshaft to the front as far as possible and check the reading on the dial indicator. The distance that it moves is the endplay. If it's greater than specified, check the crankshaft thrust surfaces for wear. If no wear is evident, new thrust washers should correct the endplay.

3   If a dial indicator isn't available, feeler gauges can be used. Gently pry or push the crankshaft all the way to the front of the engine. Slip feeler gauges between the crankshaft and the front face of the thrust main bearing to determine the clearance **(see illustration)**. The thrust bearing is number three (center).

4   Check the main bearing caps to see if they're marked to indicate their locations. They should be numbered consecutively from the front

2B

13.5 If the main bearing caps are difficult to remove, work them forward and back using the main bearing cap bolts as levers

14.1a A hammer and a large punch can be used to knock the core plugs sideways in their bores

14.1b Pull the core plugs from the block with pliers

of the engine to the rear. If they aren't, mark them with number stamping dies or a center-punch. Main bearing caps generally have a cast-in arrow, which points to the front of the engine. Loosen the main bearing cap bolts 1/4-turn at a time each, starting with the front and rear caps and working toward the center, until they can be removed by hand. Note if any stud bolts are used and make sure they're returned to their original locations when the crankshaft is reinstalled.

5   Gently tap the caps with a soft-face hammer, then separate them from the engine block. If necessary, use the bolts as levers to remove the caps **(see illustration)**. Try not to drop the bearing inserts if they come out with the caps.

6   Carefully lift the crankshaft out of the engine. It may be a good idea to have an assistant available, since the crankshaft is quite heavy. With the bearing inserts in place in the engine block and main bearing caps or cap assembly, return the caps to their respective locations on the engine block and tighten the bolts finger tight.

---

14   Engine block - cleaning

Refer to illustrations 14.1a, 14.1b, 14.8 and 14.10
Caution: *The core plugs (also known as freeze or soft plugs) may be difficult or impossible to retrieve if they're driven into the block coolant passages.*

1   Using the wide end of a punch **(see illustration)** tap in on the outer edge of the core plug to turn the plug sideways in the bore. Then,

using a pair of pliers, pull the core plug from the engine block **(see illustration)**. Don't worry about the condition of the old core plugs as they are being removed because they will be replaced on reassembly with new plugs.

2   Using a gasket scraper, remove all traces of gasket material from the engine block. Be very careful not to nick or gouge the gasket sealing surfaces.

3   Remove the main bearing caps or cap assembly and separate the bearing inserts from the caps and the engine block. Tag the bearings, indicating which cylinder they were removed from and whether they were in the cap or the block, then set them aside.

4   Remove all of the threaded oil gallery plugs from the block. The plugs are usually very tight - they may have to be drilled out and the holes retapped. Use new plugs when the engine is reassembled.

5   If the engine is extremely dirty it should be taken to an automotive machine shop to be steam cleaned or hot tanked.

6   After the block is returned, clean all oil holes and oil galleries one more time. Brushes specifically designed for this purpose are available at most auto parts stores. Flush the passages with warm water until the water runs clear, dry the block thoroughly and wipe all machined surfaces with a light, rust preventive oil. If you have access to compressed air, use it to speed the drying process and to blow out all the oil holes and galleries. **Warning:** *Wear eye protection when using compressed air!*

7   If the block isn't extremely dirty or sludged up, you can do an adequate cleaning job with hot soapy water and a stiff brush. Take plenty of time and do a thorough job. Regardless of the cleaning method used, be sure to clean all oil holes and galleries very thoroughly, dry the block completely and coat all machined surfaces with light oil.

8   The threaded holes in the block must be clean to ensure accurate torque readings during reassembly. Run the proper size tap into each of the holes to remove rust, corrosion, thread sealant or sludge and restore damaged threads **(see illustration)**. If possible, use compressed air to clear the holes of debris produced by this operation. Now is a good time to clean the threads on the head bolts and the main bearing cap bolts as well.

9   Reinstall the main bearing caps and tighten the bolts finger tight.

10   After coating the sealing surfaces of the new core plugs with Permatex no. 2 sealant, install them in the engine block **(see illustration)**. Make sure they're driven in straight or leakage could result. Special tools are available for this purpose, but a large socket, with an outside diameter that will just slip into the core plug, a 1/2-inch drive extension and a hammer will work just as well.

11   Apply non-hardening sealant (such as Permatex no. 2 or Teflon pipe sealant) to the new oil gallery plugs and thread them into the holes in the block. Make sure they're tightened securely.

12   If the engine isn't going to be reassembled right away, cover it with a large plastic trash bag to keep it clean.

14.8 All bolt holes in the block - particularly the main bearing cap and head bolt holes - should be cleaned and restored with a tap (be sure to remove debris from the holes after this is done)

14.10 A large socket on an extension can be used to drive the new core plugs into the bores

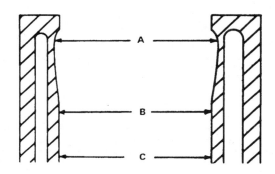

15.4a Measure the diameter of each cylinder just under the wear ridge (A), at the center (B) and at the bottom (C)

15   Engine block - inspection

Refer to illustrations 15.4a, 15.4b, 15.4c, 15.12a and 15.12b

1   Before the block is inspected, it should be cleaned (see Section 14).

2   Visually check the block for cracks, rust and corrosion. Look for stripped threads in the threaded holes. It's also a good idea to have the block checked for hidden cracks by an automotive machine shop that has the special equipment to do this type of work. If defects are found, have the block repaired, if possible, or replaced.

3   Check the cylinder bores for scuffing and scoring.

4   Measure the diameter of each cylinder at the top (just under the ridge area), center and bottom of the cylinder bore, parallel to the crankshaft axis **(see illustrations)**.

5   Next, measure each cylinder's diameter at the same three locations across the crankshaft axis. Compare the results to the Specifications.

6   If the required precision measuring tools aren't available, the piston-to-cylinder clearances can be obtained, though not quite as accurately, using feeler gauge stock. Feeler gauge stock comes in 12-inch lengths and various thicknesses and is generally available at auto parts stores.

7   To check the clearance, select a feeler gauge and slip it into the cylinder along with the matching piston. The piston must be positioned exactly as it normally would be. The feeler gauge must be between the piston and cylinder on one of the thrust faces (90-degrees to the piston pin bore).

8   The piston should slip through the cylinder (with the feeler gauge

15.4b The ability to "feel" when the telescoping gauge is at the correct point will be developed over time, so work slowly and repeat the check until you're satisfied the bore measurement is accurate

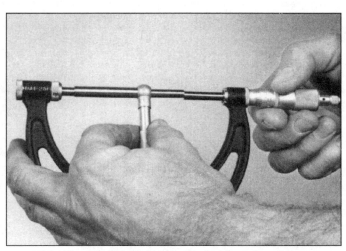

15.4c The gauge is then measured with a micrometer to determine the bore size

15.12a Check the block deck for distortion with a precision straightedge and a feeler gauge

15.12b Lay the straightedge across the block, diagonally and from end-to-end when making the check

16.3a A "bottle brush" hone will produce better results if you've never honed cylinders before

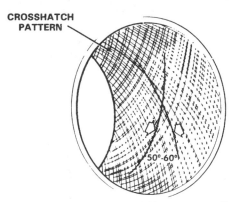

16.3b The cylinder hone should leave a smooth, crosshatch pattern with the lines intersecting at approximately a 60-degree angle

in place) with moderate pressure.

9   If it falls through or slides through easily, the clearance is excessive and a new piston will be required. If the piston binds at the lower end of the cylinder and is loose toward the top, the cylinder is tapered. If tight spots are encountered as the piston/feeler gauge is rotated in the cylinder, the cylinder is out-of-round.

10   Repeat the procedure for the remaining pistons and cylinders.

11   If the cylinder walls are badly scuffed or scored, or if they're out-of-round or tapered beyond the limits given in the Specifications, have the engine block rebored and honed at an automotive machine shop. If a rebore is done, oversize pistons and rings will be required.

12   Using a precision straightedge and a feeler gauge, check the block deck (the surface that mates with the cylinder head) for distortion **(see illustrations)**. If it's distorted beyond the specified limit, it can be resurfaced by an automotive machine shop.

13   If the cylinders are in reasonably good condition and not worn to the outside of the limits, and if the piston-to-cylinder clearances can be maintained properly, then they don't have to be rebored. Honing is all that's necessary (see Section 16).

---

16   Cylinder honing

Refer to illustrations 16.3a and 16.3b

1   Prior to engine reassembly, the cylinder bores must be honed so the new piston rings will seat correctly and provide the best possible combustion chamber seal. **Note:** *If you don't have the tools or don't want to tackle the honing operation, most automotive machine shops will do it for a reasonable fee.*

2   Before honing the cylinders, install the main bearing caps (without bearing inserts) and tighten the bolts to the torque listed in this Chapter's Specifications.

3   Two types of cylinder hones are commonly available - the flex hone or "bottle brush" type and the more traditional surfacing hone with spring-loaded stones. Both will do the job, but for the less experienced mechanic the "bottle brush" hone will probably be easier to use. You'll also need some kerosene or honing oil, rags and an electric drill motor. Proceed as follows:

  a) Mount the hone in the drill motor, compress the stones and slip it into the first cylinder (see illustration). Be sure to wear safety goggles or a face shield!

  b) Lubricate the cylinder with plenty of honing oil, turn on the drill and move the hone up-and-down in the cylinder at a pace that will produce a fine crosshatch pattern on the cylinder walls. Ideally, the crosshatch lines should intersect at approximately a 60-degrees angle (see illustration). Be sure to use plenty of lubricant and don't take off any more material than is absolutely necessary to produce the desired finish. Note: Piston ring manufacturers may specify a smaller crosshatch angle than the traditional 60-degrees - read and follow any instructions included with the new rings.

  c) Don't withdraw the hone from the cylinder while it's running. Instead, shut off the drill and continue moving the hone up-and-down in the cylinder until it comes to a complete stop, then compress the stones and withdraw the hone. If you're using a "bottle brush" type hone, stop the drill motor, then turn the chuck in the normal direction of rotation while withdrawing the hone from the cylinder.

  d) Wipe the oil out of the cylinder and repeat the procedure for the remaining cylinders.

4   After the honing job is complete, chamfer the top edges of the cylinder bores with a small file so the rings won't catch when the pistons are installed. Be very careful not to nick the cylinder walls with the end of the file.

17.4a The piston ring grooves can be cleaned with a special tool, as shown here . . .

17.4b . . . or a section of a broken ring

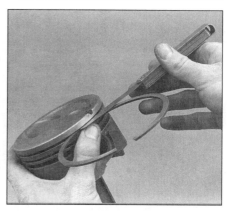

17.10 Check the ring side clearance with a feeler gauge at several points around the groove

2B

5   The entire engine block must be washed again very thoroughly with warm, soapy water to remove all traces of the abrasive grit produced during the honing operation. **Note:** *The bores can be considered clean when a lint-free white cloth - dampened with clean engine oil - used to wipe them out doesn't pick up any more honing residue, which will show up as gray areas on the cloth. Be sure to run a brush through all oil holes and galleries and flush them with running water.*

6   After rinsing, dry the block and apply a coat of light rust preventive oil to all machined surfaces. Wrap the block in a plastic trash bag to keep it clean and set it aside until reassembly.

17 Pistons/connecting rods - inspection

Refer to illustrations 17.4a, 17.4b, 17.10 and 17.11

1   Before the inspection process can be carried out, the piston/connecting rod assemblies must be cleaned and the original piston rings removed from the pistons. **Note:** *Always use new piston rings when the engine is reassembled.*

2   Using a piston ring installation tool, carefully remove the rings from the pistons. Be careful not to nick or gouge the pistons in the process.

3   Scrape all traces of carbon from the top of the piston. A hand-held wire brush or a piece of fine emery cloth can be used once the majority of the deposits have been scraped away. Do not, under any circumstances, use a wire brush mounted in a drill motor to remove deposits from the pistons. The piston material is soft and may be eroded away by the wire brush.

4   Use a piston ring groove cleaning tool to remove carbon deposits from the ring grooves. If a tool isn't available, a piece broken off the old ring will do the job. Be very careful to remove only the carbon deposits - don't remove any metal and do not nick or scratch the sides of the ring grooves **(see illustrations)**.

5   Once the deposits have been removed, clean the piston/rod assemblies with solvent and dry them with compressed air (if available). **Warning:** *Wear eye protection when using compressed air!* Make sure the oil return holes in the back sides of the ring grooves and the oil hole in the lower end of each rod are clear.

6   If the pistons and cylinder walls aren't damaged or worn excessively, and if the engine block is not rebored, new pistons won't be necessary. Normal piston wear appears as even vertical wear on the piston thrust surfaces and slight looseness of the top ring in its groove. New piston rings, however, should always be used when an engine is rebuilt.

7   Carefully inspect each piston for cracks around the skirt, at the pin bosses and at the ring lands.

8   Look for scoring and scuffing on the thrust faces of the skirt, holes in the piston crown and burned areas at the edge of the crown. If the skirt is scored or scuffed, the engine may have been suffering from overheating and/or abnormal combustion, which caused excessively

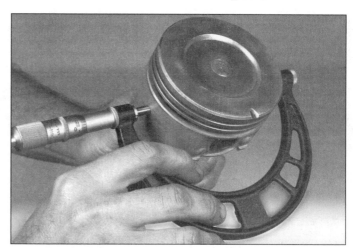

17.11 Measure the piston diameter at a 90-degree angle to the piston pin and in line with it

high operating temperatures. The cooling and lubrication systems should be checked thoroughly. A hole in the piston crown is an indication that abnormal combustion (preignition) was occurring. Burned areas at the edge of the piston crown are usually evidence of spark knock (detonation). If any of the above problems exist, the causes must be corrected or the damage will occur again. The causes may include intake air leaks, incorrect fuel/air mixture, incorrect ignition timing and EGR system malfunctions.

9   Corrosion of the piston, in the form of small pits, indicates that coolant is leaking into the combustion chamber and/or the crankcase. Again, the cause must be corrected or the problem may persist in the rebuilt engine.

10   Measure the piston ring side clearance by laying a new piston ring in each ring groove and slipping a feeler gauge in beside it **(see illustration)**. Check the clearance at three or four locations around each groove. Be sure to use the correct ring for each groove - they are different. If the side clearance is greater than specified, new pistons will have to be used.

11   Check the piston-to-bore clearance by measuring the bore (see Section 15) and the piston diameter. Make sure the pistons and bores are correctly matched. Measure the piston across the skirt, at a 90-degree angle to the piston pin, the specified distance down from the top of the piston or the lower edge of the oil ring groove **(see illustration)**. Subtract the piston diameter from the bore diameter to obtain the clearance. If it's greater than specified, the block will have to be rebored and new pistons and rings installed.

12   Check the piston-to-rod clearance by twisting the piston and rod

18.1 The oil holes should be chamfered so sharp edges don't gouge or scratch the new bearings

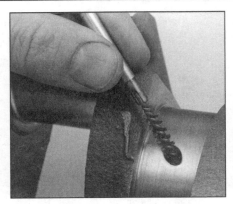

18.2 Use a wire or stiff plastic bristle brush to clean the oil passages in the crankshaft

18.4 Rubbing a penny lengthwise on each journal will reveal its condition - if copper rubs off and is embedded in the crankshaft, the journals should be reground

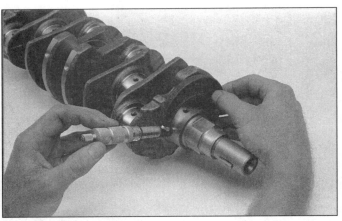

18.6 Measure the diameter of each crankshaft journal at several points to detect taper and out-of-round conditions

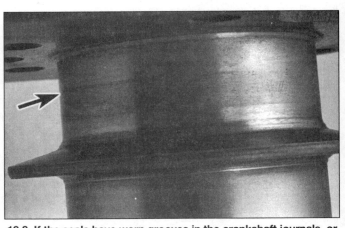

18.8 If the seals have worn grooves in the crankshaft journals, or if the seal contact surfaces are nicked or scratched, the new seals will leak

in opposite directions. Any noticeable play indicates excessive wear, which must be corrected. The piston/connecting rod assemblies should be taken to an automotive machine shop to have the pistons and rods re-sized and new pins installed.

13   If the pistons must be removed from the connecting rods for any reason, they should be taken to an automotive machine shop. While they are there have the connecting rods checked for bend and twist, since automotive machine shops have special equipment for this purpose. **Note:** *Unless new pistons and/or connecting rods must be installed, do not disassemble the pistons and connecting rods.*

14   Check the connecting rods for cracks and other damage. Temporarily remove the rod caps, lift out the old bearing inserts, wipe the rod and cap bearing surfaces clean and inspect them for nicks, gouges and scratches. After checking the rods, replace the old bearings, slip the caps into place and tighten the nuts finger tight. **Note:** *If the engine is being rebuilt because of a connecting rod knock, be sure to install new rods*

18   Crankshaft - inspection

Refer to illustrations 18.1, 18.2, 18.4, 18.6 and 18.8

1   Remove all burrs from the crankshaft oil holes with a stone, file or scraper **(see illustration).**

2   Clean the crankshaft with solvent and dry it with compressed air (if available). Be sure to clean the oil holes with a stiff brush and flush them with solvent **(see illustration).**

3   Check the main and connecting rod bearing journals for uneven wear, scoring, pits and cracks.

4   Rub a penny across each journal several times **(see illustration).** If a journal picks up copper from the penny, it's too rough and must be reground.

5   Check the rest of the crankshaft for cracks and other damage. It should be magnafluxed to reveal hidden cracks - an automotive machine shop will handle the procedure.

6   Using a micrometer, measure the diameter of the main and connecting rod journals and compare the results to the Specifications **(see illustration).** By measuring the diameter at a number of points around each journal's circumference, you'll be able to determine whether or not the journal is out-of-round. Take the measurement at each end of the journal, near the crank throws, to determine if the journal is tapered. Crankshaft runout should be checked also, but large V-blocks and a dial indicator are needed to do it correctly. If you don't have the equipment, have a machine shop check the runout.

7   If the crankshaft journals are damaged, tapered, out-of-round or worn beyond the limits given in the Specifications, have the crankshaft reground by an automotive machine shop. Be sure to use the correct size bearing inserts if the crankshaft is reconditioned.

8   Check the oil seal journals at each end of the crankshaft for wear and damage **(see illustration).** If the seal has worn a groove in the journal, or if it's nicked or scratched, the new seal may leak when the engine is reassembled. In some cases, an automotive machine shop may be able to repair the journal by pressing on a thin sleeve. If repair isn't feasible, a new or different crankshaft should be installed.

9   Examine the main and rod bearing inserts (see Section 19).

19.1a Before discarding the used bearings examine them for indications of any possible problems with the crankshaft, noting the bearing location it came from

19   Main and connecting rod bearings - inspection and selection

Inspection

Refer to illustrations 19.1a, 19.1b, 19.8a, 19.8b and 19.11

1   Even though the main and connecting rod bearings should be replaced with new ones during the engine overhaul, the old bearings should be retained for close examination, as they may reveal valuable information about the condition of the engine **(see illustrations)**.

2   Bearing failure occurs because of lack of lubrication, the presence of dirt or other foreign particles, overloading the engine and corrosion. Regardless of the cause of bearing failure, it must be corrected before the engine is reassembled to prevent it from happening again.

3   When examining the bearings, remove them from the engine block, the main bearing caps, the connecting rods and the rod caps and lay them out on a clean surface in the same general position as their location in the engine. This will enable you to match any bearing problems with the corresponding crankshaft journal.

4   Dirt and other foreign particles get into the engine in a variety of ways. It may be left in the engine during assembly, or it may pass through filters or the PCV system. It may get into the oil, and from there into the bearings. Metal chips from machining operations and normal engine wear are often present. Abrasives are sometimes left in engine components after reconditioning, especially when parts are not thoroughly cleaned using the proper cleaning methods. Whatever the source, these foreign objects often end up embedded in the soft bearing material and are easily recognized. Large particles will not embed in the bearing and will score or gouge the bearing and journal. The best prevention for this cause of bearing failure is to clean all parts thoroughly and keep everything spotlessly clean during engine assembly. Frequent and regular engine oil and filter changes are also recommended.

5   Lack of lubrication (or lubrication breakdown) has a number of interrelated causes. Excessive heat (which thins the oil), overloading (which squeezes the oil from the bearing face) and oil leakage or throw off (from excessive bearing clearances, worn oil pump or high engine speeds) all contribute to lubrication breakdown. Blocked oil passages, which usually are the result of misaligned oil holes in a bearing shell, will also oil starve a bearing and destroy it. When lack of lubrication is the cause of bearing failure, the bearing material is wiped or extruded from the steel backing of the bearing. Temperatures may increase to the point where the steel backing turns blue from overheating.

6   Driving habits can have a definite effect on bearing life. Full throttle, low speed operation (lugging the engine) puts very high loads on bearings, which tends to squeeze out the oil film. These loads cause the bearings to flex, which produces fine cracks in the bearing face (fatigue failure). Eventually the bearing material will loosen in pieces and tear away from the steel backing. Short trip driving leads to corrosion of bearings because insufficient engine heat is produced to drive off

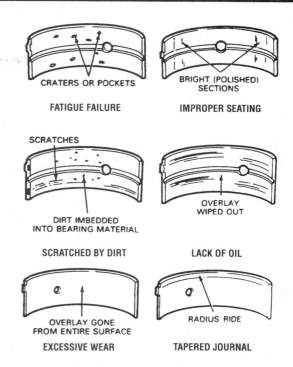

19.1b Typical bearing failures

19.8a The main bearing size marks are stamped in the oil pan rail area near the number 1 main bearing cap (the most forward main bearing)

the condensed water and corrosive gases. These products collect in the engine oil, forming acid and sludge. As the oil is carried to the engine bearings, the acid attacks and corrodes the bearing material.

7   Incorrect bearing installation during engine assembly will lead to bearing failure as well. Tight fitting bearings leave insufficient bearing oil clearance and will result in oil starvation. Dirt or foreign particles trapped behind a bearing insert result in high spots on the bearing which lead to failure.

Selection

8   If the original bearings are worn or damaged, or if the oil clearances are incorrect (see Section 22 or 24), the number stamped on the oil pan rail of the block **(see illustrations)** and the following procedures should be used to select the correct new bearings for engine reassembly. However, if the crankshaft has been reground, new undersize bearings must be installed. The automotive machine shop that reconditions the crankshaft will provide or help you select the correct size bearings. Regardless of how the bearing sizes are determined, measure the oil clearance with Plastigage to ensure the bearings are the right size.

Size mark	Main bearing bore diameter (inches)	Crankshaft main bearing journal diameter (inches)	Size mark	Crankshaft bearing size marks (upper and lower sides)	Oil Clearance (inches)
1	2.2044 - 2.2047	2.0440 - 2.0444	— —	Blue	0.0009 - 0.0019
1	2.2044 - 2.2047	2.0444 - 2.0448	—	Black	0.0008 - 0.0018
2	2.2041 - 2.2012	2.0440 - 2.0444	— —	Black	0.0009 - 0.0019
2	2.2041 - 2.2012	2.0444 - 2.0448	—	Brown	0.0008 - 0.0018
3	2.2038 - 2.2041	2.0440 - 2.0444	— —	Brown	0.0009 - 0.0019
3	2.2038 - 2.2041	2.0444 - 2.0448	—	Green	0.0008 - 0.0018
*Under-size 0.0098	2.2038 - 2.2047	2.0342 - 2.0350	None	Stamp of size	0.0008 - 0.0035
*Under-size 0.0197	2.2038 - 2.2047	2.0243 - 2.0251	None	Stamp of size	0.0008 - 0.0035

The specifications for the two available undersizes are only for use in the 1.6L SOHC engine.

19.8b Main bearing selection table

Main bearings

9   If you need to use a STANDARD size main bearing, install one that has the same number as the original bearing.

10   If the number on the original main bearing has been obscured, install one that has the same number as the number at the front end (the timing belt end) of the block stamped into the oil pan gasket deck surface.

11   Locate the main journal grade marks, seen as a single or double dash mark as shown in the bearing selection table, on the crankshaft as well **(see illustration)**.

Connecting rod bearings

12   If you need to use a STANDARD size rod bearing, install one that has the same number as the number stamped into the connecting rod cap.

All bearings

13   Remember, the oil clearance is the final judge when selecting new bearing sizes. If you have any questions or are unsure which bearings to use, get help from a dealer parts or service department or other parts supplier.

20   Engine overhaul - reassembly sequence

1   Before beginning engine reassembly, make sure you have all the necessary new parts, gaskets and seals as well as the following items on hand:

  Common hand tools
  A torque wrench
  Piston ring installation tool
  Piston ring compressor
  Short lengths of rubber or plastic hose to fit over connecting rod bolts
  Plastigage
  Feeler gauges
  A fine-tooth file
  New engine oil
  Engine assembly lube or moly-base grease
  Gasket sealant
  Thread locking compound

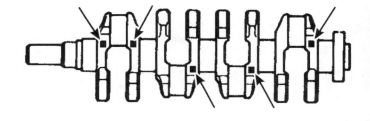

19.11 The corresponding mark for main bearing selection is located on each crankshaft counterweight, indicated by a single or double dash mark

2   In order to save time and avoid problems, engine reassembly must be done in the following general order:

  Piston rings
  Crankshaft and main bearings
  Piston/connecting rod assemblies
  Rear main oil seal
  Cylinder head and rocker arms or lifters (Part A)
  Camshaft(s) (Part A)
  Oil pump (Part A)
  Oil pick-up tube
  Oil pan (Part A)
  Timing belt and pulleys (Part A)
  Valve cover(s) (Part A)
  Timing belt cover(s) (Part A)
  Intake and exhaust manifolds (Part A)
  Flywheel/driveplate (Part A)

21   Piston rings - installation

Refer to illustrations 21.3, 21.4, 21.7a, 21.7b and 21.10

1   Before installing the new piston rings, the ring end gaps must be

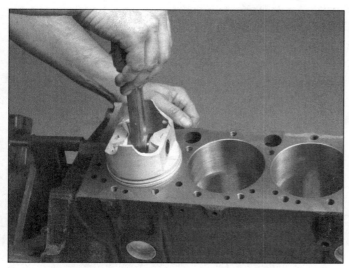

21.3 When checking piston ring end gap, the ring must be square in the cylinder bore (this is done by pushing the ring down with the top of a piston as shown)

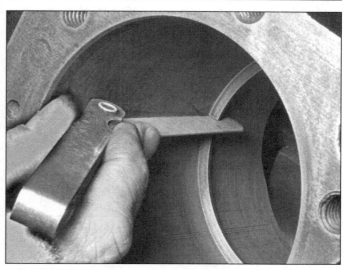

21.4 With the ring square in the cylinder, measure the end gap with a feeler gauge

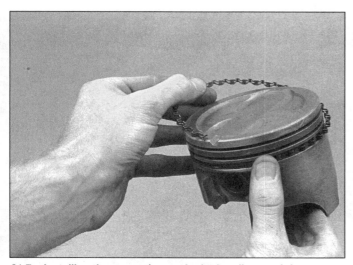

21.7a Installing the spacer/expander in the oil control ring groove

21.7b DO NOT use a piston ring installation tool when installing the oil ring side rails

2B

checked. It's assumed that the piston ring side clearance has been checked and verified correct (see Section 17).

2   Lay out the piston/connecting rod assemblies and the new ring sets so the ring sets will be matched with the same piston and cylinder during the end gap measurement and engine assembly.

3   Insert the top (number one) ring into the first cylinder and square it up with the cylinder walls by pushing it in with the top of the piston **(see illustration)**. The ring should be near the bottom of the cylinder, at the lower limit of ring travel.

4   To measure the end gap, slip feeler gauges between the ends of the ring until a gauge equal to the gap width is found **(see illustration)**. The feeler gauge should slide between the ring ends with a slight amount of drag. Compare the measurement to the Specifications. If the gap is larger or smaller than specified, double-check to make sure you have the correct rings before proceeding.

5   Repeat the procedure for each ring that will be installed in the first cylinder and for each ring in the remaining cylinders. Remember to keep rings, pistons and cylinders matched up.

6   Once the ring end gaps have been checked/corrected, the rings can be installed on the pistons.

7   The oil control ring (lowest one on the piston) is usually installed first. It's composed of three separate components. Slip the spacer/expander into the groove **(see illustration)**. If an anti-rotation tang is used, make sure it's inserted into the drilled hole in the ring groove. Next, install the lower side rail. Don't use a piston ring installation tool on the oil ring side rails, as they may be damaged. Instead, place one end of the side rail into the groove between the spacer/expander and the ring land, hold it firmly in place and slide a finger around the piston while pushing the rail into the groove **(see illustration)**. Next, install the upper side rail in the same manner.

8   After the three oil ring components have been installed, check to make sure that both the upper and lower side rails can be turned smoothly in the ring groove.

9   The number two (middle) ring is installed next. It's usually stamped with a mark which must face up, toward the top of the piston. **Note:** *Always follow the instructions printed on the ring package or box - different manufacturers may require different approaches. Do not mix up the top and middle rings, as they have different cross sections.*

10   Use a piston ring installation tool and make sure the identification mark is facing the top of the piston, then slip the ring into the middle groove on the piston. Don't expand the ring any more than necessary

21.10 Installing the compression rings with a ring expander - the mark (arrow) must face up

22.10 Lay the Plastigage strips (arrow) on the main bearing journals, parallel to the crankshaft centerline

to slide it over the piston **(see illustration)**.
11   Install the number one (top) ring in the same manner. Make sure the mark is facing up. Be careful not to confuse the number one and number two rings.
12   Repeat the procedure for the remaining pistons and rings.

---

22   Crankshaft - installation and main bearing oil clearance check

Refer to illustrations 22.10, 22.12 and 22.14
1   Crankshaft installation is the first major step in engine reassembly. It's assumed at this point that the engine block and crankshaft have been cleaned, inspected and repaired or reconditioned.
2   Position the engine with the bottom facing up.
3   Remove the main bearing cap bolts and lift out the caps. Lay the caps out in the proper order to ensure correct installation.
4   If they're still in place, remove the old bearing inserts from the block and the main bearing caps. Wipe the main bearing surfaces of the block and caps with a clean, lint-free cloth. They must be kept spotlessly clean!

Main bearing oil clearance check

5   Clean the back sides of the new main bearing inserts and lay the bearing half with the oil groove and hole in each main bearing saddle in the block (on all engines covered by this manual, the bearings with oil holes go in the block and those without oil holes go in the caps). Lay the other bearing half from each bearing set in the corresponding main bearing cap. Make sure the tab on each bearing insert fits into the recess in the block or cap. Also, the oil holes in the block must line up with the oil holes in the bearing insert. **Caution:** *Do not hammer the bearings into place and don't nick or gouge the bearing faces. No lubrication should be used at this time.*
6   The thrust bearings (washers) must be installed in the number two main bearing saddle (on the cylinder block side). Be sure to install them with the oil grooves facing out (away from the main bearing saddle). Apply a thin film of moly-based grease or engine assembly lube to the back sides of the thrust bearings to hold them in place.
7   Clean the faces of the bearings in the block and the crankshaft main bearing journals with a clean, lint-free cloth. Check or clean the oil holes in the crankshaft, as any dirt here can go only one way - straight through the new bearings.
8   Once you're certain the crankshaft is clean, carefully lay it in position in the main bearings. No lubricant should be used at this time.
9   Before the crankshaft can be permanently installed, the main bearing oil clearance must be checked.
10   Trim several pieces of the appropriate size Plastigage (they must

be slightly shorter than the width of the main bearings) and place one piece on each crankshaft main bearing journal, parallel with the journal axis **(see illustration)**.
11   Clean the faces of the bearings in the caps and install the caps in their respective positions (don't mix them up) with the arrows pointing toward the front of the engine. Don't disturb the Plastigage. Apply a light coat of oil to the bolt threads and the under sides of the bolt heads, then install them.
12   Following the recommended sequence **(see illustration)**, tighten the main bearing cap bolts, in three steps, to the torque listed in this Chapter's Specifications. Don't rotate the crankshaft at any time during this operation!
13   Remove the bolts and carefully lift off the main bearing caps. Keep them in order. Don't disturb the Plastigage or rotate the crankshaft. If any of the main bearing caps are difficult to remove, tap them gently from side-to-side with a soft-face hammer to loosen them.
14   Compare the width of the crushed Plastigage on each journal to the scale printed on the Plastigage envelope to obtain the main bearing oil clearance **(see illustration)**. Check the Specifications to make sure it's correct.
15   If the clearance is not as specified, the bearing inserts may be the wrong size which means different ones will be required (see Section 19). Before deciding that different inserts are needed, make sure that no dirt or oil was between the bearing inserts and the caps or block when the clearance was measured. If the Plastigage is noticeably wider at one end than the other, the journal may be tapered (see Section 18).
16   Carefully scrape all traces of the Plastigage material off the main bearing journals and/or the bearing faces. Don't nick or scratch the bearing faces.

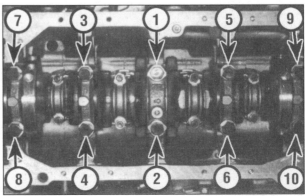

22.12 Main bearing cap tightening sequence

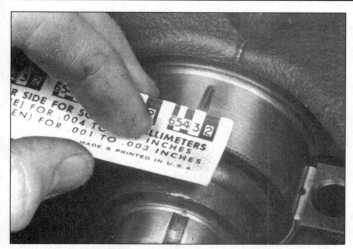

22.14 Compare the width of the crushed Plastigage to the scale on the envelope to determine the main bearing oil clearance (always take the measurement at the widest point of the Plastigage); be sure to use the correct scale - standard and metric ones are included

23.3 After removing the retainer from the block, support it on two wood blocks and drive out the old seal with a punch and hammer

Final crankshaft installation

17   Carefully lift the crankshaft out of the engine. Clean the bearing faces in the block, then apply a thin, uniform layer of clean moly-base grease or engine assembly lube to each of the bearing surfaces. Coat the thrust washers as well.

18   Lubricate the crankshaft surfaces that contact the oil seals with moly-base grease, engine assembly lube or clean engine oil.

19   Make sure the crankshaft journals are clean, then lay the crankshaft back in place in the block. Clean the faces of the bearings in the caps or cap assembly, then apply the same lubricant to them. Install the caps in their respective positions with the arrows pointing toward the front of the engine. **Note:** *If you haven't already done so, be sure to install the thrust washers in the number two main bearing saddle. The grooves in the washers must face away from the saddle.*

20   Apply a light coat of oil to the bolt threads and the under sides of the bolt heads, then install them. Tighten all except the number two cap bolts (the one with the thrust washers on the block side) to the torque listed in this Chapter's Specifications (work from the center out and approach the final torque in three steps). Tighten the number two cap bolts to 10-to-12 ft-lbs. Tap the ends of the crankshaft forward and backward with a lead or brass hammer to line up the thrust washer and crankshaft surfaces. Re-tighten all main bearing cap bolts to the specified torque, following the recommended sequence.

21   Rotate the crankshaft a number of times by hand to check for any obvious binding.

22   Check the crankshaft endplay with a feeler gauge or a dial indicator (see Section 13). The endplay should be correct if the crankshaft thrust faces aren't worn or damaged and new thrust washers have been installed.

23   Install a new rear main oil seal, then bolt the retainer to the block (see Section 23).

---

23   Rear main oil seal installation

Refer to illustrations 23.3 and 23.5

1   The crankshaft must be installed first and the main bearing caps bolted in place, then the new seal should be installed in the retainer and the retainer bolted to the block.

2   Check the seal contact surface on the crankshaft very carefully for scratches and nicks that could damage the new seal lip and cause oil leaks. If the crankshaft is damaged, the only alternative is a new or different crankshaft.

3   The old seal can be removed from the retainer by driving it out from the back side with a hammer and punch **(see illustration)**. Be sure to note how far it's recessed into the bore before removing it; the new seal will have to be recessed an equal amount. Be very careful not to scratch or otherwise damage the bore in the retainer or oil leaks could develop.

4   Make sure the retainer is clean, then apply a thin coat of engine oil to the outer edge of the new seal. The seal must be pressed squarely into the bore, so hammering it into place isn't recommended. If you don't have access to a press, sandwich the housing and seal between two smooth pieces of wood and press the seal into place with the jaws of a large vise. The pieces of wood must be thick enough to distribute the force evenly around the entire circumference of the seal. Work slowly and make sure the seal enters the bore squarely.

5   As a last resort, the seal can be tapped into the retainer with a hammer. Use a block of wood to distribute the force evenly and make sure the seal is driven in squarely **(see illustration)**.

6   The seal lips must be lubricated with clean engine oil or multi-purpose grease before the seal/retainer is slipped over the crankshaft and bolted to the block. Use a new gasket and make sure the dowel pins are in place before installing the retainer.

7   Tighten the bolts a little at a time until they're all at the torque listed in the Chapter 2 Part A Specifications.

23.5 Drive the new seal into the retainer with a wood block or a section of pipe, if you have one large enough - make sure you don't cock the seal in the retainer bore

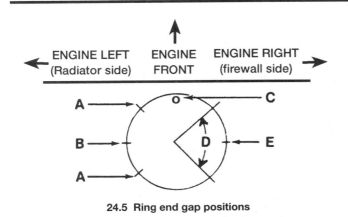

24.5 Ring end gap positions

A   *Oil ring side rail gaps*
B   *Middle compression ring gaps*
C   *Dimple in the piston (indicating front of engine)*
D   *Oil spacer/expander gap*
E   *Top compression ring gap*

24   Pistons/connecting rods - installation and rod bearing oil clearance check

Refer to illustrations 24.5, 24.9, 24.13 and 24.17

1   Before installing the piston/connecting rod assemblies, the cylinder walls must be perfectly clean, the top edge of each cylinder must be chamfered, and the crankshaft must be in place.
2   Remove the cap from the end of the number one connecting rod (refer to the marks made during removal). Remove the original bearing inserts and wipe the bearing surfaces of the connecting rod and cap with a clean, lint-free cloth. They must be kept spotlessly clean.

Connecting rod bearing oil clearance check

3   Clean the back side of the new upper bearing insert, then lay it in place in the connecting rod. Make sure the tab on the bearing fits into the recess in the rod so the oil holes line up. Don't hammer the bearing insert into place and be very careful not to nick or gouge the bearing face. Don't lubricate the bearing at this time.
4   Clean the back side of the other bearing insert and install it in the rod cap. Again, make sure the tab on the bearing fits into the recess in the cap, and don't apply any lubricant. It's critically important that the mating surfaces of the bearing and connecting rod are perfectly clean and oil free when they're assembled.
5   Position the piston ring gaps at staggered intervals around the piston **(see illustration)**.
6   Slip a section of plastic or rubber hose over each connecting rod cap bolt.
7   Lubricate the piston and rings with clean engine oil and attach a piston ring compressor to the piston. Leave the skirt protruding about 1/4-inch to guide the piston into the cylinder. The rings must be compressed until they're flush with the piston.
8   Rotate the crankshaft until the number one connecting rod journal is at BDC (bottom dead center) and apply a coat of engine oil to the cylinder walls.
9   With the mark on top of the piston **(see illustration)** facing the front (timing belt end) of the engine, gently insert the piston/connecting rod assembly into the number one cylinder bore and rest the bottom edge of the ring compressor on the engine block.
10   Tap the top edge of the ring compressor to make sure it's contacting the block around its entire circumference.
11   Gently tap on the top of the piston with the end of a wooden or plastic hammer handle **(see illustration 24.9)** while guiding the end of the connecting rod into place on the crankshaft journal. The piston rings may try to pop out of the ring compressor just before entering the cylinder bore, so keep some pressure on the ring compressor. Work slowly, and if any resistance is felt as the piston enters the cylinder,

24.9 The piston can be driven gently into the cylinder bore with the end of a wooden or plastic hammer handle

stop immediately. Find out what's hanging up and fix it before proceeding. Do not, for any reason, force the piston into the cylinder - you might break a ring and/or the piston.
12   Once the piston/connecting rod assembly is installed, the connecting rod bearing oil clearance must be checked before the rod cap is permanently bolted in place.
13   Cut a piece of the appropriate size Plastigage slightly shorter than the width of the connecting rod bearing and lay it in place on the number one connecting rod journal, parallel with the journal axis **(see illustration)**.
14   Clean the connecting rod cap bearing face, remove the protective hoses from the connecting rod bolts and install the rod cap. Make sure the mating mark on the cap is on the same side as the mark on the connecting rod. Check the cap to make sure the front mark is facing the timing belt end of the engine.
15   Apply a light coat of oil to the under sides of the nuts, then install and tighten them to the torque listed in this Chapter's Specifications. Use a thin-wall socket to avoid erroneous torque readings that can result if the socket is wedged between the rod cap and nut. If the socket tends to wedge itself between the nut and the cap, lift up on it slightly until it no longer contacts the cap. Do not rotate the crankshaft at any time during this operation.
16   Remove the nuts and detach the rod cap, being very careful not

24.13 Lay the Plastigage strips on each rod bearing journal, parallel to the crankshaft centerline

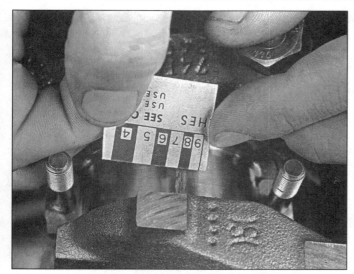

24.17 Measuring the width of the crushed Plastigage to determine the rod bearing oil clearance (be sure to use the correct scale - standard and metric ones are included)

to disturb the Plastigage.

17   Compare the width of the crushed Plastigage to the scale printed on the Plastigage envelope to obtain the oil clearance **(see illustration)**. Compare it to the Specifications to make sure the clearance is correct.

18   If the clearance is not as specified, the bearing inserts may be the wrong size (which means different ones will be required). Before deciding that different inserts are needed, make sure that no dirt or oil was between the bearing inserts and the connecting rod or cap when the clearance was measured. Also, recheck the journal diameter. If the Plastigage was wider at one end than the other, the journal may be tapered (see Section 18).

Final connecting rod installation

19   Carefully scrape all traces of the Plastigage material off the rod journal and/or bearing face. Be very careful not to scratch the bearing - use your fingernail or the edge of a credit card.

20   Make sure the bearing faces are perfectly clean, then apply a uniform layer of clean moly-base grease or engine assembly lube to both of them. You'll have to push the piston into the cylinder to expose the face of the bearing insert in the connecting rod - be sure to slip the protective hoses over the rod bolts first.

21   Slide the connecting rod back into place on the journal, remove the protective hoses from the rod cap bolts, install the rod cap and tighten the nuts to the torque listed in this Chapter's Specifications.

22   Repeat the entire procedure for the remaining pistons/connecting rods.

23   The important points to remember are:
a) Keep the back sides of the bearing inserts and the insides of the connecting rods and caps perfectly clean when assembling them.
b) Make sure you have the correct piston/rod assembly for each cylinder.
c) The dimple on the piston must face the front (timing belt end) of the engine.
d) Lubricate the cylinder walls with clean oil.
e) Lubricate the bearing faces when installing the rod caps after the oil clearance has been checked.

24   After all the piston/connecting rod assemblies have been properly installed, rotate the crankshaft a number of times by hand to check for any obvious binding.

25   As a final step, the connecting rod side clearance (endplay) must be checked (see Section 12).

26   Compare the measured side clearance to the Specifications to make sure it's correct. If it was correct before disassembly and the original crankshaft and rods were reinstalled, it should still be right. If new rods or a new crankshaft were installed, the side clearance may be inadequate. If so, the rods will have to be removed and taken to an automotive machine shop for re-sizing.

---

25   Initial start-up and break-in after overhaul

Warning: *Have a fire extinguisher handy when starting the engine for the first time.*

1   Once the engine has been installed in the vehicle, double-check the engine oil and coolant levels.

2   With the spark plugs out of the engine and the ignition system disabled (see Section 3), crank the engine until oil pressure registers on the gauge or the light goes out.

3   Install the spark plugs, hook up the plug wires and restore the ignition system functions (see Section 3).

4   Start the engine. It may take a few moments for the fuel system to build up pressure, but the engine should start without a great deal of effort.

5   After the engine starts, it should be allowed to warm up to normal operating temperature. While the engine is warming up, make a thorough check for fuel, oil and coolant leaks.

6   Shut the engine off and recheck the engine oil and coolant levels.

7   Drive the vehicle to an area with minimum traffic, accelerate at full throttle from 30 to 50 mph, then allow the vehicle to slow to 30 mph with the throttle closed. Repeat the procedure 10 or 12 times. This will load the piston rings and cause them to seat properly against the cylinder walls. Check again for oil and coolant leaks.

8   Drive the vehicle gently for the first 500 miles (no sustained high speeds) and keep a constant check on the oil level. It is not unusual for an engine to use oil during the break-in period.

9   At approximately 500 to 600 miles, change the oil and filter.

10   For the next few hundred miles, drive the vehicle normally. Do not pamper it or abuse it.

11   After 2000 miles, change the oil and filter again and consider the engine broken in.

2B

Notes

Chapter 3 Cooling, heating and air conditioning systems

Contents

3

Specifications

General

Radiator cap pressure rating	14 psi
Thermostat rating (opening temperature)	176 to 183-degrees F
Cooling system capacity	See Chapter 1
Cooling system testing pressure	13 psi
Refrigerant capacity	1.32 lbs
Refrigerant oil capacity (complete system)	5.10 ounces

Torque specifications

	Ft-lbs (unless otherwise indicated)
Condenser inlet pipe fitting nuts...	106 inch-lbs
Coolant pipe bolts	18
Evaporator outlet-to-compressor suction pipe nut	18
Expansion valve fitting nuts...	71 inch-lbs
Thermostat cover nuts..	18
Water pump-to-engine block bolts	18

1   General information

Engine cooling system

All vehicles covered by this manual employ a pressurized engine cooling system with thermostatically controlled coolant circulation. An impeller type water pump mounted on the drivebelt end of the block pumps coolant through the engine. The coolant flows around each cylinder and toward the transaxle end of the engine. Cast-in coolant passages direct coolant around the intake and exhaust ports, near the spark plug areas and in close proximity to the exhaust valve guides.

A wax pellet type thermostat is located in a housing on the other end of the engine. During warm up, the closed thermostat prevents coolant from circulating through the radiator. As the engine nears normal operating temperature, the thermostat opens and allows hot coolant to travel through the radiator, where it's cooled before returning to the engine.

The cooling system is sealed by a pressure type radiator cap, which raises the boiling point of the coolant and increases the cooling efficiency of the radiator. If the system pressure exceeds the cap pressure relief value, the excess pressure in the system forces the spring-loaded valve inside the cap off its seat and allows the coolant to escape through the overflow tube into a coolant reservoir. When the system cools, the excess coolant is automatically drawn from the reservoir back into the radiator.

The coolant reservoir serves as both the point at which fresh coolant is added to the cooling system to maintain the proper fluid level and as a holding tank for overheated coolant.

This type of cooling system is known as a closed design because coolant that escapes past the pressure cap is saved and reused.

3.7a The thermostat housing (arrow) on DOHC engines is located on the left end of the cylinder head, near the distributor

3.7b On the SOHC engine, the thermostat housing is located near the distributor also

Heating system

The heating system consists of a blower fan and heater core located in the heater box, the hoses connecting the heater core to the engine cooling system and the heater/air conditioning control head on the dashboard. Hot engine coolant is circulated through the heater core. When the heater mode is activated, a flap opens to expose the heater box to the passenger compartment. A fan switch on the control head activates the blower motor, which forces air through the core, heating the air.

Air conditioning system

The air conditioning system consists of a condenser mounted in front of the radiator, an evaporator mounted adjacent to the heater core, a compressor mounted on the engine, a receiver-drier which contains a high pressure relief valve and the plumbing connecting all of the above components.

A blower fan forces the warmer air of the passenger compartment through the evaporator core (sort of a radiator-in-reverse), transferring the heat from the air to the refrigerant. The liquid refrigerant boils off into low pressure vapor, taking the heat with it when it leaves the evaporator.

2   Antifreeze - general information

Warning: *Do not allow antifreeze to come in contact with your skin or painted surfaces of the vehicle. Rinse off spills immediately with plenty of water. Antifreeze is highly toxic if ingested. Never leave antifreeze lying around in an open container or in puddles on the floor; children and pets are attracted by it's sweet smell and may drink it. Check with local authorities about disposing of used antifreeze. Many communities have collection centers which will see that antifreeze is disposed of safely.*

The cooling system should be filled with a water/ethylene glycol based antifreeze solution, which will prevent freezing down to at least -20-degrees F, or lower if local climate requires it. It also provides protection against corrosion and increases the coolant boiling point.

The cooling system should be drained, flushed and refilled at the specified intervals (see Chapter 1). Old or contaminated antifreeze solutions are likely to cause damage and encourage the formation of corrosion and scale in the system. Use distilled water with the antifreeze.

Before adding antifreeze, check all hose connections, because antifreeze tends to leak through very minute openings. Engines don't normally consume coolant, so if the level goes down, find the cause and correct it.

The exact mixture of antifreeze-to-water which you should use depends on the relative weather conditions. The mixture should contain at least 50-percent antifreeze, but should never contain more than 70-percent antifreeze. Consult the mixture ratio chart on the antifreeze container before adding coolant. Hydrometers are available at most auto parts stores to test the coolant. Use antifreeze which meets the vehicle manufacturer's specifications.

3   Thermostat - check and replacement

Warning: *Do not remove the radiator cap, drain the coolant or replace the thermostat until the engine has cooled completely. Do not allow antifreeze to come in contact with your skin or painted surfaces of the vehicle. Rinse off spills immediately with plenty of water. Antifreeze is highly toxic if ingested. Never leave antifreeze lying around in an open container or in puddles on the floor; children and pets are attracted by it's sweet smell and may drink it. Check with local authorities about disposing of used antifreeze. Many communities have collection centers which will see that antifreeze is disposed of safely.*

Check

1   Before assuming the thermostat is to blame for a cooling system problem, check the coolant level, drivebelt tension (see Chapter 1) and temperature gauge operation.
2   If the engine seems to be taking a long time to warm up (based on heater output or temperature gauge operation), the thermostat is probably stuck open. Replace the thermostat with a new one.
3   If the engine runs hot, use your hand to check the temperature of the upper radiator hose. If the hose isn't hot, but the engine is, the thermostat is probably stuck closed, preventing the coolant inside the engine from escaping to the radiator. Replace the thermostat. **Caution:** *Don't drive the vehicle without a thermostat. The computer may stay in open loop, causing emissions and fuel economy to suffer.*
4   If the upper radiator hose is hot, it means that the coolant is flowing and the thermostat is open. Consult the *Troubleshooting* section at the front of this manual for cooling system diagnosis.

Replacement

Refer to illustrations 3.7a, 3.7b and 3.11
5   Disconnect the negative battery cable from the battery.
6   Drain the cooling system (see Chapter 1). If the coolant is relatively new or in good condition, save it and reuse it.
7   Follow the upper radiator hose (DOHC engine) or the lower radiator hose (SOHC engine) to the engine to locate the thermostat housing **(see illustrations)**.
8   Loosen the hose clamp and detach the hose from the fitting. If the hose is stuck, grasp it near the end with a pair of adjustable pliers and twist it to break the seal, then pull it off. If the hose is old or deteriorated, cut it off and install a new one.

3.11 Note the position of the air bleed valve (arrow) and how the thermostat is installed

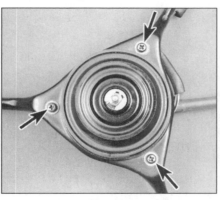

4.3 Disconnect the electrical connector for the fan and make a connection directly to the battery - if the fan does not work, replace the motor

4.8 Look on the left side of the fan shroud to find the main cooling fan electrical connector and disconnect it

9   If the outer surface of the large fitting that mates with the hose is deteriorated (corroded, pitted, etc.) it may be damaged further by hose removal. If it is, the thermostat housing cover will have to be replaced.

10   Remove the bolts/nuts and detach the thermostat cover **(see illustrations 3.7a and 3.7b)**. If the cover is stuck, tap it with a soft-face hammer to jar it loose. Be prepared for some coolant to spill as the gasket seal is broken.

11   Note the position of the air bleed valve and how the thermostat is installed **(see illustration)**, then remove the thermostat and all traces of old gasket material and sealant from the housing and cover with a gasket scraper.

12   Apply a thin, uniform layer of RTV sealant to both sides of the new gasket and position it on the housing.

13   Install the new thermostat in the housing. Make sure the air bleed valve faces up and the spring end is directed into the engine.

14   Install the thermostat cover and bolts. Tighten the bolts to the torque listed in this Chapter's Specifications.

15   Reattach the hose to the fitting and tighten the hose clamp securely. Reconnect the electrical connector for the cooling fan switch.

16   Refill the cooling system (see Chapter 1).

17   Start the engine and allow it to reach normal operating temperature, then check for leaks and proper thermostat operation (as described in Steps 3 and 4).

---

4   Engine cooling fan(s) - check and replacement

Refer to illustrations 4.3, 4.8, 4.9a, 4.9b, 4.14, 4.16 and 4.17

Check

1   The engine cooling fan(s) are controlled by a temperature relay which is mounted on the left engine compartment relay center. On the 1.6L SOHC engine the radiator fan operates together with the condenser fan (if your vehicle has air conditioning) all the time. On the 1.6L and 1.8L DOHC engines the two fans operate separately When the coolant reaches a predetermined temperature, the switch opens the ground return for the fan motor relay, completing the circuit.

2   First, check the fuses (see Chapter 12).

3   To test the fan motor, unplug the electrical connector and use fused jumper wires **(see illustration)** to connect the fan directly to the battery. If the fan still does not work, replace the motor.

4   If the motor tested okay, the fault lies in the radiator fan thermoswitch, the relay or the wiring harness (see Chapter 12).

5   Turn on the ignition switch, unplug the electrical connector from the radiator fan thermoswitch **(see illustration 5.4)** and, using a jumper wire, connect the terminals together.

6   If the fan does not operate, check the wiring and the relay (see Chapter 12). If it does operate, replace the radiator fan thermoswitch.

4.9a Remove the two upper mounting bolts . . .

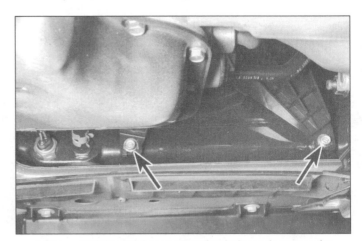

4.9b . . . and the two lower mounting bolts and remove the fan assembly

Replacement
Main cooling fan

7   Disconnect the negative battery cable from the battery.

8   Unplug the cooling fan electrical connector **(see illustration)**.

9   Remove the radiator fan shroud bolts **(see illustrations)**.

10   Remove the fan assembly from the vehicle.

11   Installation is the reverse of removal.

3

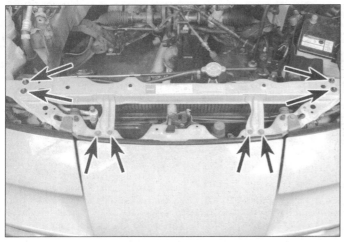

4.14 Remove the radiator support by removing the four bolts at the front and the two bolts on each end of the support (arrows)

4.16 Disconnect the electrical connector for the auxiliary fan located on the fan shroud, near the hood latch

4.17 Remove the four condenser fan mounting nuts (the two lower nuts are shown here)

5.4 The radiator fan thermoswitch is located on the left side of the lower tank of the radiator

1   *Radiator fan thermoswitch*
2   *Transmission fluid cooler line*

Air conditioning condenser fan

12   Air conditioned models have an additional fan located in front of the condenser.
13   Disconnect the negative battery cable from the battery.
14   Remove the radiator support **(see illustration).**
15   Remove the hood latch.
16   Disconnect the fan motor electrical connector **(see illustration).**
17   Remove the four nuts holding the condenser fan to the condenser **(see illustration).** Remove the assembly.
18   Installation is the reverse of the removal procedure.

---

5   Radiator - removal and installation

Refer to illustration 5.4
Warning: *Do not start this procedure until the engine is completely cool. Do not allow antifreeze to come in contact with your skin or painted surfaces of the vehicle. Rinse off spills immediately with plenty of water. Antifreeze is highly toxic if ingested. Never leave antifreeze lying around in an open container or in puddles on the floor; children and pets are attracted by it's sweet smell and may drink it. Check with local authorities about disposing of used antifreeze. Many communities have collection centers which will see that antifreeze is disposed of safely.*

Removal

1   Disconnect the negative battery cable from the battery.
2   Raise the front of the vehicle and support it securely on jack-stands. Remove the lower splash shields.
3   Drain the cooling system (see Chapter 1). If the coolant is relatively new or in good condition, save it and reuse it.
4   Disconnect the electrical connector from the radiator fan thermoswitch **(see illustration).**
5   Disconnect the coolant reservoir hose from the radiator. Loosen the upper and lower radiator hose clamps, then detach the radiator hoses from the fittings. If they're stuck, grasp each hose near the end with a pair of adjustable pliers and twist it to break the seal, then pull it off - be careful not to damage the radiator fittings! If the hoses are old or deteriorated, cut them off and install new ones.
6   Remove the radiator support **(see illustration 4.14).**
7   Disconnect the electrical connector(s) from the cooling fan(s) **(see illustrations 4.8 and 4.16).**
8   If the vehicle is equipped with an automatic transaxle, disconnect the transmission fluid cooler lines and plug the lines and fittings **(see illustration 5.4).**
9   Carefully lift out the radiator. Don't spill coolant on the vehicle or scratch the paint. Remove the bolts securing the cooling fan to the ra-

diator and pull it free.

10   With the radiator removed, it can be inspected for leaks and damage. If it needs repair, have a radiator shop or dealer service department perform the work, as special techniques are required.

11   Bugs and dirt can be removed from the radiator with a garden hose or a soft brush. Don't bend the cooling fins as this is done.

Installation

12   Installation is the reverse of the removal procedure. Be sure the rubber cushions are seated properly at the base of the radiator.

13   After installation, fill the cooling system with the proper mixture of antifreeze and water (see Chapter 1).

14   Start the engine and check for leaks. Allow the engine to reach normal operating temperature, indicated by the upper radiator hose becoming hot. Recheck the coolant level and add more if required.

15   If you're working on an automatic transaxle equipped vehicle, check and add fluid as needed (see Chapter 1).

---

6   Coolant reservoir - removal and installation

Warning: *Do not start this procedure until the engine is completely cool. Do not allow antifreeze to come in contact with your skin or painted surfaces of the vehicle. Rinse off spills immediately with plenty of water. Antifreeze is highly toxic if ingested. Never leave antifreeze lying around in an open container or in puddles on the floor; children and pets are attracted by it's sweet smell and may drink it. Check with local authorities about disposing of used antifreeze. Many communities have collection centers which will see that antifreeze is disposed of safely.*

1   Disconnect the hose from the radiator filler neck and inspect the hose for cracks.

2   Follow the hose from the filler neck to the reservoir cap and lift the cap off the coolant reservoir and withdraw the overflow hose.

3   Remove the hold down bolt.

4   Slide the coolant reservoir straight up from its guides to remove it.

5   Pour the coolant into a container. Wash out and inspect the reservoir for cracks and chafing. Replace it if it's damaged.

6   Installation is the reverse of removal.

---

7   Water pump - check

1   A failure in the water pump can cause serious engine damage due to overheating.

2   There are two ways to check the operation of the water pump while it's installed on the engine. If the pump is defective, it should be replaced with a new or rebuilt unit.

3   With the engine running at normal operating temperature, squeeze the upper radiator hose. If the water pump is working properly, a slight pressure surge should be felt as the hose is released. **Warning:** *Keep your hands away from the fan blades!*

4   Remove the timing belt cover(s) (see Chapter 2A). Water pumps are equipped with weep or vent holes. If a failure occurs in the pump seal, coolant will leak from the hole. In most cases you'll need a flashlight to find the hole on the water pump from underneath to check for leaks. On both the SOHC and DOHC engines any water coming from this hole is vented to the outside of the timing belt cover on the back side of the engine in order to not damage the timing belt.

5   If the water pump shaft bearings fail there may be a howling sound at the drivebelt end of the engine while it's running. Don't mistake drivebelt slippage, which causes a squealing sound, for water pump bearing failure.

---

8   Water pump - removal and installation

Refer to illustration 8.6

Warning: *Wait until the engine is completely cool before beginning this procedure. Do not allow antifreeze to come in contact with your skin or painted surfaces of the vehicle. Rinse off spills immediately with plenty*

8.6 After removing the timing belt (and power steering pump bracket on DOHC models), unscrew the four bolts and remove the water pump from the engine block

of water. Antifreeze is highly toxic if ingested. Never leave antifreeze lying around in an open container or in puddles on the floor; children and pets are attracted by it's sweet smell and may drink it. Check with local authorities about disposing of used antifreeze. Many communities have collection centers which will see that antifreeze is disposed of safely.

Removal

1   Disconnect the negative battery cable from the battery.

2   Drain the cooling system (see Chapter 1). If the coolant is relatively new or in good condition, save it and reuse it.

3   Remove the two bolts from the power steering pump bracket. Do not disconnect the fluid lines. Set the power steering pump out of the way.

4   Remove the timing belt cover(s) (see Chapter 2A).

5   Remove the timing belt (see Chapter 2A).

6   Remove the water pump mounting bolts and detach the water pump from the engine **(see illustration)**. If the water pump is stuck, gently tap it with a soft faced hammer to break the seal.

Installation

7   Clean the bolt threads and the threaded holes in the engine to remove corrosion and sealant. Remove all traces of old gasket material from the sealing surfaces.

8   Compare the new pump to the old one to make sure they're identical.

9   Apply a thin film of RTV sealant to the new gasket and install it on the pump.

10   Carefully mate the pump to the engine.

11   Install the bolts. Tighten them to the torque listed in this Chapter's Specifications. Don't over-tighten them or the pump may be damaged.

12   Reinstall all parts removed for access to the pump.

13   Refill the cooling system (see Chapter 1) and check the timing belt tension (see Chapter 2A). Run the engine and check for leaks.

---

9   Coolant temperature sending unit - check and replacement

Warning: *The engine must be completely cool before removing the sending unit.*

Check

1   If the coolant temperature gauge is inoperative, check the fuses first (see Chapter 12).

2   If the temperature indicator shows excessive temperature after running awhile, see the *Troubleshooting* section in the front of the manual.

3

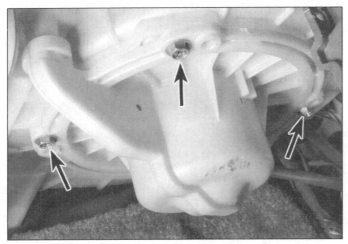

10.3 Remove the four bolts holding the blower motor in place and remove the blower motor assembly

10.4 Disconnect the electrical connector from the blower motor

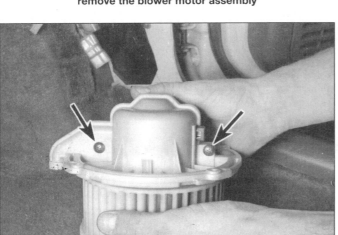

10.5 Remove the two screws that hold the case halves around the blower motor

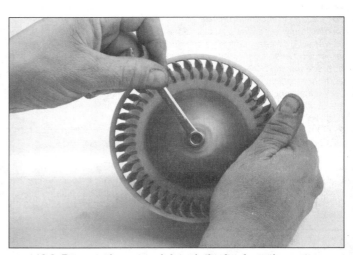

10.6 Remove the nut and detach the fan from the motor

3   If the temperature gauge indicates Hot shortly after the engine is started cold, disconnect the wire at the coolant temperature sending unit - it's located on the thermostat housing **Note**: *There are two sensors at the thermostat housing. One is the sending unit for the instrument panel gauge and the other is the sensor for the signal to the ECM. The smaller of the two (the one with the yellow/black wire) is for the operation of the gauge..* If the gauge reading drops, replace the sending unit. If the reading remains high, the wire to the gauge may be shorted to ground or the gauge is faulty.

4   If the coolant temperature gauge fails to indicate after the engine has been warmed up (approximately 10 minutes) and the fuses checked out okay, shut off the engine. Disconnect the wire at the sending unit and using a jumper wire, connect it to a clean ground on the engine. Turn on the ignition without starting the engine. If the gauge now indicates Hot, replace the sending unit.

5   If the gauge still does not work, the circuit may be open or the gauge may be faulty. See Chapter 12 for additional information.

Replacement

6   With the engine completely cool, remove the cap from the radiator to release any pressure, then reinstall the cap. This reduces coolant loss during sending unit replacement.

7   Disconnect the electrical connector from the sending unit. **Note**: *There are two sensors at the thermostat housing. One is for the instrument panel gauge and the other is for the signal to the ECM. The smaller of the two (the one with the yellow/black wire) is for the opera-*

tion of the gauge.

8   Prepare the new sending unit for installation by wrapping the threads with Teflon tape.

9   Unscrew the sending unit from the engine and quickly install the new one to prevent coolant loss.

10   Tighten the sending unit securely and connect the electrical connector.

11   Check the coolant level and add, if necessary. Start the engine and check for leaks and proper gauge operation.

10   Blower motor - removal and installation

Refer to illustrations 10.3, 10.4, 10.5 and 10.6

1   Disconnect the negative cable from the battery.

2   Locate the blower motor on passenger side behind the glove compartment. Removing the glove compartment makes access to the blower motor easier, but isn't absolutely necessary.

3   Remove the four blower motor retaining screws **(see illustration)** and lower the unit from the housing.

4   Disconnect the blower motor electrical connector **(see illustration)**.

5   Remove the two screws that hold the case halves together and separate the case to take out the blower motor **(see illustration)**.

6   If you are replacing the motor, detach the fan and transfer it to the

11.3 Squeeze the hose clamps with pliers and gently pull off the heater hoses from the heater core tubes on the firewall (sometimes it may be necessary to twist the hoses to break the seal before the hoses can be removed)

new motor **(see illustration)**.
7   Installation is the reverse of removal.
8   Run the blower and check for proper operation.

---

11   Heater core - removal and installation

Refer to illustrations 11.3 and 11.5
1   Disconnect the negative cable from the battery.
2   Drain the cooling system (see Chapter 1).
3   Working in the engine compartment, disconnect the heater hoses where they enter the firewall **(see illustration)**.
4   Remove the instrument panel (see Chapter 11).
5   Disconnect the evaporator case from the firewall (see Section 18). If the vehicle is not equipped with air conditioning, disconnect the blower motor-to-heater case duct **(see illustration)**.
6   Disconnect the temperature control cable and the mode control cable at the heater case **(see illustration 11.5)**.
7   Remove the nuts at the firewall attaching the heater unit and re-move the heater unit from the vehicle **(see illustration 11.5)**.
8   Remove the center floor duct from the heater unit **(see illustration 11.5)**.
9   Remove the screws and clips and separate the two halves of the heater assembly. Take out the old heater core and install the new unit.
10   Reassemble the heater unit and check the operation of the con-

3

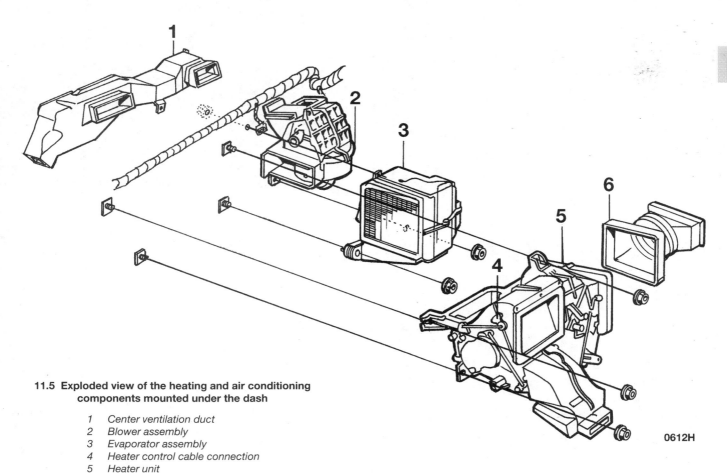

11.5 Exploded view of the heating and air conditioning components mounted under the dash

1   Center ventilation duct
2   Blower assembly
3   Evaporator assembly
4   Heater control cable connection
5   Heater unit
6   Duct

0612H

12.4   Remove the four screws holding the control assembly in the dash

12.5a   Using a small screwdriver to release the clips on the electrical connectors in the control assembly, disconnect the front half of the switch and remove it by pulling out towards you

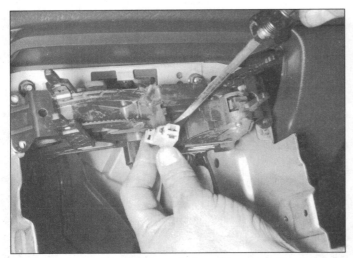

12.5b   On the back half of the switch, pull the connector towards the dash to remove it from the control assembly

12.5c   The remaining electrical connectors must be pulled out the back of the control assembly also

12.6   Use a small screwdriver to pry up the clips that hold the cables from the heater case to the control assembly - shown here are two of the three to be removed (the third is the same type of clip but located on the underside of the control assembly)

trol flaps. If any parts bind, correct the problem before installation.
11   Reinstall the remaining parts in the reverse order of removal.
12   Refill the cooling system (see Chapter 1), reconnect the battery and run the engine. Check for leaks and proper system operation.

---

12   Air conditioner and heater control assembly - removal and installation

---

Refer to illustrations 12.4, 12.5a, 12.5b, 12.5c and 12.6
1   Disconnect the negative cable from the battery.
2   Remove the knobs from the levers of the heater control unit.
3   Remove the ashtray and the trim panels which surround the radio and heater control assembly (see Chapter 11).
4   Remove the four screws holding the control unit in the dash and pull the assembly from the dash **(see illustration)**.
5   Disconnect the electrical connectors from the control assembly **(see illustrations)**.
6   Remove the three retaining clips holding the cables for the temperature, mode control and fresh/recirculated air levers **(see illustration)**.
7   Remove the control assembly.

8   Adjustment for the temperature, mode control and fresh/recirculated air control cables are as follows:

a   Place the temperature control lever all the way to the left position (cold).

b   Place the mode control lever all the way to the right position (defrost).

c   Place the fresh/recirculating lever all the way to the left position (fresh).

9   Pull all three cables out to full length from their housings.

10   Attach the cables to their respective levers and attach the clips.

11   Check for full travel and proper operation.

---

13   Air conditioning system - check and maintenance

Warning: *The air conditioning system is under high pressure. Do not loosen any fittings or remove any components until after the system has been discharged. Air conditioning refrigerant should be properly discharged into an EPA-approved container at a dealer service department or an automotive air conditioning repair facility. Always wear eye protection when disconnecting air conditioning system fittings.*

1   The following maintenance checks should be performed on a regular basis to ensure that the air conditioner continues to operate at peak efficiency.

a) Check the compressor drivebelt. If it's worn or deteriorated, replace it (see Chapter 1).

b) Check the drivebelt tension and, if necessary, adjust it (see Chapter 1).

c) Check the system hoses. Look for cracks, bubbles, hard spots and deterioration. Inspect the hoses and all fittings for oil bubbles and seepage. If there's any evidence of wear, damage or leaks, replace the hose(s).

d) Inspect the condenser fins for leaves, bugs and other debris. Use a "fin comb" or compressed air to clean the condenser.

e) Make sure the system has the correct refrigerant charge.

f) Check the evaporator housing drain tube for blockage. Long term non-use can cause hardening, and subsequent failure, of the seals.

2   Because of the complexity of the air conditioning system and the special equipment necessary to service it, in-depth troubleshooting and repairs are not included in this manual. However, simple checks and component replacement procedures are provided in this Chapter. For more complete information on the air conditioning system, refer to the *Haynes Automotive Heating and Air Conditioning Manual.*

3   The most common cause of poor cooling is simply a low system refrigerant charge. If a noticeable drop in cool air output occurs, one of the following quick checks will help you determine if the refrigerant level is low.

4   Warm the engine up to normal operating temperature.

5   Place the air conditioning temperature selector at the coldest setting and put the blower at the highest setting. Open the doors (to make sure the air conditioning system doesn't cycle off as soon as it cools the passenger compartment).

6   With the compressor engaged - the clutch will make an audible click and the center of the clutch will rotate - inspect the sight glass, if equipped. If the refrigerant looks foamy, it's low. Have the system charged by a dealer service department or other qualified repair shop.

7   If there's no sight glass, feel the inlet and outlet pipes at the compressor. One side should be much colder than the other. If there's no perceptible difference between the two pipes, there's something wrong with the compressor or the system. It might be a low charge - it might be something else. Take the vehicle to a dealer service department or other qualified repair shop.

---

14   Air conditioning receiver/drier - removal and installation

Refer to illustration 14.3

Warning: *The air conditioning system is under high pressure. Do not*

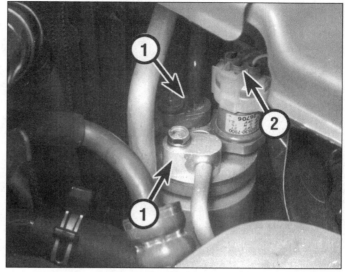

14.3 Disconnect the two refrigerant lines and the electrical connector at the pressure switch

1   *Refrigerant lines*
2   *Pressure switch electrical connector*

loosen any fittings or remove any components until after the system has been discharged. Air conditioning refrigerant should be properly discharged into an EPA-approved container at a dealer service department or an automotive air conditioning repair facility. Always wear eye protection when disconnecting air conditioning system fittings.

1   Have the refrigerant discharged at a dealer service department or an automotive air conditioning repair facility.

2   The receiver/drier, which acts as a reservoir and filter for the refrigerant, is located in the right front corner of the engine compartment. The receiver/drier bracket is attached to the right side of the air conditioning condenser.

3   Detach the refrigerant lines and electrical connector from the receiver/drier **(see illustration)**. Immediately cap the open fittings to prevent the entry of dirt and moisture.

4   Remove the radiator support **(see illustration 4.14)**.

5   Remove the receiver/drier mounting bolts and detach it from the condenser.

6   Install new O-rings on the lines and lubricate them with clean refrigerant oil.

7   Installation is the reverse of removal. **Note:** *Do not remove the sealing caps until you are ready to reconnect the lines.*

8   If a new receiver/drier is installed, add one fluid ounce of refrigerant oil to the system.

9   Have the system evacuated, charged and leak tested by the shop that discharged it.

---

15   Air conditioning compressor - removal and installation

Refer to illustrations 15.3, 15.8a and 15.8b

Warning: *The air conditioning system is under high pressure. Do not loosen any fittings or remove any components until after the system has been discharged. Air conditioning refrigerant should be properly discharged into an EPA-approved container at a dealer service department or an automotive air conditioning repair facility. Always wear eye protection when disconnecting air conditioning system fittings.*

1   Have the refrigerant discharged at a dealer service department or an automotive air conditioning repair facility.

2   Disconnect the negative cable from the battery and remove the battery (see Chapter 5).

15.3 Locate the wires on top of the air conditioning compressor, follow them back and unplug the electrical connector

15.8a Remove the compressor mounting bracket with the compressor by removing the bolts that hold the bracket to the block . . .

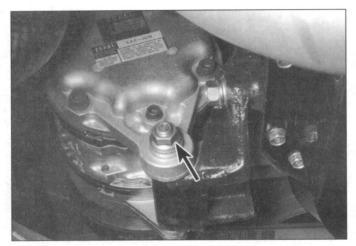

15.8b . . . then, from underneath the vehicle, remove the lower mounting bolt (the lower mounting bracket will stay attached to the block) and remove the air conditioning compressor from the vehicle

3   Disconnect the electrical connector from the compressor clutch **(see illustration)**.
4   On SOHC engines, remove the compressor/power steering belt from the pulleys by loosening the power steering pump adjustment and pivot bolts and moving the power steering pump towards the engine.
5   On DOHC engines, remove the serpentine belt (see Chapter 1)
6   Detach the refrigerant lines from the compressor and immediately cap the open fittings to prevent the entry of dirt and moisture.
7   Raise the vehicle and support it securely on jackstands.
8   Remove the mounting bolts **(see illustrations)** and lower the compressor from the engine compartment. **Note:** *Keep the compressor level during handling and storage. If the compressor seized or you find metal particles in the refrigerant lines, the system must be flushed out by an air conditioning technician and the receiver/drier must be replaced* (see Section 14).
9   Prior to installation, turn the center of the clutch six times to disperse any oil that has collected in the head.
10   Install the compressor in the reverse order of removal.
11   If you are installing a new compressor, refer to the manufacturer's instructions for adding refrigerant oil to the system. **Note:** *Drain out any oil that is present in the compressor, then add 1.7 ounces of new refrig-*

erant oil to the compressor.
12   Have the system evacuated, charged and leak tested by the shop that discharged it.

16   Air conditioning condenser - removal and installation

Warning: *The air conditioning system is under high pressure. Do not loosen any fittings or remove any components until after the system has been discharged. Air conditioning refrigerant should be properly discharged into an EPA-approved container at a dealer service department or an automotive air conditioning repair facility. Always wear eye protection when disconnecting air conditioning system fittings.*
1   Have the refrigerant discharged at a dealer service department or an automotive air conditioning repair facility.
2   Remove the radiator support **(see illustration 4.14)**.
3   Remove the hood latch.
4   Disconnect the condenser fan electrical connector (see Section 4).
5   Disconnect the electrical connector from the receiver/drier (see Section 14). Also detach the refrigerant outlet line from the receiver/drier.
6   Disconnect the compressor discharge line from the condenser.
7   Immediately cap the open fittings to prevent the entry of dirt and moisture.
8   Lift out the condenser and the receiver/drier. Store the condenser upright to prevent oil loss.
9   If a new condenser is to be installed, add one ounce of new refrigerant oil to the system.
10   Installation is the reverse of removal.
11   Have the system evacuated, charged and leak tested by the shop that discharged it.

17   Air conditioning expansion valve - removal and installation

Refer to illustration 17.3
Warning: *The air conditioning system is under high pressure. Do not loosen any fittings or remove any components until after the system has been discharged. Air conditioning refrigerant should be properly discharged into an EPA-approved container at a dealer service department or an automotive air conditioning repair facility. Always wear eye protection when disconnecting air conditioning system fittings.*
1   Have the refrigerant discharged at a dealer service department or an automotive air conditioning repair facility.

2   Disconnect the cable from the negative terminal of the battery.
3   Remove the two nuts that secure the evaporator inlet fitting to the expansion valve **(see illustration)**.
4   Remove the expansion valve from the evaporator inlet.
5   Installation is the reverse of the removal. **Note:** *Always use new O-rings when reassembling air conditioning components.*

---

18   Air conditioning evaporator - removal and installation

Warning: *The air conditioning system is under high pressure. Do not loosen any fittings or remove any components until after the system has been discharged. Air conditioning refrigerant should be properly discharged into an EPA-approved container at a dealer service department or an automotive air conditioning repair facility. Always wear eye protection when disconnecting air conditioning system fittings.*

1   Have the refrigerant discharged at a dealer service department or an automotive air conditioning repair facility.
2   Disconnect the cable from the negative terminal of the battery.
3   Remove the expansion valve (see Section 17)
4   Immediately cap the open fittings to prevent the entry of dirt and moisture and remove the inlet and outlet grommets.
5   Remove the glovebox (see Chapter 11) and the instrument panel lower support.
6   Remove the evaporator case retaining nuts from the firewall in the engine compartment **(see illustration 11.5)**.
7   Disconnect all electrical connectors from the air conditioning thermostatic switch and the blower motor resistor.
8   Remove the evaporator case assembly **(see illustration 11.5)**.
9   Split the evaporator case by removing the clips and lifting the upper case half off.
10   Separate the evaporator core from the lower case half.
11   Check the evaporator fins for blockage; if they are dirty clean

17.3 Remove the two nuts (arrows) that hold the evaporator inlet fitting, pull the lines off and remove the expansion valve

them with compressed air - never use water for this purpose!
12   Check fittings for cracks and signs of wear; replace parts as necessary.
13   Installation is the reverse of the removal procedure. Be sure to replace all O-rings removed during disassembly with new ones.
14   If a new evaporator was installed, add 1.7 ounces of new refrigerant oil to the system.
15   Have the system evacuated, charged and leak tested by the shop that discharged it.

3

Notes

Chapter 4   Fuel and exhaust systems

Contents

4

Specifications

Fuel pressure

Fuel system pressure (at idle)
 1990 and 1991 models only
  Vacuum hose detached .... 38 to 49 psi
  Vacuum hose attached.. 35 to 40 psi
 1993 1.6L engine only
  Vacuum hose detached .... 38 to 50 psi
  Vacuum hose attached.. 30 to 40 psi
 All others
  Vacuum hose detached .... 49 to 51 psi
  Vacuum hose attached.. 38 to 42 psi
Fuel system hold pressure .... 21 psi
Fuel pump pressure (maximum)...................................... 60 psi
Fuel pump hold pressure... 50 psi

Injector resistance

SOHC engines .... 12.7 ohms
DOHC engines .... 2.1 ohms

Torque specifications   Ft-lbs
Air intake plenum-to-intake manifold bolts 17
Throttle body-to-air intake plenum bolts 16

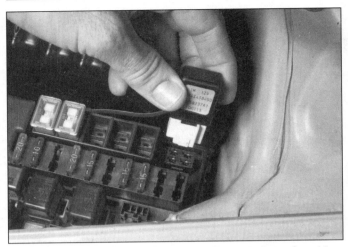

2.3 Remove the fuel pump relay from the control panel next to the battery

3.2 Jumping the fuel pump terminals on the control panel

1   General information

The fuel system consists of a fuel tank, an electric fuel pump (located in the fuel tank), a fuel pump relay, fuel injectors, an air cleaner assembly and a throttle body unit. The fuel injection components are all equipped with a Multi Point Fuel Injection (MPFI) system.

Multi Point Fuel Injection (MPFI) system

Multi Point Fuel Injection uses timed impulses to inject the fuel directly into the intake port of each cylinder. The injectors are controlled by the Electronic Control Module (ECM). The ECM monitors various engine parameters and delivers the exact amount of fuel required into the intake ports. The throttle body serves only to control the amount of air passing into the system. Because each cylinder is equipped with its own injector, much better control of the fuel/air mixture ratio is possible.

Fuel pump and lines

Fuel is circulated from the fuel tank to the fuel injection system, and back to the fuel tank, through a pair of metal lines running along the underside of the vehicle. An electric fuel pump is located inside the fuel tank. A vapor return system routes all vapors back to the fuel tank through a separate return line.

The fuel pump will operate as long as the engine is cranking or running and the ECM is receiving ignition reference pulses from the electronic ignition system. If there are no reference pulses, the fuel pump will shut off after two or three seconds.

Exhaust system

The exhaust system includes an exhaust manifold fitted with an exhaust oxygen sensor, a catalytic converter, an exhaust pipe, and a muffler.

The catalytic converter is an emission control device added to the exhaust system to reduce pollutants. A single-bed converter is used in combination with a three-way (reduction) catalyst. Refer to Chapter 6 for more information regarding the catalytic converter.

2   Fuel pressure relief procedure

Refer to illustration 2.3

Warning 1: *Gasoline is extremely flammable, so take extra precautions when you work on any part of the fuel system. Don't smoke or allow open flames or bare light bulbs near the work area, and don't work in a garage where a natural gas-type appliance (such as a water heater or clothes dryer) with a pilot light is present. If you spill any fuel on your*

skin, rinse it off immediately with soap and water. When you perform any kind of work on the fuel system, wear safety glasses and have a Class B type fire extinguisher on hand.*
Warning 2: *After the fuel pressure has been relieved, wrap shop towels around any fuel connection you'll be disconnecting. They'll absorb the residual fuel that may leak out, reducing the risk of fire and preventing contact with your skin.*

1   Before servicing any fuel system component, you must relieve the fuel pressure to minimize the risk of fire or personal injury.
2   Remove the fuel filler cap – this will relieve any pressure built up in the tank.
3   Remove the fuel pump relay from the main relay panel **(see illustration)**. **Note:** *Consult your owner's manual for the exact location of the fuel pump relay if the information is not stamped onto the relay cover.*
4   Start the engine and wait for the engine to stall, then turn off the ignition key.
5   The fuel system is now depressurized. **Note:** *Place a rag around the fuel line before removing any hose clamp or fitting to prevent any residual fuel from spilling onto the engine.*

3   Fuel pump/fuel pressure – check

Warning: *Gasoline is extremely flammable, so take extra precautions when you work on any part of the fuel system. Don't smoke or allow open flames or bare light bulbs near the work area, and don't work in a garage where a natural gas-type appliance (such as a water heater or clothes dryer) with a pilot light is present. If you spill any fuel on your skin, rinse it off immediately with soap and water. When you perform any kind of work on the fuel system, wear safety glasses and have a Class B type fire extinguisher on hand.*
Note 1: *To perform the fuel pressure test, you will need to obtain a fuel pressure gauge and adapter set (fuel line fittings).*
Note 2: *The fuel pump will operate as long as the engine is cranking or running and the ECM is receiving ignition reference pulses from the electronic ignition system. If there are no reference pulses, the fuel pump will shut off after two or three seconds.*

Preliminary inspection

Refer to illustrations 3.2 and 3.3

1   Should the fuel system fail to deliver the proper amount of fuel, or any fuel at all, inspect it as follows. Remove the fuel filler cap. Have an assistant turn the ignition key to the On position while you listen at the fuel filler opening. You should hear a whirring sound that lasts for a couple of seconds.
2   If you don't hear anything, remove the fuel pump relay and install a jumper wire onto the terminals of the connector that correspond to the red/white wire and the black/red wire of the fuel pump relay wire

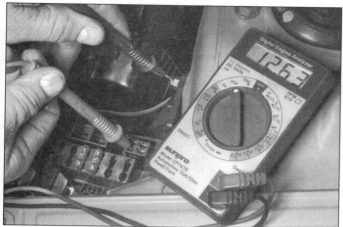

3.3 With the ignition key OFF, probe the supply terminal for the fuel pump relay on the control panel – there should be for battery voltage present

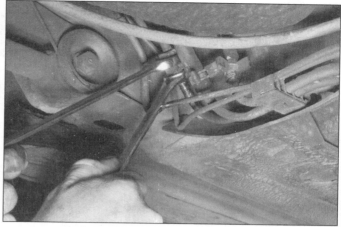

3.8a Using a backup wrench, disconnect the fuel feed line near the fuel tank . . .

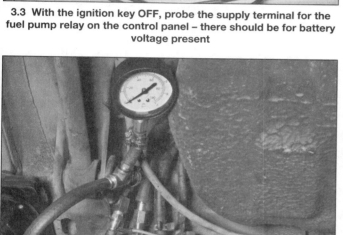

3.8b . . . and, using the correct adapters, attach a fuel pressure gauge

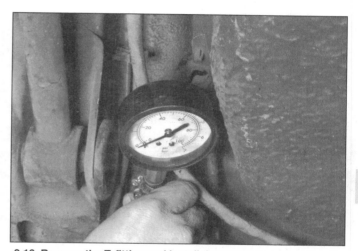

3.16 Remove the T-fitting and install the pressure gauge directly to the fuel feed line

harness **(see illustration)**. Listen at the fuel filler opening again – if you now hear the whirring sound, the fuel pump relay or its control circuit is faulty. If there still is no whirring sound, there is a problem in the fuel pump circuit from the control panel to the fuel pump, or a defective fuel pump.

3   To check for power to the fuel pump relay terminal on the control panel, probe the connector terminal that corresponds to the fuel pump relay red/white wire with a voltmeter **(see illustration)**. There should be battery voltage present.

4   If there is no voltage present, check the fuse(s) and the wiring circuit for the fuel pump relay (see Chapter 12). If the voltage reading is correct and the fuel pump only runs with the jumper wire in place, replace the fuel pump relay with a new one.

5   If there is voltage present, check for battery voltage at the fuel pump electrical connector. If there is voltage present at the fuel pump connector, replace the fuel pump.

Operating pressure check
Refer to illustrations 3.8a and 3.8b

6   Relieve the fuel system pressure (see Section 2).
7   Detach the cable from the negative battery terminal.
8   Using a tee (three-way) fitting, a short section of high-pressure fuel hose and clamps, attach a fuel pressure gauge in the fuel feed line near the fuel tank **(see illustrations)**.
9   Attach the cable to the negative battery terminal, then start the engine.
10   Note the fuel pressure and compare it with the pressure listed in

this Chapter's Specifications.
11   If the system fuel pressure is less than specified:
 a) Inspect the system for a fuel leak. Repair any leaks and recheck the fuel pressure.
 b) If the pressure is still low, check the fuel pump output pressure (see below) and the fuel pressure regulator (see Section 16).
12   If the pressure is higher than specified, replace the fuel filter and recheck the fuel pressure. If it's still too high, check the fuel pressure regulator (see Section 16).
13   Turn the ignition switch to Off, wait five minutes and recheck the pressure. Compare the reading with the hold pressure listed in this Chapter's specifications. If the hold pressure is less than specified:
 a) Inspect the lines for a leak. Repair any leaks and recheck the fuel pressure.
 b) Check the fuel pressure regulator (see Section 16).
 c) Check the fuel injectors for leaks (see Section 17).

Fuel pump output pressure check
Refer to illustration 3.16

Warning: *For this test it is necessary to use a fuel pressure gauge with a bleeder valve in order to relieve the fuel pressure after the test is completed (the normal procedure for pressure relief will not work because the gauge is connected directly to the the fuel pump).*

14   Relieve the system fuel pressure (see Section 2).
15   Detach the cable from the negative battery terminal.
16   Attach a fuel pressure gauge directly to the fuel fuel feed line (in the same location as shown in Step 8) **(see illustration)**.

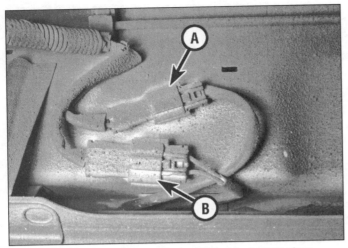

5.6 Fuel pump and sending unit electrical connectors

A   *Fuel pump connector*
B   *Fuel level sending unit connector*

17   Attach the cable to the negative battery terminal.
18   Using a jumper wire, bridge the terminals of the fuel pump relay **(see illustration 3.2)**.
19   Note the pressure reading on the gauge and compare the reading to the value listed in this Chapter's Specifications.
20   If the indicated pressure is less than specified, inspect the fuel line for leaks between the pump and gauge. If no leaks are found, replace the fuel pump.
21   Turn the ignition key to Off and wait five minutes. Note the reading on the gauge and compare it to the hold pressure listed in this Chapter's Specifications. If the hold pressure is less than specified, check the fuel line between the pump and gauge for leaks. If no leaks are found, replace the fuel pump.
22   Remove the jumper wire and reinstall the fuel pump relay.
23   Open the bleeder valve on the gauge and allow the pressurized fuel drain into an approved fuel container. Remove the gauge and reconnect the fuel line.

4   Fuel lines and fittings – inspection and replacement

Warning: *Gasoline is extremely flammable, so take extra precautions when you work on any part of the fuel system. Don't smoke or allow open flames or bare light bulbs near the work area, and don't work in a garage where a natural gas-type appliance (such as a water heater or clothes dryer) with a pilot light is present. If you spill any fuel on your skin, rinse it off immediately with soap and water. When you perform any kind of work on the fuel system, wear safety glasses and have a Class B type fire extinguisher on hand.*

Inspection

1   Once in a while, you will have to raise the vehicle to service or replace some component (an exhaust pipe hanger, for example). Whenever you work under the vehicle, always inspect fuel lines and all fittings and connections for damage or deterioration.
2   Check all hoses and pipes for cracks, kinks, deformation or obstructions.
3   Make sure all hoses and pipe clips attach their associated hoses or pipes securely to the underside of the vehicle.
4   Verify all hose clamps attaching rubber hoses to metal fuel lines or pipes are snug enough to assure a tight fit between the hoses and pipes.

Replacement

5   If you must replace any damaged sections, use original equipment replacement hoses or pipes constructed from exactly the same

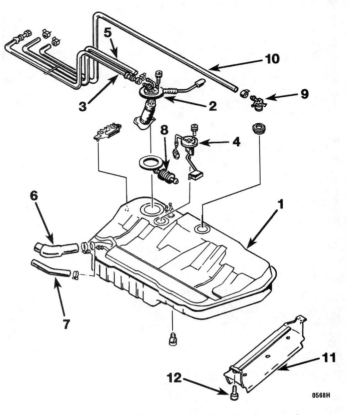

5.7 Exploded view of the fuel tank and components

1	Fuel tank	8	Tank pressure control (TPC) valve (Vin 8 only)
2	Fuel pump	9	Fuel tank vent valve
3	Fuel feed hose	10	Fuel vapor hose
4	Fuel tank sender	11	Exhaust pipe heat shield
5	Fuel return hose	12	Exhaust pipe heat shield bolt
6	Fuel filler hose		
7	Fuel breather hose		

material as the section you are replacing. Do not install substitutes constructed from inferior or inappropriate material or you could cause a fuel leak or a fire.
6   Always, before detaching or disassembling any part of the fuel system, note the routing of all hoses and pipes and the orientation of all clamps and clips to assure that replacement sections are installed in exactly the same manner.
7   Before detaching any part of the fuel system, be sure to relieve the fuel system pressure (see Section 2). Also cover the fitting being disconnected with a rag to absorb any fuel that may spray out.

5   Fuel tank – removal and installation

Refer to illustrations 5.6, 5.7 and 5.10
Warning: *Gasoline is extremely flammable, so take extra precautions when you work on any part of the fuel system. Don't smoke or allow open flames or bare light bulbs near the work area, and don't work in a garage where a natural gas-type appliance (such as a water heater or clothes dryer) with a pilot light is present. If you spill any fuel on your skin, rinse it off immediately with soap and water. When you perform any kind of work on the fuel system, wear safety glasses and have a Class B type fire extinguisher on hand.*
Note: *Don't begin this procedure until the fuel gauge indicates the tank is empty or nearly empty. If the tank must be removed when it's full (for example, if the fuel pump malfunctions), siphon any remaining fuel from the tank prior to removal.*

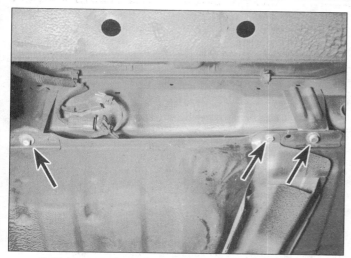

5.10 Remove the bolts from the perimeter of the tank

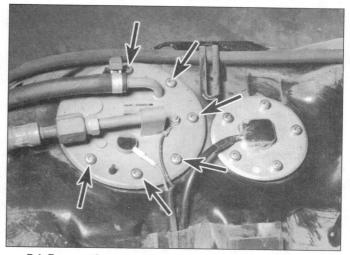

7.4 Remove the screws (arrows) that retain the fuel pump assembly to the fuel tank

1   Unless the vehicle has been driven far enough to completely empty the tank, it's a good idea to siphon the residual fuel out before removing the tank from the vehicle. **Warning:** *DO NOT start the siphoning action by mouth! Use a siphoning kit, available at most auto parts stores.*
2   Relieve the fuel pressure (see Section 2).
3   Detach the cable from the negative terminal of the battery.
4   Raise the vehicle and place it securely on jackstands.
5   Remove the center section of the exhaust system.
6   Locate the electrical connectors for the electric fuel pump and fuel gauge sending unit in front of the tank **(see illustration)**, and unplug them.
7   Disconnect the fuel feed and return lines, the vapor return line and the filler neck and vent tubes **(see illustration)**.
8   Support the fuel tank with a piece of wood and a floor jack.
9   Remove the two bolts and separate the parking brake cables from the fuel tank (if necessary).
10   Remove the retaining bolts from the perimeter of the tank **(see illustration)**.
11   Remove the tank from the vehicle.
12   Installation is the reverse of removal.

6   Fuel tank cleaning and repair – general information

1   All repairs to the fuel tank or filler neck should be carried out by a professional who has experience in this critical and potentially dangerous work. Even after cleaning and flushing of the fuel system, explosive fumes can remain and ignite during repair of the tank.
2   If the fuel tank is removed from the vehicle, it should not be placed in an area where sparks or open flames could ignite the fumes coming out of the tank. Be especially careful inside garages where a natural gas-type appliance is located, because the pilot light could cause an explosion.

7   Fuel pump – removal and installation

Refer to illustrations 7.4 and 7.6

Warning: *Gasoline is extremely flammable, so take extra precautions when you work on any part of the fuel system. Don't smoke or allow open flames or bare light bulbs near the work area, and don't work in a garage where a natural gas-type appliance (such as a water heater or clothes dryer) with a pilot light is present. If you spill any fuel on your skin, rinse it off immediately with soap and water. When you perform any kind of work on the fuel system, wear safety glasses and have a Class B type fire extinguisher on hand.*

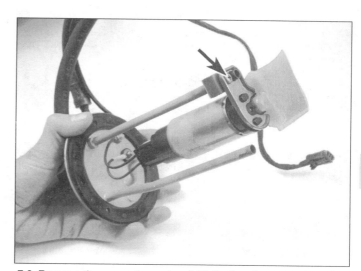

7.6 Remove the screw (arrow) and lift the bracket to gain access to the fuel tank filter

Removal

1   Relieve the fuel pressure (see Section 2).
2   Remove the cable from the negative battery terminal.
3   Remove the fuel tank (see Section 5).
4   Remove the screws from the top of the fuel pump assembly **(see illustration)**.
5   Pull the fuel pump assembly out of the tank.
6   Inspect the filter on the lower end of the fuel pump **(see illustration)**. If it's dirty, remove it, clean it with solvent and blow it out with compressed air. If it's too dirty to be cleaned, replace it.
7   If you have to separate the fuel pump from the bracket, remove the retaining screw **(see illustration 7.6)** and slide the pump away from the bottom support. Care should be taken to prevent damage to the rubber insulator and fuel strainer during removal. After the pump is clear of the bottom support, pull it out of the rubber connector.

Installation

8   Position a new rubber gasket around the opening of the fuel tank and guide the fuel pump assembly into the tank.
9   Install the screws and tighten them securely.
10   Install the fuel tank (see Section 5).

4

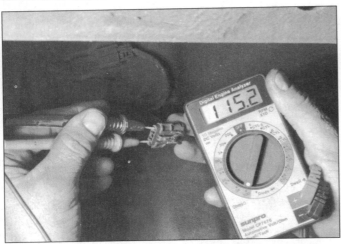

8.3 Check the resistance of the fuel level sending unit. The resistance is high, therefore the tank is nearly empty

8.8 Carefully remove the sending unit without damaging the float at the end of the assembly

8   Lift the sending unit from the tank. Carefully angle the sending unit out of the opening without damaging the fuel level float located at the bottom of the assembly **(see illustration)**.
9   Installation is the reverse of removal. Be sure to install a new rubber gasket, and tighten the screws securely.

9   Air cleaner housing – removal and installation

Refer to illustration 9.5
1   Detach the cable from the negative terminal of the battery.
2   Remove the battery from the vehicle, if necessary (see Chapter 5).
3   Loosen the clamp(s) from the air intake duct on the throttle body and the air cleaner housing and remove the air intake duct from the engine compartment.
4   Remove the air filter (see Chapter 1).
5   Remove the three bolts from the air cleaner assembly **(see illustration)** and lift the complete air cleaner housing from the engine compartment.
6   Installation is the reverse of removal.

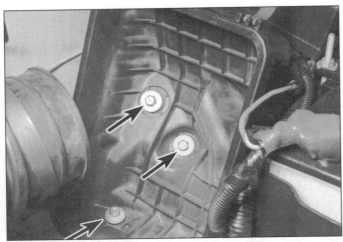

9.5 Remove the bolts (arrows) from the air cleaner housing and lift the assembly from the engine compartment

8   Fuel level sending unit – check and replacement

Refer to illustrations 8.3 and 8.8

Check

1   Raise the vehicle and support it securely on jackstands.
2   Disconnect the electrical connector for the fuel level sending unit **(see illustration 5.6).**
3   Position the ohmmeter probes into the electrical connector and check the resistance **(see illustration)**. Use the 200-ohm scale on the ohmmeter.
4   With the fuel tank completely full, the resistance should be about 2.0 to 3.0 ohms. With the fuel tank nearly empty, the resistance of the sending unit should be about 115 to 120 ohms.
5   If the readings are incorrect, replace the sending unit. **Note:** *A more accurate check of the sending unit can be made by removing it from the fuel tank and checking its resistance while manually operating the float arm.*

Replacement

6   Remove the fuel tank from the vehicle (see Section 5).
7   Remove the screws that secure the fuel level sending unit to the fuel tank **(see illustration 7.4)**. **Note:** *The fuel level sending unit (smaller diameter) is located next to the fuel pump.*

10   Accelerator cable – removal, installation and adjustment

Refer to illustrations 10.2, 10.3 and 10.5

Removal

1   Remove the accelerator cable from the two retainer clips on the firewall and the bolt and bracket on the air intake plenum.
2   Detach the accelerator cable from the throttle lever **(see illustration)**.
3   Loosen the accelerator cable locknut and remove the cable from the bracket **(see illustration)**.
4   Detach the screws and the clips retaining the lower instrument trim panel on the driver's side and remove the trim piece (see Chapter 11).
5   Pull the cable end out and then up from the accelerator pedal recess **(see illustration)**.
6   Push the cable through the firewall into the engine compartment.

Installation

7   Installation is the reverse of removal. Be sure the cable is routed correctly.
8   If necessary, at the engine compartment side of the firewall, apply sealant around the accelerator cable to prevent water from entering the passenger compartment.

10.2 Rotate the throttle lever and remove the cable end from the slotted portion of the throttle lever

10.3 Unscrew the locknut from the cable housing, pull the cable housing out of the bracket and slide the cable through the slot

| A) | Adjusting nut | B) | Locknut |

10.5 Working inside the driver's compartment, pull the accelerator cable end out and then lift the cable out of the recess (arrow) in the pedal

Adjustment

9   Loosen the locknut and turn the adjusting nut until there is approximately 3/8-inch of deflection when you push down on the exposed portion of the cable. Tighten the locknut.

10   Have an assistant operate the accelerator pedal and make sure the throttle opens and closes completely without binding.

---

11   Electronic Fuel Injection (EFI) system – general information

Electronic fuel injection provides optimum fuel/air mixture ratios at all stages of combustion and offers immediate throttle response characteristics. It also enables the engine to run at the leanest possible fuel/air mixture ratio, reducing exhaust gas emissions.

These models are equipped with a Multi Port Fuel Injection (MPFI) system. The MPFI systems are controlled by an Electronic Control Module (ECM) or computer located under the dash on the driver's side. The ECM monitors engine performance and adjusts the air/fuel mixture according to the information it receives from the information sensors (oxygen sensor, Intake Air Temperature (IAT) sensor, Throttle Position Sensor (TPS) etc. See Chapter 6 for additional information and descriptions of the information sensors and the ECM control system.

An electric fuel pump located in the fuel tank pumps fuel to the fuel injection system through the fuel feed line and an in-line fuel filter. The fuel pump will operate as long as the engine is cranking or running and the ECM is receiving ignition reference pulses from the electronic ignition system. If there are no reference pulses, the fuel pump will shut off after 2 or 3 seconds.

The throttle body has a throttle valve to control the amount of air delivered to the engine. The Throttle Position Sensor (TPS) and Idle Air Control (IAC) valves are located on the throttle body.

The fuel rail is mounted on the top of the intake manifold. It distributes fuel to the individual injectors. Fuel is delivered to the input end of the rail by the fuel feed line. At the other end of the fuel rail is the fuel pressure regulator, which keeps the pressure to the injectors at the required level. The excess fuel is bled off through the pressure regulator and is returned to the fuel tank via a separate line.

4

---

12   Fuel injection system – check

Refer to illustrations 12.6, 12.7, 12.8 and 12.9

Warning: *Gasoline is extremely flammable, so take extra precautions when you work on any part of the fuel system. Don't smoke or allow open flames or bare light bulbs near the work area, and don't work in a garage where a natural gas-type appliance (such as a water heater or clothes dryer) with a pilot light is present. If you spill any fuel on your skin, rinse it off immediately with soap and water. When you perform any kind of work on the fuel system, wear safety glasses and have a Class B type fire extinguisher on hand.*

Note: *the following procedure is based on the assumption that the fuel pump is working and the fuel pressure is adequate (see Section 3).*

1   Check all electrical connectors that are related to the system. Loose electrical connectors and poor grounds can cause many problems that resemble more serious malfunctions.

2   Check to see that the battery is fully charged, as the control unit and sensors depend on an accurate supply voltage in order to properly meter the fuel.

3   Check the air filter element – a dirty or partially blocked filter will severely impede performance and economy (see Chapter 1).

4   If a blown fuse is found, replace it and see if it blows again. If it does, search for a grounded wire in the harness to the fuel pump.

5   Check the air intake duct to the intake plenum for leaks, which will result in an excessively lean mixture. Also check the condition of the vacuum hoses connected to the intake manifold.

6   Remove the air intake duct from the throttle body and check for dirt, carbon or other residue build-up in the throttle body, particularly around the throttle plate. If it's dirty, clean it with carburetor cleaner

12.6 Clean the throttle body with carburetor cleaner to remove sludge deposits

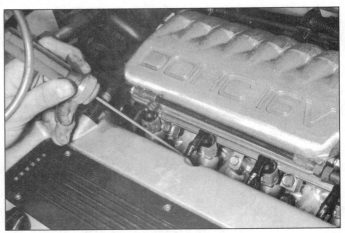

12.7 Use a stethoscope or screwdriver to determine if the injectors are working properly – they should make a steady clicking sound that rises and falls with engine speed changes

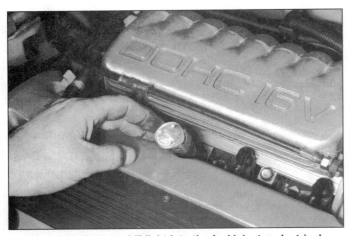

12.8 Install the "noid" light into the fuel injector electrical connector and check to see that it blinks when the engine is running

12.9 Measuring the resistance of an injector

and a toothbrush **(see illustration)**.

7   With the engine running, place a stethoscope against each injector, one at a time, and listen for a clicking sound, indicating operation **(see illustration)**. If you don't have a stethoscope, place the tip of a screwdriver against the injector and press your ear against the handle.

8   If an injector isn't functioning (not clicking), purchase a special injector test light (sometimes called a "noid" light) and install it into the injector electrical connector **(see illustration)**. Start the engine and make sure the noid light flashes. This will test for the proper voltage signal to the injector.

9   With the engine turned Off and the fuel injector electrical connectors disconnected, measure the resistance of each injector **(see illustration)**. Compare your findings with the resistance values listed in this Chapter's Specifications. If the resistance of an injector is not as specified, it is probably faulty.

10   Check the fuel pressure (see Section 3) and the fuel pressure regulator (see Section 16).

11   All other checks to the system should be left to a dealer service department or other qualified repair shop, as there is a chance that the control unit may be damaged if the tests are not performed properly.

---

13   Throttle body – check, removal and installation

Check

1   Detach the air intake duct from the throttle body (see Section 9)

and move the duct out of the way.

2   Have an assistant depress the throttle pedal while you watch the throttle valve. Check that the throttle valve moves smoothly when the throttle is moved from closed (idle position) to fully open (wide open throttle). **Note:** *Spray carburetor cleaner into the throttle body, especially around the shaft area, to free-up any binding caused by the accumulation of carbon deposits or sludge buildup* **(see illustration 12.6)**.

3   Wiggle the throttle lever while watching the throttle shaft inside the bore. If it appears worn (loose), replace the throttle body unit.

Removal and installation

Refer to illustration 13.10

4   Disconnect the cable from the negative terminal of the battery.

5   Unplug the Idle Air Control (IAC) valve and the Throttle Position Sensor (TPS) electrical connectors.

6   Mark and disconnect any vacuum hoses connected to the throttle body.

7   Disconnect the accelerator cable from the throttle lever, then detach the cable housing from its bracket (see Section 10).

8   Remove the breather hose.

9   Detach the air intake duct (see Section 9).

10   Remove the throttle body bolts and detach the throttle body **(see illustration)**. Clean off all traces of old gasket material

11   Install the throttle body and a new gasket and tighten the bolts to the torque listed in this Chapter's Specifications.

12   The rest of the procedure is the reverse of removal.

13.10   Remove the throttle body bolts (arrows) and lift the throttle body off the air intake plenum (the two bottom bolts are not visible in this photo)

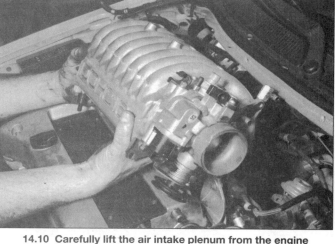

14.10   Carefully lift the air intake plenum from the engine compartment (DOHC engine shown)

15.2   With the ignition key ON (engine not running), check for battery voltage at the IAC valve electrical connector

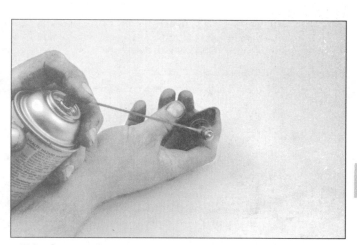

15.3a   Spray carburetor cleaner directly into the IAC valve pintle to remove excess carbon deposits

14   Air intake plenum – removal and installation

Refer to illustration 14.10

1   Disconnect the cable from the negative terminal of the battery.
2   Remove the accelerator cable (see Section 10).
3   Remove the throttle body (see Section 13).
4   Remove the EGR valve (see Chapter 6).
5   Raise the vehicle and secure it on jackstands.
6   Drain the coolant from the radiator and the engine block (see Chapter 1).
7   Working under the engine, remove the bolts from the lower section of the air intake plenum. Lower the vehicle.
8   Working inside the engine compartment, remove the plenum bolts that are accessible from the top.
9   Disconnect any coolant lines or electrical connectors from the air intake plenum. Also mark and detach all vacuum lines that may interfere with removal.
10   Remove the air intake plenum **(see illustration)** and gaskets. If the plenum sticks, use a block of wood and a hammer to dislodge it. Do not pry between the sealing flanges, as this will damage the machined surfaces and vacuum leaks may develop.
11   Remove all traces of old gasket material from the plenum and intake manifold mating surfaces. It's a good idea to stuff rags into the intake manifold openings to prevent debris and old gasket material from falling in.
12   Install the new gaskets and set the plenum into position.

13   Install the plenum bolts and tighten them to the torque listed in this Chapter's Specifications.
14   The rest of the procedure is the reverse of removal.

15   Idle Air Control (IAC) valve – check, removal and installation

Refer to illustrations 15.2, 15.3.a, 15.3b, 15.9 and 15.10

Check

1   The idle air control valve (IAC) controls the engine idle speed. This output actuator is mounted on the throttle body and is controlled by voltage pulses sent from the ECM (computer). The IAC valve pintle moves in or out allowing more or less intake air into the system according to the engine conditions. To increase idle speed, the ECM retracts the IAC valve pintle away from the seat and allows more air to bypass the throttle bore. To decrease idle speed, the ECM extends the IAC valve pintle towards the seat, reducing the air flow.
2   To check the system, first check for the voltage signal from the ECM. Turn the ignition key On (engine not running) and with a voltmeter, probe the terminals of the IAC valve electrical connector **(see illustration)**. It should read battery voltage on one terminal while the others read less than battery voltage. This indicates that the valve is receiving the proper signal from the ECM.
3   Next, remove the valve (see Step 4) and inspect it:
   a) Check the pintle for excessive carbon deposits. If necessary,

4

15.3b Spray carburetor cleaner into the IAC valve housing and check for clogged air passages in the air intake plenum

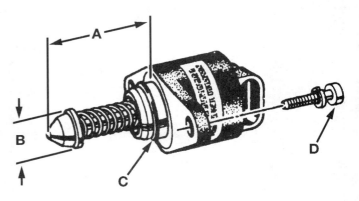

15.9 Typical IAC valve

A	Distance of pintle extension	C O-ring
B	Diameter of pintle	D Screw and washer

clean it with carburetor cleaner spray **(see illustration)**. Also clean the IAC valve housing to remove any deposits **(see illustration)**.

b) Next, apply battery voltage to the IAC valve and observe that the valve pintle retracts with the voltage signal. If there is no movement from the valve, replace it with a new one.

Removal

4   Unplug the electrical connector from the Idle Air Control (IAC) valve.
5   Remove the two IAC valve attaching screws and withdraw the valve.
6   Check the condition of the rubber O-ring. If it's hardened or deteriorated, replace it.
7   Clean the sealing surface and the bore of the idle air/vacuum signal housing assembly to ensure a good seal. **Caution:** *The IAC valve itself is an electrical component and must not be soaked in any liquid cleaner, as damage may result.*
8   Before installing the IAC valve, the position of the pintle must be checked. If the pintle is extended too far, damage to the assembly may occur.

Installation

9   Measure the distance from the gasket mounting surface of the IAC valve to the tip of the pintle **(see illustration)**.
10   If the distance is greater than 1-1/8 inch, reduce it by applying firm hand pressure on the pintle **(see illustration)** to retract it (a slight side-to-side motion may help).
11   Position the new O-ring on the IAC valve. Lubricate the O-ring with a light film of engine oil.
12   Install the IAC valve and tighten the screws securely.
13   Plug in the electrical connector at the IAC valve assembly. **Note:** *No adjustment is made to the IAC assembly after reinstallation. The IAC resetting is controlled by the ECM when the engine is started.*

16   Fuel pressure regulator – check and replacement

Warning: *Gasoline is extremely flammable, so take extra precautions when you work on any part of the fuel system. Don't smoke or allow open flames or bare light bulbs near the work area, and don't work in a garage where a natural gas-type appliance (such as a water heater or clothes dryer) with a pilot light is present. If you spill any fuel on your skin, rinse it off immediately with soap and water. When you perform any kind of work on the fuel system, wear safety glasses and have a Class B type fire extinguisher on hand.*

Check

Refer to illustrations 16.5 and 16.10
Note: *This procedure assumes the fuel filter is in good condition.*

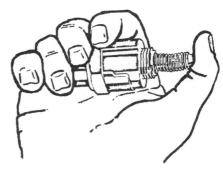

15.10 To adjust an IAC valve, retract the pintle by exerting firm pressure while using a slight side-to side movement

1   Relieve the fuel system pressure (see Section 2).
2   Detach the cable from the negative battery terminal.
3   Disconnect the fuel line and install a fuel pressure gauge (see Section 3). Reconnect the battery cable.
4   Start the engine and check for leakage around the gauge connections.
5   Disconnect the vacuum hose from the fuel pressure regulator and hook up a hand-held vacuum pump to the port on the fuel pressure regulator **(see illustration)**.
6   Read the fuel pressure gauge with vacuum applied to the pressure regulator and also with no vacuum applied. The fuel pressure should decrease as vacuum increases (and increase as vacuum decreases). Compare your readings with the values listed in this Chapter's Specifications.
7   Reconnect the vacuum hose to the regulator and check the fuel pressure at idle, comparing your reading with the value listed in this Chapter's Specifications. Disconnect the vacuum hose and watch the gauge – the pressure should jump up considerably as soon as the hose is disconnected. If it doesn't, proceed to Step 10.
8   If the fuel pressure is low, pinch the fuel return line shut and watch the gauge. If the pressure doesn't rise, the fuel pump is defective or there is a restriction in the fuel feed line. If the pressure rises sharply, replace the pressure regulator.
9   If the fuel pressure is too high, turn the engine off. Disconnect the fuel return line and blow through it to check for a blockage. If there is no blockage, replace the fuel pressure regulator.
10   Connect a vacuum gauge to the vacuum hose to the pressure regulator. Start the engine and check for vacuum **(see illustration)**. If

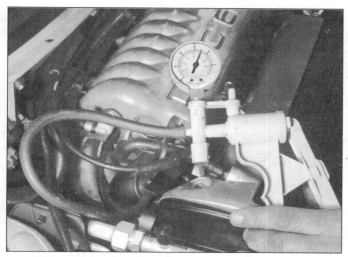

16.5 Carefully watch the fuel pressure gauge as vacuum is applied – fuel pressure should decrease as vacuum increases (DOHC engine shown)

16.10 Make sure there is vacuum to the fuel pressure regulator at idle (SOHC engine shown)

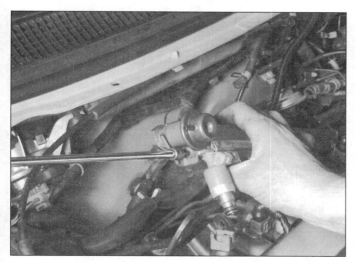

16.16 Remove the Torx bolt from the fuel pressure regulator

17.6 Remove the bolts (arrows) that hold the fuel rail to the intake manifold

4

there isn't vacuum present, check for a clogged hose or vacuum port. If the amount of vacuum is adequate, replace the fuel pressure regulator.

Replacement

Refer to illustration 16.16

11   Relieve the fuel pressure from the system (see Section 2). Disconnect the cable from the negative terminal of the battery.
12   Clean any dirt from around the fuel pressure regulator.
13   Remove the air intake plenum (see Section 14).
14   Detach the vacuum hose from the regulator.
15   Detach the fuel return line from the pressure regulator.
16   Unbolt the fuel rail (see Section 17). Lift the fuel rail up and remove the bolt that retains the fuel pressure regulator **(see illustration)**.
17   Install new O-rings and lubricate them with a light coat of oil.
18   Installation is the reverse of removal. Tighten the pressure regulator mounting bolt and the fuel return line securely.

---

17   Fuel rail and injectors – check, removal and installation

Warning: *Gasoline is extremely flammable, so take extra precautions when you work on any part of the fuel system. Don't smoke or allow*

open flames or bare light bulbs near the work area, and don't work in a garage where a natural gas-type appliance (such as a water heater or clothes dryer) with a pilot light is present. If you spill any fuel on your skin, rinse it off immediately with soap and water. When you perform any kind of work on the fuel system, wear safety glasses and have a Class B type fire extinguisher on hand.

Fuel rail and related components

Refer to illustrations 17.6 and 17.7
Caution: *To prevent dirt from entering the engine, the area around the injectors should be cleaned before servicing.*
Note: *An eight-digit identification number is stamped on the side of the fuel rail assembly. Refer to this number if servicing or parts replacement is required.*

1   Relieve the fuel system pressure (see Section 2). Detach the negative battery cable from the battery.
2   Remove the air intake plenum (see Section 14).
3   Remove the fuel lines at the fuel rail (see Section 4).
4   Remove the vacuum line at the regulator.
5   Label and unplug the injector electrical connectors.
6   Remove the fuel rail retaining bolts **(see illustration)**.

17.7 Lift the fuel rail assembly off the manifold (if necessary, use a prybar on the fuel rail mount)

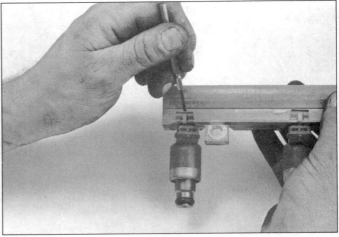

17.8 Separate the injectors from the rail

7   Carefully remove the fuel rail with the injectors **(see illustration)**. **Caution:** *Use care when handling the fuel rail assembly to avoid damaging the injectors.*

Fuel injectors

Refer to illustrations 17.8 and 17.9

8   To remove the fuel injectors, spread open the end of the injector clip slightly **(see illustration)** and remove it from the fuel rail, then extract the injector.
9   Inspect the injector O-ring seal(s). These should be replaced whenever the fuel rail is removed **(see illustration)**.
10   Install the new O-ring(s) on the injector(s) and lubricate them with engine oil.
11   Install the injectors on the fuel rail.
12   Secure the injectors with the retaining clips.
13   Installation is the reverse of removal.

---

18   Exhaust system servicing – general information

Warning: *Inspection and repair of exhaust system components should be done only after enough time has elapsed after driving the vehicle to allow the system components to cool completely. Also, when working under the vehicle, make sure it is securely supported on jackstands.*
1   The exhaust system consists of the exhaust manifold(s), the catalytic converter, the muffler, the tailpipe and all connecting pipes, brackets, hangers and clamps. The exhaust system is attached to the body with mounting brackets and rubber hangers. If any of the parts are improperly installed, excessive noise and vibration will be transmitted to the body.
2   Conduct regular inspections of the exhaust system to keep it safe and quiet. Look for any damaged or bent parts, open seams, holes, loose connections, excessive corrosion or other defects which could allow exhaust fumes to enter the vehicle. Deteriorated exhaust system components should not be repaired; they should be replaced with new parts.
3   If the exhaust system components are extremely corroded or rusted together, welding equipment will probably be required to remove them. The convenient way to accomplish this is to have a muffler repair shop remove the corroded sections with a cutting torch. If, however, you want to save money by doing it yourself (and you don't

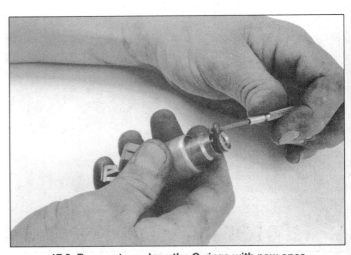

17.9 Be sure to replace the O-rings with new ones

have a welding outfit with a cutting torch), simply cut off the old components with a hacksaw. If you have compressed air, special pneumatic cutting chisels can also be used. If you do decide to tackle the job at home, be sure to wear safety goggles to protect your eyes from metal chips and work gloves to protect your hands.
4   Here are some simple guidelines to follow when repairing the exhaust system:
  a) Work from the back to the front when removing exhaust system components.
  b) Apply penetrating oil to the exhaust system component fasteners to make them easier to remove.
  c) Use new gaskets, hangers and clamps when installing exhaust systems components.
  d) Apply anti-seize compound to the threads of all exhaust system fasteners during reassembly.
  e) Be sure to allow sufficient clearance between newly installed parts and all points on the underbody to avoid overheating the floor pan and possibly damaging the interior carpet and insulation. Pay particularly close attention to the catalytic converter and heat shield.

Chapter 5 Engine electrical systems

Contents

Specifications

Ignition coil

Primary resistance..	1.2 to 1.5 ohms
Secondary resistance..	10,200 to 13,800 ohms
Insulation resistance	More than 10M ohms

Ignition timing .... 10-degrees BTDC at 700 rpm

Alternator brush length (minimum) 1/16-inch

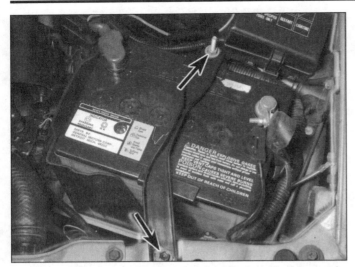

2.3 Remove the battery hold-down clamp nut and bolt (arrows) from the engine compartment

1   General information

Ignition system

The ignition system is composed of the battery, distributor, coil, ignition switch, spark plugs and the primary (low tension) and secondary (high tension) wiring circuits.

The engines covered by this manual are equipped with an HEI (High Energy Ignition) system. All models use a separately mounted coil. Each vehicle is equipped with an electronic spark timing (EST) system and an electronic control module (ECM) which monitors data from the various engine sensors, computes the desired spark timing and signals the distributor to change the timing according to the driving conditions and vehicle speed.

The secondary (spark plug) wire used with the HEI system is a carbon impregnated cord conductor encased in an 8 mm (5/16-inch) diameter rubber jacket with an outer silicon jacket. This type of wire will withstand very high temperatures and still provide insulation for the HEI's high voltage. For more information on spark plug wiring, refer to Chapter 1. **Warning:** *Because of the very high voltage generated by the HEI system, extreme care should be taken whenever an operation involving ignition components is performed. This not only includes the distributor coil, control module and spark plug wires, but related wires that are connected to the system as well (such as plug connections, tachometer and testing equipment). Consequently, before any work is performed, the ignition should be turned OFF and the negative battery cable disconnected.*

Charging system

The charging system consists of a belt-driven alternator with an integral voltage regulator and the battery. These components work together to supply electrical power for the ignition system, the lights and all accessories.

There are three models of alternators used. Earlier models (1990) use the Delco Remy CS-121 model (85 amp for models with automatic transmission, 61 amps for models with manual transmission) and later models (1991 through 1993 models) are equipped with the Nippondenso 10211-7950 (1.6L engines – 75 amps) and Nippondenso 10211-8350 (1.8L engines – 85 amps). All types use a conventional pulley and fan.

Starting system

The starting circuit consists of the battery, starter motor, ignition

switch and other related electrical wiring. The starter motor is equipped with a solenoid mounted directly to the assembly. Parts are available for repair of the motor and solenoid as separate units.

2   Battery – removal and installation

Refer to illustration 2.3

1   Disconnect both cables from the battery terminals. **Caution:** *Always disconnect the negative cable first and hook it up last or the battery may be shorted by the tool being used to loosen the cable clamps.*
2   The battery is located at the front of the engine compartment. It is held in place by a hold-down clamp.
3   Remove the battery hold-down clamp nut and bolt **(see illustration)**.
4   Lift out the battery. Be careful – it's heavy.
5   While the battery is out, inspect the carrier (tray) for corrosion.
6   If you are replacing the battery, make sure that you get one that's identical, with the same dimensions, amperage rating, cold cranking rating, etc.
7   Installation is the reverse of removal.

3   Battery – emergency jump starting

Refer to the *Booster battery (jump) starting* procedure at the front of this manual.

4   Battery cables – check and replacement

1   Periodically inspect the entire length of each battery cable for damage, cracked or burned insulation and corrosion. Poor battery cable connections can cause starting problems and decreased engine performance.
2   Check the cable-to-terminal connections at the ends of the cables for cracks, loose wire strands and corrosion. The presence of white, fluffy deposits under the insulation at the cable terminal connection is a sign that the cable is corroded and should be replaced. Check the terminals for distortion, missing mounting bolts and corrosion.
3   When removing the cables, always disconnect the negative cable first and hook it up last or the battery may be shorted by the tool used to loosen the cable clamps. Even if only the positive cable is being replaced, be sure to disconnect the negative cable from the battery first (see Chapter 1 for further information regarding battery cable removal).
4   Disconnect the old cables from the battery, then trace each of them to their opposite ends and detach them from the starter solenoid and ground terminals. Note the routing of each cable to ensure correct installation.
5   If you are replacing either or both of the old cables, take them with you when buying new cables. It is vitally important that you replace the cables with identical parts. Cables have characteristics that make them easy to identify: positive cables are usually red, larger in cross-section and have a larger diameter battery post clamp; ground cables are usually black, smaller in cross-section and have a slightly smaller diameter clamp for the negative post.
6   Clean the threads of the solenoid or ground connection with a wire brush to remove rust and corrosion. Apply a light coat of battery terminal corrosion inhibitor, or petroleum jelly, to the threads to prevent future corrosion.
7   Attach the cable to the solenoid or ground connection and tighten the mounting nut/bolt securely.
8   Before connecting a new cable to the battery, make sure that it reaches the battery post without having to be stretched.
9   Connect the positive cable first, followed by the negative cable.

6.3 To use a calibrated ignition tester, simply disconnect a spark plug wire, clip the tester to a convenient ground (like a valve cover bolt) and operate the starter - if there's enough power to fire the plug, sparks will be visible between the electrode tip and the tester body

---

5   Ignition system – general information and precautions

Warning: *Because of the very high voltage generated by the HEI system, extreme care should be taken whenever an operation involving ignition components is performed. This not only includes the distributor, coil, control module and spark plug wires, but related wires that are connected to the system as well (such as plug connections, tachometer and testing equipment). Consequently, before any work is performed, the ignition should be turned OFF and the negative battery cable disconnected.*

1   Engines covered by this manual are equipped with a High Energy Ignition (HEI) system.

2   HEI equipped vehicles use a special HEI distributor with Electronic Spark Timing (EST). HEI distributors are equipped with a separate coil. All spark timing changes in the HEI/EST distributor are carried out by the Electronic Control Module (ECM), which monitors data from various engine sensors, computes the desired spark timing and signals the distributor to change the timing accordingly. No vacuum or mechanical advance is used.

3   When working on the ignition system, take the following precautions:

a) Don't keep the ignition switch on for more than ten seconds if the engine won't start.

b) Always connect a tachometer in accordance with the tool manufacturer's instructions. Some tachometers may be incompatible with this ignition system. Consult a dealer service department before buying a tachometer for use with this vehicle.

c) Never allow the ignition coil terminals to touch ground. Grounding the coil could result in damage to the module or the ignition coil.

d) Don't disconnect the battery when the engine is running.

---

6   Ignition system – check

Refer to illustrations 6.3 and 6.5

Warning: *Because of the very high voltage generated by the ignition system, extreme care should be taken whenever an operation is performed involving ignition components. This not only includes the coil, control module and spark plug wires, but related items connected to*

the system as well, such as the electrical connections, tachometer and any test equipment.

1   With the ignition switch turned to the "ON" position, a "CHECK ENGINE" light should glow on the instrument panel. This is a basic check for battery voltage to the ignition system and the ECM.

2   Check all ignition wiring connections for tightness, cuts, corrosion or any other signs of a bad connection. A faulty or poor connection at a spark plug could result in a misfire. Also check for carbon deposits inside the spark plug boots.

3   Use a calibrated ignition tester to verify adequate available secondary voltage at the spark plug **(see illustration)**.

4   Using an ohmmeter, check the resistance of the spark plug wires (see Chapter 1). Each wire should have slightly different resistance values depending on its length. Refer to the Specifications listed in Chapter 1 for the correct values.

5   An accompanying diagnostic chart **(see illustration)** diagrams the following testing procedures for the HEI ignition system. Also shown are the terminal pin designations for testing the ignition module.

6   Test 1: Two wires are checked to ensure that an open is not present in a spark plug wire. Test 1A: If spark occurs with the four-terminal distributor connector disconnected, pick-up coil output is too low for EST operation.

7   Test 2: A spark indicates that the problem must be the distributor cap or rotor. **Note:** *A few sparks followed by no spark is the same condition as no spark at all.*

8   Test 3 **(see illustration 6.5)**: Normally, there should be battery voltage at the "C" and "+" terminals. Low voltage indicates an open or high resistance circuit from the distributor to the coil or ignition switch. If the "C" terminal voltage is low, but the "+" terminal voltage is 10 volts or more, the circuit from "C" terminal to the ignition coil or ignition coil primary winding is open.

9   Test 4 checks for a shorted module or a grounded circuit from the ignition coil to the module. The distributor module should be turned off, so normal voltage should be about 12-volts. If the module is turned on, the voltage will be low, but above one volt. This could cause the ignition coil to fail from excessive heat. With an open ignition coil primary winding, a small amount of voltage will leak through the module from the "BAT" to the tach terminal.

10   Applying a voltage (1.5 to 8-volts) to module terminal "P" should turn the module on and the tach terminal voltage should drop to about 7 to 9-volts. **Note:** *On 1993 models, apply only 1.5 volts to the "P" terminal.*

11   Test 5 will determine whether the module or coil is faulty or if the pick-up coil is not generating the proper signal to turn the module on. This test can be performed by using a DC battery with a rating of 1.5-volts. The use of the test light is to allow the "P" terminal to be probed more easily.

12   Test 6 should turn off the module and cause a spark. If no spark occurs, the fault is most likely in the ignition coil because most module problems would have been found before this point in the procedure. A GM HEI module tester (Kent Moore J-24642-F or equivalent) can determine which is at fault. If you cannot obtain the module tester, take the vehicle to a dealer service department or other repair shop.

---

7   Ignition coil – check, removal and installation

Refer to illustrations 7.4, 7.5 and 7.7

1   Disconnect the cable from the negative terminal of the battery.

Check

2   Check the coil for opens and grounds by performing the following three tests with an ohmmeter.

3   Using the ohmmeter's high scale, hook up the ohmmeter leads to the coil body (negative probe) and to the top, left terminal on the coil connector (positive probe). The ohmmeter should indicate a very high, or infinite, resistance value. If it doesn't, replace the coil. This checks the coil body insulation resistance.

4   Next check the coil primary resistance. Using the low scale, con-

5

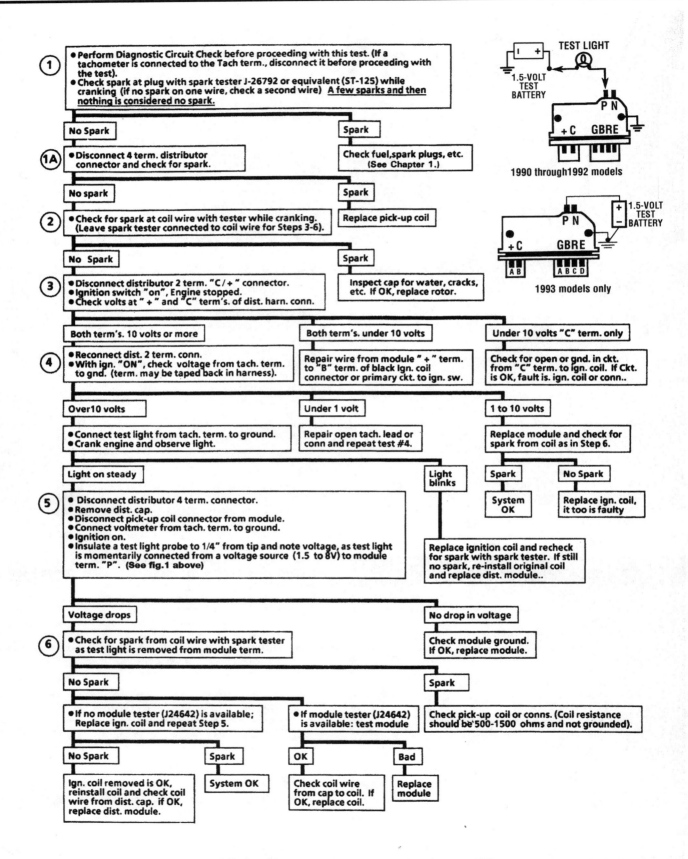

① • Perform Diagnostic Circuit Check before proceeding with this test. (If a tachometer is connected to the Tach term., disconnect it before proceeding with the test).
• Check spark at plug with spark tester J-26792 or equivalent (ST-125) while cranking (if no spark on one wire, check a second wire) A few sparks and then nothing is considered no spark.

TEST LIGHT

1.5-VOLT TEST BATTERY

1990 through1992 models

| No Spark | Spark |

1A • Disconnect 4 term. distributor connector and check for spark.

Check fuel,spark plugs, etc. (See Chapter 1.)

| No spark | Spark |

1.5-VOLT TEST BATTERY

1993 models only

② • Check for spark at coil wire with tester while cranking. (Leave spark tester connected to coil wire for Steps 3-6).

Replace pick-up coil

| No Spark | Spark |

③ • Disconnect distributor 2 term. "C / + " connector.
• Ignition switch "on", Engine stopped.
• Check volts at " + " and "C" term's. of dist. harn. conn.

Inspect cap for water, cracks, etc. If OK, replace rotor.

| Both term's. 10 volts or more | Both term's. under 10 volts | Under 10 volts "C" term. only |

④ • Reconnect dist. 2 term. conn.
• With ign. "ON", check voltage from tach. term. to gnd. (term. may be taped back in harness).

Repair wire from module " + " term. to "B" term. of black Ign. coil connector or primary ckt. to ign. sw.

Check for open or gnd. in ckt. from "C" term. to ign. coil. If Ckt. is OK, fault is. ign. coil or conn..

| Over10 volts | Under 1 volt | 1 to 10 volts |

• Connect test light from tach. term. to ground.
• Crank engine and observe light.

Repair open tach. lead or conn and repeat test #4.

Replace module and check for spark from coil as in Step 6.

| Light on steady | Light blinks | Spark | No Spark |

⑤ • Disconnect distributor 4 term. connector.
• Remove dist. cap.
• Disconnect pick-up coil connector from module.
• Connect voltmeter from tach. term. to ground.
• Ignition on.
• Insulate a test light probe to 1/4" from tip and note voltage, as test light is momentarily connected from a voltage source (1.5 to 8V) to module term. "P". (See fig.1 above)

System OK

Replace ign. coil, it too is faulty

Replace ignition coil and recheck for spark with spark tester. If still no spark, re-install original coil and replace dist. module..

| Voltage drops | No drop in voltage |

⑥ • Check for spark from coil wire with spark tester as test light is removed from module term.

Check module ground. If OK, replace module.

| No Spark | Spark |

• If no module tester (J24642) is available; Replace ign. coil and repeat Step 5.

• If module tester (J24642) is available: test module

Check pick-up coil or conns. (Coil resistance should be 500-1500 ohms and not grounded).

| No Spark | Spark | OK | Bad |

Ign. coil removed is OK, reinstall coil and check coil wire from dist. cap. if OK, replace dist. module.

System OK

Check coil wire from cap to coil. If OK, replace coil.

Replace module

6.5 Diagnostic flow chart for checking the ignition system on the HEI system

7.4 Checking the coil primary resistance (arrows)

7.5 Checking the coil secondary resistance (arrows)

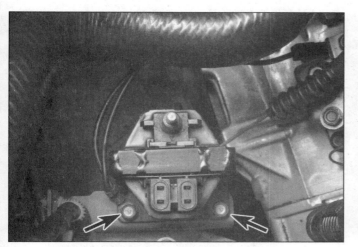

7.7 The coil is retained by two bolts (arrows)

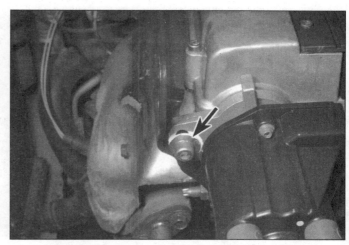

8.4 Mark the position of the hold-down bolt in relation to the distributor.

5

8.5 Also mark the relationship of the rotor to the distributor

nect the probes to the indicated terminals (see illustration). The ohmmeter should indicate a very low, or zero, resistance value. Refer to the Specifications listed in this Chapter. If it doesn't, replace the coil.

5   Next, check the coil secondary resistance. Using the high scale, hook up the leads as illustrated (see illustration). The ohmmeter

should not indicate an infinite resistance. Refer to the Specifications listed in this Chapter. If it does, replace the coil.

Removal and installation

6   Unplug the coil high tension wire and both electrical leads from the coil.
7   Unscrew the mounting bolts (see illustration) and remove the coil from the engine.
8   Installation is the reverse of the removal procedure.

---

8   Distributor – removal and installation

Refer to illustrations 8.4 and 8.5

Removal

1   Detach the cable from the negative terminal of the battery.
2   Unplug the electrical connectors from the side of the distributor base.
3   Remove the distributor cap and move it out of the way (leave the spark plug wires connected).
4   Mark the position of the distributor housing in relation to the engine (see illustration).
5   Mark the position of the rotor in relation to the distributor (see illustration).

9.2 Make sure the mark on the pulley (arrow) is bright enough to be detected under the timing light (use a spot of white paint if necessary) - also, check the increments on the timing cover to distinguish the 0-degree mark as well as the 10-degrees BTDC mark

6   Remove the distributor hold-down bolt and clamp.
7   Remove the distributor. **Caution:** *Avoid turning the crankshaft while the distributor is removed. Turning the crankshaft while the distributor is removed will necessitate retiming the engine.*

Installation (crankshaft not turned after distributor removal)

8   Position the rotor in the exact location it was in when the distributor was removed.
9   Insert the distributor into its hole in the cylinder head. To mesh the tangs at the bottom of the distributor with the slot in the end of the camshaft it may be necessary to turn the rotor slightly.
10   With the base of the distributor seated against the cylinder head, turn the distributor housing to align the marks made on the distributor base and the hold-down bolt.
11   Tighten the hold-down bolt securely.
12   Reconnect the ignition wiring harness.
13   Install the distributor cap.
14   Reconnect the coil connector.
15   Check the ignition timing (see Section 9).

Installation (crankshaft turned after distributor removal)

16   Remove the number one spark plug.
17   Place your finger over the spark plug hole while turning the crankshaft with a wrench on the pulley bolt at the front of the engine.
18   When you feel compression, continue turning the crankshaft slowly until the timing mark on the vibration damper is aligned with the "0" on the engine timing indicator.
19   Position the rotor pointing toward the number one spark plug wire terminal on the distributor cap.
20   Perform Steps 9 through 15.

9   Ignition timing – adjustment

Refer to illustrations 9.2 and 9.4
Note: *It is imperative that the procedures included on the Vehicle Emissions Control Information label be followed when adjusting the ignition timing. The label will include all information concerning preliminary steps to be performed before adjusting the timing, as well as the timing specifications.*

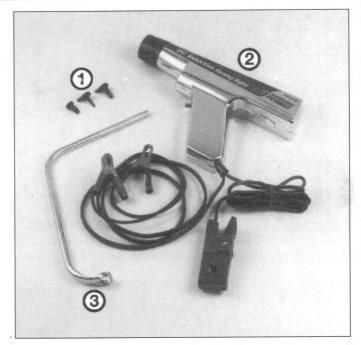

9.4 Tools needed to check and adjust the ignition timing

1   ***Vacuum plugs*** *- Vacuum hoses will, in most cases, have to be disconnected and plugged. Molded plugs in various shapes and sizes are available for this*
2   ***Inductive pick-up timing light*** *- Flashes a bright, concentrated beam of light when the number one spark plug fires. Connect the leads according to the instructions supplied with the light*
3   ***Distributor wrench*** *- On some models, the hold-down bolt for the distributor is difficult to reach and turn with conventional wrenches or sockets. A special wrench like this must be used*

1   Locate the VECI label under the hood and read through and perform all preliminary instructions concerning ignition timing.
2   Locate the timing mark pointer plate located beside the crankshaft pulley **(see illustration)**. The 0 mark represents Top Dead Center (TDC). The pointer plate will be marked in either one or two-degree increments and should have the proper timing mark for your particular engine noted. If not, count back from the 0 mark the correct number of degrees BTDC, as noted on the VECI label, and mark the plate.
3   Locate the notch on the crankshaft pulley and mark it with chalk or a dab of paint so it will be visible under the timing light.
4   With the ignition off, connect the pick-up lead of the timing light to the number one spark plug. Use an inductive-type pick-up **(see illustration)**. Do not pierce the wire or attempt to insert a wire between the boot and the spark plug wire. Connect the timing light power leads according to the manufacturer's instructions.
5   Use a jumper wire and bridge the diagnostic terminal (see illustration 2.6 in Chapter 6).
6   Start the engine, aim the timing light at the timing mark by the crankshaft pulley and note which timing mark the notch on the pulley is lining up with.
7   If the notch is not lining up with the correct mark, loosen the distributor hold-down bolt and rotate the distributor until the notch is lined up with the correct timing mark.
8   Retighten the hold-down bolt and recheck the timing.
9   Turn off the engine and disconnect the timing light. Reconnect the number one spark plug wire, if removed. Remove the jumper wire from the diagnostic terminal.

10.1 Disconnect the four-wire electrical connector from the ignition module

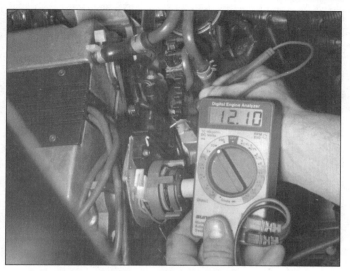

10.4a Check for battery voltage at the pink wire (terminal +)

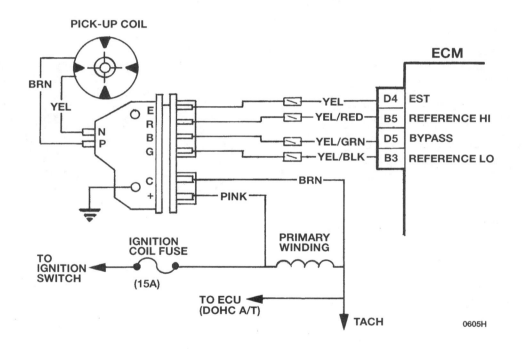

10.4b Schematic of the ignition module and the pick-up coil

10   Ignition module – check and replacement

Refer to illustrations 10.1, 10.4a, 10.4b, 10.9a, 10.9b, 10.15 and 10.16

Check

1   Disconnect the four-wire electrical connector from the distributor **(see illustration)**.
2   Check for a spark at the coil and spark plug wires (see Section 6).
3   If there is no spark, remove the distributor cap. Reconnect the distributor electrical connector.
4   With the ignition switch turned On, check for battery voltage at the module positive (+) terminal (pink wire) **(see illustrations)**. **Note:**

The wire color is the single most important feature for distinguishing the correct terminal. Be sure to clean the harness and check the wire colors carefully.

5   If the reading is less than ten volts, there is a fault in the wire between the module positive (+) terminal and the ignition coil positive connector or the ignition coil and primary circuit-to-ignition switch.
6   If the reading is ten volts or more, check the "C" terminal (brown wire) on the module **(see illustration10.4b)**.
7   If the reading is less than one volt, there is an open or grounded wire in the distributor-to-coil "C" terminal connection or ignition coil or an open primary circuit in the coil itself.

10.9a Unplug the pick-up coil electrical connector from the ignition module

10.9b Connect a test light to a 1.5 volt battery and touch the tip of the test light to terminal P of the ignition module - check for a drop in voltage (from terminal C [brown wire]) and a spark across the coil secondary tower to the coil body as contact is made

10.15 Remove the ignition module screws

10.16 Be sure to coat the backside of the ignition module with silicone dielectric grease before installing it

8   If the reading is one to ten volts, replace the module with a new one and check for a spark (see Section 6). If there is a spark, the module was faulty and the system is now operating properly. If there is no spark, there is a fault in the ignition coil.

9   If the reading in Step 4 is 10 volts or more, unplug the pick-up coil connector from the module **(see illustration)**. Check the "C" terminal (brown wire) voltage with the ignition switch On and watch the voltage reading as a test light is momentarily (five seconds or less) connected between a 1.5-volt test battery positive (+) terminal and the module "P" (brown wire) (pick-up coil) terminal **(see illustration)**.

10   If there is no drop in voltage, check the module ground and, if it is good, replace the module with a new one.

11   If the voltage drops, check for spark at the coil wire as the test light is removed from the module terminal. If there is no spark, the module is faulty and should be replaced with a new one. If there is a spark, the pick-up coil or connections are faulty or not grounded.

Replacement

12   Detach the cable from the negative terminal of the battery.

13   Remove the distributor cap and rotor.

14   Disconnect the pick-up coil electrical connector from the module **(see illustration 10.9a)**.

15   Remove both module attaching screws **(see illustration)** and lift the module up and away from the distributor.

16   Do not wipe the grease from the module or the distributor base if the same module is to be reinstalled. If a new module is to be installed, a package of silicone dielectric grease will be included with it. Wipe the distributor base and the new module clean, then apply the silicone

grease on the face of the module and on the distributor base where the module seats **(see illustration)**. This grease is necessary for heat dissipation.

17   Install the module and attach the electrical connectors.

18   Install the distributor rotor and cap (see Chapter 1).

19   Attach the cable to the negative terminal of the battery.

11   Pick-up coil – check and replacement

Refer to illustrations 11.4, 11.7, 11.8, 11.9a, 11.9b, 11.9c, 11.10, 11.11, 11.12, 11.13a and 11.13b

1   Detach the cable from the negative terminal of the battery.

2   Remove the distributor cap and rotor.

3   Detach the pick-up coil electrical connector from the module **(see illustration 10.9a)**.

Check

4   Connect the ohmmeter leads to both terminals of the pick-up coil lead. Flex the leads by hand to check for intermittent opens. The ohmmeter should read one steady value between 500 and 1500 ohms as the leads are flexed by hand **(see illustration)**. If it doesn't, the pick-up coil is defective and must be replaced.

5   Connect one lead of an ohmmeter to the terminal of the pick-up

11.4 Check the resistance of the pick-up coil - it should be between 500 and 1,500 ohms

11.7 Make a mark on the distributor shaft and drive coupling so they will be assembled in the same relationship

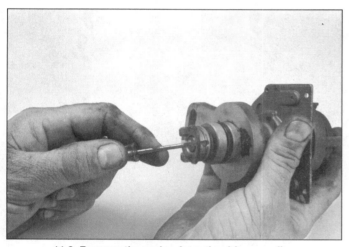

11.8 Remove the spring from the drive coupling

11.9a Use a punch and drive the retaining pin from the shaft

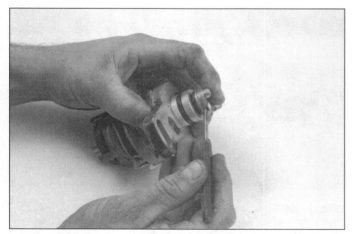

11.9b Be sure to leave the punch inside the shaft and position your finger on the coupling to prevent it from getting thrown by spring pressure from the thrust spring

11.9c Use a file and carefully remove any burrs from the distributor shaft before attempting to pull it out of the housing

coil lead and the other to ground. Flex the leads by hand to check for intermittent grounds. The ohmmeter should indicate infinite resistance at all times. If it doesn't, the pick-up coil is defective and must be replaced.

Replacement

6   Remove the distributor from the engine (see Section 8).

7   Mark the distributor drive coupling and shaft so that they can be reassembled in the same position **(see illustration)**.

8   Remove the spring from the distributor drive coupling **(see illustration)**.

9   Set the distributor on a piece of wood and, using a hammer and punch, drive out the retaining pin from the distributor shaft and drive coupling **(see illustrations)**.

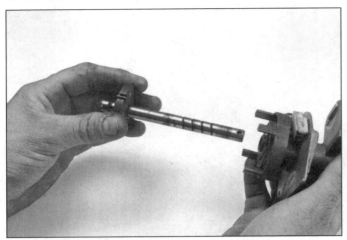

11.10 Pull the shaft from the distributor housing

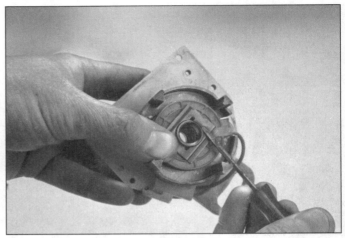

11.11 Use a small screwdriver and pry the rectangular clip from the distributor

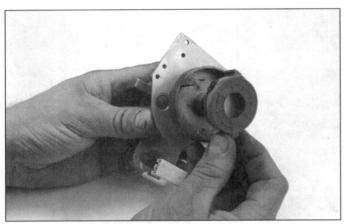

11.12 Lift the pick-up coil from the distributor

11.13a Exploded view of the distributor components

10   Remove the distributor shaft **(see illustration)**.
11   Remove the rectangular clip from the top of the pick-up coil **(see illustration)**.
12   Lift the pick-up coil assembly straight up and remove it from the distributor **(see illustration)**.
13   Reassembly is the reverse of disassembly **(see illustrations)**.

12   Charging system – general information and precautions

The charging system consists of a belt-driven alternator with an integral voltage regulator and the battery. These components work together to supply electrical power for the ignition system, the lights and all accessories.

All alternators installed on models with the 1.6L engine use rivets instead of screws. Alternators on models with 1.8L engines use conventional through-bolts to secure the two halves, and they are serviceable. These alternators incorporate a heavy-duty bearing design in the slip ring end casting. Alternators on models with 1.6L engines should be considered non-serviceable and, if defective, should be exchanged as cores for new or rebuilt units.

The purpose of the voltage regulator is to limit the alternator's voltage to a preset value. This prevents power surges, circuit overloads, etc., during peak voltage output. The voltage regulator is contained within the alternator housing.

The charging system does not ordinarily require periodic mainte-

11.13b Be sure to replace the O-ring in the groove in the distributor housing - these O-rings often look OK but are actually hardened and cracked

nance. The drivebelts, electrical wiring and connections should, however, be inspected at the intervals suggested in Chapter 1.

Take extreme care when making circuit connections to a vehicle equipped with an alternator and note the following. When making connections to the alternator from a battery, always match correct polarity. Before using arc welding equipment to repair any part of the vehicle,

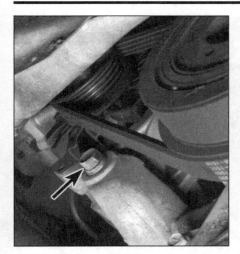

14.6 Location of the alternator lower mounting bolt (arrow) - 1.6L engine

15.2 Remove the nuts and detach the rear cover from the alternator

15.3 Once the rear cover is removed, remove the five screws that retain the voltage regulator and the brush holder

disconnect the wires from the alternator and the battery terminals. Never start the engine with a battery charger connected. Always disconnect both battery cables before using a battery charger.

The charging indicator light on the dash lights up when the ignition switch is turned on and goes out when the engine starts. If the lamp stays on or comes on once the engine is running, a charging system problem has occurred. See Section 13 for charging system diagnosis.

13 Charging system – check

1   If a malfunction occurs in the charging circuit, do not immediately assume that the alternator is causing the problem. First check the following items:
 a) The battery cables where they connect to the battery. Make sure the connections are clean and tight.
 b) The battery electrolyte specific gravity. If it is low, charge the battery.
 c) Check the alternator external wiring and connections. They must be in good condition.
 d) Check the drivebelt condition and tension (see Chapter 1).
 e) Make sure the alternator mounting bolts are tight.
 f) Run the engine and check the alternator for abnormal noise (may be caused by a loose drive pulley, loose mounting bolts, worn or dirty bearings, defective diode or defective stator).
2   Using a voltmeter, check the battery voltage with the engine off. It should be approximately 12-volts.
3   Start the engine and check the battery voltage again. It should now be approximately 14 to 15-volts.

14 Alternator – removal and installation

Note: *There are three different model alternators installed on the vehicles covered by this manual. The alternators installed on models with 1.6L engines are NOT serviceable. In the event the alternator becomes defective, exchange the alternator for a new or rebuilt one at your local auto parts store or dealer parts department.*

1.6L engine
Refer to illustration 14.6
1   Detach the cable from the negative terminal of the battery.
2   Remove the drivebelt (1990 and 1991 models) or serpentine drivebelt (1992 and 1993 models) (see Chapter 1).

3   Raise the vehicle and support it securely on jackstands.
4   Remove the splash shield from the inner fender panel on the passenger side of the vehicle (see Chapter 11).
5   Detach the electrical connector from the back of the alternator. Also remove the nut and detach the battery positive cable from the back of the alternator.
6   Working under the vehicle, remove the alternator lower mounting bolt **(see illustration)**.
7   Working inside the engine compartment, remove the rear mounting bolt and the alternator brace, if equipped.
8   Detach any wiring harness routing clips and remove the alternator from the vehicle.
9   Installation is the reverse of the removal procedure.

1.8L engine
10   Detach the cable from the negative terminal of the battery.
11   Remove the serpentine drivebelt (see Chapter 1).
12   Remove the electrical connector from the oxygen sensor (see Chapter 6).
13   Remove the five bolts from the heat shield and lift it from the engine compartment.
14   Remove the wiring harness retainer from the power steering pump.
15   Remove the three bolts from the power steering pump, any electrical connectors and then remove the pump and set it to one side (don't disconnect the hoses).
16   Detach the alternator electrical connectors from the rear of the alternator.
17   Remove the upper mounting bolt.
18   Raise the vehicle and support it securely on jackstands.
19   Remove the splash shield from the inner fender panel on the passenger side of the vehicle (see Chapter 11).
20   Remove the alternator lower mounting bolt.
21   Remove the alternator from the vehicle.
22   Installation is the reverse of the removal procedure.

15 Voltage regulator and alternator brushes (1.8L engine only) – check and replacement

Refer to illustrations 15.2, 15.3 and 15.4
1   Remove the alternator from the vehicle (see Section 14).
2   Remove the nuts and separate the end cover from the alternator body **(see illustration)**.
3   Remove the five screws and lift the brush holder and the voltage regulator assembly off the main alternator body **(see illustration)**.

18.3 Lift the rubber boot off the solenoid electrical harness and remove the nut from the solenoid post

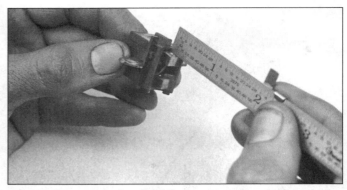

15.4 Measure the length of the brushes - they shouldn't be shorter than 1/16-inch

Check

4   Measure the length of the brushes **(see illustration)**. They should not be shorter than 1/16-inch (1.5 mm).
5   If the brushes are too short, replace them with new ones.

Replacement

6   Unsolder the brush wire from the brush holder assembly.
7   Remove the brushes from the holder.
8   When soldering the new brushes to the brush holder, leave about 13/32-inch of the brushes protruding from the holder, then solder the wires to the holder.
9   The remainder of installation is the reverse of removal.

16   Starting system – general information

The function of the starting system is to crank the engine rapidly enough to allow it to start. The starting system is composed of the starter motor, solenoid and battery. The battery supplies the electrical energy to the solenoid, which then completes the circuit to the starter motor, which does the actual work of cranking the engine.

The solenoid and starter motor are mounted together at the lower rear side of the engine. No periodic lubrication or maintenance is required.

The electrical circuitry of the vehicle is arranged so that the starter motor can only be operated when the clutch pedal is depressed (manual transmission) or the transmission selector lever is in Park or Neutral (automatic transmission).

Never operate the starter motor for more than 10 seconds at a time without pausing to allow it to cool for at least two minutes. Excessive cranking can cause overheating, which can seriously damage the starter.

17   Starter motor – testing in vehicle

1   If the starter motor does not turn at all when the ignition switch is operated, make sure the shift lever is in Neutral or Park (automatic transmission) or that the clutch pedal is depressed (manual transmission).
2   Make sure the battery is charged and that all cables, both at the battery and starter solenoid terminals, are secure.
3   If the starter motor spins but the engine is not cranking, the overrunning clutch in the starter motor is slipping and the motor must be removed from the engine for replacement.
4   If, when the switch is actuated, the starter motor does not operate at all but the solenoid clicks, then the problem lies with either the battery, the main solenoid contacts or the starter motor itself. **Note:** *Before diagnosing starter problems, make sure the battery is fully charged.*
5   If the solenoid plunger cannot be heard when the switch is actuated, the solenoid itself is defective or the solenoid circuit is open.
6   To check the solenoid, connect a jumper wire between the bat-

tery (+) and the "S" terminal on the solenoid. If the starter motor now operates, the solenoid is OK and the problem is in the ignition switch, neutral start switch or in the wiring.
7   If the starter motor still does not operate, remove the starter/solenoid for disassembly, testing and repair.
8   If the starter motor cranks the engine at an abnormally slow speed, first make sure that the battery is charged and that all terminal connections are tight. If the engine is partially seized, or has the wrong viscosity oil in it, it will crank slowly.
9   Run the engine until normal operating temperature is reached, then disconnect the coil wire from the distributor cap and ground it on the engine.
10   Connect a voltmeter positive lead to the starter motor terminal of the solenoid and then connect the negative lead to ground.
11   Crank the engine and take the voltmeter readings as soon as a steady figure is indicated. Do not allow the starter motor to turn for more than 10 seconds at a time. A reading of 9-volts or more, with the starter motor turning at normal cranking speed, is normal. If the reading is 9-volts or more but the cranking speed is slow, the motor is faulty. If the reading is less than 9-volts and the cranking speed is slow, the solenoid contacts are probably burned.

18   Starter motor – removal and installation

Refer to illustration 18.3
1   Detach the cable from the negative terminal of the battery.
2   Raise the vehicle and place it securely on jackstands.
3   Detach the wires from the starter solenoid **(see illustration)**.
4   Remove the two bolts, nuts and washersl holding the starter to the engine.
5   Remove the starter from the engine.
6   Installation is the reverse of removal.

19   Starter solenoid – removal and installation

1   Disconnect the cable from the negative terminal of the battery.
2   Remove the starter motor (see Section 18).

Removal

3   Disconnect the strap from the solenoid to the starter motor terminal.
4   Remove the two screws which secure the solenoid to the starter motor.
5   Pull and lift slightly to disengage the flange from the starter body.

Installation

6   Make sure the return spring is in position on the solenoid, then insert the solenoid body into the starter housing and make sure the slotted portion of the solenoid arm aligns with the lever of the starter motor.
7   Install the two solenoid screws and connect the motor strap.

Chapter 6
Emissions and engine control systems

Contents

6

---

1 General information

Refer to illustration 1.6

To prevent pollution of the atmosphere from incompletely burned and evaporating gases, and to maintain good driveability and fuel economy, a number of emission control devices and systems are incorporated.
They include the:

Electronic Spark Timing (EST) system
Secondary Air system (1990 and 1991 engines only)
Exhaust Gas Recirculation (EGR) system
Evaporative Emission Control System (EECS)
Positive Crankcase Ventilation (PCV) system
Transmission Converter Clutch (TCC) system (1.8L engine only)
Catalytic converter (CAT)
Air conditioning (AC) control

All of these systems are linked, directly or indirectly, to the Computer Command Control (CCC or C3) system. The Sections in this Chapter include general descriptions, checking procedures within the scope of the home mechanic and component replacement procedures (when possible) for each of the systems listed above.

Before assuming that an emissions control system is malfunctioning, check the fuel and ignition systems carefully. The diagnosis of some emission control devices requires specialized tools, equipment and training. If checking and servicing become too difficult or if a procedure is beyond the scope of your skills, consult your dealer service department.

This doesn't mean, however, that emission control systems are particularly difficult to maintain and repair. You can quickly and easily perform many checks and do most (if not all) of the regular maintenance at home with common tune-up and hand tools. **Note**: *The most frequent cause of emissions problems is simply a loose or broken vacuum hose or wiring connection, so always check the hose and wiring connections first.*

Pay close attention to any special precautions outlined in this

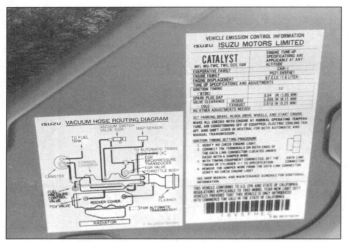

1.6 The Vehicle Emission Control Information (VECI) label is located on the underside of the hood and contains information on idle speed adjustment, ignition timing, location of the emission devices on your vehicle, vacuum line routing, etc.

Chapter. It should be noted that the illustrations of the various systems may not exactly match the system installed on your vehicle because of changes made by the manufacturer during production or from year-to-year.

A Vehicle Emissions Control Information (VECI) label is located in the engine compartment **(see illustration)**. This label contains important emissions specifications and ignition timing procedures, as well as a vacuum hose schematic and emissions components identification

guide. When servicing the engine or emissions systems, the VECI label in your particular vehicle should always be checked for up-to-date information.

2 Computer Command Control (CCC) system and trouble codes

Refer to illustrations 2.1a, 2.1b and 2.6

The Computer Command Control (CCC) system consists of an Electronic Control Module (ECM) and information sensors which monitor various functions of the engine and send data back to the ECM **(see illustrations)**.

This system is equipped with an Engine Control Module (ECM) with an Erasable Programmable Read Only Memory (EEPROM). The calibrations (parameters) are stored in the ECM within the EEPROM. If the ECM must be replaced, it is necessary to have the EEPROM programmed with a special scanning tool called TECH #1 available only at dealer service department. **Note**: *The EEPROM is not replaceable on these vehicles. In the event of any malfunction with the EEPROM (Code 51), the vehicle must be taken to a dealership service department for diagnosis and repair.*

The ECM controls the following systems:
Electronic spark timing
Exhaust gas recirculation
Canister purge
Engine cooling fan
Idle Air Control (IAC)
Transmission converter clutch
Air conditioning clutch control
Secondary air system
The CCC system is analogous to the central nervous system in

2.1a Emission and engine control components on the 1.6L SOHC engine

1	IAT sensor	7	Distributor	13	Charcoal canister
2	MAP sensor	8	Coolant temperature sensor	14	Purge control valve
3	EGR backpressure transducer	9	Fuel injector	15	Relay control center (air conditioner fuses)
4	EGR valve (behind air intake plenum)	10	Air intake plenum		
5	TPS sensor	11	Power steering pressure sensor		
6	IAC valve	12	PCV valve		

2.1b Emission and engine control components on the 1.6L DOHC engine

1	IAT sensor	6	EGR backpressure transducer	11	Fuel injector
2	EGR valve (under the air intake plenum)	7	Main relay control center	12	PCV valve
3	MAP sensor	8	Coolant temperature sensor	13	Charcoal canister
4	TPS sensor	9	Distributor	14	Relay control center (air conditioner fuses)
5	IAC valve	10	Oxygen sensor (in exhaust manifold, but not visible in photo)		

2.6 The assembly Line Data Link (ALDL) is located under the passenger side glovebox behind the kick panel - to activate the diagnostic codes, jump terminals #1 and #3 (the two outer terminals)

the human body. The sensors (nerve endings) constantly relay information to the ECM (brain), which processes the data and, if necessary, sends out a command to change the operating parameters of the engine (body).

Here's a specific example of how one portion of this system operates: An oxygen sensor, located in the exhaust manifold, constantly monitors the oxygen content of the exhaust gas. If the percentage of oxygen in the exhaust gas is incorrect, an electrical signal is sent to the ECM. The ECM takes this information, processes it and then sends a

command to the fuel injection system, telling it to change the air/fuel mixture. This happens in a fraction of a second and it goes on continuously when the engine is running. The end result is an air/fuel mixture ratio which is constantly maintained at a predetermined ratio, regardless of driving conditions.

One might think that a system which uses an on-board computer and electrical sensors would be difficult to diagnose. This is not necessarily the case. The CCC system has a built-in diagnostic feature which indicates a problem by flashing a CHECK ENGINE light on the instrument panel. When this light comes on during normal vehicle operation, a fault in one of the information sensor circuits or the ECM itself has been detected. More importantly, a trouble code is stored in the ECM's memory.

To retrieve this information from the ECM memory, you must use a short jumper wire to ground the diagnostic terminal. This terminal is part of an electrical connector known as the Assembly Line Data Link (ALDL) **(see illustration)**. The ALDL is located underneath the dashboard, to the right of the passenger seat, tucked into the corner. To use the ALDL, remove the right side kick panel (see Chapter 11). There will be either two or three harness connectors grouped together. These connectors will access the various computers (ECM for the CCC system, ECU for the transaxle control system and the SRS or airbag system). It is important to determine the correct connector for the engine management codes (CCC system). Look for a clear plastic cover that completely covers the electrical connector. The other connectors will have different colors. With the electrical connector exposed to view, push one end of the jumper wire into the diagnostic terminal and the other end into the ground terminal; numbers 1 and 3.

When the diagnostic terminal is grounded with the ignition ON and the engine stopped, the system will enter the Diagnostic Mode. **Caution:** *Don't start or crank the engine with the diagnostic terminal*

6

grounded. In this mode the ECM will display a "Code 12" by flashing the CHECK ENGINE light, indicating that the system is operating. A code 12 is simply one flash, followed by a brief pause, then two flashes in quick succession. This code will be flashed three times. If no other codes are stored, Code 12 will continue to flash until the diagnostic terminal ground is removed.

After flashing Code 12 three times, the ECM will display any stored trouble codes. Each code will be flashed three times, then Code 12 will be flashed again, indicating that the display of any stored trouble codes has been completed.

When the ECM sets a trouble code, the CHECK ENGINE light will come on and a trouble code will be stored in memory. If the problem is intermittent, the light will go out after 10 seconds, when the fault goes away. However, the trouble code will stay in the ECM memory until the battery voltage to the ECM is interrupted. Removing battery voltage for 10 seconds will clear all stored trouble codes. Trouble codes should always be cleared after repairs have been completed. **Caution:** *To prevent damage to the ECM, the ignition switch must be OFF when disconnecting or connecting power to the ECM.*

Following is a list of the typical trouble codes which may be encountered while diagnosing the Computer Command Control System. Also included are simplified troubleshooting procedures. If the problem persists after these checks have been made, more detailed service procedures will have to be done by a dealer service department.

Trouble code	Circuit or system	Probable cause
Code 12 (1 flash, pause, 2 flashes)	No distributor reference pulses to ECM	This code will flash whenever the diagnostic terminal is grounded with the ignition turned ON and the engine not running. If additional trouble codes are stored in the ECM they will appear after this code has flashed three times. If this code appears while the engine is running, no reference pulses from the distributor are reaching the ECM.
Code 13 (1 flash, pause, 3 flashes)	Oxygen sensor circuit (non-heated type)	Check for a sticking or misadjusted throttle position sensor (TPS). Check the wiring and connectors from the oxygen sensor (see Section 4). Replace the oxygen sensor.*
Code 14 (1 flash, pause, 4 flashes)	Coolant sensor/high or low temp	If the engine is experiencing cooling system problems the problem must be rectified before continuing. Check all wiring and connectors associated with the coolant temperature sensor. Replace the coolant temperature sensor.*
Code 21 (2 flashes, pause, 1 flash)	Throttle position sensor/voltage high or low	Check for a sticking or misadjusted TPS plunger. Check all wiring and connections between the TPS and the ECM. Adjust or replace the TPS (see Section 4).*
Code 23 (2 flashes, pause, 3 flashes)	Intake Air Temperature (IAT) sensor circuit voltage high or low	Check for continuity in the signal wire and the ground wire. Check the operation of the IAT sensor (see Section 4).
Code 24 (2 flashes, pause, 4 flashes)	Vehicle speed sensor	A fault in this circuit should be indicated only when the vehicle is in motion. Disregard Code 24 if it is set when the drive wheels are not turning. Check the connections at the ECM. Check the TPS setting.
Code 32 (3 flashes, pause, 2 flashes)	EGR (Exhaust gas recirculation)	EVRV shorted to ground on start-up, switch not closed after the ECM has commanded the EGR for a specified period of time or the EGR solenoid circuit is open for specified period of time (see Section 7). Replace the EGR valve.*
Code 33 (3 flashes, pause, 3 flashes)	MAP sensor voltage high or low	Check the vacuum hoses from the MAP sensor (see Section 4). Check the electrical connections at the ECM. Replace the MAP sensor.*
Code 42 (4 flashes, pause, 2 flashes)	Electronic Spark Timing circuit	Electronic Spark Timing (EST) bypass circuit or EST circuit is grounded or open. A malfunctioning ignition module can cause this code.
Code 44 (4 flashes, pause, 4 flashes)	Oxygen sensor indicates lean exhaust (heated type)	Check the ECM electrical connections. Check for vacuum leakage at the throttle body base gasket, vacuum hoses or the intake manifold gasket. Replace the oxygen sensor (see Section 4).*
Code 45 (4 flashes, pause, 5 flashes)	Oxygen sensor indicates rich exhaust	Possible rich or leaking injector, high fuel pressure or faulty TPS. Also, check the evaporative charcoal canister and its components for the presence of fuel. Replace the oxygen sensor (see Section 4).*
Code 51 (5 flashes, pause, 1 flash)	ECM or EEPROM	Be sure that the ECM ground connections are tight. If they are, replace the ECM (see Section 3).

* Component replacement may not cure the problem in all cases. For this reason, you may want to seek professional advice before purchasing replacement parts.

3.6 Remove the two nuts (arrows) and separate the ECM from the bracket

4.2a The coolant temperature sensor (arrow) is located toward the front of the engine on SOHC engines - the resistance of the sensor is being checked

3 Electronic Control Module (ECM) - replacement

Refer to illustration 3.6

Note: *This system is equipped with an Engine Control Module (ECM) with an Erasable Programmable Read Only Memory (EEPROM). The calibrations (parameters) are stored in the ECM within the EEPROM. If the ECM must be replaced, it is necessary to have the EEPROM programmed with a special scanning tool called TECH #1 available only at dealer service departments. The EEPROM is not replaceable on these vehicles. In the event of any malfunction with the EEPROM (Code 51), the vehicle must be taken to a dealer service department for diagnosis and repair.*

1   The Electronic Control Module (ECM) is located inside the passenger compartment under the dashboard on the driver's side (left side).
2   Disconnect the negative battery cable from the battery.
3   Remove the screws from the trim panel under the left side of the dash.
4   Remove the trim panel to expose the components under the dash (see Chapter 11).
5   Unplug both electrical connectors from the ECM. **Caution**: *The ignition switch must be turned OFF when pulling out or plugging in the electrical connectors to prevent damage to the ECM.*
6   Remove the retaining nuts **(see illustration)** from the bracket that retains the ECM.
7   Carefully slide the ECM down far enough to clear the fuse panel.
Note: *Avoid any static electricity damage to the computer by using gloves and a special anti-static pad to store the ECM once it is removed.*
8   Installation is the reverse of removal.

4 Information sensors

Note: *See component location illustrations in Section 2 for additional information on the location of the following information sensors.*

Engine coolant temperature sensor

Refer to illustrations 4.2a, 4.2b, 4.3 and 4.4

General description

1   The coolant sensor is a thermistor (a resistor which varies the value of its voltage output in accordance with temperature changes). The change in the resistance values will directly affect the voltage signal from the coolant sensor. As the sensor temperature DECREASES, the resistance values will INCREASE. As the sensor temperature IN-CREASES, the resistance values will DECREASE. A failure in the

4.2b Check the resistance of the coolant temperature sensor with the engine completely cold and then with the engine at operating temperature (DOHC engine shown, distributor removed for clarity)

coolant sensor circuit should set a Code 14. This code indicates a failure in the coolant temperature circuit, so in most cases the appropriate solution to the problem will be either repair of a wire or replacement of the sensor.

Check

2   To check the sensor, check the resistance value of the coolant temperature sensor **(see illustrations)** while it is completely cold (50 to 80-degrees F = 2,400 to 5,600 ohms). Next, start the engine and warm it up until it reaches operating temperature. The resistance should be lower (180 to 200-degrees F = 200 to 300 ohms). **Note**: *Access to the coolant temperature sensor makes it difficult to position electrical probes on the terminals. If necessary, remove the sensor and perform the tests in a pan of heated water to simulate the conditions.*

Replacement

3   Before installing the new sensor, wrap the threads with Teflon sealing tape to prevent leakage and thread corrosion **(see illustration)**.
4   To remove the sensor, release the locking tab, unplug the electrical connector **(see illustration)**, then carefully unscrew the sensor. Be prepared for some coolant spillage. **Caution**: *Handle the coolant sensor with care. Damage to this sensor will affect the operation of the entire fuel injection system.*
5   Installation is the reverse of removal.

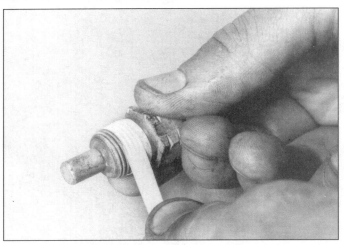

4.3 To prevent leakage, wrap the threads of the coolant temperature sensor with Teflon tape before installing it

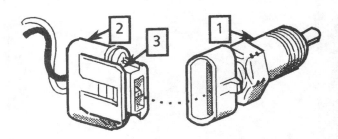

4.4 To remove the engine coolant temperature sensor (1), pry open the locking tab (3) with a small screwdriver and unplug the electrical connector (2), then carefully unscrew the sensor with a deep socket or wrench

Manifold Absolute Pressure (MAP) sensor

Refer to illustrations 4.8a, 4.8b, and 4.8c

General description

6   The Manifold Absolute Pressure (MAP) sensor monitors the intake manifold pressure changes resulting from changes in engine load and speed and converts the information into a voltage output. The ECM uses the MAP sensor to control fuel delivery and ignition timing. The ECM will receive information as a voltage signal that will vary from 1.0 to 1.5 volts at closed throttle (high vacuum) and 4.0 to 4.5 volts at wide open throttle (low vacuum).

7   A failure in the MAP sensor circuit should set a Code 33.

Check and replacement

8   The accompanying diagnostic chart and photos outline the testing procedures for the MAP sensor **(see illustrations)**. To replace the MAP sensor, detach the hose and electrical connector and remove the two screws. Installation is the reverse of removal.

Oxygen sensor

Refer to illustration 4.9 and 4.11

General description and check

9   The oxygen sensor, which is located in the exhaust manifold **(see illustration)**, monitors the oxygen content of the exhaust gas stream. The oxygen content in the exhaust reacts with the oxygen sensor to produce a voltage output which varies from 0.1-volt (high oxygen, lean mixture) to 0.9-volts (low oxygen, rich mixture). The ECM constantly monitors this variable voltage output to determine the ratio of oxygen to fuel in the mixture. The ECM alters the air/fuel mixture ratio by controlling the pulse width (open time) of the fuel injectors. A mixture ratio

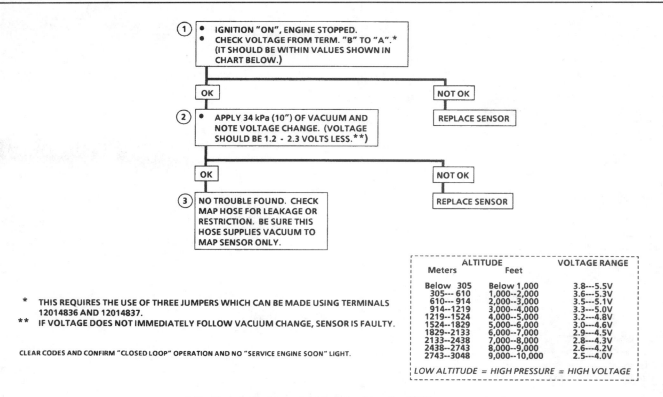

4.8a Diagnostic flow chart for checking the MAP sensor output

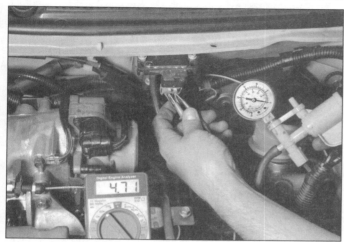

4.8b Using a voltmeter, probe the backside of the MAP sensor electrical connector at the gray/red wire (B terminal - signal wire) and the gray wire (A terminal - ground wire) and check for voltage - it should be between 2.5 to 5.5-volts (depending on the altitude)

4.8c Next, apply vacuum and check the MAP sensor voltage - it should be between 1.2 and 2.3 volts lower than the previous check

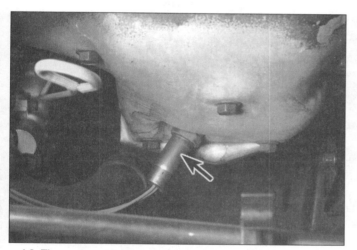

4.9 The oxygen sensor is located in the exhaust manifold - be careful when working on a hot engine

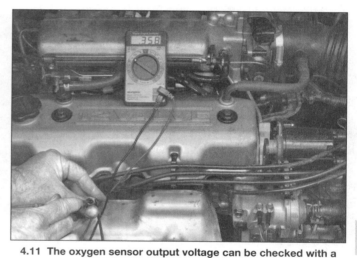

4.11 The oxygen sensor output voltage can be checked with a digital voltmeter set on the low scale

of 14.7 parts air to 1 part fuel is the ideal mixture ratio for minimizing exhaust emissions, thus allowing the catalytic converter to operate at maximum efficiency. It is this ratio of 14.7 to 1 which the ECM and the oxygen sensor attempt to maintain at all times.

10   The oxygen sensor produces no voltage when it is below its normal operating temperature of about 600-degrees F. During this initial period before warm-up, the ECM operates in open loop mode.

11   If the engine reaches normal operating temperature and/or has been running for two or more minutes, and if the oxygen sensor is producing a steady signal voltage between 0.35 and 0.55-volts **(see illustration)**, even though the TPS indicates that the engine is not at idle, the ECM will set a Code 13.

12   A delay of two minutes or more between engine start-up and normal operation of the sensor, followed by a low voltage signal or a short in the sensor circuit, will cause the ECM to set a Code 44. If a high voltage signal occurs, the ECM will set a Code 45. **Note:** *1990 models use an unheated oxygen sensor. 1991 through 1993 models are equipped with a four-wire electrical connector with a special heating element installed in the oxygen sensor that helps speed the warm-up for quicker response.*

13   When any of the above codes occur, the ECM operates in the open loop mode - that is, it controls fuel delivery in accordance with a programmed default value instead of feedback information from the oxygen sensor.

14   The proper operation of the oxygen sensor depends on four conditions:

a) **Electrical** - The low voltages generated by the sensor depend upon good, clean connections which should be checked whenever a malfunction of the sensor is suspected or indicated.

b) **Outside air supply** - The sensor is designed to allow air circulation to the internal portion of the sensor. Whenever the sensor is removed and installed or replaced, make sure the air passages are not restricted.

c) **Proper operating temperature** - The ECM will not react to the sensor signal until the sensor reaches approximately 600-degrees F. This factor must be taken into consideration when evaluating the performance of the sensor.

d) **Unleaded fuel** - The use of unleaded fuel is essential for proper operation of the sensor. Make sure the fuel you are using is of this type.

15   In addition to observing the above conditions, special care must be taken whenever the sensor is serviced.

a) The oxygen sensor has a permanently attached pigtail and electrical connector which should not be removed from the sensor. Damage or removal of the pigtail or electrical connector can adversely affect operation of the sensor.

b) Grease, dirt and other contaminants should be kept away from the electrical connector and the louvered end of the sensor.

6

4.25 Use sharp electrical probes to pierce the wires on the backside of the TPS electrical connector to read signal voltage

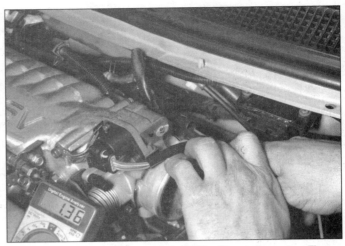

4.27 Check the resistance of the TPS with an ohmmeter. First, ground the negative probe and open and close the throttle while checking each terminal to determine the correct one. Next, observe the fluctuation in resistance from closed to wide open throttle.

c) Do not use cleaning solvents of any kind on the oxygen sensor.
d) Do not drop or roughly handle the sensor.
e) The silicone boot must be installed in the correct position to prevent the boot from being melted and to allow the sensor to operate properly.

Replacement

Note: *Because it is installed in the exhaust manifold or pipe, which contracts when cool, the oxygen sensor may be very difficult to loosen when the engine is cold. Rather than risk damage to the sensor (assuming you are planning to reuse it in another manifold or pipe), start and run the engine for a minute or two, then shut it off. Be careful not to burn yourself during the following procedure.*

16   Disconnect the cable from the negative terminal of the battery.
17   Raise the vehicle and place it securely on jackstands.
18   Follow the wire from the sensor and unplug the electrical connector.
19   Unscrew the sensor from the exhaust manifold.
20   Anti-seize compound must be used on the threads of the sensor to facilitate future removal. The threads of new sensors will already be coated with this compound, but if an old sensor is removed and reinstalled, recoat the threads.
21   Install the sensor and tighten it securely. **Caution**: *Excessive force may damage the threads.*
22   Reconnect the electrical connector.
23   Lower the vehicle and reconnect the cable to the negative terminal of the battery.

Throttle Position Sensor (TPS)
General description

Refer to illustrations 4.25 and 4.27
24   The Throttle Position Sensor (TPS) is located on the end of the throttle shaft on the throttle body. By monitoring the output voltage from the TPS, the ECM can determine fuel delivery based on throttle valve angle (driver demand). A broken or loose TPS can cause intermittent bursts of fuel from the injector and an unstable idle because the ECM thinks the throttle is moving.

Check

25   To check the TPS, turn the ignition switch to On (engine not running) and connect the probes of a voltmeter into the ground wire (terminal B) and signal wire (terminal A) on the backside of the electrical connector **(see illustration)**. **Note**: *The signal wire on 1990 models is a tan/blue wire and on all others it is a blue/red wire. The ground wire is a black/white wire on all models.*
26   The sensor should read 0.25 to 0.98-volts at idle. Have an assistant depress the accelerator pedal to simulate full throttle and the sensor should increase voltage to 4.0 to 4.8-volts. If the TPS voltage read-

ings are incorrect, replace it with a new unit.
27   Next, check the TPS sensor resistance. First disconnect the electrical connector and connect the probes **(see illustration)** to the terminals. Slowly move the throttle valve and observe a distinct change in the resistance values as the sensor travels from idle to full throttle. The resistance should range from 1,100 to 5,600 ohms.
28   A problem in any of the TPS circuits will set a Code 21. Once a trouble code is set, the ECM will use an artificial default value for TPS and some vehicle performance will return.

Replacement

29   Refer to Chapter 4 for the TPS replacement procedure.

Park/Neutral Position switch
General description

30   The Park/Neutral Position (PNP) switch (sometimes referred to as the neutral safety switch), located on the transaxle indicates to the ECM when the transmission is in Park or Neutral. This information is used for Transmission Converter Clutch (TCC), Exhaust Gas Recirculation (EGR) and Idle Air Control (IAC) valve operation. For example, if the signal wire (pink/purple wire) becomes grounded (closed) while in DRIVE, the EGR may be rendered inoperative, resulting in a detonation problem. On the other hand, the signal wire may become permanently "open", causing the idle to drop when the transmission is shifted into DRIVE. **Caution**: *The vehicle should not be driven with the Park/Neutral switch disconnected because idle quality will be adversely affected and a false Code 24 (failure in the Vehicle Speed Sensor circuit) may be set.*
31   The switch is closed to ground in Park or Neutral and open in Drive ranges. Because this system requires a special SCAN tool, have any failures diagnosed by a dealer service department or other repair shop.

Replacement and adjustment

32   Refer to Chapter 7B, *Neutral safety switch - check, adjustment and replacement* for the replacement or adjustment procedure.

Air conditioning control
Air conditioning clutch control

Refer to illustrations 4.34a and 4.34b
Note: *Refer to Chapter 12 for additional information on the location of the relays.*
33   During air conditioning operation, the ECM controls the application of the air conditioning compressor clutch. The ECM controls the air conditioning clutch control relay to delay clutch engagement after the air conditioning is turned On to allow the IAC valve to adjust the

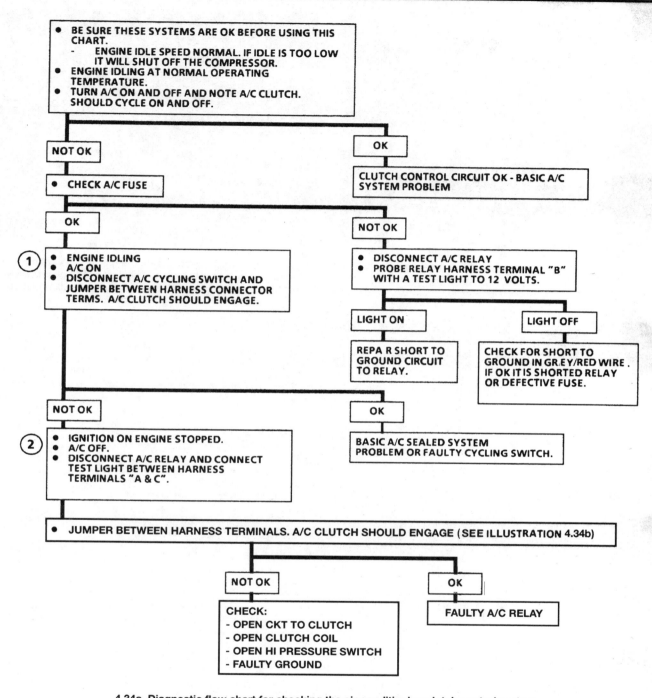

4.34a Diagnostic flow chart for checking the air conditioning clutch control system

idle speed of the engine to compensate for the additional load. The ECM also controls the relay to disengage the clutch in the event of an excessively high or low pressure within the system or an overheating problem.

34   The accompanying diagnostic chart and photo outline the testing procedures for the air conditioning clutch control **(see illustrations)**.

Air conditioning "On" signal

35   Turning on the air conditioning supplies battery voltage to the air conditioning compressor clutch and to terminal B8 (green/orange wire) of ECM electrical connector through green wire to the air conditioner compressor relay to increase idle air rate and maintain idle speed.

36   In most cases, if the air conditioning does not function, the problem is probably related to the air conditioning system relays and switches and not the ECM.

37   If the air conditioning is operating properly and idle is too low when the air conditioning compressor turns on or is too high when the air conditioning compressor turns off, check for an open circuit in the gray/ red wire between the air conditioning control relay and the ECM.

Vehicle Speed Sensor (VSS)
General description

38   The Vehicle Speed Sensors (VSS) are located in the instrument panel behind the cluster and on the transaxle. The transaxle sensor

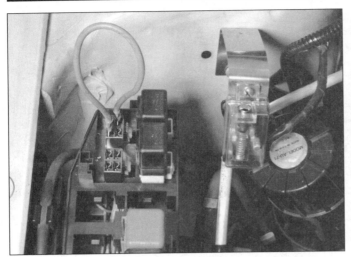

4.34b Check the air conditioner clutch by jumping the harness and applying voltage directly to the clutch - you should hear a loud "clunk" when it engages

4.46 The IAT sensor is located on the rear of the intake plenum - if the probes (arrows) of the voltmeter can't be correctly positioned, remove the sensor and use simulated conditions to check the resistance

signals the vehicle speed until about 11 mph and from there the sensor located in the instrument cluster signals speeds of 12 mph or greater. The sensor is a magnetic reed type and it sends a pulsing voltage signal to the ECM, which the ECM converts to miles per hour. The VSS is part of the Transmission Converter Clutch (TCC) system. Any problems with the VSS will usually set a code 24.

Check

39   To check the vehicle speed sensors, remove the electrical connector in the wiring harness near the sensor. The signal wire should have 10-volts or more available. If there is no voltage available, have the ECM diagnosed by a dealer service department or other repair shop.

Replacement

40   To replace the VSS in the instrument cluster, remove the instrument cluster (see Chapter 12), detach the sensor retaining screw and bracket and unplug the sensor. Trace the pigtail of the VSS to its electrical connector in the main wiring harness and unplug it. To remove the transaxle mounted VSS, unplug the electrical connector, unscrew the mounting bolt and remove the sensor from the transaxle.
41   Installation is the reverse of removal.

Intake Air Temperature (IAT) Sensor
Refer to illustration 4.46

General description

42   The Intake Air Temperature (IAT) sensor is located on the side of the air intake plenum. This sensor acts as a resistor which changes value according to the temperature of the air entering the engine. Low temperatures produce a high resistance value (for example, at -40-degrees F the resistance is 100,700 ohms) while high temperatures produce low resistance values (at 212-degrees F the resistance is 177 ohms). The ECM supplies approximately 5-volts (signal voltage) to the IAT sensor. The voltage leaving the sensor will change according to the temperature of the incoming air. The voltage will be high when the air temperature is cold and low when the air temperature is warm. Any problems with the IAT sensor will usually set a code 23.

Check

43   To check the IAT sensor, disconnect the electrical connector from the sensor and turn the ignition key On but do not start the engine.
44   Measure the voltage (signal voltage) on terminal A. There should be approximately 5-volts present.
45   If the signal voltage is not correct, have the ECM diagnosed by a dealer service department or other repair shop.

46   Measure the resistance across the sensor terminals **(see illustration)**. The resistance should be HIGH when the air temperature is LOW. Next, start the engine and let it idle (cold). Allow the engine to reach normal operating temperature. Turn the ignition Off, disconnect the IAT sensor and measure the resistance across the terminals. The resistance should be LOW when the air temperature is HIGH. If the sensor does not exhibit this change in resistance, replace it.

Replacement

47 Prepare the new IAT sensor by wrapping the threads with Teflon sealing tape.
48   Unscrew the sensor from the intake plenum.
49   Carefully thread the new sensor in to the intake plenum, then tighten it securely. Plug in the electrical connector.

Power steering pressure switch
Refer to illustrations 4.54 and 4.57

General description

50   Turning the steering wheel increases power steering fluid pressure and engine load. The pressure switch will close before the load can cause an idle problem.
51   The power steering switch is normally open to ground. The blue wire carries battery voltage. Closing the switch will cause the voltage to drop to 1-volt or less.
52   A pressure switch that will not open or an open circuit from the ECM will cause timing to retard at idle and this will affect idle quality.
53   A pressure switch that will not close (or an open circuit caused by wiring problems) may cause the engine to die when the power steering system is used heavily.

Check

54   The accompanying diagnostic chart **(see illustration)** outlines the testing procedure for the power steering pressure switch.

Replacement

55   Disconnect the cable from the negative terminal of the battery.
56   Without disconnecting the hoses, remove the power steering pump (see Chapter 10).
57   Unscrew the switch from the pump **(see illustration)**. Be prepared for fluid spillage.
58   Wrap the threads of the new switch with Teflon sealing tape. Install the switch and tighten it securely.
59   Install the power steering pump, add fluid (see Chapter 1) and bleed the system (see Chapter 10).

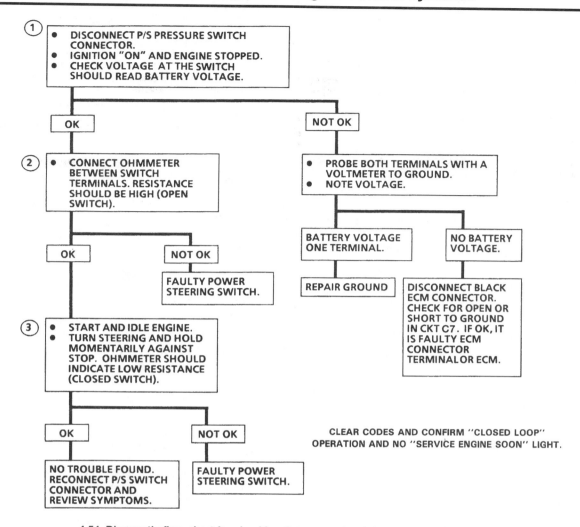

4.54 Diagnostic flow chart for checking the power steering pressure switch

4.57 The power steering pressure switch (arrow) is threaded into the bottom of the power steering pump

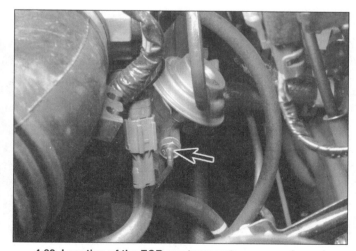

4.60 Location of the EGR gas temperature sensor (arrow)

EGR gas temperature sensor (California models only)

Refer to illustration 4.60

60   The EGR valve is equipped with a temperature sensor mounted at the base of the EGR valve (**see illustration**). This sensor is designed to work at very high temperatures much like the coolant temperature and air intake temperature sensors. The ECM monitors the signal from the EGR gas temperature sensor to determine if the valve is open or closed. With the EGR valve open, the temperatures will be very high. With the EGR valve closed, the temperatures will be low. This sensor

6

can detect if the EGR valve is stuck open or even if the orifice is slightly restricted. Any problems with the EGR system will set a code 32 (see Section 2). In the event of any EGR gas temperature sensor problem, have the system diagnosed by a dealer service department or other repair shop.

5   Electronic Spark Timing (EST)

General description

1   To provide improved engine performance, fuel economy and control of exhaust emissions, the Electronic Control Module (ECM) controls distributor spark advance (ignition timing) with the Electronic Spark Timing (EST) system.

2   The EST system consists of the distributor, ignition module, the ECM and the connecting wires. The terminals for the EST are lettered on the module, P and N. The distributor terminal electrical connector is lettered left-to-right, +-C-G-B-R-E **(see illustration 6.5** in Chapter 5). These circuits perform the following functions:

a) Terminal P - EST. This circuit triggers the HEI module. The ECM doesn't know what the actual timing is, but it does know when it gets the reference signal. It advances or retards the spark from that point. If the base timing is set incorrectly, the entire spark curve will be incorrect.

b) Terminal R - Distributor Reference High. This provides the ECM with rpm and crankshaft position information.

c) Terminal B - Bypass. At about 400 rpm the ECM applies 5-volts to this circuit to switch spark timing control from the HEI module to the ECM. An open or grounded bypass circuit will set a Code 42 and the engine will run at base timing, plus a small amount of advance built into the HEI module.

d) Terminal G - Reference Ground Low. This wire is grounded in the distributor and insures that the ground circuit has no voltage drop which could affect performance. If it is open, it may cause poor performance.

e) Terminal + Supply voltage. This wire provides battery voltage to the module.

f) Terminal C - Tachometer. This wire receives a voltage signal from the tachometer.

3   The ECM receives a reference pulse from the distributor, which indicates both engine rpm and crankshaft position. The ECM then determines the proper spark advance for the engine operating conditions and sends an EST pulse to the distributor.

Check

4   The ECM will set spark timing at a specified value when the diagnostic "Test" terminal in the ALDL electrical connector is grounded **(see illustration 2.6).** To check for EST operation, the timing should be checked at 1500 rpm with the terminal ungrounded. Then ground the test terminal (see Section 2). If the timing changes at 1500 rpm, the EST is operating. A fault in the EST system will usually set Trouble Code 42.

5   Refer to Chapter 5 for the ignition timing adjustment procedure and more information on the ignition system.

6   Secondary air system (1990 and 1991 engines only)

Refer to illustration 6.1

General description

1   The secondary air control system is used to control intake air to the secondary intake valves when the engine speed is above 5000 rpm. This system allows reduced intake air at idle to stabilize idle quality and then activates to allow more airflow to improve engine performance at high rpm. The system consists of the secondary port intake valves mounted in the lower intake manifold and a vacuum operated diaphragm which moves the secondary valve linkage **(see illustration).** The vacuum to the diaphragm is controlled by a vacuum switching solenoid which is activated by the ECM.

Check

2   Raise the vehicle and support it securely on jackstands. Disconnect the vacuum hose from the secondary intake air control solenoid **(see illustration 6.1)** and connect a vacuum gauge to the hose. With the engine idling, vacuum should be about 10 inches Hg.

3   If the vacuum is incorrect, repair the hose or the manifold. If the vacuum is correct, connect a vacuum pump (hand-held type) to the control solenoid on the intake manifold side.

4   With the ignition key On (engine not running), apply vacuum and observe the actuator linkage on the vacuum actuator. The linkage should not move.

5   If the linkage moves, disconnect the solenoid electrical connector and repeat the test. If the linkage continues to move, there is a leak in the solenoid diaphragm and the solenoid must be replaced with a new part. If the linkage does not move, then there is a problem with the electrical circuit from the ECM and/or the ECM itself.

6   If the linkage originally did not move (see Step 4), ground the diagnostic terminal #1 and #3 **(see illustration 2.6)** and apply vacuum while observing the linkage. The linkage should move.

7   If the linkage does not move, connect a vacuum pump directly to the vacuum actuator and observe that the linkage moves smoothly. If it does not move, check for a hose leaking or linkage binding or possibly a faulty vacuum actuator.

8   If the linkage does move, check for the voltage to the solenoid.

a) Disconnect the solenoid electrical connector and turn the ignition key On (engine not running)

b) Ground the diagnostic terminal **(see illustration 2.6).**

c) Connect a test light across the terminals and watch for a light

9   If the light comes on, then the solenoid is faulty. Replace it with a new part.

10   If the light remains off, check the ignition switch electrical circuit (see Chapter 12).

Replacement

11   To replace either the vacuum actuator or the solenoid, simply detach the vacuum hose and/or the electrical connector, remove the mounting screws and remove the component. If you're removing the vacuum actuator, you'll have to pry the actuator rod from the secondary air valve linkage. Installation is the reverse of removal.

7   Exhaust Gas Recirculation (EGR) system

General description

Refer to illustration 7.2

1   The EGR system is used to lower NOx (oxides of nitrogen) emission levels caused by high combustion temperatures. It does this by decreasing combustion temperatures. Under certain driving conditions (depending on engine rpm, engine load and engine temperature), the exhaust gases are mixed with the intake air/fuel mixture to pre-heat the mixture and reduce the high rate of combustion created by the volatile mixture. This will decrease the NOx compounds that are expelled into the atmosphere.

2   The EGR system consists of a backpressure EGR valve, a backpressure transducer, a ported manifold vacuum source tube and an Electronic Vacuum Regulator Valve (EVRV) solenoid which controls this vacuum source **(see illustration).** Any trouble with the EGR system will usually set a Code 32 in the self diagnosis system on 1991 through 1993 models only.

3   The EGR valve is controlled by a normally open EVRV (solenoid) which allows vacuum to pass. Under certain conditions, the ECM energizes the EVRV (solenoid) to cut off the flow of vacuum to the backpressure transducer. In this state, vacuum is not transmitted to the EGR valve and it remains closed (no EGR). These conditions are:

a) Engine coolant is low (below 113-degrees F)

b) The TPS is at idle position

c) When the engine is running under low load

d) When intake manifold pressure is low

Other than these conditions, the EGR valve is controlled by the

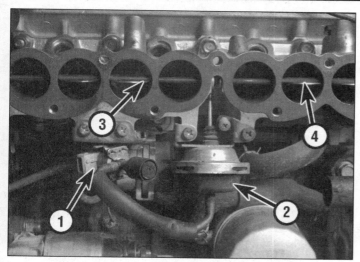

6.1 The secondary air system is positioned below the intake manifold on the DOHC engine and any testing must be performed from under the vehicle

1 Secondary intake air control solenoid	2 Vacuum actuator
	3 Secondary air valves

movement of the backpressure transducer which senses exhaust backpressure.

4   Too much EGR flow tends to weaken combustion, causing the engine to run rough or stop. When EGR flow is excessive, the engine

can stop after a cold start or at idle after deceleration, the vehicle can surge at cruising speeds or the idle may be rough. If the EGR valve remains constantly open, the engine may not idle at all.

5   Too little or no EGR flow allows combustion temperatures to get too high during acceleration and load conditions. This can cause spark knock (detonation), engine overheating or emission test failure.

Check

Refer to illustration 7.6

6   The accompanying diagnostic chart (see illustration) outlines the testing procedures for the EGR valve.

7   If a Code 32 is displayed by the CHECK ENGINE light, there are several possibilities for EGR failure. Engine coolant temperature sensor, TPS, MAP sensor, TCC system and the engine rpm govern the parameters the EGR system use for distinguishing the correct EGR On time. First check all the components of the EGR system before checking the information sensors and output devices of the CCC system.

8   The EGR vacuum control solenoid uses an ECM-controlled pulse width to modulate the EGR solenoid. The valve is normally open and the vacuum source is a ported signal. The ECM will turn the EGR On and Off (this is called the "duty cycle") by grounding circuit D-12 (white/green wire). The duty cycle should be zero percent (no EGR) when in Park or Neutral, when the TPS input is below the specified value or when Wide Open Throttle (WOT) is indicated.

9   The following checks will help you pinpoint problems in the EGR system. Where the procedure says to lift up on the EGR valve diaphragm, it's a good idea to wear a heat-resistant glove to prevent burns.

EGR valve

Refer to illustration 7.11

10   With the engine operating at normal temperature, accelerate the engine and observe that the EGR valve diaphragm moves.

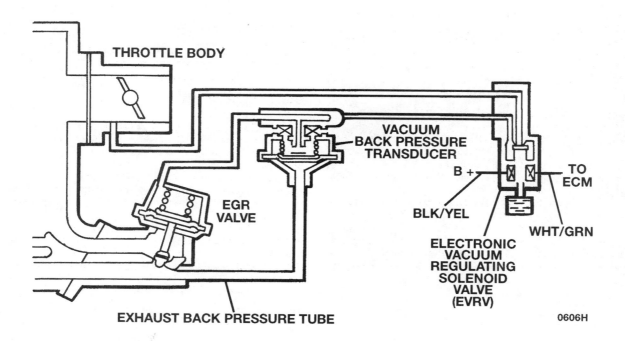

7.2 Schematic of a typical EGR system

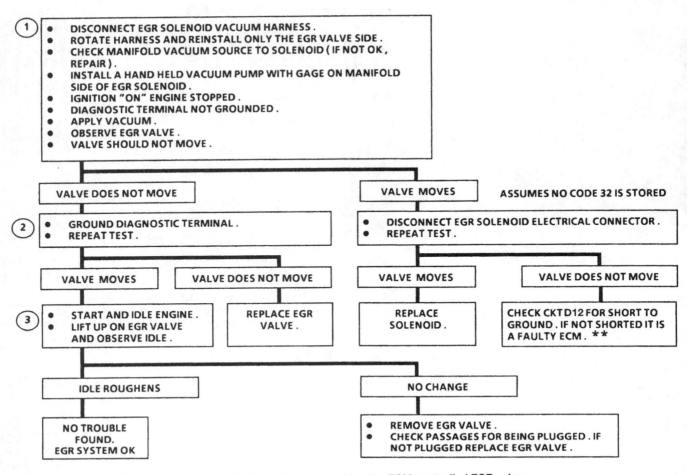

1
- DISCONNECT EGR SOLENOID VACUUM HARNESS.
- ROTATE HARNESS AND REINSTALL ONLY THE EGR VALVE SIDE.
- CHECK MANIFOLD VACUUM SOURCE TO SOLENOID (IF NOT OK , REPAIR).
- INSTALL A HAND HELD VACUUM PUMP WITH GAGE ON MANIFOLD SIDE OF EGR SOLENOID.
- IGNITION "ON" ENGINE STOPPED.
- DIAGNOSTIC TERMINAL NOT GROUNDED.
- APPLY VACUUM.
- OBSERVE EGR VALVE.
- VALVE SHOULD NOT MOVE.

VALVE DOES NOT MOVE

VALVE MOVES   ASSUMES NO CODE 32 IS STORED

2
- GROUND DIAGNOSTIC TERMINAL.
- REPEAT TEST.

- DISCONNECT EGR SOLENOID ELECTRICAL CONNECTOR.
- REPEAT TEST.

VALVE MOVES   **VALVE DOES NOT MOVE**   **VALVE MOVES**   **VALVE DOES NOT MOVE**

3
- START AND IDLE ENGINE.
- LIFT UP ON EGR VALVE AND OBSERVE IDLE.

REPLACE EGR VALVE.

REPLACE SOLENOID.

CHECK CKT D12 FOR SHORT TO GROUND. IF NOT SHORTED IT IS A FAULTY ECM. **

IDLE ROUGHENS   **NO CHANGE**

NO TROUBLE FOUND. EGR SYSTEM OK

- REMOVE EGR VALVE.
- CHECK PASSAGES FOR BEING PLUGGED. IF NOT PLUGGED REPLACE EGR VALVE.

7.6 Diagnostic flow chart for checking the ECM-controlled EGR valve

7.11 Apply vacuum directly to the EGR valve and observe that the valve diaphragm moves up and down freely without any binding (the valve should also hold vacuum)

11 Turn the ignition key Off. Disconnect the vacuum hose from the EGR valve. Using a hand-held vacuum pump **(see illustration)** apply vacuum and observe that the EGR diaphragm moves.

12 In both tests, the EGR valve should move freely and not bind or stick in any way or the valve must be replaced.

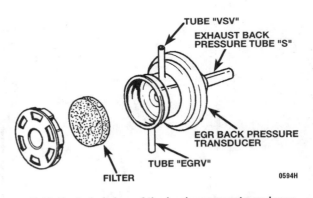

7.13 Exploded view of the backpressure transducer

Backpressure transducer (modulator)

Refer to illustration 7.13

13 Remove all the vacuum hoses from the transducer and, while blocking port VSV **(see illustration)**, blow air into port EGRV.

14 Air should pass through the filter (top section) of the EGR valve.

15 Connect a vacuum pump to port VSV and plug port EGRV **(see illustration 7.13)**.

16 Blow air into tube S and apply vacuum. The valve should hold vacuum.

17 If the backpressure transducer fails any of these tests, replace it.

7.19a Check the resistance of the EVRV with an ohmmeter - it should be between 33 and 42 ohms (DOHC engine shown)

7.19b Checking the EVRV on an SOHC engine

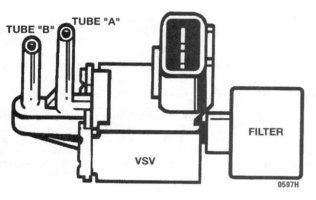

7.20 A typical EVRV

Electronic Vacuum Regulating Valve (EVRV)

Refer to illustrations 7.19a, 7.19b and 7.20

18   Disconnect the vacuum hoses and the electrical connector from the EVRV.

19   Using an ohmmeter, check the resistance between the two terminals **(see illustrations)**. It should be 33 to 42 ohms.

20   Blow air into port A **(see illustration)** and make sure air comes out of the filter (lower section).

21   Reconnect the electrical connector and ground the ALDL diagnostic terminal **(see illustration 2.6)**.

22   Blow air into port A and make sure air comes out of port B.

23   If the EVRV fails any of these tests, replace it with a new part.

Component replacement

EGR valve

24   When buying a new EGR valve, make sure that you have the right EGR valve. Use the stamped code located on the top of the EGR valve.

25   Detach the cable from the negative terminal of the battery.

26   Remove the air cleaner housing and air intake ducts (see Chapter 4).

27   Detach the vacuum line from the EGR valve.

28   Remove the EGR valve mounting bolts.

29   Remove the EGR valve and gasket from the manifold. Discard the gasket.

30   With a wire wheel or scraper, remove all exhaust deposits from the EGR valve mounting surface on the manifold and, if you plan to

reuse the same valve, the mounting surface of the valve itself. Look for exhaust deposits in the valve outlet. Remove deposit build-up with a screwdriver. **Caution:** *Never wash the valve in solvents or degreaser - both agents will permanently damage the diaphragm. Sand blasting is also not recommended because it will affect the operation of the valve.*

31   If the EGR passage contains an excessive build-up of deposits, clean it out with a wire wheel. Make sure that all loose particles are completely removed to prevent them from clogging the EGR valve or from being ingested into the engine.

32   Installation is the reverse of removal.

Electronic Vacuum Regulator Valve (EVRV)

33   Detach the cable from the negative terminal of the battery.

34   Unplug the electrical connector from the solenoid.

35   Clearly label and detach both vacuum hoses.

36   Remove the solenoid mounting screw and remove the solenoid.

37   Installation is the reverse of removal.

EGR backpressure transducer

38   Detach the cable from the negative terminal of the battery.

39   Remove the air ducts from the intake system (see Chapter 4).

40   Remove the vacuum hoses from the transducer.

41   Remove the bolts and separate the transducer from the brace.

42   Installation is the reverse of removal.

Hoses

43   When replacing hoses, use hose identified with the word *Fluorelastomer*. Use the VECI label as a hose routing guide. For further information regarding hose inspection and service, see Chapter 1.

6

---

8   Evaporative Emission Control System (EECS)

Refer to illustration 8.10

General description

1   This system is designed to trap and store fuel vapors that evaporate from the fuel tank, throttle body and intake manifold.

2   The Evaporative Emission Control System (EECS) consists of a charcoal-filled canister and the lines connecting the canister to the fuel tank, ported vacuum and intake manifold vacuum. **Note:** *1.6L SOHC engines are not equipped with ECM controlled EECS systems. The purge control valve is controlled by manifold vacuum only.*

3   Fuel vapors are transferred from the fuel tank, throttle body and intake manifold to a canister where they are stored when the engine is not operating. When the engine is running, the fuel vapors are purged from the canister by intake air flow and consumed in the normal combustion process.

8.10 Apply vacuum to the control vacuum signal tube and make sure the canister holds vacuum

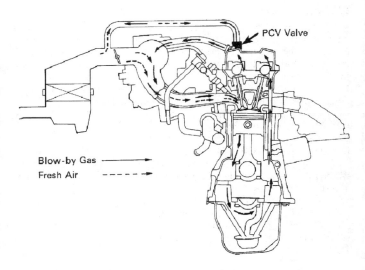

9.1 Gas flow in a typical PCV system

Check

4   Poor idle, stalling and poor driveability can be caused by an inoperative purge valve, a damaged canister, split or cracked hoses or hoses connected to the wrong tubes.

5   Evidence of fuel loss or fuel odor can be caused by fuel leaking from fuel lines or the throttle body, a cracked or damaged canister, an inoperative bowl vent valve, an inoperative purge valve, disconnected, misrouted, kinked, deteriorated or damaged vapor or control hoses or an improperly seated air cleaner or air cleaner gasket.

6   Inspect each hose attached to the canister for kinks, leaks and breaks along its entire length. Repair or replace as necessary.

7   Inspect the canister. If it is cracked or damaged, replace it.

8   Look for fuel leaking from the bottom of the canister. If fuel is leaking, replace the canister and check the hoses and hose routing.

9   Apply a short length of hose to the lower tube of the purge valve assembly and attempt to blow through it. Little or no air should pass into the canister (a small amount of air will pass because the canister has a constant purge hole).

10   With a hand vacuum pump, apply vacuum through the control vacuum signal tube to the purge valve diaphragm **(see illustration)**.

11   If the diaphragm does not hold vacuum for at least 20 seconds, the diaphragm is leaking and the canister must be replaced.

12   If the diaphragm holds vacuum, again try to blow through the hose while vacuum is still being applied. An increased flow of air should be noted. If it isn't, replace the canister.

13   On vehicles equipped with ECM controlled EVRV solenoids (purge valves), check for a voltage signal from the ECM (white/red wire or white/orange wire) on the EVRV solenoid (purge valve) electrical connector.

14   Connect a vacuum gauge on the manifold side of the EVRV (purge valve) and check for vacuum. Verify that there is 10 inches Hg of vacuum available at the EVRV solenoid. If not, check for any damaged hoses or blocked vacuum ports.

Component replacement

15   Clearly label, then detach, all vacuum lines from the canister.

16   Loosen the canister mounting clamp bolt and pull the canister out.

17   Installation is the reverse of removal.

---

9   Positive Crankcase Ventilation (PCV) system

Refer to illustration 9.1

1   To reduce hydrocarbon (HC) emissions, crankcase blow-by gas is routed to the intake manifold for combustion in the cylinders **(see illustration)**.

2   The main components of the PCV system are the PCV valve, a fresh air filtered inlet and the hoses connecting these components with the engine.

3   If abnormal operating conditions arise, the system is designed to allow excessive amounts of blow-by gas to flow back through the crankcase vent tube and into the intake plenum, to be consumed by normal combustion.

4   Checking and replacement of the PCV valve is covered in Chapter 1.

5   Since this system directs the blow-by gas into the plenum and through the throttle body, an oily residue build-up in that area can occur over time. Consequently, it's a good idea to periodically clean this residue from the throttle body. Refer to Chapter 4 for the throttle body cleaning procedure.

---

10   Transmission Converter Clutch (TCC) system (1.8L engine only)

General description

1   The Transmission Converter Clutch (TCC) uses a single solenoid-operated valve in the automatic transmission to mechanically couple the engine flywheel to the output shaft of the transmission through the torque converter. This reduces the slippage losses in the converter, reducing emissions because engine rpm at any given speed is reduced. It also increases fuel economy. The TCC system is only installed on later models equipped with the 1.8L DOHC engine and the JF403E transaxle. Torque converter clutch apply should occur in third gear or overdrive only. Also, the TCC system will not activate until the transaxle fluid temperature has reached approximately 176-degrees F.

2   For the converter clutch to operate properly, two conditions must be met:

a) The engine must be warmed up before the clutch can apply. The engine coolant temperature sensor and the ATF temperature sensor tells the ECM when the engine is at operating temperature.

b) The vehicle must be traveling at the necessary minimum speed to raise the pressure to the level necessary to apply the valve. If the hydraulic pressure is correct, the ECM signals the solenoid(s) to apply the converter clutch. After the converter clutch applies, the ECM uses the information from the TPS to release the clutch when the car is accelerating or decelerating at a certain rate.

3   Another switch used in the TCC circuit is a brake switch which opens the power supply to the TCC solenoid when the brake is applied.

Check

4   If the converter clutch is applied at all times, the engine will stall immediately, just like a manual transmission with the clutch engaged.

6   If the converter clutch does not apply, fuel economy may be lower than expected. If the Vehicle Speed Sensor (VSS) (see Section 4) fails, the TCC will not apply.

7   A TCC-equipped transmission has different operating characteristics than an automatic transmission without TCC. If you detect a "chuggle" or "surge" condition, perform the following check.

9   Connect a tachometer.

10   Drive the vehicle until normal operating temperature is reached, then maintain a 50 to 55 mph speed.

11   Lightly touch the brake pedal and check it for a slight bumpy sensation, indicating that the TCC is releasing. A slight increase in rpm should also be noted.

12   Release the brake and check for reapplication of the converter clutch and a slight decrease in engine rpm.

13   If the TCC fails to perform satisfactorily during this test, take your vehicle to a dealer service department or other repair shop to have the TCC serviced.

11   Catalytic converter

General description

1   The catalytic converter is an emission control device added to the exhaust system to reduce pollutants from the exhaust gas stream. A single-bed converter design is used in combination with a three-way (reduction) catalyst. The catalytic coating on the three-way catalyst contains platinum and rhodium, which lowers the levels of oxides of nitrogen (NOx) as well as hydrocarbons (HC) and carbon monoxide (CO).

Check

2   The test equipment for a catalytic converter is expensive and highly sophisticated. If you suspect that the converter on your vehicle is malfunctioning, take it to a dealer or authorized emissions inspection facility for diagnosis and repair.

3   Whenever the vehicle is raised for servicing of underbody components, check the converter for leaks, corrosion and other damage. If damage is discovered, the converter should be replaced.

4   Although catalytic converters don't break too often, they do become plugged. The easiest way to check for a restricted converter is to use a vacuum gauge to diagnose the effect of a blocked exhaust on intake vacuum.

   a) Open the throttle until the engine speed is about 2000 RPM.
   b) Release the throttle quickly.
   c) If there is no restriction, the gauge will quickly drop to not more than 2 in Hg or more above its normal reading.
   d) If the gauge does not show 5 in Hg or more above its normal reading, or seems to momentarily hover around its highest reading for a moment before it returns, the exhaust system, or the converter, is plugged (or an exhaust pipe is bent or dented, or the core inside the muffler has shifted)

Replacement

5   Because the converter part of the exhaust system, converter replacement requires removal of the exhaust pipe assembly (see Chapter 4). Take the vehicle, or the exhaust system, to a dealer service department or a muffler shop.

6

Notes

Chapter 7 Part A Manual transaxle

Contents

7A

Specifications

Torque specifications   Ft-lbs (unless otherwise indicated)
Transaxle-to-engine bolts.. 55

1 General information

The vehicles covered by this manual are equipped with either a 5-speed manual or a 3- or 4-speed automatic transaxle. Information on the manual transaxle is included in this Part of Chapter 7. Service procedures for the automatic transaxle are contained in Chapter 7, Part B.

The manual transaxle is a compact, two-piece, lightweight aluminum alloy housing containing both the transmission and differential assemblies.

Because of the complexity, unavailability of replacement parts and special tools necessary, internal repair procedures for the manual transaxle are not recommended for the home mechanic. For readers who wish to tackle a transaxle rebuild, a brief *Manual transaxle overhaul - general information* Section is provided. The bulk of information

in this Chapter is devoted to removal and installation, replacement and adjustment procedures.

2 Oil seal replacement

Refer to illustrations 2.4, 2.6, 2.10a, 2.10b and 2.11

1   Oil leaks frequently occur due to wear of the driveaxle seals and/or the speedometer drive gear O-ring. Replacement of these seals is relatively easy, since the repairs can usually be performed without removing the transaxle from the vehicle.

2   The driveaxle seals are located at the sides of the transaxle, where the driveaxles are attached. If leakage at the seal is suspected, raise the vehicle and support it securely on jackstands. If the seal is

2.4 Carefully lever the old seal out of the transaxle with a seal removal tool, a large screwdriver or a pry bar - make sure you don't damage the seal bore

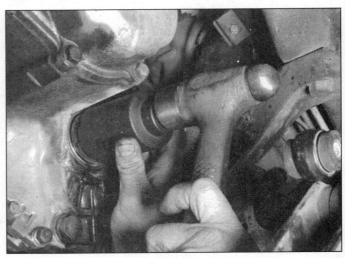

2.6 Using a large section of pipe or a large deep socket as a drift, install the new oil seal - drive it into the bore squarely and make sure that it is completely seated

2.10a Remove the hold-down bolt and clamp (arrows) . . .

2.10b . . . and remove the speedometer pinion gear housing

leaking, lubricant will be found on the side of the transaxle.

3   Remove the driveaxle (see Chapter 8).

4   Using an oil seal removal tool, a screwdriver or a prybar, carefully pry the oil seal out of the transaxle bore **(see illustration)**.

5   If the oil seal cannot be removed with a screwdriver or prybar, a special oil seal removal tool (available at auto parts stores) will be required.

6   Using a large section of pipe or a large deep socket as a drift, install the new oil seal. Drive it into the bore squarely and make sure that it is completely seated **(see illustration)**. Lubricate the lip of the new seal with multi-purpose grease.

7   Install the driveaxle(s). Be careful not to damage the lip of the new seal.

8   The speedometer cable is threaded onto the speedometer pinion gear housing, which is located on top of the differential (the rear portion of the transaxle housing) just to the left of the rear mount. To get at it, you'll need to raise the front of the vehicle and place it securely on jackstands. Look for lubricant around the pinion housing to determine if the O-ring is leaking.

9   Unscrew the threaded fitting that attaches the speedometer cable to the pinion housing and disconnect the cable.

10   Remove the pinion gear housing hold-down bolt and clamp and

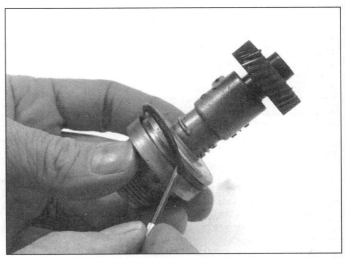

2.11 Using a small screwdriver, remove the old O-ring

3.1 To disconnect the shift cables from the transaxle, remove these clips (arrows), slide the ends of the cables off the selecting levers, pull off the retaining clips and detach the cables from their brackets

3.3a To disconnect the shift cables from the shift lever base, loosen these nuts (arrows)

3.3b Remove this clip (arrow) from the passenger side cable and this nut (arrow) from the clevis bolt underneath the shift lever, then disconnect both shift cables from the shift lever

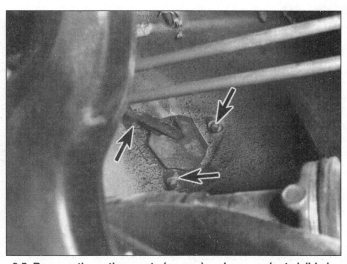

3.5 Remove these three nuts (arrows) and screws (not visible in this photo - the screws must be backed out from inside the vehicle) and detach the cover from the floor

7A

remove the housing **(see illustrations)**.
11   Using a small screwdriver, remove the old O-ring **(see illustration)**.
12   Coat the new O-ring with clean engine oil and install it on the pinion gear housing.
13   Installation is the reverse of removal.

---

3   Shift cables - replacement and adjustment

Refer to illustrations 3.1, 3.3a, 3.3b and 3.5
1   Disconnect the shift cables and retaining clips at the transaxle **(see illustration)**.
2   Remove the console and the shifter boot (see Chapter 11).
3   Disconnect the shift cables from the shift lever base and from the shift lever **(see illustrations)**.
4   Remove the right side sill plate, peel back the carpet on the right side of the floor in front of the passenger seat all the way to the center tunnel and peel back the carpet over the center tunnel.
5   Remove the shift cable cover screws **(see illustration)** and detach the cover from the floor.

6   Remove the shift cables by pulling them through the firewall from the passenger side.
7   Installation is the reverse of removal. Be sure to adjust the cables when you're done.
8   To adjust the shift cables:
   a)   Place the transaxle in Neutral.
   b)   Turn the adjusting nuts on the left (driver's side) cable until the shift lever is at a right angle to the base (vertical), as viewed from the side.
   c)   Turn the adjusting nuts on the right (passenger's side) cable until the shift lever is at a right angle to the base (vertical), as viewed from the rear.
   d)   After the shift lever is adjusted correctly, tighten the adjusting nuts.

---

4   Shift lever - removal and installation

Refer to illustration 4.3
1   Remove the center console.
2   Disconnect the shift cables **(see illustrations 3.3a and 3.3b)**.

4.3 Shift lever base mounting bolts (arrows)

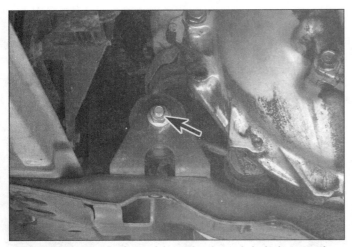

6.16 Remove the nut (arrow) from the through-bolt that attaches the torque rod to the center crossmember bracket, remove the through bolt, pivot the forward end of the torque rod up and slide it off the through-bolt that attaches it to the transaxle (see previous photo)

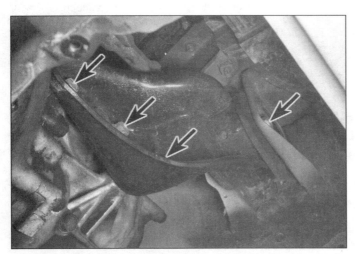

6.18 Remove the three bolts (left arrows) from the front transaxle mounting bracket (the right arrow points to the transaxle mount-to-body through-bolt, which only needs to be unscrewed if the mount is to be replaced)

6.15 Remove the nut (lower left arrow) from the through-bolt that attaches the torque rod to the transaxle, remove the bolts (upper left arrows) from the torque rod-to-block bracket and remove the bracket; to remove the through-bolt, disconnect the forward end of the torque rod (see next photo), then unscrew the through-bolt (lower right arrow)

3   Remove the shift lever base mounting bolts **(see illustration)**.
4   Installation is the reverse of removal.

---

5   Transaxle mount - check and replacement

1   Refer to Chapter 2 Part A, Section 18 for the check and replacement procedure for the torque rod and the engine mounts.
2   The other transaxle mount bolts to the transaxle and has a large circular insulator on the other end, which is attached to a flange on the body and is secured by a through-bolt. Check this mount following the procedure described in Chapter 2A, Section 18.
3   If the mount has to be removed or replaced, support the transaxle with a floor jack and remove the three bolts securing the bracket to the engine, and the through-bolt securing the mount to the body **(see illustration 6.18)**.

---

6   Manual transaxle - removal and installation

Removal

Refer to illustrations 6.15, 6.16, 6.18, 6.19, 6.20, 6.22, 6.23 and 6.24
1   Remove the battery (see Chapter 5).
2   Remove the ignition coil (see Chapter 5) and the battery tray.
3   Remove the air cleaner assembly (see Chapter 4).
4   Clearly label all electrical connections and grounds, then unplug and unbolt them from the transaxle.
5   Disconnect the shift cables (see Section 3).
6   Disconnect the clutch cable (see Chapter 8).
7   Disconnect the speedometer cable (see Section 2).
8   Loosen the front wheel lug nuts, raise the front of the vehicle and place it securely on jackstands. Remove the front wheels.
9   Remove the front under covers.
10   Remove the front exhaust pipe (see Chapter 4).
11   Drain the transaxle fluid.
12   Disconnect the tie-rod ends from the steering knuckles (see Chapter 10).
13   Remove the driveaxles (see Chapter 8).
14   Support the engine with an engine hoist or a floor jack. If you use a floor jack, place the jack under the engine oil pan. Put a block of wood between the jack and the pan to protect the pan from damage.
15   Remove the nut from the through-bolt that attaches the torque rod to the transaxle **(see illustration)**, then remove the bolts from the

6.19 Remove these rear engine mount bolts (arrows) and remove the mount

6.20 Remove these rear stiffener plate bolts (arrows) and remove the stiffener (engine removed for clarity)

6.22 Remove these center crossmember bolts (arrows) from the front lower crossmember and remove the two rear bolts (not visible in this photo)

6.23 Remove these flywheel access cover bolts (arrows) and remove the cover

7A

torque rod-to-block bracket and remove the bracket.

16   Remove the nut from the through-bolt that attaches the torque rod to the center crossmember bracket **(see illustration)**, remove the through bolt, pivot the forward end of the torque rod up and slide it off the through-bolt that attaches it to the transaxle **(see illustration 6.15)**.

17   Loosen the hex on the torque rod-to-transaxle through-bolt **(see illustration 6.15)**. Unscrew and remove the bolt from the transaxle.

18   Remove the three bolts from the front transaxle mounting bracket **(see illustration)**.

19   Remove the rear engine mount **(see illustration)**.

20   Remove the rear stiffener plate **(see illustration)**.

21   Support the transaxle with a jack (preferably a special jack made for this purpose). Safety chains will help steady the transaxle on the jack.

22   Remove the center crossmember **(see illustration)**.

23   Remove the flywheel access cover **(see illustration)**.

24   Remove the transaxle-to-engine bolts **(see illustration)**.

25   Make a final check that all wires and hoses have been disconnected from the transaxle and then move the transaxle and jack toward the side of the vehicle until the transaxle is clear of the engine. Keep the transaxle level as this is done.

26   Pull the transaxle away from the engine. Once the input shaft is clear of the clutch pressure plate, lower the transaxle and remove it from under the vehicle.

6.24 Remove the transaxle-to-engine bolts (arrows) and remove the transaxle from the engine (engine/transaxle assembly removed from the vehicle for clarity)

27   The clutch components can now be inspected (see Chapter 8). In most cases, new clutch components should be routinely installed whenever the transaxle is removed.

Installation

28   If you removed any clutch components, install them (see Chapter 8).

29   With the transaxle secured to the jack as on removal, raise it into position and then carefully slide it forward, engaging the input shaft with the clutch splines. Do not use excessive force to install the transaxle - if the input shaft does not slide into place, readjust the angle of the transaxle so it is level and/or turn the input shaft so the splines engage properly with the clutch.

30   Install the transaxle-to-engine bolts. Tighten the bolts to the torque listed in this Chapter's Specifications. Also install the stiffener plate.

31   Install the transaxle and engine mount nuts and bolts. Tighten all nuts and bolts securely.

32   Install the center crossmember. Tighten all nuts and bolts securely.

33   Remove the jacks supporting the transaxle and the engine.

34   Install the various items removed previously, referring to Chapter 8 for the installation of the driveaxles.

35   Make a final check that all wires, hoses and the speedometer cable have been connected and that the transaxle has been filled with the specified lubricant to the proper level (see Chapter 1). Lower the vehicle.

36   Connect the negative battery cable. Road test the vehicle to check for proper transaxle operation and check for leakage.

7   Manual transaxle overhaul - general information

1   Overhauling a manual transaxle is a difficult job for the do-it-yourselfer. It involves the disassembly and reassembly of many small parts. Numerous clearances must be precisely measured and, if necessary, changed with select-fit spacers and snap-rings. As a result, if transaxle problems arise, it can be removed and installed by a competent do-it-yourselfer, but overhaul should be left to a transmission repair shop. Rebuilt transaxles may be available - check with your dealer parts department and auto parts stores. At any rate, the time and money involved in an overhaul is almost sure to exceed the cost of a rebuilt unit.

2   Nevertheless, it's not impossible for an inexperienced mechanic to rebuild a transaxle if the special tools are available and the job is done in a deliberate step-by-step manner so nothing is overlooked.

3   The tools necessary for an overhaul include internal and external snap-ring pliers, a bearing puller, a slide hammer, a set of pin punches, a dial indicator and possibly a hydraulic press. In addition, a large, sturdy workbench and a vise or transaxle stand will be required.

4   During disassembly of the transaxle, make careful notes of how each piece comes off, where it fits in relation to other pieces and what holds it in place.

5   Before taking the transaxle apart for repair, it will help if you have some idea of what area of the transaxle is malfunctioning. Certain problems can be closely tied to specific areas in the transaxle, which can make component examination and replacement easier. Refer to the *Troubleshooting* section at the front of this manual for information regarding possible sources of trouble.

Chapter 7 Part B Automatic transaxle

Contents

Specifications

Torque specifications

	Ft-lbs
Torque converter-to-driveplate bolts	31
Transaxle-to-engine bolts	31

1   General information

All vehicles covered in this manual come equipped with either a 5-speed manual or a 3- or 4-speed automatic transaxle. All information on the automatic transaxle is included in this Part of Chapter 7. Information for the manual transaxle can be found in Part A of this Chapter.

Because of the complexity of the automatic transaxles covered in this manual and the specialized equipment necessary to perform most service operations, this Chapter contains only those procedures related to general diagnosis, routine maintenance, adjustment and removal and installation.

If the transaxle requires major repair work, it should be left to a dealer service department or an automotive or transmission repair shop. You can, however, remove and install the transaxle yourself and save the expense, even if the repair work is done by a transmission shop.

2   Diagnosis - general

Note: *Automatic transaxle malfunctions may be caused by five general conditions: poor engine performance, improper adjustments, hydraulic malfunctions, mechanical malfunctions or malfunctions in the computer or its signal network. Diagnosis of these problems should always begin with a check of the easily repaired items: fluid level and condition (see Chapter 1), shift linkage adjustment and throttle linkage adjustment. Next, perform a road test to determine if the problem has been corrected or if more diagnosis is necessary. If the problem persists after the preliminary tests and corrections are completed, additional diagnosis should be done by a dealer service department or transmission repair shop. Refer to the* Troubleshooting *section at the front of this manual for information on symptoms of transaxle problems.*

Preliminary checks

1   Drive the vehicle to warm the transaxle to normal operating temperature.
2   Check the fluid level as described in Chapter 1:
   a) If the fluid level is unusually low, add enough fluid to bring the level within the designated area of the dipstick, then check for external leaks (see below).
   b) If the fluid level is abnormally high, drain off the excess, then check the drained fluid for contamination by coolant. The presence of engine coolant in the automatic transmission fluid indicates that a failure has occurred in the internal radiator walls that separate the coolant from the transmission fluid (see Chapter 3).
   c) If the fluid is foaming, drain it and refill the transaxle, then check for coolant in the fluid, or a high fluid level.
3   Check the engine idle speed. **Note:** *If the engine is malfunctioning, do not proceed with the preliminary checks until it has been repaired and runs normally.*
4   Check the throttle valve cable for freedom of movement. Adjust it if necessary (see Section 4). **Note:** *The throttle cable may function properly when the engine is shut off and cold, but it may malfunction once the engine is hot. Check it cold and at normal engine operating temperature.*
5   Inspect the shift control linkage (see Section 3). Make sure that it's properly adjusted and that the linkage operates smoothly.

Fluid leak diagnosis

6   Most fluid leaks are easy to locate visually. Repair usually consists of replacing a seal or gasket. If a leak is difficult to find, the following procedure may help.
7   Identify the fluid. Make sure it's transmission fluid and not engine oil or brake fluid (automatic transmission fluid is a deep red color).
8   Try to pinpoint the source of the leak. Drive the vehicle several miles, then park it over a large sheet of cardboard. After a minute or two, you should be able to locate the leak by determining the source of the fluid dripping onto the cardboard.
9   Make a careful visual inspection of the suspected component and

the area immediately around it. Pay particular attention to gasket mating surfaces. A mirror is often helpful for finding leaks in areas that are hard to see.
10   If the leak still cannot be found, clean the suspected area thoroughly with a degreaser or solvent, then dry it.
11   Drive the vehicle for several miles at normal operating temperature and varying speeds. After driving the vehicle, visually inspect the suspected component again.
12   Once the leak has been located, the cause must be determined before it can be properly repaired. If a gasket is replaced but the sealing flange is bent, the new gasket will not stop the leak. The bent flange must be straightened.
13   Before attempting to repair a leak, check to make sure that the following conditions are corrected or they may cause another leak. **Note:** *Some of the following conditions cannot be fixed without highly specialized tools and expertise. Such problems must be referred to a transmission shop or a dealer service department.*

Gasket leaks

14   Check the pan periodically. Make sure the bolts are tight, no bolts are missing, the gasket is in good condition and the pan is flat (dents in the pan may indicate damage to the valve body inside).
15   If the pan gasket is leaking, the fluid level or the fluid pressure may be too high, the vent may be plugged, the pan bolts may be too tight, the pan sealing flange may be warped, the sealing surface of the transaxle housing may be damaged, the gasket may be damaged or the transaxle casting may be cracked or porous. If sealant instead of gasket material has been used to form a seal between the pan and the transaxle housing, it may be the wrong sealant.

Seal leaks

16   If a transaxle seal is leaking, the fluid level or pressure may be too high, the vent may be plugged, the seal bore may be damaged, the seal itself may be damaged or improperly installed, the surface of the shaft protruding through the seal may be damaged or a loose bearing may be causing excessive shaft movement.
17   Make sure the dipstick tube seal is in good condition and the tube is properly seated. Periodically check the area around the speedometer gear or sensor for leakage. If transmission fluid is evident, check the O-ring for damage.

Case leaks

18   If the case itself appears to be leaking, the casting is porous and will have to be repaired or replaced.
19   Make sure the oil cooler hose fittings are tight and in good condition.

Fluid comes out vent pipe or fill tube

20   If this condition occurs, the transaxle is overfilled, there is coolant in the fluid, the case is porous, the dipstick is incorrect, the vent is plugged or the drain-back holes are plugged.

3   Shift lever - removal and installation

1   Remove the ashtray (see Chapter 11).
2   Remove the shifter trim bezel (see Chapter 11).
3   Remove the heater control knobs (see Chapter 3).
4   Remove the radio bezel (see Chapter 11).
5   Remove the two retaining screws from the shift lever knob and pull the knob off the shift lever.
6   Remove the six lower console retaining screws (see Chapter 11) and lift up the console far enough to unplug the electrical connector for the economy switch, if equipped. Remove the console.
7   Remove the four shift indicator retaining screws and remove the indicator.
8   Disconnect the park/lock cable from the shift lever (see Section 5).
9   Remove the shift lock-out module (1990 and 1991 models) or the shift lock control module (1992 and 1993 models) from the shift lever and unplug the electrical connectors.

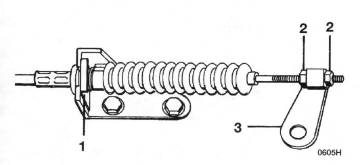

4.5 On 1990 and 1991 models, remove the C-clip (1) from the bracket on the transaxle, loosen the adjustment nut and locknut (2) on the shift lever at the transaxle (3) and disconnect the shift control cable from the shift lever (later models use a slightly different arrangement for attaching the cable to the lever)

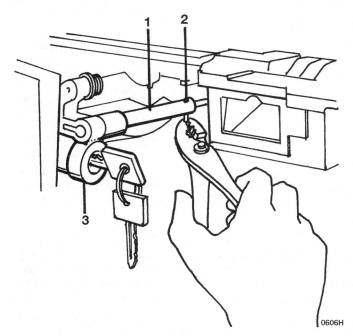

5.10 Remove the roll pin (1) from the park/lock cable (2) at the ignition switch (3)

10   Disconnect the shift control cable from the shift lever (see Section 4).
11   Remove the shift lever mounting bolts and remove the shift lever assembly.
12   Remove the solenoid and switch assembly from the shift lever.
13   Installation is the reverse of removal. Be sure to adjust the shift control cable (see Section 4) and the park/lock cable (see Section 5).

4   Shift control cable - replacement and adjustment

Replacement
Refer to illustration 4.5
1   Refer to Steps 1 through 7 in Section 3.
2   Disconnect the shift control cable from the shift lever and from the bracket on the shift lever base.
3   Remove the three bolts for the cable grommet cover in the tunnel (see Section 3 in Chapter 7 Part A) and remove the cover and grommet.
4   Remove the intake air duct, the air breather tube and the air cleaner assembly (see Chapter 4).
5   On 1990 and 1991 models, remove the C-clip from the bracket on the transaxle, remove the nut from the selector lever on the transaxle and disconnect the shift control cable from the shift lever on the transaxle **(see illustration)**. 1992 and 1993 models use a slightly different setup to attach the cable to the transaxle shift lever.
6   Remove the shift lever assembly mounting bolts (see Section 3), pull the shift lever assembly rearward and remove the cable by pulling it through the bulkhead.
7   Installation is the reverse of removal. Be sure to adjust the shift control (select) cable before you install the air cleaner assembly, air breather tube and intake air duct.

Adjustment
8   Turn the ignition key to the Lock position.
9   Put the shift lever in the Park position.
10   Loosen the adjuster nuts (1990 and 1991 models) or nut (1992 and 1993 models) at the shift lever on the transaxle.
11   Verifty that the shift lever on the transaxle is in the Park position.
12   On 1990 and 1991 models, pull the cable forward and tighten the forward adjuster nut until it contacts the shift lever on the transaxle, then tighten the rear nut until it contacts the shift lever.
13   If the shift lever on the transaxle isn't in the Park position on 1992 and 1993 models, rotate the lever clockwise until it's in the Park position and tighten the adjustment nut.
14   The remainder of installation is the reverse of removal (see Chapter 4).

5   Park/lock cable - check, replacement and adjustment

Note: *This cable prevents the ignition key from being turned to Lock in any shift lever position other than Park, and prevents the shift lever from being moved out of the Park position when the key is in the Lock position.*

Check
1   With the shift lever in the Park position, you should be able to turn the ignition key to the Lock position.
2   With the ignition key in the Lock position, you should not be able to move the shift lever out of the Park position.
3   With the ignition key in the Acc or the Run position, and with the shift lever in any range other than the Park position, you should not be able to turn the ignition key to the Lock position. The shift lever must be in the Park position for the ignition key to turn to the Lock position.
4   If any of the above conditions are incorrect, you should adjust or, if necessary, replace the park/lock cable.

Replacement
5   Refer to Steps 1 through 7 in Section 3.

1990 and 1991 models
Refer to illustration 5.10
6   Remove the left switch panel and cigarette lighter panel (see Chapter 11).
7   Remove the hood release handle.
8   Remove the lower dash and lower steering column trim (see Chapter 11).
9   Disconnect the park/lock cable from the shift lever.
10   Remove the roll pin from the park/lock cable at the ignition switch **(see illustration)**.
11   Detach the park/lock cable from its retaining bracket.
12   Remove the park/lock cable.
13   Installation is the reverse of removal. But after you've attached the new cable - and before you put any of the trim pieces back on - be sure to adjust the cable (see below).
14   After the cable is adjusted, the remainder of installation is the reverse of removal.

7B

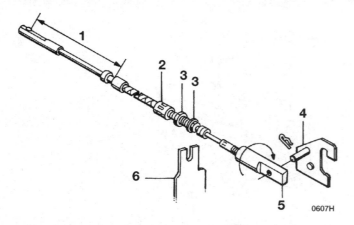

5.28 To adjust the park/lock cable on 1992 and 1993 models, turn the cable eye end clockwise until it reaches the end face of the park/lock cable threads, turn the eye end counterclockwise 1/2 to 1 full turn, then turn the park/lock cable adjustment nuts so that the cable length at the ignition switch end is 2-11/16 inches

1	Park/lock cable	5	Cable eye end
2	Cable adjustment nuts	6	Cable length at the
3	Cable bracket on		ignition switch end
	shift lever		of cable
4	Park/lock cable cam		

1992 and 1993 models

15   Remove the four shift indicator retaining screws and the shift indicator from the shift lever.
16   Pry off the switch bezel from the instrument panel with a small screwdriver and unplug the electrical connectors from the switches (see Chapter 11).
17   Pry off the cigarette lighter bezel from the instrument panel and unplug the cigarette lighter electrical connector (see Chapter 11).
18   Remove the hood latch release handle screws and detach the handle from the hood latch release cable.
19   Remove the knee bolster (see Chapter 11).
20   Remove the steering column covers (see Chapter 12).
21   Remove the roll pin and the park/lock cable from the ignition switch **(see illustration 5.10)**.
22   Loosen the park/lock cable adjustment nuts at the shift lever bracket.
23   Remove the retaining clip and disconnect the park/lock cable from the park/lock cable cam at the shift lever.
24   Detach the park/lock cable from the shift lever bracket and remove the cable from under the instrument panel.

Adjustment

Refer to illustration 5.28
25   Place the shift lever in Park.
26   Turn the ignitition key to the Lock position.
27   On 1990 and 1991 models, pull the park/lock cable forward at the shift lever bracket and tighten the forward adjuster nut until it contacts the bracket, then tighten the rear nut until it contacts the shift lever bracket and tighten both adjuster nuts.
28   On 1992 and 1993 models, turn the eye end (the shift lever end) of the park/lock cable clockwise until it reaches the end face of the park/lock cable threads. Then turn the eye end in (counterclockwise) 1/2 to 1 turn. Turn the park/lock cable adjustment nuts until the cable length at the ignition switch end is 2-11/16 inches **(see illustration)**.

6   Shift lock solenoid - check and replacement

Check

1   When an ignition "On" signal and a "Park" signal are received by

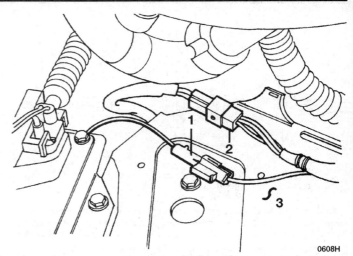

7.3 The electrical connectors for the neutral safety switch (1) and the kickdown solenoid (2) are located under the battery tray (3) on three-speed models

the shift lock control module, the module energizes the shift lock solenoid, which locks the shift lever button, which in turn locks the shift lever in the "P" position. The shift lock control module de-energizes the shift lock solenoid whenever a "Brake" signal is received, at which time the shift lever button is released and the shift lever is free to move out of the "P" position.
2   Checking the operation of the module is beyond the scope of the home mechanic. However, checking the operation of the solenoid is easy.
3   To gain access to the solenoid, refer to Steps 1 through 6 in Section 3.
4   Unplug the electrical connector to the solenoid and apply battery voltage to the connector terminals. If the solenoid clicks, it's working; if it doesn't, it's defective.

Replacement

5   Simply remove the two solenoid mounting screws and remove the solenoid. Installation is the reverse of removal.

7   Neutral safety switch - check, replacement and adjustment

Check

Refer to illustration 7.3
1   Verify the engine starts in the Park and Neutral positions.
2   Verify that the back-up light is on when the shift control lever is in the Reverse position.
3   If the neutral safety switch isn't operating correctly, unplug the electrical connector for the switch **(see illustration)** and check the continuity between each terminal:
   a) In the Park position, there should be continuity between terminals A and B, but no continuity between terminals C and D.
   b) In the Reverse position, there should be no continuity between terminals A and B, but there should be continuity between terminals C and D.
   c) In the Neutral position, there should be continuity between terminals A and B, but no continuity between terminals C and D.
4   If the switch checks out, inspect the electrical wiring and connectors to and from the switch; if it doesn't check out, replace it.

Replacement

Three-speed models

5   Detach the cable from the negative battery terminal.
6   Remove the battery (see Chapter 5).
7   Unplug the electrical connector for the switch at the left fender

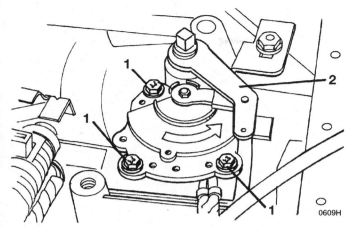

7.18 To remove the neutral safety switch on four-speed models, rotate the manual shift shaft lever (1) counterclockwise until the manual shift shaft is in the first gear position, then remove the three retaining bolts (2)

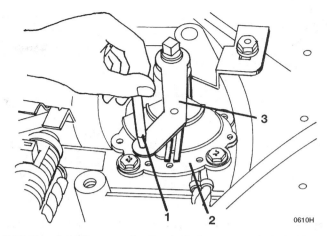

7.22 To adjust the neutral safety switch on four-speed models, insert a drift punch (1) into the adjustment holes in the switch (2) and the switch lever (3)

(1990 and 1991 models) or underneath the right side of the battery tray (1992 and 1993 models).

8   Raise the vehicle and place it securely on jackstands.

9   Remove the six splash shield screws and remove the splash shield.

10   Unscrew and remove the switch.

11   Installation is the reverse of removal. Be sure to apply Loctite pipe sealant (GM part no. 1052080) or the equivalent to the threaded portion of the new switch.

12   After installation is completed, check the new switch as follows: Apply the parking brake and block the wheels. Place the shift lever in the Park position, turn the ignition key to the Start position and verify that the starter motor operates. Stop the engine and turn the ignition key to the On position. Move the shift lever from the Park position to the Neutral position, turn the ignition key to the Start position and verify that the starter motor operates. Finally, verify that the starter motor DOES NOT operate in "D," "2," "L" or "R."

Four-speed models

Refer to illustration 7.18

13   Detach the cable from the negative battery terminal.

14   Remove the intake air duct, the air breather tube and the air cleaner assembly (see Chapter 4).

15   Disconnect the shift control cable from the transaxle shift lever (see Section 3).

16   Unplug the electrical connectors for the switch.

17   Remove the manual shift shaft nut and remove the transaxle shift lever.

18   Rotate the manual shift shaft lever counterclockwise until the manual shift shaft is in the first gear position **(see illustration)**.

19   Remove the three neutral safety switch retaining screws and remove the switch. Installation is the reverse of removal

Adjustment (four-speed models only)

Refer to illustration 7.22

20   Align the manual shift shaft lever pin with the slot provided in the switch lever and install the three switch retaining screws. Don't tighten the screws until the switch is adjusted.

21   Rotate the manual shift shaft lever clockwise until the manual shift shaft is in the Neutral position.

22   Insert a small drift punch or a piece of wire into the adjustment holes in the switch and the switch lever **(see illustration)**.

23   Tighten the switch retaining screws to the torque listed in this Chapter's Specifications.

24   The remainder of installation is the reverse of removal.

8   Kickdown switch and solenoid (three-speed models) - check, adjustment and replacement

Check and adjustment

1   While driving the vehicle at cruising speeds (NOT wide open throttle), with the shift lever in the "D" range, verify that the 3-2 and 2-1 downshifts occur within the specified range: The 3-2 downshift should occur between 12 and 18 mph; the 2-1 downshift should occur between 7 and 12 mph. If the downshifts occur, but not at the specified vehicle speeds, take the vehicle to a dealer service department or other repair shop; diagnosis is beyond the scope of the home mechanic. If the downshifts don't occur at all, perform the following diagnostic procedure:

2   Check the fuses (see Chapter 12).

3   Turn the ignition switch to On. Using a digital multimeter, check for voltage in the kickdown solenoid switch (black and yellow) wire at the connector (don't unplug the connector - insert the meter probes through the backside of the connector). If no voltage is present, repair the open(s) in the black and yellow wire between the junction block and the kickdown switch.

4   Slowly depress the accelerator pedal with your hand. If you don't hear a click, hold the pedal down and readjust the switch by loosening the locknut and rotating it in a clockwise direction until you hear a click. Rotate the switch an extra one-half turn clockwise, past the point at which you heard the click. Retighten the locknut. If you can't get the switch to click by adjusting it, replace the switch.

5   If you hear a clicking sound as the pedal approaches the wide-open throttle position, proceed to the next Step.

6   Check for voltage in the kickdown solenoid (blue and white) wire with your multimeter with the accelerator pedal pressed to the wide-open throttle position (don't unplug the connector - insert the meter probes through the backside of the connector). If no voltage is present, repair the open(s) in the blue and white wire between the kickdown switch and the kickdown solenoid. If voltage is present, proceed to the next Step.

7   Unplug the kickdown solenoid connector, hook up your multimeter between the solenoid terminal and ground and measure resistance. If the resistance isn't between 3.2 and 3.7 ohms, replace the kickdown solenoid; if the resistance is within this range, the downshift system is operating properly. Further diagnosis is beyond the scope of the home mechanic. Take the vehicle to a dealer and have it professionally diagnosed.

Replacement

Switch

8   Disconnect the cable from the negative battery terminal.

7B

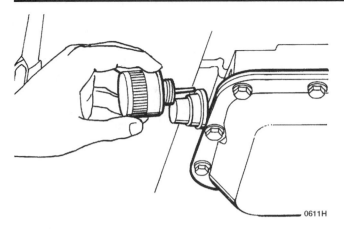

8.17 To remove the kickdown solenoid from the transaxle, simply unscrew it

9   Unplug the electrical connector for the kickdown switch, which is located on the upper end of the accelerator pedal.
10   Loosen the kickdown switch locknuts.
11   Turn the switch counterclockwise to unscrew and remove it from its mounting bracket.
12   Installation is the reverse of removal. Make sure you screw in the switch until you hear a click, then rotate it another half turn.

Solenoid

Refer to illustration 8.17
13   Remove the battery (see Chapter 5).
14   Unplug the electrical connector for the solenoid **(see illustration 7.3)**.
15   Raise the vehicle and place it securely on jackstands.
16   Remove the six splash shield retaining screws and remove the left splash shield.
17   Unscrew and remove the kickdown solenoid **(see illustration)**.
18   Inspect the O-ring for cracks, tears or other damage. If it's damaged or otherwise deteriorated, replace it.
19   Installation is the reverse of removal.

---

9   Automatic transaxle - removal and installation

Removal

1   Remove the battery (see Chapter 5).
2   Remove the intake air tube, air breather tube and air cleaner assembly (see Chapter 4).
3   Mark and disconnect all electrical connectors attached to the transaxle.
4   Disconnect the shift control cable from the shift lever on the transaxle and detach the cable from all brackets on the transaxle (see Section 3). Disconnect the park/lock cable (see Section 4).
5   Disconnect the breather hose from the vent pipe on top of the transaxle.
6   Disconnect the speedometer cable from the transaxle.
7   Remove the left transaxle mount through-bolt.
8   Remove the four upper transaxle-to-engine bolts from the transaxle.
9   Loosen the front wheel lug nuts, raise the vehicle and support it securely on jackstands. Remove the front wheels and remove both splash shields.
10   Drain the transaxle fluid (see Chapter 1).
11   Remove both driveaxles (see Chapter 8).
12   Remove the front transaxle mount through-bolt.
13   Remove the damper from the rear mount through-bolt.
14   Remove the rear transaxle mount through-bolt.
15   Remove the two front center crossmember mounting bolts.

16   Remove the front portion of the exhaust pipe (the part between the exhaust manifold and the rear part of the exhaust pipe) (see Chapter 4).
17   Remove the two rear center crossmember mounting bolts and remove the center crossmember.
18   Remove the starter motor (see Chapter 5).
19   Support the engine using a hoist from above or a 4x4 wood post across the engine compartment, or a jack and a block of wood under the oil pan to spread the load.
20   Support the transaxle with a jack - preferably a special jack made for this purpose. Safety chains will help steady the transaxle on the jack. If you use a floor jack, be sure to use a block of wood between the jack head and the transaxle pan to protect the pan and valve body from damage.
21   Remove the rear mount-to-transaxle case bolt.
22   Remove the front mount retaining bolt.
23   Remove the front mount bracket from the engine.
24   Remove the torque converter cover.
25   Mark the relationship of the torque converter to the driveplate so they can be installed in the same position.
26   Remove the torque converter-to-driveplate bolts. Turn the crankshaft for access to each one in turn.
27   Disconnect the oil cooler lines from the transaxle. Plug the lines to prevent leaks and to prevent contaminants from entering the lines.
28   Remove the two rear mount transaxle bolts.
29   Remove any other chassis or suspension components which will interfere with transaxle removal.
30   Remove the rest of the bolts securing the transaxle to the engine.
31   Lower the transaxle slightly, then disconnect and plug the transaxle cooler lines if you haven't already done so.
32   Remove the transaxle fluid filler tube if it gets in the way.
33   Move the transaxle to the side to disengage it from the engine block dowel pins and make sure the torque converter is detached from the driveplate. Secure the torque converter to the transaxle so that it will not fall out during removal. Lower the transaxle from the vehicle.

Installation

34   Make sure that the torque converter hub is securely engaged in the pump prior to installation. Rotate the converter while pushing it in to confirm this.
35   With the transaxle secured to the jack, raise it into position. Be sure to keep it level so the torque converter does not slide forward. Connect the cooler lines.
36   Move the transaxle carefully into place until the dowel pins are engaged and the torque converter is engaged.
37   Turn the torque converter to line up the bolt holes with the holes in the driveplate. The match marks on the torque converter and driveplate, made during step 5, must also be in alignment.
38   Install the transaxle-to-engine bolts and nuts. Tighten the bolts and nuts to the torque listed in this Chapter's Specifications.
39   Install the torque converter-to-driveplate bolts. Tighten the bolts to the torque listed in this Chapter's Specifications.
40   Install any suspension and chassis components which were removed. Tighten the bolts and nuts to the torque values listed in the Chapter 10 Specifications section.
41   Remove the jacks supporting the transaxle and the engine.
42   Install the fluid filler tube, if you removed it.
43   Install the starter (see Chapter 5).
44   Connect the vacuum hose(s).
45   Connect the shift control and park/lock cables (see Sections 4 and 5).
46   Plug in the transaxle electrical connectors.
47   Install the torque converter cover.
48   Connect the driveaxles to the transaxle (see Chapter 8).
49   Connect the speedometer cable.
50   Adjust the shift control and park/lock cables (see Sections 3 and 4).
51   Install any exhaust system components which were removed.
52   Lower the vehicle.
53   Fill the transaxle (see Chapter 1). Run the vehicle and check for fluid leaks.

Chapter 8   Clutch and driveaxles

Contents

Specifications

Clutch

Pedal freeplay	See Chapter 1
Pedal height	See Chapter 1

Torque specifications

	Ft-lbs
Clutch pressure plate-to-flywheel bolts	13
Driveaxle/hub nut	137
Intermediate shaft bracket bolts	30
Wheel lug nuts	See Chapter 1

---

1   General information

The information in this Chapter deals with the components from the rear of the engine to the front wheels, except for the transaxle, which is dealt with in Chapter 7A and 7B. For the purposes of this Chapter, these components are grouped into two categories: Clutch and driveaxles. Separate Sections within this Chapter offer general descriptions and checking procedures for both groups.

Since nearly all the procedures covered in this Chapter involve working under the vehicle, make sure it's securely supported on sturdy jackstands or a hoist where the vehicle can be easily raised and lowered.

8

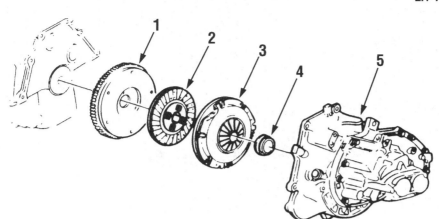

2.1 An exploded view of the clutch assembly

1 *Flywheel*
2 *Clutch disc*
3 *Pressure plate*
4 *Release bearing*
5 *Transaxle*

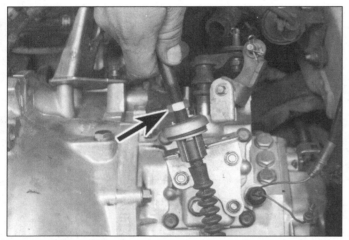

3.1 Pull back on the clutch cable housing and loosen the adjustment nut (arrow), detach the cable end from the release lever, then remove the cable from its bracket

2 Clutch - description and check

Refer to illustration 2.1

1   All vehicles with a manual transaxle use a single dry plate, diaphragm spring type clutch **(see illustration)**. The clutch disc has a splined hub which allows it to slide along the splines of the transaxle input shaft. The clutch and pressure plate are held in contact by spring pressure exerted by the diaphragm in the pressure plate.

2   The clutch release system is cable-actuated. The system consists of the clutch pedal, the cable, a clutch release lever and the clutch release (or throw-out) bearing.

3   When pressure is applied to the clutch pedal to release the clutch, the cable moves the release lever, which pivots, moving the release bearing. The bearing pushes against the fingers of the diaphragm spring of the pressure plate assembly, which in turn releases the clutch plate.

4   Terminology can be a problem regarding the clutch components because common names have in some cases changed from that used by the manufacturer. For example, the driven plate is also called the clutch plate or disc, the pressure plate assembly is sometimes referred to as the clutch cover, the clutch release bearing is sometimes called a throw-out bearing, and so on.

5   Other than replacing components that have obvious damage, some preliminary checks should be performed to diagnose a clutch

system failure.

a)   To check "clutch spin down time," run the engine at normal idle speed with the transaxle in Neutral (clutch pedal up - engaged). Disengage the clutch (pedal down), wait several seconds and shift the transaxle into Reverse. No grinding noise should be heard. A grinding noise would most likely indicate a problem in the pressure plate or the clutch disc.

b)   To check for complete clutch release, run the engine (with the parking brake applied to prevent movement) and hold the clutch pedal approximately 1/2-inch from the floor. Shift the transaxle between 1st gear and Reverse several times. If the shift is not smooth, component failure is indicated.

c)   Visually inspect the clutch pedal bushing at the top of the clutch pedal to make sure there is no sticking or excessive wear.

3 Clutch cable - removal and installation

Refer to illustration 3.1

1   Pull back on the clutch cable housing and loosen the adjustment nut **(see illustration)**.

2   Detach the cable from the release arm, then pull the cable housing out of the bracket.

3   Remove the cable retaining bolt at the clutch pedal.

4   Remove the cable by pulling it through the hole in the firewall.

5   Installation is the reverse of removal. Make sure the rubber grommet is securely seated in the hole in the firewall.

6   When you're done, refer to Chapter 1 and adjust the cable.

4 Clutch release bearing and lever - removal, inspection and installation

Warning: *Dust produced by clutch wear and deposited on clutch components may contain asbestos, which is hazardous to your health. DO NOT blow it out with compressed air and DO NOT inhale it. DO NOT use gasoline or petroleum-based solvents to remove the dust. Brake system cleaner should be used to flush it into a drain pan. After the clutch components are wiped clean with a rag, dispose of the contaminated rags and cleaner in a labeled, covered container.*

Removal

Refer to illustrations 4.3a, 4.3b and 4.3c

1   Disconnect the negative cable from the battery.

2   Remove the transaxle (see Chapter 7 Part A).

3   Remove the retaining spring from the clutch fork and slide the release bearing off the transaxle front bearing retainer **(see illustrations)**.

4.3a Pry the retaining spring from the clutch release fork, . . .

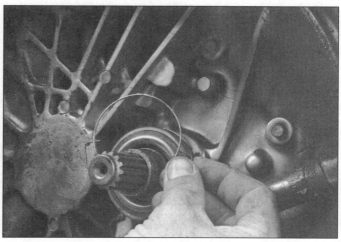

4.3b . . . remove the spring . . .

4.3c . . . and remove the release bearing from the transaxle front bearing retainer

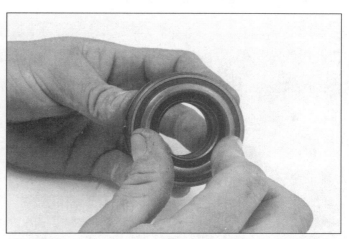

4.4 Hold the bearing by the outer race and rotate the inner race while applying pressure - if the bearing doesn't turn smoothly or if it's noisy, replace it

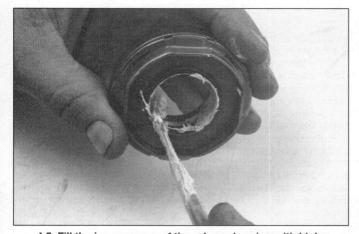

4.5 Fill the inner groove of the release bearing with high-temperature grease (also apply a light coat of the same grease to the transaxle input shaft splines and the front bearing retainer)

Inspection

Refer to illustration 4.4

4   Hold the bearing by the outer race and rotate the inner race while applying pressure **(see illustration)**. If the bearing doesn't turn

smoothly or if it's noisy, replace the bearing/hub assembly with a new one. Wipe the bearing with a clean rag and inspect it for damage, wear and cracks. Don't immerse the bearing in solvent - it's sealed for life and to do so would ruin it. Also check the release lever and fork for cracks and bends.

Installation

Refer to illustrations 4.5, 4.6 and 4.7

5   Fill the inner groove of the release bearing with high-temperature grease. Also apply a light coat of the same grease to the transaxle front bearing retainer **(see illustration)** and the input shaft splines.

6   Install the release bearing on the input shaft sleeve. Make sure the bearing pads are aligned with the fork ends **(see illustration)**.

7   Insert the ends of the retaining spring into the clutch fork holes **(see illustration)**. Make sure the spring seats in the groove of the bearing and the ends of the spring are properly engaged with the forks.

8   Apply a light coat of high-temperature grease to the face of the release bearing where it contacts the pressure plate diaphragm fingers.

9   The remainder of installation is the reverse of the removal procedure.

---

5   Clutch components - removal, inspection and installation

Warning: *Dust produced by clutch wear and deposited on clutch components may contain asbestos, which is hazardous to your health. DO*

8

4.6 Make sure the flats (arrows) on the clutch release bearing are aligned with the ends of the clutch release forks

4.7 Make sure the ends of the spring are inserted into the holes in the fork ends and the spring is properly engaged with the fork ends

5.6 If you're going to reuse the same pressure plate, look for alignment marks between the pressure plate and the flywheel - if there aren't any, make your own so they'll be in the same relationship to each other after reassembly

5.7 Clutch pressure plate-to-flywheel bolts (arrows)

NOT blow it out with compressed air and DO NOT inhale it. DO NOT use gasoline or petroleum-based solvents to remove the dust. Brake system cleaner should be used to flush the dust into a drain pan. After the clutch components are wiped clean with a rag, dispose of the contaminated rags and cleaner in a labeled, covered container.

Removal

Refer to illustrations 5.6 and 5.7

1 Access to the clutch components is normally accomplished by removing the transaxle, leaving the engine in the vehicle. If, of course, the engine is being removed for major overhaul, then the opportunity should always be taken to check the clutch for wear and replace worn components as necessary. However, the relatively low cost of the clutch components compared to the time and labor involved in gaining access to them warrants their replacement any time the engine or transaxle is removed, unless they are new or in near-perfect condition. The following procedures assume that the engine will stay in place.

2 Disconnect the clutch cable (see Section 3).

3 Remove the transaxle from the vehicle (see Chapter 7, Part A). Support the engine while the transaxle is out. Preferably, an engine hoist should be used to support it from above. However, if a jack is used underneath the engine, make sure a piece of wood is used between the jack and oil pan to spread the load. **Caution:** *The pick-up for*

the oil pump is very close to the bottom of the oil pan. If the pan is bent or distorted in any way, engine oil starvation could occur.

4 The clutch release fork and release bearing can remain attached to the transaxle for the time being.

5 To support the clutch disc during removal, install a clutch alignment tool through the clutch disc hub.

6 Carefully inspect the flywheel and pressure plate for indexing marks. The marks are usually an X, an O or a white letter. If they cannot be found, scribe marks yourself so the pressure plate and the flywheel will be in the same alignment during installation **(see illustration)**.

7 Slowly loosen the pressure plate-to-flywheel bolts **(see illustration)**. Work in a diagonal pattern and loosen each bolt a little at a time until all spring pressure is relieved. Then hold the pressure plate securely and completely remove the bolts, followed by the pressure plate and clutch disc.

Inspection

Refer to illustrations 5.10, 5.12a and 5.12b

8 Ordinarily, when a problem occurs in the clutch, it can be attributed to wear of the clutch driven plate assembly (clutch disc). However, all components should be inspected at this time.

9 Inspect the flywheel for cracks, heat checking, score marks and other damage. If the imperfections are slight, a machine shop can resurface it to make it flat and smooth. Refer to Chapter 2A for the flywheel removal procedure.

5.10 Inspect the lining on the clutch disc for evidence of excessive wear, such as smeared friction material, chewed-up rivets, worn hub splines and distorted damper cushions or springs

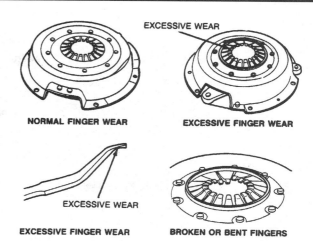

5.12a Replace the pressure plate if any of these conditions are noted

5.12b Inspect the pressure plate friction surface for score marks, cracks and evidence of overheating

5.14 Center the clutch disc in the pressure plate with a clutch alignment tool

10   Inspect the lining on the clutch disc. There should be at least 1/16-inch of lining above the rivet heads. Check for loose rivets, distortion, cracks, broken springs and other obvious damage **(see illustration)**. As mentioned above, ordinarily the clutch disc is replaced as a matter of course, so if in doubt about its condition, replace it with a new one.

11   The release bearing should be replaced along with the clutch disc (see Section 4).

12   Check the machined surface and the diaphragm spring fingers of the pressure plate **(see illustrations)**. If the surface is grooved or otherwise damaged, replace the pressure plate assembly. Also check for obvious damage, distortion, cracking, etc. Light glazing can be removed with emery cloth or sandpaper. If a new pressure plate is indicated, new or factory rebuilt units are available.

Installation

Refer to illustration 5.14

13   Before installation, carefully wipe the flywheel and pressure plate machined surfaces clean with brake system cleaner. It's important that no oil or grease is on these surfaces or the lining of the clutch disc. Handle these parts only with clean hands.

14   Position the clutch disc and pressure plate against the flywheel, with the clutch disc held in place with an alignment tool **(see illustration)**. Make sure it's installed properly (most replacement clutch plates will be marked "flywheel side" or something similar - if not marked, in-

stall the clutch disc with the damper springs or cushions toward the transaxle).

15   Tighten the pressure plate-to-flywheel bolts only finger tight, working around the pressure plate.

16   Center the clutch disc by ensuring the alignment tool is through the splined hub and into the recess in the crankshaft. Wiggle the tool up, down or side-to-side as needed to bottom the tool. Tighten the pressure plate-to-flywheel bolts a little at a time, working in a criss-cross pattern to prevent distortion of the cover. After all of the bolts are snug, tighten them to the torque listed in this Chapter's Specifications. Remove the alignment tool.

17   Using high-temperature grease, lubricate the inner groove of the release bearing (see Section 4). Also place a light coat of grease on the release lever contact areas, the input shaft splines and the input shaft bearing retainer.

18   Install the clutch release bearing (see Section 4).

19   Install the transaxle and all components removed previously, tightening all fasteners to the proper torque specifications.

6   Clutch start switch - check, replacement and adjustment

Check

1   Before checking the clutch start switch for correct operation, make sure the clutch cable is properly adjusted (see Chapter 1).

8

2   Verify that the engine will not start when the clutch pedal is released.

3   Verify that the engine will start when the clutch pedal is depressed all the way.

4   If the engine won't start with the pedal depressed, or starts with the pedal released, unplug the electrical connector to the switch (located near the top of the clutch pedal) and check continuity between the connector terminals with the clutch pedal depressed.

5   If there's continuity between the terminals with the pedal depressed, the switch is okay but needs to be adjusted (see below); if there's no continuity between the terminals with the pedal depressed, replace the switch. If there's continuity between the terminals when the clutch pedal is released, replace the switch.

Replacement

Adjustable switch

6   Unplug the switch electrical connector, if you haven't already done so.

7   Remove the front locknut, if equipped.

8   Remove the switch from its bracket.

9   Remove the rear locknut and remove the switch .

10   Installation is the reverse of removal.

Non-adjustable switch

11   The non-adjustable switch is mounted vertically at the upper end of the clutch pedal lever, just like a conventional adjustable switch. However, the plunger is attached to the top of the clutch pedal lever by a clevis arrangement.

12   Unplug the switch electrical connector, if you haven't already done so.

13   Remove the mounting bolt to the right of the switch.

14   Disengage the plunger from the clutch pedal lever.

15   Remove the switch.

16   Installation is the reverse of removal.

Adjustment

Note: *Some clutch switches are not adjustable. If the switch on your vehicle isn't adjustable (i.e. has no locknut and threaded adjuster sleeve to adjust plunger length) and it doesn't work as described in Step 5, replace it.*

17   Adjust clutch pedal freeplay (see Chapter 1).

18   Loosen the locknut and screw the switch in or out until continuity is as described in Steps 4 and 5. Tighten the locknut.

---

7   Driveaxles - general information and inspection

---

1   Power is transmitted from the transaxle to the wheels through a pair of driveaxles. The inner end of each driveaxle is splined to the differential side gears. The driveaxles can be pulled out to replace the oil seals (see Chapter 7A). The outer ends of the driveaxles are splined to the front hubs and locked in place by a large nut.

2   Each driveaxle assembly consists of an inner and outer constant velocity (CV) joint connected together by an axleshaft. The inner ends of the driveaxles are equipped with either a tri-pot or a double-offset (ball-and-cage) type CV joint, depending on the engine/transaxle combination. Double-offset CV joints are used on models equipped with a manual transaxle; tri-pots are used on models with an automatic transaxle. Either design is capable of both angular and axial motion. In other words, the inner CV joints are free to slide in-and-out as the driveaxle moves up-and-down with the wheel. These joints can be disassembled and cleaned in the event of a boot failure, but if any parts are damaged, the joints must be replaced as a unit (see Section 10).

3   The outer CV joints on all models, a ball-and-socket design, are also capable of angular - but not axial - movement. These joints can also be cleaned and repacked if an outer boot is torn, but they're not serviceable.

4   The boots should be inspected periodically for damage and leaking lubricant. Torn CV joint boots must be replaced immediately or the CV joints can be damaged. Boot replacement involves removal of the

8.2 Unstake the driveaxle hub nut before attempting to loosen it

8.3 To prevent the hub from turning while you're loosening the driveaxle hub nut, wedge a prybar between two of the wheel studs and allow the prybar to rest against the ground or the floorpan of the vehicle

driveaxle (see Section 8). **Note:** *Some auto parts stores carry "split" type replacement boots, which can be installed without removing the driveaxle from the vehicle. This is a convenient alternative; however, the driveaxle should be removed and the CV joint disassembled and cleaned to ensure the joint is free from contaminants such as moisture and dirt which will accelerate CV joint wear.* The most common symptom of worn or damaged CV joints, besides lubricant leaks, is a clicking noise in turns, a clunk when accelerating after coasting and vibration at highway speeds. To check for wear in the CV joints and driveaxle shafts, grasp each axle (one at a time) and rotate it in both directions while holding the CV joint housings, feeling for play indicating worn splines or sloppy CV joints. Also check the axleshafts for cracks, dents and distortion.

---

8   Driveaxle - removal and installation

Note: *Not all of the steps in this procedure apply to all models. Read through the procedure carefully and determine which steps apply to the vehicle being worked on before actually beginning any work.*

Removal

Refer to illustrations 8.2, 8.3, 8.6, 8.9, 8.10 and 8.11

1   Disconnect the cable from the negative terminal of the battery.

2   Unstake the driveaxle hub nut **(see illustration)**.

8.6 To loosen the driveaxle from the hub splines, tap the end of the driveaxle with a soft-faced hammer or a hammer and a brass punch

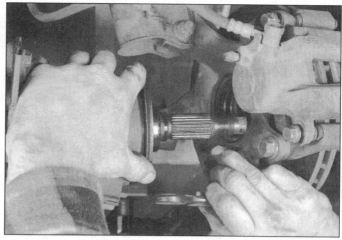

8.9 Pull out on the steering knuckle and detach the driveaxle from the hub

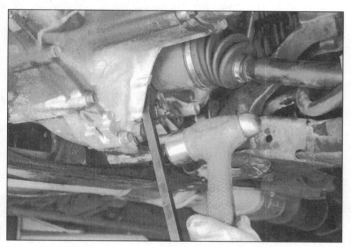

8.10 If you're removing the left driveaxle, or the right driveaxle on a model without an intermediate shaft, place a prybar between the CV joint and the transaxle housing and give the prybar a sharp rap with a hammer as shown - this is the only way to unseat the square-cut snap-ring that locks the splined inner end of the CV joint to the side gear

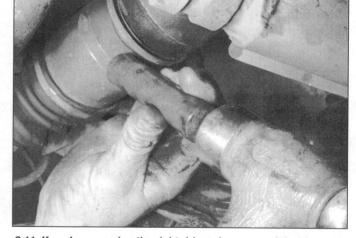

8.11 If you're removing the right driveaxle on a model with a 1.8L engine and a manual transaxle, tap the inner CV joint with a brass punch - it should come out easily

3   Loosen the driveaxle hub nut. To prevent the hub from turning, wedge a prybar between two of the wheel studs and allow the prybar to rest against the ground or the floorpan of the vehicle **(see illustration).**

4   Set the parking brake, loosen the front wheel lug nuts, raise the vehicle and support it securely on jackstands. Remove the wheel. Remove the driveaxle hub nut and washer. Discard the old hub nut - you'll need a new one for reassembly.

5   It's not absolutely necessary that you drain the transaxle lubricant prior to removing a driveaxle, but if the mileage on the odometer indicates that the transaxle is nearing the lubricant-change interval prescribed in Chapter 1, now is a good time to do it.

6   To loosen the driveaxle from the hub splines, tap the end of the driveaxle with a soft-faced hammer or a hammer and a brass punch **(see illustration).** If the driveaxle is stuck in the hub splines and won't move, it may be necessary to remove the brake disc (see Chapter 9) and push it from the hub with a two-jaw puller.

7   Remove the engine undercover(s). Place a drain pan underneath the transaxle just in case any lubricant leaks out.

8   Remove the pinch bolt securing the balljoint to the control arm,

then pry the control arm down to separate the components (see Chapter 10).

9   Pull out on the steering knuckle and detach the driveaxle from the hub **(see illustration).**

10   Before you remove the driveaxle, look for lubricant leakage in the area around the differential seal. If there's evidence of a leak, you'll want to replace the seal after removing the driveaxle (see Chapter 7 Part A). If you're removing the left driveaxle, or the right driveaxle on a model without an intermediate shaft (models with a 1.8L engine), carefully place a prybar between the inner CV joint and the transaxle housing and give the prybar a sharp rap with a hammer as shown **(see illustration).** Don't even bother trying to pry the inner CV joint loose any other way - the square-cut snap-ring that locks the splined inner end of the CV joint into the side gear cannot be disengaged by mere prying.

11   If you're removing the right driveaxle on a model with a 1.8L engine and a manual transaxle, note that the driveaxle isn't attached directly to the transaxle - it's attached to an intermediate shaft that is, in turn, attached to the transaxle. To separate the driveaxle from the intermediate shaft, tap the inner CV joint off the intermediate shaft with a brass punch **(see illustration).**

12   Should it become necessary to move the vehicle while the driveaxle is out, place a large bolt with two large washers (one on each side of the hub) through the hub and tighten the nut securely.

13   If you noted evidence of a leaking driveaxle seal, refer to Chapter

9.4 Remove these two bolts (arrows) to detach the intermediate shaft bearing bracket from the block

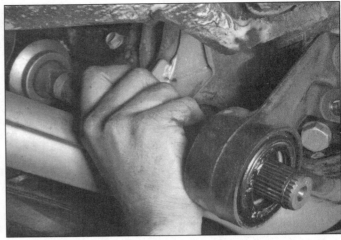

9.5 Pull the intermediate shaft out of the differential side gear to remove it

7A for the seal replacement procedure. If you need to replace the right driveaxle seal on a model with a 1.8L engine and a manual transaxle, you'll also need to remove the intermediate shaft (see Section 9).

Installation

Caution: *If you removed the snap-rings that lock the left inner CV joint and the right intermediate shaft into the differential side gears on a vehicle with a 1.8L engine and a manual transaxle, make sure you don't interchange them. The left snap-ring is larger and stronger than the right snap-ring, and can be identified by a blue paint mark.*

14   Installation is the reverse of removal, but with the following additional points:

  a) When installing the left driveaxle, or the right driveaxle on a model without an intermediate shaft, push it in sharply to seat the snap-ring on the inner CV joint in the groove in the differential side gear.

  b) When installing the right driveaxle/intermediate shaft assembly on a model with a 1.8L engine and manual transaxle, make sure the inner end of the driveaxle is fully seated in the center bearing bracket.

  c) Tighten the NEW driveaxle hub nut to the torque listed in this Chapter's Specifications, then stake the nut.

  d) Install the wheel and lug nuts, lower the vehicle and tighten the lug nuts to the torque listed in the Chapter 1 Specifications.

  e) Add transaxle/differential lubricant (see Chapter 1).

9   Intermediate shaft - removal and installation

Refer to illustrations 9.4 and 9.5

Note: *This procedure applies only to models with a 1.8L engine and a manual transaxle. Other models don't use this setup.*

1   Remove the right driveaxle (see Section 8).

2   It's not absolutely necessary that you drain the transaxle lubricant prior to removing the intermediate shaft, but if the mileage on the odometer indicates that the transaxle is nearing the lubricant-change interval prescribed in Chapter 1, now is a good time to do it. It's also a good idea to place a drain pan underneath the transaxle to catch any lubricant that leaks out.

3   Before removing the shaft, check the oil seal for evidence of leakage. Refer to Chapter 7A for the seal replacement procedure.

4   Remove the two center bearing bracket retaining bolts **(see illustration)**.

5   Pull the intermediate shaft out of the differential side gear **(see illustration)**, then remove it from the vehicle.

6   Check the center bearing for smooth operation. If it feels rough or sticky, replace the intermediate shaft.

7   Installation is the reverse of removal.

10.3a Pry up the retaining tabs on the boot clamps . . .

10   Driveaxle boot replacement and CV joint overhaul

Note: *If the CV joints must be overhauled (usually due to torn boots), explore all options before beginning the job. Complete rebuilt driveaxles are available on an exchange basis, which eliminates much time and work. Whichever route you choose to take, check on the cost and availability of parts before disassembling the vehicle.*

Outer CV joint

Removal

Refer to illustrations 10.3a, 10.3b, 10.4 and 10.5

Note: *The following procedure applies to driveaxle assemblies with axleshafts thicker than their splined ends, i.e. equal length driveaxles used on models equipped with a DOHC engine and a manual transaxle. If the driveaxle is fitted to a model equipped with a SOHC engine and a manual transaxle, or to a vehicle with an automatic transaxle, you may not be able to remove the outer CV joint from the axleshaft as described below. In that event, you'll have to remove the inner CV joint and the inner CV joint boot as described later in this Section, slide off or cut off the old boot and install the new boot by sliding it on from the inner end of the axleshaft.*

1   Remove the driveaxle (see Section 8).

2   Mount the driveaxle in a vice with wood lined jaws (to prevent

10.3b . . . then open the clamps and remove them from the boot

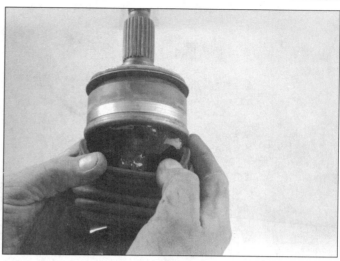

10.4 Pry the edge of the boot loose from the CV joint and pull it off the joint

10.5 Carefully drive the outer CV joint off the axleshaft with a brass bar and a hammer. Make sure you strike the inner race only - be careful not to damage the splines or the cage.

10.10 Wrap the axleshaft splines with tape to prevent damage to the boot when installing it

8

damage to the axleshaft). Check the CV joint for excessive play in the radial direction, which indicates worn parts. Check for smooth operation throughout the full range of motion for each CV joint. If a boot is torn, the recommended procedure is to disassemble the joint, clean the components and inspect for damage due to loss of lubrication and possible contamination by foreign matter.

3   Using a small screwdriver, pry up on the boot clamp retaining tabs to loosen them and slide them off **(see illustrations)**.

4   Pry up on the edge of the boot and pull it off the CV joint **(see illustration)**.

5   Carefully drive the CV joint off the axleshaft with a brass bar and a hammer **(see illustration)**. Strike the inner race only - be careful not to damage the splines or the cage.

6   Remove the boot.

Check

7   Clean the CV joint thoroughly with solvent to remove all grease. Blow the solvent out of the joint with compressed air, if available. **Warning:** *Wear eye protection!* Check for cracks, pitting, scoring and other signs of wear.

8   If there's any sign of damage or excessive wear, replace the outer

CV joint as an assembly. There are no parts available separately, so it can't be overhauled.

Installation

Refer to illustrations 10.10 and 10.11

9   Pack the CV joint with the CV joint grease included in the boot kit.

10   Slide the new boot and small clamp onto the axleshaft. It's a good idea to wrap the splined end of the axleshaft with tape to protect the small end of the new boot from damage **(see illustration)**. Partially fill the boot with CV joint grease. Place the large boot clamp onto the axleshaft.

11   Install the CV joint assembly onto the axleshaft and, using a brass hammer, drive the joint onto the shaft **(see illustration)**. Complete the procedure by performing Steps 36, 37 and 38.

Inner CV joint

Tri-pot type (models with an automatic transaxle)

Disassembly

Refer to illustrations 10.12, 10.13, 10.14 and 10.15

12   After removing the boot clamps **(see illustrations 10.3a and**

10.11 To install the outer CV joint onto the axleshaft, place the axleshaft in a bench vise and tap the joint onto the shaft splines with a hammer and a brass punch

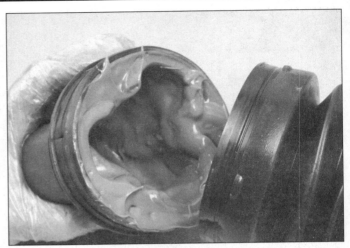

10.12 Once the boot is detached from the inner CV joint housing, the housing can be removed

10.13 Use a center-punch to place marks (arrows) on the tri-pot and the driveaxle to ensure that they're properly reassembled

10.14 Remove the snap-ring from the groove in the end of the axleshaft

10.3b), pull the boot back from the inner CV joint and slide the joint housing off **(see illustration)**.

13   Use a center punch to mark the tri-pot and axleshaft to ensure that they are reassembled properly **(see illustration)**.

14   Remove the snap-ring from the end of the axleshaft with a pair of snap-ring pliers **(see illustration)**.

15   Use a hammer and a brass punch to drive the tri-pot joint from the driveaxle **(see illustration)**.

Check

16   Clean all components with solvent to remove the grease, and check for cracks, pitting, scoring and other signs of wear.

Reassembly

Refer to illustrations 10.17, 10.19a, 10.19b and 10.19c

17   Slide the clamps and boot onto the axleshaft. It's a good idea to wrap the axleshaft splines with tape to prevent damaging the boot **(see illustration 10.10)**. Place the tri-pot on the shaft **(see illustration)** and install the snap-ring. Apply grease to the tri-pot assembly, the inside of the joint housing and the inside of the boot.

18   Slide the boot into place, making sure both ends seat in their grooves.

19   Equalize the pressure in the boot, then tighten and secure the boot clamps **(see illustrations)**. Proceed to Step 39.

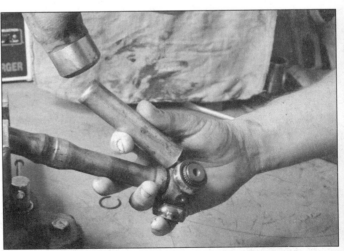

10.15 Drive the tri-pot joint from the axleshaft with a brass punch and hammer - make sure you don't damage the bearing surfaces or the splines on the shaft

10.17 Install the tri-pot with the chamfered (tapered) ends of the splines facing toward the axleshaft

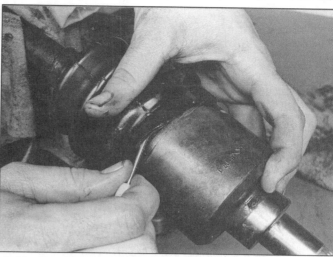

10.19a Equalize the pressure inside the boot by inserting a small, DULL screwdriver between the boot and the CV joint housing

10.19b To install the new clamps, bend the tang down and . . .

10.19c . . . tap the tabs down to hold it in place

10.20 Remove both boot clamps, then slide the boot down the axleshaft so it's out of the way

Double-offset (ball-and-cage) type (models with a manual transaxle)

Disassembly

Refer to illustrations 10.20, 10.21, 10.22, 10.23 and 10.24

20   Remove both boot clamps **(see illustrations 10.3a and 10.3b)** and discard them. Slide the boot out of the way **(see illustration)**.

21   Mark the shaft, the inner race, the cage and the outer race (housing) so they can be reassembled in the same way **(see illustration)**.

22   Pry the wire ring bearing retainer from the housing **(see illustration)**.

23   Pull the housing off the inner bearing assembly **(see illustration)**.

24   Remove the snap-ring from the groove in the axleshaft with a pair of snap-ring pliers **(see illustration)**.

25   Slide the inner race off the axleshaft.

26   Using a screwdriver or piece of wood, pry the ball bearings from the cage. Be careful not to scratch the inner race, the ball bearings or the cage.

27   Remove the cage.

Inspection

Refer to illustrations 10.28a and 10.28b

28   Clean the components with solvent to remove all traces of grease. Inspect the cage and races for pitting, score marks, cracks and

8

10.21 Mark the shaft, inner race, cage and outer race (housing) so they can be reassembled in the same relationship to each other

10.22 Pry the retainer from the housing with a small screwdriver

10.23 Slide the housing off the bearing assembly - some of the ball bearings may fall out when the race is removed, so be ready to catch them

10.24 Remove the snap-ring from the groove in the axleshaft with a pair of snap-ring pliers

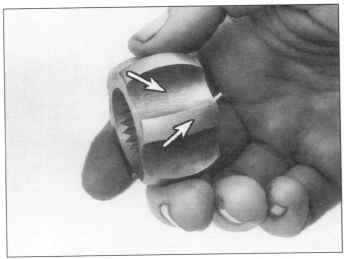

10.28a Inspect the inner race lands and grooves for pitting, score marks, cracks and other signs of wear and damage

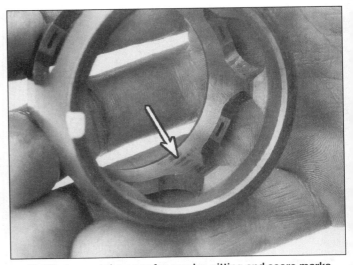

10.28b Inspect the cage for cracks, pitting and score marks (shiny, polished spots are normal and will not adversely affect CV joint performance)

10.34 Pack the inner race and cage assembly with grease, by hand, until grease is worked completely into the assembly (also note that the larger diameter side, or "bulge," is facing out

other signs of wear and damage. Shiny, polished spots are normal and will not adversely affect CV joint performance **(see illustrations).**

Reassembly

Refer to illustration 10.34

29   Wrap the axleshaft splines with tape to avoid damaging the boot. Slide the small boot clamp and boot onto the axleshaft **(see illustra-**tion 10.10)**, then remove the tape. Slide the large boot clamp over the boot.

30   Install the cage (outer race) assembly on the axleshaft with the smaller diameter side of the cage facing toward the boot.

31   Install the inner race onto the axleshaft with the matchmark on the race (or the larger diameter side) aligned with the mark on the end of the axleshaft.

32   Install the snap-ring in the groove. Make sure it's completely seated by pushing on the inner race.

33   Move the cage up over the inner race, aligning the match marks. Press the ball bearings into the cage windows with your thumbs. If they won't stay in place, apply CV joint grease to hold them.

34   Fill the outer race and boot with CV joint grease (normally included with the new boot kit). Pack the inner race and cage assembly with grease, by hand, until grease is worked completely into the assembly **(see illustration).**

35   Slide the inner race, balls and cage into the CV joint housing and install the wire ring bearing retainer.

36   Wipe any excess grease from the axle boot groove on the outer race. Seat the small diameter of the boot in the recessed area on the axleshaft. Push the other end of the boot onto the CV joint housing and move the race in or out until there's no deformation (distortion or dents) in the boot.

37   Equalize the pressure in the boot by inserting a dull screwdriver between the boot and the outer race **(see illustration 10.19a)**. Don't damage the boot with the tool.

38   Install the boot clamps **(see illustrations 10.19b and 10.19c)**.

All inner CV joints

39   Install a new circlip on the inner CV joint stub axle.

40   Install the driveaxle (see Section 8).

Notes

Chapter 9   Brakes

Contents

Specifications

General

Brake fluid type...	See Chapter 1
Brake pedal height.......................................	6.22 inches
Power brake booster pushrod-to-master	
Cylinder piston clearance	0.0 inch
Brake light switch-to-pedal clearance...............	0.020 to 0.040 inch

Disc brakes

Minimum brake pad thickness	See Chapter 1
Disc thickness*	
Standard	0.866 inch
Minimum	0.811 inch
Disc runout limit...	0.006 inch

Drum brakes

Minimum brake shoe lining thickness	See Chapter 1
Drum inside diameter*	
Standard..	7.87 inch
Maximum..	7.93 inch

* Note: If different specifications are cast into the disc or drum, they supersede information printed here.

Torque specifications

	Ft lbs (unless otherwise indicated)
Caliper mounting bolts	36
Caliper bracket-to-steering knuckle bolts	76
Brake hose-to-caliper banjo fitting bolt..	22
Wheel cylinder mounting bolts	89 in-lbs
Brake hose-to-wheel cylinder fitting..	11
Master cylinder-to-brake booster nuts	115 in-lbs
Power brake booster mounting nuts	115 in-lbs
Wheel lug nuts	See Chapter 1

9

2.5 Before you remove the caliper, use a C-clamp to push the piston back into its bore - otherwise, the caliper and new pads may not fit over the brake disc

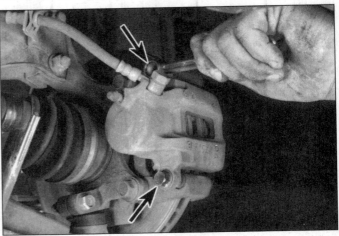

2.6a Remove the caliper mounting bolts (arrows) . . .

1   General information

The vehicles covered by this manual are equipped with hydraulically operated front and rear brake systems. The front brakes are disc type and the rear brakes are drum type. Both the front and rear brakes are self adjusting. The disc brakes automatically compensate for pad wear, while the drum brakes incorporate an adjustment mechanism which is activated as the parking brake is applied.

Hydraulic system

The hydraulic system consists of two separate circuits. The master cylinder has separate reservoirs for the two circuits, and, in the event of a leak or failure in one hydraulic circuit, the other circuit will remain operative. A dual proportioning valve on the firewall provides brake balance between the front and rear brakes.

Power brake booster

The power brake booster, utilizing engine manifold vacuum and atmospheric pressure to provide assistance to the hydraulically operated brakes, is mounted on the firewall in the engine compartment.

Parking brake

The parking brake operates the rear brakes only, through cable actuation. It's activated by a lever mounted in the center console.

Service

After completing any operation involving disassembly of any part of the brake system, always test drive the vehicle to check for proper braking performance before resuming normal driving. When testing the brakes, perform the tests on a clean, dry, flat surface. Conditions other than these can lead to inaccurate test results.

Test the brakes at various speeds with both light and heavy pedal pressure. The vehicle should stop evenly without pulling to one side or the other. Avoid locking the brakes, because this slides the tires and diminishes braking efficiency and control of the vehicle.

Tires, vehicle load and wheel alignment are factors which also affect braking performance.

2   Disc brake pads - replacement

Refer to illustrations 2.5 and 2.6a through 2.6h
Warning: *Disc brake pads must be replaced on both front or rear wheels at the same time - never replace the pads on only one wheel. Also, the dust created by the brake system may contain asbestos, which is harmful to your health. Never blow it out with compressed air and don't inhale any of it. An approved filtering mask should be worn when working on the brakes. Do not, under any circumstances, use petroleum-based solvents to clean brake parts. Use brake system cleaner only! When servicing the disc brakes, use only high-quality, na-*

2.6b . . . lift off the caliper . . .

2.6c . . . and hang it out of the way with a piece of wire

2.6d Remove the outer brake pad . . .

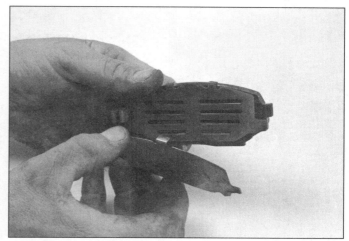

2.6e Remove the shim from the outer brake pad backing plate . . .

tionally recognized brand-name pads.
Note: *This procedure applies to both the front and rear disc brakes.*
1 Remove the cap from the brake fluid reservoir.
2 Loosen the wheel lug nuts, raise the front or rear of the vehicle and support it securely on jackstands. Block the wheels at the opposite end.
3 Remove the wheels. Work on one brake assembly at a time, using the assembled brake for reference if necessary.
4 Inspect the brake disc carefully as outlined in Section 4. If machining is necessary, follow the information in that Section to remove the disc, at which time the pads can be removed as well.
5 Push the piston back into its bore to provide room for the new brake pads. A C-clamp can be used to accomplish this **(see illustration).** As the piston is depressed to the bottom of the caliper bore, the fluid in the master cylinder will rise. Make sure that it doesn't overflow. If necessary, siphon off some of the fluid.
6 Follow the accompanying photos, beginning with **illustration 2.6a,** for the actual pad replacement procedure. Be sure to stay in order and read the caption under each illustration.
7 When reinstalling the caliper, be sure to tighten the mounting bolts to the torque listed in this Chapter's Specifications. After the job has been completed, firmly depress the brake pedal a few times to bring the pads into contact with the disc. Check the level of the brake fluid, adding some if necessary. Check the operation of the brakes carefully before placing the vehicle into normal service.

2.6f . . . and remove the inner brake pad (the shim isn't removable from this pad)

2.6g Inspect the upper and lower anti-rattle springs (arrows) - make sure they're in good shape and properly installed as shown

2.6h Make sure the new pads are properly seated between the anti-rattle springs, then reinstall the caliper

9

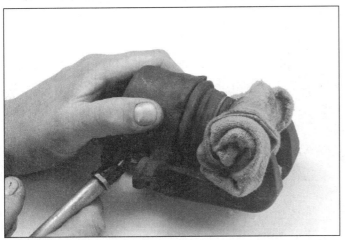

3.4 To remove the piston from the caliper, place a wood block or a bundle of rags between the piston and caliper, then apply compressed air to the brake fluid hose connection on the caliper body (use only enough pressure to ease the piston out of its bore)

3.5 Peel the piston boot from its groove in the piston bore - you should be able to get the old boot out without using any tools, but if you find it necessary to pry it out, use a small screwdriver and make sure you don't damage the bore

---

3   Disc brake caliper - removal, overhaul and installation

Warning: *Dust created by the brake system may contain asbestos, which is harmful to your health. Never blow it out with compressed air and don't inhale any of it. An approved filtering mask should be worn when working on the brakes. Do not, under any circumstances, use petroleum-based solvents to clean brake parts. Use brake system cleaner only!*

Note: *If an overhaul is indicated (usually because of fluid leakage), explore all options before beginning the job. New and factory rebuilt calipers are available on an exchange basis, which makes this job quite easy. If it's decided to rebuild the calipers, make sure a rebuild kit is available before proceeding. Always rebuild the calipers in pairs - never rebuild just one of them!*

Removal

1   Remove the bolt and disconnect the brake hose from the caliper.
2   Plug the brake hose to keep contaminants out of the brake system and to prevent losing any more brake fluid than is necessary.
3   Refer to Section 3 for the *front caliper removal procedure* (it's part of the brake pad replacement procedure).

Overhaul

Refer to illustrations 3.4, 3.5, 3.7, 3.10, 3.11 and 3.12

4   To remove the piston from the caliper, apply compressed air to the brake fluid hose connection on the caliper body **(see illustration).** Use only enough pressure to ease the piston out of its bore. **Warning:** *Be careful not to place your fingers between the piston and the caliper as the piston may come out with some force.*
5   Remove the piston boot **(see illustration).**
6   Inspect the mating surfaces of the piston and caliper bore wall. If there is any scoring, rust, pitting or bright areas, replace the complete caliper unit with a new one.
7   If these components are in good condition, remove the piston seal from the caliper bore using a wooden or plastic tool **(see illustration).** Metal tools may damage the cylinder bore.
8   Wash all the components in clean brake fluid or brake cleaner.
9   Submerge the new piston seal in brake fluid and install it into the groove in the caliper bore.
10   Install the big end of the new piston dust boot into its groove in the caliper bore **(see illustration).**
11   Place the caliper in a vise. Place the piston against the end of the new dust boot, apply a small burst of compressed air to the caliper bore to inflate the boot and push the piston through the small end of

3.7 To remove the seal from the caliper bore, use a plastic or wooden tool, such as a pencil

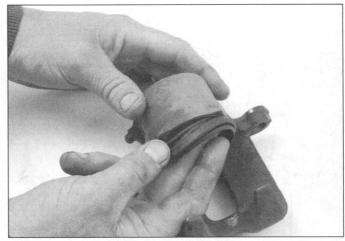

3.10 Install the big end of the new dust boot into the caliper - make sure the ridge around the big end is fully seated in its groove in the piston bore

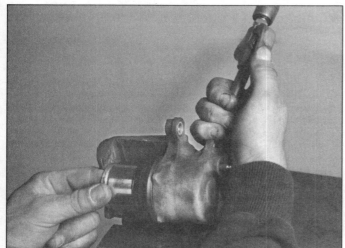

3.11 Place the piston against the open small end of the new dust boot, apply a small burst of compressed air to the caliper bore to inflate the boot and push the piston through the small end of the boot as the boot inflates

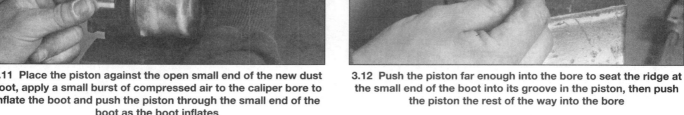

3.12 Push the piston far enough into the bore to seat the ridge at the small end of the boot into its groove in the piston, then push the piston the rest of the way into the bore

the boot as the boot inflates **(see illustration)**. **Warning:** *Once the piston has been inserted into the boot, stop applying compressed air. Also, don't place your fingers between the piston and the caliper frame. Although it's possible to push the piston through the boot without first inflating the boot with compressed air, it's extremely difficult.*

12   Coat the sides of the piston with clean brake fluid, then carefully push the piston far enough into the bore to seat the small end of the boot into its groove near the outer end of the piston **(see illustration)**. Now depress the piston the rest of the way into the bore. Apply firm - but not excessive - pressure to the piston; make sure that it remains square to the bore as it goes in. Don't try to force the piston into the bore if it becomes cocked.

Installation

13   Install the caliper by reversing the removal procedure. Make sure you install new copper sealing washers at the banjo fitting for the brake hose-to-caliper connection. Tighten the banjo bolt to the torque listed in this Chapter's Specifications.

14   Bleed the brake circuit according to the procedure in Section 9. Make sure there are no leaks from the hose connections. Test the brakes carefully before returning the vehicle to normal service.

4   Brake disc - inspection, removal and installation

Inspection

Refer to illustrations 4.3, 4.4a, 4.4b, 4.5a and 4.5b

1   Loosen the wheel lug nuts, raise the vehicle and support it securely on jackstands. Remove the wheel and install the lug nuts to hold the disc in place.

2   Remove the brake caliper (see Section 3). It isn't necessary to disconnect the brake hose. After removing the caliper bolts, suspend the caliper out of the way with a piece of wire **(see illustration 2.6c)**.

3   Visually inspect the disc surface for score marks and other damage. Light scratches and shallow grooves are normal after use and may not always be detrimental to brake operation, but deep scoring - over 0.039-inch (1.0 mm) - requires disc removal and refinishing by an automotive machine shop. Be sure to check both sides of the disc **(see illustration)**. If pulsating has been noticed during application of the brakes, suspect disc runout.

4   To check disc runout, place a dial indicator at a point about 1/2-inch from the outer edge of the disc **(see illustration)**. Set the indicator to zero and turn the disc. The indicator reading should not exceed the specified allowable runout limit. If it does, the disc should be refinished

4.3 The brake pads on this vehicle were obviously neglected, as they wore down to the rivets and cut deep grooves into the disc - wear this severe means the disc must be replaced

4.4a To check disc runout, mount a dial indicator as shown and rotate the disc

9

4.4b Using a swirling motion, remove the glaze from the disc surface with sandpaper or emery cloth

4.5a The minimum wear (or discard) thickness is cast into the inside of the disc

by an automotive machine shop. **Note:** *The discs should be resurfaced regardless of the dial indicator reading, as this will impart a smooth finish and ensure a perfectly flat surface, eliminating any brake pedal pulsation or other undesirable symptoms related to questionable discs. At the very least, if you elect not to have the discs resurfaced, remove the glaze from the surface with emery cloth using a swirling motion* **(see illustration)**.

5   It's absolutely critical that the disc not be machined to a thickness under the specified minimum allowable disc refinish thickness. The minimum wear (or discard) thickness is cast into the inside of the disc **(see illustration)**. The disc thickness can be checked with a micrometer **(see illustration)**.

Removal

Refer to illustration 4.6
6   Remove the caliper bracket **(see illustration)**.
7   Remove the lug nuts which were put on to hold the disc in place and remove the disc from the hub. If the disc is stuck to the hub and won't come off, thread bolts into the holes provided and tighten them. Alternate between the bolts, turning them 1/4-turn at a time, until the disc is free.

Installation

8   Place the disc in position over the threaded studs.
9   Install the caliper bracket, pads and caliper over the disc and position it on the steering knuckle. Tighten the caliper bracket bolts to the

torque listed in this Chapter's Specifications.
10   Install the wheel, then lower the vehicle to the ground. Tighten the lug nuts to the torque listed in the Chapter 1 Specifications. Depress the brake pedal a few times to bring the brake pads into contact with the disc. Bleeding won't be necessary unless the brake hose was disconnected from the caliper. Check the operation of the brakes carefully before driving the vehicle.

---

5   Drum brake shoes - replacement

Refer to illustrations 5.4a through 5.4w
Warning: *Drum brake shoes must be replaced on both wheels at the same time - never replace the shoes on only one wheel. Also, the dust created by the brake system may contain asbestos, which is harmful to your health. Never blow it out with compressed air and don't inhale any of it. An approved filtering mask should be worn when working on the brakes. Do not, under any circumstances, use petroleum-based solvents to clean brake parts. Use brake system cleaner only!*
Caution: *Whenever the brake shoes are replaced, the return and hold-down springs should also be replaced. Due to the continuous heating/cooling cycle the springs are subjected to, they lose tension over a period of time and may allow the shoes to drag on the drum and wear at a much faster rate than normal. When replacing the rear brake shoes, use only high-quality, nationally recognized brand-name parts.*
1   Loosen the wheel lug nuts, raise the rear of the vehicle and sup-

4.5b The disc thickness can be checked with a micrometer

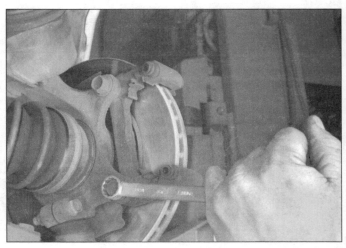

4.6 To remove the caliper bracket, unscrew the two bolts that hold it to the steering knuckle

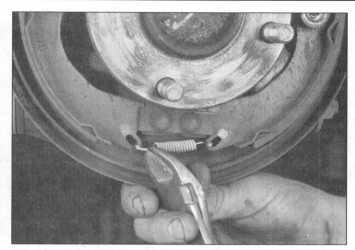

5.4a Unhook and remove the return spring from the lower ends of the two brake shoes (diagonal cutting pliers work well for gripping the spring)

5.4b Unhook and remove the automatic adjuster spring from the automatic adjuster lever

port it securely on jackstands. Block the front wheels to keep the vehicle from rolling.

2   Release the parking brake.

3   Remove the wheel. **Note:** *All four rear brake shoes must be replaced at the same time, but to avoid mixing up parts, work on only one brake assembly at a time.*

4   Follow the accompanying illustrations for the brake shoe replacement procedure **(see illustrations 5.4a through 5.4w)**. Be sure to stay in order and read the caption under each illustration. **Note:** *If the brake drum cannot be easily pulled off the axle and shoe assembly, make sure the parking brake is completely released. If the drum still cannot be pulled off, the brake shoes will have to be retracted. This is done by first removing the plug from the backing plate. With the plug removed, push the lever off the adjuster star wheel with a narrow screwdriver while turning the adjuster wheel with another screwdriver, moving the shoes away from the drum. The drum should now come off.*

5   Before reinstalling the drum, it should be checked for cracks, score marks, deep scratches and hard spots, which will appear as small discolored areas. If the hard spots cannot be removed with fine emery cloth or if any of the other conditions listed above exist, the drum must be taken to an automotive machine shop to have it turned.

5.4c Remove the automatic adjuster lever (arrow)

5.4d Using a brake hold-down spring tool, remove the trailing (rear) shoe retainer and spring

5.4e Remove the leading (front) shoe retainer and spring

5.4f Note how the tangs on the ends of the adjuster mechanism engage their respective slots in the leading and trailing brake shoes, then spread the two brake shoes apart and remove the adjuster

9

5.4g Unhook and remove the upper return spring

5.4h Pull back the spring on the end of the parking brake cable with a pair of pliers and disconnect the parking brake lever from the cable

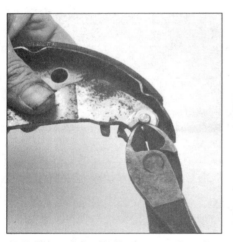

5.4i Remove the E-clip that attaches the parking brake lever to the trailing brake shoe (don't lose the washer or the E-clip - you'll need them for reattaching the lever to the shoe)

5.4j Drive out the parking brake lever pivot pin with a punch and install it in the new trailing shoe

5.4k Install the parking brake lever on the new trailing shoe, then install the washer and a new E-clip on the parking brake lever pivot pin - pinch the ends of the E-clip tight to make sure it stays on

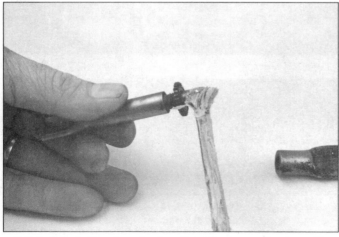

5.4l Lubricate the star-wheel on the adjuster mechanism with high-temperature grease

5.4m Lubricate the friction surfaces of the brake backing plate with high-temperature grease

5.4n To attach the parking brake lever to the parking brake cable, pull back the spring with a pair of pliers, grasp the plug on the end of the cable with a pair of locking pliers and pull on the plug until the gap between the plug and the spring is wide enough to for the cable to slide into place (this operation can be tricky - it's not a bad idea to have a helper standing by just in case you need three hands)

5.4o Install the trailing shoe and secure it with the hold-down spring and retainer

5.4p Make sure the upper end of the trailing shoe is properly engaged with the slot in the rear wheel cylinder piston

5.4q Hook the rear end of the upper return spring into its hole (right arrow) in the trailing shoe, hook the front end of the spring into its hole (left arrow) in the leading shoe and place the leading shoe into position (but don't install the hold-down spring yet)

5.4r When you install the adjuster mechanism, make sure both ends of the adjuster are properly engaged with their respective notches (arrows) in the leading and trailing shoes; and make sure the leading shoe is properly engaged with the slot in the front piston of the wheel cylinder

5.4s Install the front hold-down spring and retainer

5.4t To install the lower return spring, hook each end into its hole (arrows)

9

5.4u Install the auto adjuster lever over the parking brake lever pivot pin, and with its notch engaged with the rear end of the adjuster mechanism as shown, hook the rear end of the auto adjuster spring into the hole (arrow) in the lever

5.4v Hook the forward end of the auto adjuster spring into its hole (arrow) in the leading shoe

5.4w That's all there is to it! Now compare your work with this photo and make sure you have assembled everything correctly

Note: *Professionals recommend resurfacing the drums each time a brake job is done. Resurfacing will eliminate the possibility of out-of-round drums. If the drums are worn so much that they can't be resurfaced without exceeding the maximum allowable diameter (stamped into the drum), then new ones will be required. At the very least, if you elect not to have the drums resurfaced, remove the glaze from the surface with emery cloth using a swirling motion.*

6   Install the brake drum on the axle flange.

7   Mount the wheel, install the lug nuts, then lower the vehicle. Tighten the lug nuts to the torque listed in the Chapter 1 Specifications.

8   Make a number of forward and reverse stops and operate the parking brake to adjust the brakes until satisfactory pedal action is obtained.

9   Check the operation of the brakes carefully before driving the vehicle.

---

6   Wheel cylinder - removal, overhaul and installation

Note: *If an overhaul is indicated (usually because of fluid leaks or sticky operation), explore all options before beginning the job. New wheel cylinders are available, which makes this job quite easy. If it's decided to rebuild the wheel cylinder, make sure a rebuild kit is available before proceeding. Never overhaul only one wheel cylinder - always rebuild both of them at the same time.*

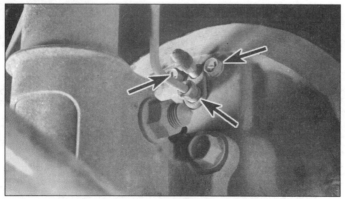

6.4 Disconnect the brake line fitting (lower arrow), then remove the two wheel cylinder retaining bolts (upper arrows)

Removal
Refer to illustration 6.4

1   Raise the rear of the vehicle and support it securely on jackstands. Block the front wheels to keep the vehicle from rolling.

2   Remove the brake shoe assembly (see Section 5).

3   Remove all dirt and foreign material from around the wheel cylinder.

4   Disconnect the brake line **(see illustration)** with a flare-nut wrench, if available. Don't pull the brake line away from the wheel cylinder.

5   Remove the wheel cylinder mounting bolts.

6   Detach the wheel cylinder from the brake backing plate and place it on a clean workbench. Immediately plug the brake line to prevent fluid loss and contamination.

Overhaul
Refer to illustration 6.7

7   Remove the bleeder screw, cups, pistons, boots and spring assembly from the wheel cylinder body **(see illustration)**.

8   Clean the wheel cylinder with brake fluid, denatured alcohol or brake system cleaner. **Warning:** *Do not, under any circumstances, use petroleum-based solvents to clean brake parts!*

9   Use compressed air to dry the wheel cylinder and blow out the passages. **Warning:** *Wear eye protection when using compressed air.*

10   Check the bore for corrosion and score marks. Crocus cloth can be used to remove light corrosion and stains, but the cylinder must be replaced with a new one if the defects cannot be removed easily, or if

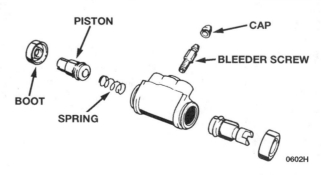

6.7 An exploded view of the wheel cylinder assembly

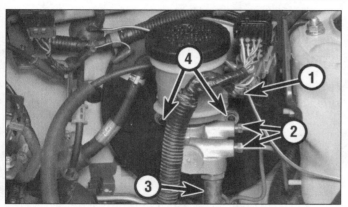

7.2 To remove the master cylinder, unplug the electrical connector (1) for the brake fluid level switch, disconnect the two front brake line fittings (2) from the master cylinder, disconnect the two rear brake line fittings (3) from the proportioning valve and remove the two nuts (4) that attach the master cylinder to the brake booster

the bore is scored.

11 Lubricate the new cups with brake fluid.

12 Assemble the brake cylinder components **(see illustration 6.7)**. Make sure the cup lips face in.

Installation

13 Place the wheel cylinder in position and install the bolts finger tight. Connect the brake line to the cylinder, being careful not to cross-thread the fitting. Tighten the wheel cylinder bolts to the torque listed in this Chapter's Specifications.

14 Tighten the brake line. Install the brake shoes, brake drum and wheel. Tighten the lug nuts to the torque listed in the Chapter 1 Specifications.

15 Bleed the brakes (see Section 9).

16 Check the operation of the brakes carefully before driving the vehicle.

---

7   Master cylinder - removal, overhaul and installation

Note: *Before deciding to overhaul the master cylinder, check on the availability and cost of a new or factory rebuilt unit and also the availability of a rebuild kit.*

Removal

Refer to illustration 7.2

1   The master cylinder is located in the engine compartment, mounted on the power brake booster. First, remove the top of the air cleaner and the air duct (see Chapter 4).

2   Unplug the electrical connector for the brake fluid level switch **(see illustration)**.

3   Remove as much fluid as possible from the reservoir with a syringe.

4   Place rags under the fittings and prepare caps or plastic bags to cover the ends of the lines once they're disconnected. **Caution:** *Brake fluid will damage paint. Cover all body parts and be careful not to spill fluid during this procedure.* Loosen the fittings at the ends of the brake lines where they enter the master cylinder. To prevent rounding off the flats, use a flare-nut wrench, which wraps around the fitting hex.

5   Pull the brake lines away from the master cylinder and plug the ends to prevent contamination.

6   Remove the nuts attaching the master cylinder to the power booster. Pull the master cylinder off the studs to remove it. Again, be careful not to spill the fluid as this is done.

Overhaul

Refer to illustrations 7.8a, 7.8b, 7.11, 7.12a, 7.12b and 7.13

7   Before disassembling the master cylinder, buy the rebuild kit,

7.8a Remove the reservoir retaining screw (pin on SOHC models) . . .

7.8b . . . pull off the reservoir and remove the reservoir grommets (arrows) (the lower arrow points to the stopper bolt which must be removed before the pistons can be removed from the master cylinder)

7.11 Use a Phillips head screwdriver to push the pistons into the cylinder, then remove the stopper bolt and snap-ring

which will contain the necessary replacement parts and any instructions which may be specific to your model.

8   Remove the reservoir retaining screw (or pin, on SOHC models), pull off the reservoir and remove the grommets **(see illustrations)**.

9   Inspect the primary piston dust seal next to the flange. If it's cracked or torn, replace it (this seal keeps dust and dirt out of the brake booster).

10   Place the cylinder in a vise and use a punch or Phillips screwdriver to depress the pistons until they bottom against the other end of the master cylinder. Hold the pistons in this position and remove the stopper bolt from the master cylinder **(see illustration 7.8b)**.

11   Carefully remove the snap-ring at the end of the master cylinder **(see illustration)**.

9

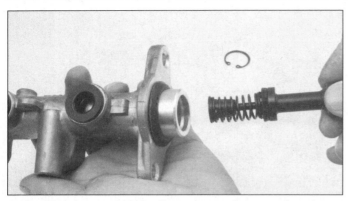

7.12a After the snap-ring has been removed, remove the primary piston assembly . . .

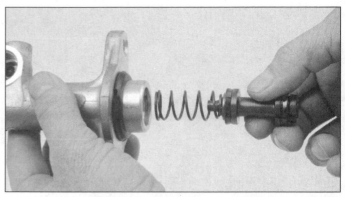

7.12b . . . then remove the secondary piston assembly - if the secondary piston sticks in the bore, carefully tap the master cylinder against a block of wood until the secondary piston assembly protrudes from the bore (pull the piston straight out - if it becomes even slightly cocked, the bore could be damaged)

12   The internal components can now be removed from the bore **(see illustrations)**. Make a note of the proper order of the components so they can be returned to their original locations. **Note:** *The two pistons and springs are different, so pay particular attention to their installed order.*

13   Remove the proportioning valves **(see illustration)**.

14   Inspect the bore of the master cylinder. Any deep score marks or other damage will mean a new master cylinder is required. DO NOT attempt to hone the bore.

15   Replace all parts included in the rebuild kit, following any instructions in the kit. Clean all reused parts with new brake fluid or brake system cleaner. **Warning:** *Do not use petroleum-based solvents. During reassembly, lubricate all parts liberally with clean brake fluid.*

16   Push the assembled components into the bore, bottoming them against the end of the master cylinder, then install the stopper bolt.

17   Install the new snap-ring, making sure it's seated properly in the groove. Install the dust seal.

18   Install the reservoir grommets, reservoir and screw (or pin), then install the proportioning values.

19   Before installing the master cylinder, it should be bench bled. Since you'll have to apply pressure to the master cylinder piston and, at the same time, control flow from the brake line outlets, the master cylinder should be mounted in a vise, with the jaws of the vise clamping on the mounting flange.

20   Insert threaded plugs into the brake line outlet holes and snug them down so no air will leak past them, but not so tight that they can't be easily loosened.

21   Fill the reservoir with brake fluid of the recommended type (see Chapter 1).

22   Remove one plug and push the piston assembly into the bore to expel the air from the master cylinder. A large Phillips screwdriver can be used to push on the piston assembly.

23   To prevent air from being drawn back into the master cylinder, the plug must be replaced and snugged down before releasing the pressure on the piston.

24   Repeat the procedure until only brake fluid is expelled from the brake line outlet hole. When only brake fluid is expelled, repeat the procedure at the other outlet hole and plug. Be sure to keep the master cylinder reservoir filled with brake fluid to prevent the introduction of air into the system.

25   Since high pressure isn't involved in the bench bleeding procedure, an alternative to the removal and replacement of the plugs with each stroke of the piston assembly is available. Before pushing in on the piston assembly, remove the plug as described in Step 22. Before releasing the piston, however, instead of replacing the plug, simply put your finger tightly over the hole to keep air from being drawn back into the master cylinder. Wait several seconds for brake fluid to be drawn from the reservoir into the bore, then depress the piston again, removing your finger as brake fluid is expelled. Be sure to put your finger back over the hole each time before releasing the piston, and when the bleeding procedure is complete for that outlet, replace the plug and tighten it before going on to the other port.

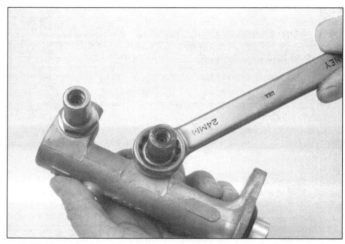

7.13 Remove the proportioning valves from the bottom of the master cylinder

Installation

26   Install the master cylinder over the studs on the power brake booster and tighten the nuts only finger-tight at this time.

27   Thread the brake line fittings into the master cylinder. Since the master cylinder is still a bit loose, it can be moved slightly so the fittings thread in easily. Don't strip the threads as the fittings are tightened.

28   Tighten the mounting nuts and the brake line fittings.

29   Fill the master cylinder reservoir with fluid, then bleed the master cylinder (only if hasn't been bench bled) and the brake system (see Section 9). To bleed the master cylinder on the vehicle, have an assistant depress the brake pedal and hold it down. Loosen the fitting to allow air and fluid to escape. Tighten the fitting, then allow your assistant to return the pedal to its rest position. Repeat this procedure on both fittings until the fluid is free of air bubbles. Check the operation of the brake system carefully before driving the vehicle.

---

8   Brake hoses and lines - inspection and replacement

Inspection

1   About every six months, with the vehicle raised and supported securely on jackstands, the rubber hoses which connect the steel brake lines with the front and rear brake assemblies should be in-

8.3 To disconnect a front brake hose from the metal brake line at the frame bracket, unscrew the threaded fitting with a flare-nut wrench

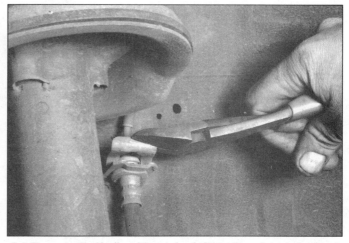

8.4 Remove the U-clip with a pair of pliers, then detach the front hose from the bracket

spected for cracks, chafing of the outer cover, leaks, blisters and other damage. These are important and vulnerable parts of the brake system and inspection should be complete. A light and mirror will be helpful for a thorough check. If a hose exhibits any of the above conditions, re-place it with a new one.

Replacement

Front brake hose

Refer to illustrations 8.3, 8.4 and 8.6

2   Loosen the wheel lug nuts, raise the vehicle and support it se-curely on jackstands. Remove the wheel.
3   At the frame bracket, hold the hose fitting with an open-end wrench and unscrew the brake line fitting from the hose (**see illustra-tion**). Use a flare-nut wrench to prevent rounding off the corners.
4   Remove the U-clip (**see illustration**) with a pair of pliers, then de-tach the hose from the bracket.
5   At the caliper end of the hose, remove the banjo fitting bolt, then detach the hose from the caliper. Discard the two copper sealing washers on either side of the fitting - they should be replaced with new ones during installation.
6   Remove the U-clip from the strut bracket (**see illustration**), then detach the hose from the bracket.

7   To install the hose, pass the caliper fitting end through the strut bracket, then connect the fitting to the caliper with the banjo bolt and two new copper washers.
8   Secure the hose to the strut bracket with the U-clip. Make sure the hose isn't twisted between the caliper and the strut bracket.
9   Route the hose into the frame bracket, again making sure it isn't twisted, then connect the brake line fitting, starting the threads by hand. Install the clip, then tighten the fitting securely.
10   Bleed the caliper (see Section 9).
11   Install the wheel and lug nuts, lower the vehicle and tighten the lug nuts to the torque specified in Chapter 1.

Rear brake hose

Refer to illustrations 8.12a and 8.12b

12   Perform Steps 2, 3 and 4 above, then repeat Steps 3 and 4 at the other end of the hose (**see illustrations**). Be sure to bleed the caliper or wheel cylinder (see Section 9).

Metal brake lines

13   When replacing brake lines, be sure to use the correct parts. Don't use copper tubing for any brake system components. Purchase steel brake lines from a dealer or auto parts store.
14   Prefabricated brake line, with the tube ends already flared and fit-

8.6 Remove the U-clip from the front strut bracket and pull the hose through the bracket

8.12a To disconnect a rear brake hose from the metal brake line at the strut bracket, break the line loose at the threaded fitting with a flare-nut wrench . . .

8.12b . . . then remove the U-clip from the bracket

9

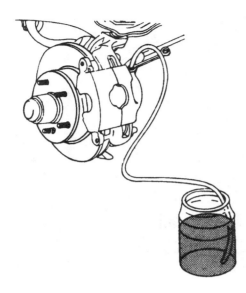

9.8 To bleed the brakes, place one end of the tubing over the bleeder valve and submerge the other end in brake fluid in the container, have an assistant pump the brakes slowly a few times and hold the pedal down, then open the bleeder valve just enough to allow fluid to flow out the valve, through the tubing and into the container, then close the bleeder valve after a few seconds; repeat this process until no more bubbles are visible in the brake fluid

tings installed, is available at auto parts stores and dealer parts departments. These lines are also bent to the proper shapes.

15   When installing the new line, make sure it's securely supported in the brackets and has plenty of clearance between moving or hot components.

16   After installation, check the master cylinder fluid level and add fluid as necessary. Bleed the brake system (see Section 9) and test the brakes carefully before driving the vehicle in traffic.

9   Brake hydraulic system - bleeding

Refer to illustration 9.8

Warning: *Wear eye protection when bleeding the brake system. If the fluid comes in contact with your eyes, immediately rinse them with water and seek medical attention.*

Note: *Bleeding the hydraulic system is necessary to remove any air that manages to find its way into the system when it's been opened during removal and installation of a hose, line, caliper or master cylinder.*

1   You'll probably have to bleed the system at all four brakes if air has entered it due to low fluid level, or if the brake lines have been disconnected at the master cylinder.

2   If a brake line was disconnected only at a wheel, then only that caliper or wheel cylinder must be bled.

3   If a brake line is disconnected at a fitting located between the master cylinder and any of the brakes, that part of the system served by the disconnected line must be bled.

4   Remove any residual vacuum from the brake power booster by applying the brake several times with the engine off.

5   Remove the master cylinder reservoir cover and fill the reservoir with brake fluid. Reinstall the cover. **Note:** *Check the fluid level often during the bleeding operation and add fluid as necessary to prevent the fluid level from falling low enough to allow air bubbles into the master cylinder.*

10.7 To disconnect the brake booster pushrod from the brake pedal, remove the retaining clip (right arrow) and pull out the clevis pin (left arrow)

6   Have an assistant on hand, as well as a supply of new brake fluid, a clear plastic container partially filled with clean brake fluid, a length of 3/16-inch plastic, rubber or vinyl tubing to fit over the bleeder valve and a wrench to open and close the bleeder valve.

7   Beginning at the right rear wheel, loosen the bleeder valve slightly, then tighten it to a point where it's snug but can still be loosened quickly and easily.

8   Place one end of the tubing over the bleeder valve and submerge the other end in brake fluid in the container **(see illustration)**.

9   Have the assistant pump the brakes slowly a few times to get pressure in the system, then hold the pedal down firmly.

10   While the pedal is held down, open the bleeder valve just enough to allow a flow of fluid to leave the valve. Watch for air bubbles to exit the submerged end of the tube. When the fluid flow slows after a couple of seconds, close the valve and have your assistant release the pedal.

11   Repeat Steps 9 and 10 until no more air is seen leaving the tube, then tighten the bleeder valve and proceed to the left rear wheel, the right front wheel and the left front wheel, in that order, and perform the same procedure. Be sure to check the fluid in the master cylinder reservoir frequently.

12   Never use old brake fluid. It contains moisture which will deteriorate the brake system components.

13   Refill the master cylinder with fluid at the end of the operation.

14   Check the operation of the brakes. The pedal should feel solid when depressed, with no sponginess. If necessary, repeat the entire process. **Warning:** *Do not operate the vehicle if you're in doubt about the effectiveness of the brake system.*

10   Power brake booster - check, removal and installation

Operating check

1   Depress the brake pedal several times with the engine off and make sure there's no change in the pedal reserve distance.

2   Depress the pedal and start the engine. If the pedal goes down slightly, operation is normal.

Airtightness check

3   Start the engine and turn it off after one or two minutes. Depress the brake pedal slowly several times. If pedal resistance increases each time (gets harder to push down), the booster is airtight.

4   Depress the brake pedal while the engine is running, then stop the

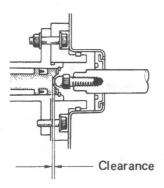

10.14a There should be zero clearance between the booster pushrod and the master cylinder pushrod, but there shouldn't be any interference either - if there is any interference, the brakes may drag; if there's much clearance, brake pedal travel will be excessive

10.14b To adjust the length of the booster pushrod, hold the serrated portion of the rod with a pair of pliers and turn the adjusting screw in or out as necessary to achieve zero clearance

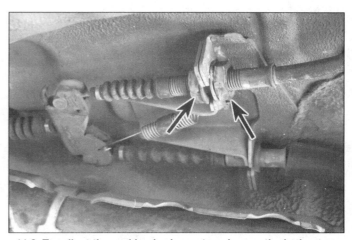

11.3 To adjust the parking brake system, loosen the locknut on the left parking brake cable (left arrow) and turn the adjuster nut (right arrow) until the parking brake lever comes up seven or eight clicks when it's applied

engine with the pedal depressed. If there's no change in the pedal reserve travel after holding the pedal for 30 seconds, the booster is airtight.

Removal

Refer to illustration 10.7

5   Power brake booster units shouldn't be disassembled. They require special tools not normally found in most automotive repair stations or shops. They're fairly complex and, because of their critical relationship to brake performance, should be replaced with a new or rebuilt one.

6   To remove the booster, first remove the brake master cylinder (see Section 7).

7   Remove the left side under-dash panel (see Chapter 11). Locate the pushrod clevis connecting the booster to the brake pedal **(see illustration)**. It's accessible from inside the vehicle, under the dash on the driver's side.

8   Remove the clevis pin retaining clip with pliers and pull out the pin.

9   Holding the clevis with pliers, unscrew the locknut with a wrench. The clevis is now loose.

10   Disconnect the hose leading from the engine to the booster. Be careful not to damage the hose when removing it from the booster fitting.

11   Remove the four nuts and washers holding the brake booster to the firewall (you may need a light to see them).

12   Slide the booster straight out from the firewall until the studs clear the holes.

Installation

Refer to illustrations 10.14a and 10.14b

13   Installation procedures are basically the reverse of removal. Tighten the clevis locknut securely and the booster mounting nuts to the torque listed in this Chapter's Specifications.

14   If the power booster unit is being replaced, the clearance between the master cylinder piston and the pushrod in the vacuum booster must be measured and, if necessary, adjusted. Using a depth micrometer or vernier calipers, measure the distance from the piston seat (recessed area) in the master cylinder to the master cylinder mounting flange. Next, measure the distance from the end of the vacuum booster pushrod to the mounting face of the booster (including gasket) where the master cylinder mounting flange seats. The measurements should be the same **(see illustration)**. If not, turn the adjusting screw on the end of the power booster pushrod until the clearance is within the specified limit **(see illustration)**.

15   After the final installation of the master cylinder and brake hoses and lines, the brake pedal height and freeplay must be adjusted and

the system must be bled. See the appropriate Sections of this Chapter for the procedures.

11   Parking brake - adjustment

Refer to illustration 11.3

1   The parking brake lever, when properly adjusted, should travel seven to eight clicks when a moderate pulling force is applied. If it travels less than seven clicks, there's a chance the parking brake might not be releasing completely and might be dragging on the drum. If the lever can be pulled up more than eight clicks, the parking brake may not hold adequately on an incline, allowing the car to roll.

2   To gain access to the parking brake cable adjuster nuts, raise the vehicle and place it securely on jackstands.

3   Loosen the cable locknut on the left cable **(see illustration)**. Tighten the adjuster nut on that cable until the parking brake lever travels the requisite seven or eight clicks. Tighten the locknut.

4   Lower the vehicle.

12   Parking brake cables - replacement

Equalizer-to-parking brake cable

Refer to illustrations 12.2 and 12.5

Note: *The following procedure applies to either rear cable.*

1   Loosen the rear wheel lug nuts, raise the rear of the vehicle and

9

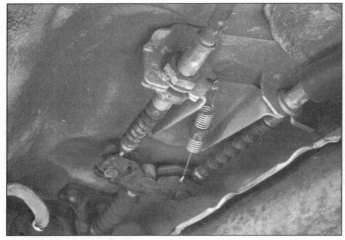

12.2 Remove the tension spring from the equalizer assembly

12.5 Remove the rear parking brake cable bracket bolt

12.13 Working inside the vehicle, release the parking brake lever so that it's in the "down" (released) position and detach the cable from the lever

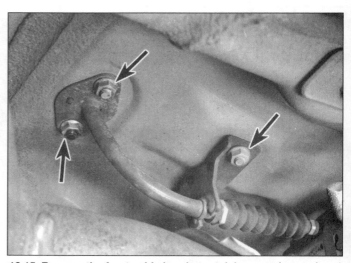

12.15 Remove the front cable bracket retaining nuts (arrows) and pull the cable through the hole in the floorpan

support it securely on jackstands. Block the front wheels. Remove the wheel.

2   Remove the tension spring **(see illustration)**.

3   Loosen the adjusting nut and locknut on the left rear cable **(see illustration 11.3)**.

4   Disconnect the rear cable from the equalizer assembly.

5   Detach the rear cable bracket **(see illustration)**.

6   Remove the brake drum and the brake shoes (see Section 5).

7   Disconnect the cable from the parking brake lever (see Section 11).

8   Pull the cable through the backing plate.

9   Installation is the reverse of removal. Be sure to adjust the parking brake when you're done (see Section 11).

Equalizer-to-brake lever cable

Refer to illustrations 12.13 and 12.15

10   Remove the center console (see Chapter 11).

11   Raise the vehicle and place it securely on jackstands.

12   Working under the vehicle, loosen the locknut and adjusting nut on the left parking brake cable **(see illustration 11.3)**.

13   Working inside the vehicle, release the parking brake lever so that it's in the "down" (released) position and detach the cable from the lever **(see illustration)**.

14   Working under the vehicle, disconnect the rear cable assembly

from the front cable assembly (see above).

15   Remove the nut from the front cable bracket and the two nuts from the flange where the cable goes through the floorpan **(see illustration)** and pull the cable through the hole in the floorpan.

16   Installation is the reverse of the removal procedure. Apply a light coat of grease to the portion of the cable end that contacts the equalizer. Be sure to adjust the parking brake when you're done (see Section 11).

13   Brake light switch - check, replacement and adjustment

Check

1   The brake light switch, which activates the brake lights at the rear of the vehicle when the pedal is depressed, is located on a bracket at the top of the brake pedal. The switch is normally open. If it's working properly, it will close the rear brake light circuit when the brake pedal is depressed.

2   To check the switch, insert the probes of a voltmeter into the backside of the electrical connector for the switch and verify that there's voltage present when the brake pedal is depressed. Or, you can use an ohmmeter: Unplug the connector and verify that there's continuity across the terminals of the switch-side connector when the

brake pedal is depressed. If the switch doesn't operate as describe, trying adjusting it, then recheck it. If it still doesn't work, replace it.

Replacement

3   Disconnect the wiring harness at the brake light switch electrical connector.
4   Loosen the locknut and unscrew the switch from the pedal bracket.
5   Installation is the reverse of removal.

Adjustment

6   Loosen the locknut and adjust the switch until the clearance between the switch plunger and the brake pedal is within the dimension listed in this Chapter's Specifications.

---

14   Brake pedal - adjustment

Refer to illustration 14.1

1   The pedal height is measured from the floor to the top of the pedal **(see illustration)**. Compare your measurement to the Specifications.
2   Loosen the brake light switch locknut (see Section 13).
3   Loosen the locknut on the pedal pushrod.
4   Turn the pedal pushrod until the pedal height is correct.
5   Tighten the pushrod locknut.
6   Adjust the brake light switch, then tighten the brake light locknut.

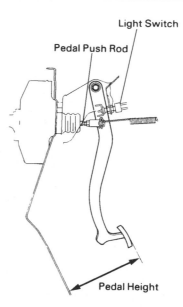

14.1 Brake pedal height is measured from the floor to the top of the pedal

9

Notes

Chapter 10
Suspension and steering systems

Contents

Specifications

Torque specifications

Ft-lbs

Front suspension

Balljoint	
Balljoint-to-control arm bolts/nuts	115
Balljoint-to-steering knuckle pinch bolt	49
Control arm	
Rear bushing-to-crossmember bolt	51
Front bushing-to-body bolt	95
Stabilizer bar	
Bar-to-control arm link bolts	19
Bar-to-crossmember bushing bracket bolts	12
Strut	
Upper mounting nuts	58
Strut-to-steering knuckle bolts/nuts	115
Damper shaft nut	43

10

Torque specifications (continued)

Ft-lbs

Rear suspension

Strut
    Upper mounting nuts 50
    Strut-to-knuckle bolts/nuts 116
    Damper shaft nut... 36
Trailing link bolts (both ends)... 94
Lateral link bolts (both ends) 94
Stabilizer bar
    Link retaining bolts... 19
    Bushing bracket bolts 71

Steering system

Supplemental Inflatable Restraint (SIR)
    inflator module mounting screws................................. 44
Steering wheel nut.. 25
U-joint pinch bolts 30
Steering gear mounting bolts 51
Tie-rod end-to-steering knuckle nut................................. 40
Power steering pump
    Adjusting and pivot bolt
        1.6L engine 11
        1.8L engine 15
    Pressure line fitting.. 25
Wheel lug nuts .... See Chapter 1

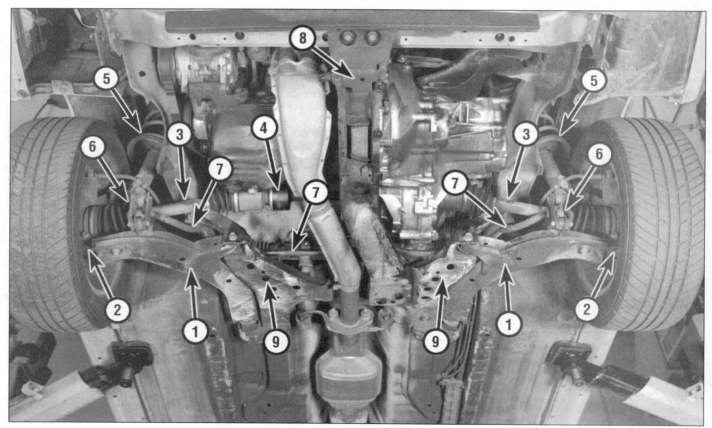

1.1 Front suspension components

1   Lower control arm
2   Balljoint
3   Driveaxle assembly

4   Intermediate shaft
      bearing support
5   Strut assembly

6   Stabilizer bar link
7   Stabilizer bar
8   Center crossmember
9   Suspension crossmember

1 General information

Refer to illustrations 1.1 and 1.2

The front suspension (**see illustration**) is a Macpherson strut design. The upper end of each strut is attached to the vehicle body. The lower end of each strut is connected to the steering knuckle. A control arm is attached to the crossmember by front and rear pivot bolts. The outer end of the control arm is attached to the steering knuckle by a balljoint bolted to the outer end of the arm. A stabilizer bar - attached to the crossmember by bushing brackets and to the control arms by links - reduces vehicle roll.

The rear suspension (**see illustration**) also utilizes strut assemblies. The upper end of each strut is attached to the vehicle body. The lower end of the strut is attached to a knuckle. The knuckle is located by a pair of lateral links on each side, and a trailing link between the body and each knuckle. A stabilizer bar is attached to the crossmember by bushing brackets and to the knuckles by links.

The power-assisted rack-and-pinion steering gear is located behind the engine/transaxle assembly on the crossmember. The steering gear actuates the tie-rods, which are attached to the steering knuckles. The steering column intermediate shaft is attached to the steering gear pinion shaft by a universal joint.

All vehicles covered by this manual are equipped with a driver's Supplemental Inflatable Restraint (SIR), i.e. an airbag. **Warning:** *When removing the steering wheel, it's critical that you follow instructions and observe all cautions and warnings. Failure to do so cause result in serious personal injury.*

Frequently, when working on the suspension or steering system components, you may come across fasteners which seem impossible to loosen. These fasteners on the underside of the vehicle are continually subjected to water, road grime, mud, etc., and can become rusted or "frozen," making them extremely difficult to remove. In order to unscrew these stubborn fasteners without damaging them (or other components), be sure to use lots of penetrating oil and allow it to soak in for a while. Using a wire brush to clean exposed threads will also ease

removal of the nut or bolt and prevent damage to the threads. Sometimes a sharp blow with a hammer and punch will break the bond between a nut and bolt threads, but care must be taken to prevent the punch from slipping off the fastener and ruining the threads. Heating the stuck fastener and surrounding area with a torch sometimes helps too, but isn't recommended because of the obvious dangers associated with fire. Long breaker bars and extension, or "cheater," pipes will increase leverage, but never use an extension pipe on a ratchet - the ratcheting mechanism could be damaged. Sometimes tightening the nut or bolt first will help to break it loose. Fasteners that require drastic measures to remove should always be replaced with new ones.

Since most of the procedures dealt with in this Chapter involve jacking up the vehicle and working underneath it, a good pair of jackstands will be needed. A hydraulic floor jack is the preferred type of jack to lift the vehicle, and it can also be used to support certain components during various operations. **Warning:** *Never, under any circumstances, rely on a jack to support the vehicle while working on it. Whenever any of the suspension or steering fasteners are loosened or removed they must be inspected and, if necessary, replaced with new ones of the same part number or of original equipment quality and design. Torque specifications must be followed for proper reassembly and component retention. Never attempt to heat or straighten any suspension or steering components. Instead, replace any bent or damaged part with a new one.*

2 Strut assembly (front) - removal, inspection and installation

Removal

Refer to illustrations 2.3 and 2.6

1   Loosen the wheel lug nuts, raise the vehicle and support it securely on jackstands. Remove the wheel.

2   Unbolt the brake hose from the caliper (see Chapter 9). Have some rags and a container handy to catch the brake fluid. Unclip the hose from the strut bracket and push it through. Plug the caliper and

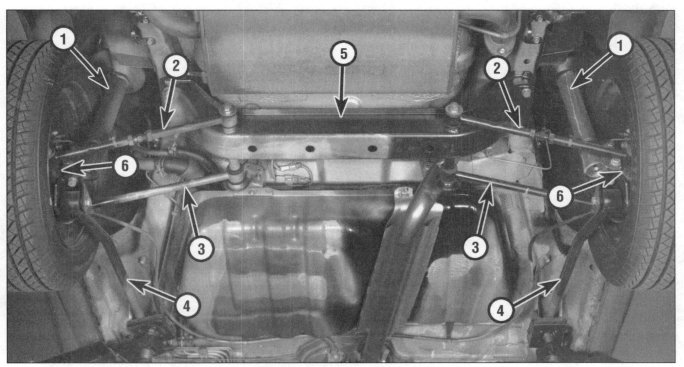

1.2 Rear suspension components

1 *Strut assembly*	3 *Front lateral link*	5 *Rear crossmember*
2 *Rear lateral link*	4 *Trailing link*	6 *Rear suspension knuckle*

10

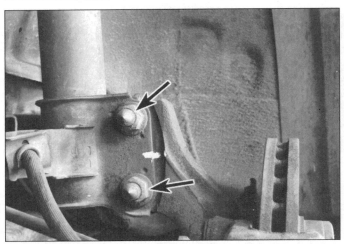

2.3 Using paint or a scribe mark the relationship of the strut to the steering knuckle then remove the bolts and nuts (arrows) that attach the strut to the knuckle

2.6 Remove the three nuts (arrows) that attach the upper end of the strut to the body

the hose to prevent leaks and to prevent contamination from entering the brake system.

3   Using paint or a sharp scribe, mark the relationship of the strut to the knuckle **(see illustration)**.

4   Remove the strut-to-knuckle nuts and knock the bolts out with a hammer and punch.

5   Separate the strut from the steering knuckle. Be careful not to overextend the inner CV joint.

6   Support the strut and spring assembly with one hand and remove the three strut-to-shock tower nuts **(see illustration)**. Remove the strut assembly.

Inspection

7   Check the strut body for leaking fluid, dents, cracks and other obvious damage which would warrant repair or replacement.

8   Check the coil spring for chips or cracks in the spring coating (this will cause premature spring failure due to corrosion). Inspect the spring seat for cuts, hardness and general deterioration.

9   If any damage or wear is evident, proceed to the strut disassembly procedure (see Section 3).

Installation

10   Guide the strut assembly up into the fenderwell and insert the three upper mounting studs through the holes in the shock tower. Once the three studs protrude from the shock tower, install the nuts so the strut won't fall back through. This is most easily accomplished with the help of an assistant, as the strut is quite heavy and awkward.

11   Slide the steering knuckle into the strut flange and insert the two bolts and nuts. Match the alignment marks and tighten the bolts/nuts to the torque listed in this Chapter's Specifications.

12   Guide the brake hose through its bracket in the strut, reconnect it to the brake caliper and tighten the banjo bolt to the torque listed in the Chapter 9 Specifications. Bleed the brakes (see Chapter 9).

13   Install the wheel and lug nuts, then lower the vehicle and tighten the lug nuts to the torque listed in the Chapter 1 Specifications.

14   Tighten the three upper mounting nuts to the torque listed in this Chapter's Specifications.

15   Drive the vehicle to an alignment shop to have the front end alignment checked, and if necessary, adjusted.

---

3   Strut - replacement

---

1   If the struts or coil springs exhibit the telltale signs of wear (leaking fluid, loss of damping capability, chipped, sagging or cracked coil springs) explore all options before beginning any work. The strut/shock

absorber assemblies are not serviceable and must be replaced if a problem develops. However, strut assemblies complete with springs may be available on an exchange basis, which eliminates much time and work. Whichever route you choose to take, check on the cost and availability of parts before disassembling your vehicle. **Warning:** *Disassembling a strut assembly is a potentially dangerous undertaking and utmost attention must be directed to the job at hand, or serious bodily injury may result. Use only a high quality spring compressor and carefully follow the manufacturer's instructions furnished with the tool. After removing the coil spring from the strut assembly, set it aside in a safe, isolated area (a steel cabinet is preferred).*

Disassembly

Refer to illustrations 3.3, 3.4, 3.5, 3.6 and 3.7

2   Remove the strut and spring assembly following the procedure described in the previous Section. Mount the strut assembly in a vise. Line the vise jaws with wood or rags to prevent damage to the unit and don't tighten the vise excessively.

3   Following the tool manufacturer's instructions, install the spring compressor (which can be obtained at most auto parts stores or equipment yards on a daily rental basis) on the spring and compress it sufficiently to relieve all pressure from the upper spring seat **(see illustration)**. This can be verified by wiggling the spring.

3.3 Install the spring compressor in accordance with the tool manufacturer's instructions and compress the spring until all pressure on the upper spring seat is relieved (you can verify this by wiggling the spring)

3.4 Remove the rubber cover and the damper shaft nut

3.5 Remove the strut support verify that the bearing in the support operates smoothly and inspect the rubber portion of the support for cracking and general deterioration - if the bearing is bad or the rubber is separated replace the support

4   Remove the rubber cover and the damper shaft nut **(see illustration)**.

5   Remove the strut support **(see illustration)**. Inspect the bearing in the support for smooth operation. If it doesn't turn smoothly, replace the strut support. Check the rubber portion of the strut support for cracking and general deterioration. If there is any separation of the rubber, replace the strut support.

6   Lift the spring seat and upper insulator from the damper shaft **(see illustration)**. Check the rubber spring seat for cracking and hardness, replacing it if necessary.

7   Carefully lift the compressed spring from the assembly **(see illustration)** and set it in a safe place, such as a steel cabinet. **Warning:** *Never place your head near the end of the spring!*

8   Slide the rubber jounce bumper off the damper shaft.

9   Remove the lower insulator and inspect it for wear, cracking and hardness. Replace it if necessary.

Reassembly

Refer to illustrations 3.11 and 3.12

10   If the lower insulator is being replaced, set it into position with the dropped portion seated in the lowest part of the seat. Extend the damper rod to its full length and install the rubber bumper.

11   Carefully place the coil spring onto the lower insulator, with the paint marks on the spring toward the lower insulator. Make sure the end of the spring rests in the lowest part of the insulator **(see illustration)**.

3.6 Remove the spring seat and the upper insulator from the damper shaft; inspect the rubber spring seat for cracking and hardness - replace it if necessary

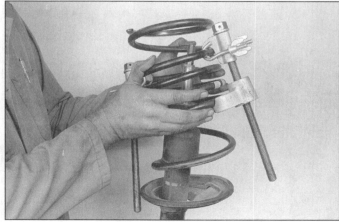

3.7 Carefully lift the compressed spring from the assembly and set it in a safe place such as a steel cabinet. Warning: Never place your head near the end of the spring!

3.11 Place the coil spring on the lower seat and insulator so that the end of the spring fits into the recessed portion of the seat (and make sure the paint marks on the spring are near the seat and insulator - not near the upper insulator and seat - or the spring will be upside down)

10

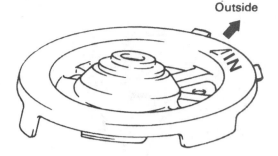

3.12 When you install the upper insulator and spring seat make sure the "IN" stamping on the spring seat faces out (in the same direction as the strut-to-knuckle flanges)

4.2 Remove the bolt and nut (arrows) and disconnect the stabilizer bar from the link plates that attach it to the control arm

4.3 Remove the bushing bracket nut (arrow) pull off the bracket and the bushing

12   Install the upper insulator and spring seat. Make sure that the "IN" stamping faces out (in the same direction as the strut-to-knuckle flange) **(see illustration)**.
13   Compress and install the coil spring, install the strut support and the strut nut and tighten the nut to the torque listed in this Chapter's Specifications.
14   Install the rubber cover.
15   Release the coil spring compressor and remove the strut assembly from the vise.
16   Install the strut assembly (see Section 2).

---

4   Front stabilizer bar and bushings - removal and installation

---

Note: *The stabilizer bar itself is fairly difficult to remove on the vehicles covered by this manual. However, the stabilizer bar bushings, which are generally the only part of the bar you should ever have to replace, can be removed without removing the stabilizer bar.*

Stabilizer bar bushings

Refer to illustrations 4.2 and 4.3
1   Loosen the wheel lug nuts, raise the front of the vehicle and support it securely on jackstands. Remove the front wheels. Apply the parking brake and block the rear wheels to keep the vehicle from rolling off the stands.
2   Disconnect both ends of the stabilizer bar from the links that attach it to the control arms **(see illustration)**.
3   Remove the bushing bracket nuts **(see illustration)** and pull off the old bushings (they're split, so you don't need to slide them all the

way to the ends of the bar).
4   Clean the bushing area of the stabilizer bar with a stiff wire brush to remove any rust or dirt.
5   Lubricate the inside and outside of the new bushing with vegetable oil (used in cooking) to simplify reassembly. **Caution:** *Don't use petroleum or mineral-based lubricants or brake fluid - they will lead to deterioration of the bushings.*
6   Installation is otherwise the reverse of removal.

Stabilizer bar

Removal

7   Loosen the wheel lug nuts, raise the front of the vehicle and support it securely on jackstands. Remove the front wheels. Apply the parking brake and block the rear wheels to keep the vehicle from rolling off the stands.
8   Remove the front exhaust pipe.
9   Disconnect the power steering lines and the intermediate shaft from the steering gear (see Section 17).
10   Remove the pinch bolts and disconnect the control arm balljoints from the steering knuckles (see Sections 5 and 6).
11   Disconnect the tie-rod ends from the steering knuckles (see Section 15).
12   Support the engine with an engine hoist from above (see Chapter 2 Part B).
13   Disconnect the engine torque rod at the center crossmember (see Chapter 2 Part A).
14   Disconnect the rear engine mount from the engine (see Chapter 2 Part A).
15   Remove the two bolts at the center crossmember and the four bolts at the suspension crossmember (see Chapter 2 Part B).
16   Remove the center crossmember, the suspension crossmember and the steering gear as an assembly.
17   Unbolt and remove the steering gear from the crossmember.
18   Unbolt and remove the stabilizer bar from the crossmember.
19   While the stabilizer bar is removed, slide the bracket bushings off and inspect them. If they're cracked, worn or deteriorated, replace them.
20   Clean the bushing area of the stabilizer bar with a stiff wire brush to remove any rust or dirt.

Installation

21   Lubricate the inside and outside of the new bushing with vegetable oil (used in cooking) to simplify reassembly. **Caution:** *Don't use petroleum or mineral-based lubricants or brake fluid - they will lead to deterioration of the bushings.*
22   Installation is otherwise the reverse of removal.

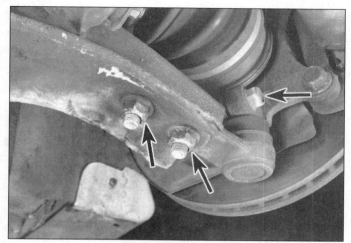

5.2 Remove the balljoint-to-steering knuckle pinch bolt (upper arrow) and remove the two nuts (lower arrows) and bolts attaching the balljoint to the control arm

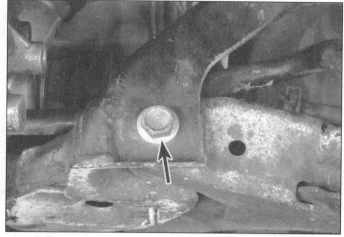

6.4 Remove the front bushing-to-body bolt (arrow)

5   Balljoints - replacement

Refer to illustration 5.2

1   Loosen the wheel lug nuts, raise the vehicle and support it securely on jackstands. Remove the wheel.
2   Remove the balljoint-to-steering knuckle pinch bolt (**see illustration**).
3   Remove the two nuts and bolts attaching the balljoint to the control arm.
4   Remove the balljoint.
5   Position the balljoint on the control arm and install the bolts and nuts, but don't tighten them yet.
6   Attach the balljoint to the steering knuckle and install the pinch bolt.
7   Tighten the balljoint-to-control arm bolts/nuts and the balljoint-to-steering knuckle pinch bolt to the torque listed in this Chapter's Specifications.
8   Install the wheel and lug nuts. Lower the vehicle and tighten the lug nuts to the torque listed in the Chapter 1 Specifications.

6   Control arm - removal, inspection and installation

Removal

Refer to illustrations 6.4 and 6.5

1   Loosen the wheel lug nuts on the side to be dismantled, raise the front of the vehicle, support it securely on jackstands and remove the wheel.
2   Disconnect the stabilizer bar links from the control arm (see Section 4).
3   Disconnect the balljoint from the steering knuckle (see Section 5).
Note: *Unless you're planning to replace either the balljoint or the control arm, it's unnecessary to disconnect the balljoint from the control arm - simply remove the pinch bolt and separate the balljoint stud from the steering knuckle.*
4   Remove the front bushing-to-body bolt (**see illustration**).
5   Remove the rear bushing-to-crossmember bolts (**see illustration**).
6   Remove the control arm.

Inspection

7   Inspect the control arm. Make sure it's straight. A bent control arm must be replaced. Inspect the control arm bushings for damage and wear. If either bushing is damaged or worn out, the control arm must be replaced. The bushings can't be replaced separately.

6.5 Remove the rear bushing-to-crossmember bolts (arrows)

Installation

8   Installation is the reverse of removal. Make sure all fasteners are tightened to the torque listed in this Chapter's Specifications.

7   Steering knuckle and hub - removal and installation

Warning: *Dust created by the brake system may contain asbestos, which is harmful to your health. Never blow it out with compressed air and don't inhale any of it. Do not, under any circumstances, use petroleum-based solvents to clean brake parts. Use brake cleaner only.*

Removal

1   Loosen the driveaxle hub nut while the vehicle is still on the ground (see Chapter 8).
2   Loosen the wheel lug nuts, raise the vehicle and support it securely on jackstands. Remove the wheel.
3   Remove the brake caliper, the caliper bracket and the brake disc (see Chapter 9). Support the caliper with a piece of wire.
4   Mark the relationship of the strut to the steering knuckle and loosen - but don't remove - the strut-to-knuckle bolts (see Section 2).

10

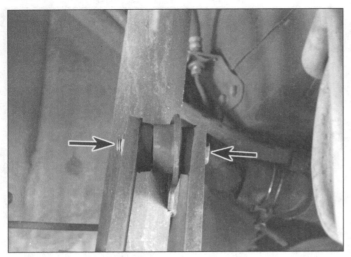

9.2 Remove the stabilizer bar-to-link bolt and nut (arrows) from each set of link plates

9.3 Remove the bolt (arrow) from each stabilizer bar bushing bracket and detach the brackets from the crossmember

10.5 Remove this bolt and nut (arrows) and disconnect the stabilizer bar link from the strut bracket

5   Disconnect the tie-rod end from the steering knuckle (see Section 15).
6   Disconnect the control arm from the steering knuckle (see Section 6).
7   Remove the driveaxle hub nut and disconnect the steering knuckle from the driveaxle (see Chapter 8). Suspend the outer end of the driveaxle with a piece of wire. **Note**: *Now would be a good time to check the driveaxle boots for damage and the transaxle side seals for leakage (see Chapter 8).*
8   Disconnect the strut from the steering knuckle (see Section 2).
9   Remove the steering knuckle.
10   Installation is the reverse of removal.
11   When you're done, drive the vehicle to a dealer or wheel alignment shop and have the toe-in checked and, if necessary, adjusted.

8   Front hub and bearing assembly - removal and installation

Due to the special tools and expertise required to press the hub and bearing from the steering knuckle, this job should be left to a professional mechanic. However, the steering knuckle and hub may be removed and the assembly taken to a dealer service department or other repair shop. See Section 7 for the steering knuckle and hub removal procedure.

9   Rear stabilizer bar and bushings - removal and installation

Refer to illustrations 9.2 and 9.3
1   Loosen the rear wheel lug nuts, raise the vehicle and support it securely on jackstands. Remove the wheels.
2   Remove the stabilizer bar-to-link bolts and nuts **(see illustration)**.
3   Unbolt the stabilizer bar bushing brackets from the crossmember **(see illustration)**.
4   Remove the stabilizer bar.
5   Inspect the stabilizer bushings for wear, hardness, distortion, cracks and other signs of deterioration. If the bushings are damaged or worn, replace them.
6   Installation is the reverse of removal. Clean the areas where the bushings contact the bar with a wire brush. If necessary, use a light coat of vegetable oil to ease bushing and U-bracket installation (don't use petroleum based products or brake fluid - they'll damage the rubber). Be sure to tighten the stabilizer bar link bolts and nuts and the stabilizer bushing bracket bolts to the torque listed in this Chapter's Specifications.

10   Strut assembly (rear) - removal, inspection and installation

Removal
Refer to illustrations 10.5, 10.6, 10.7a, 10.7b and 10.8
1   Loosen the wheel lug nuts, raise the vehicle and support it securely on jackstands. Remove the wheel.
2   Unscrew the brake line from the wheel cylinder (see Chapter 9). Use a flare nut wrench to avoid rounding off the corners of the nut.
3   Disconnect the brake line from the flexible hose at the strut bracket (see Chapter 9). Again, the use of a flare nut wrench is recommended. Plug the hose end or wrap a plastic bag tightly around the end of the hose to prevent excessive leakage and contamination.
4   Unscrew the threaded fitting that attaches the metal brake line to the brake hose at the bracket on the strut, remove the clip and disconnect the line and the hose (see Chapter 9).
5   Disconnect the stabilizer bar link from the strut bracket **(see illustration)**.
6   Mark the relationship of the strut to the knuckle, then remove the strut-to-knuckle nuts and bolts **(see illustration)**.
7   Open the rear hatch and remove the trim cover from the strut tower **(see illustrations)**.
8   Remove the three strut upper mounting nuts **(see illustration)** while an assistant supports the strut so it doesn't fall. Guide the strut out of the fenderwell.

Chapter 10 Suspension and steering systems

10.6 Mark the relationship of the strut to the knuckle then remove the strut-to-knuckle nuts and bolts (arrows)

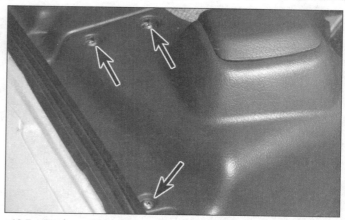

10.7a Remove these three upper trim cover screws (arrows) . . .

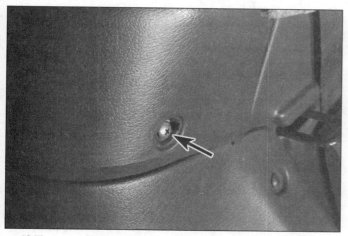

10.7b . . . and the screw on the side of the cover (arrow) and remove the trim cover

10.8 Remove the three upper mounting nuts (the two arrows plus the one not visible in this photo with a socket on it) while an assistant supports the strut so it doesn't fall

Inspection

9   Follow the inspection procedures described in Section 2. If the strut assembly must be disassembled for replacement of the strut or the coil spring, refer to Section 3.

Installation

10   Maneuver the assembly up into the fenderwell and insert the mounting studs through the holes in the body. Install the nuts, but don't tighten them yet.
11   Push the knuckle into the strut lower bracket, align the marks between the strut and the knuckle and install the bolts and nuts, tightening them to the torque listed in this Chapter's Specifications.
12   Connect the stabilizer bar link to the strut bracket.
13   Route the brake hose through its bracket on the strut, connect it to the metal brake line, tighten it securely and install the retaining clip (see Chapter 9).
14   Install the wheel and lug nuts, lower the vehicle and tighten the lug nuts to the torque listed in the Chapter 1 Specifications.
15   Tighten the three strut upper mounting nuts to the torque listed in this Chapter's Specifications.
16   Bleed the brake system at the wheel cylinder (see Chapter 9).

---

11   Rear suspension arms - removal and installation

Trailing link
Refer to illustrations 11.2a and 11.2b
1   Raise the rear of the vehicle and support it securely on jack-

stands. Block the front wheels.
2   Remove the bolts and nuts from both ends of the trailing link **(see illustrations)**.
3   Remove the trailing link.
4   Installation is the reverse of removal. Be sure to tighten the fasteners to the torque listed in this Chapter's Specifications. It's a good

11.2a Remove the bolts and nuts (arrow) from the forward end of the trailing link . . .

10

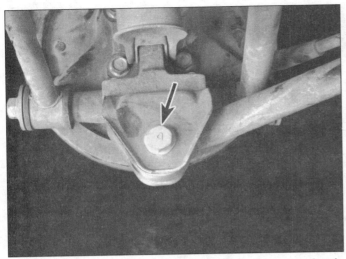

11.2b . . . and the bolts and nuts (arrows) from the rear end and remove the trailing link

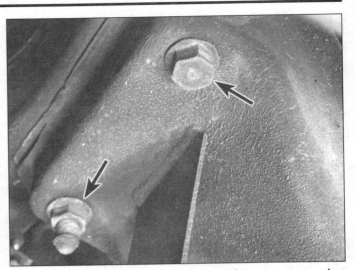

11.6a To remove either lateral link support the rear crossmember with a floor jack remove this nut and bolt (arrows) from both ends of the rear crossmember and lower the crossmember

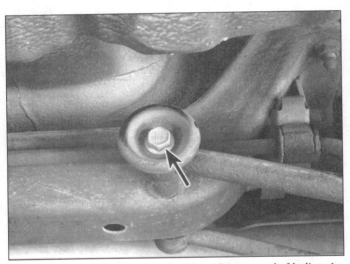

11.6b Remove the bolt (arrow) and nut (at rear end of bolt, not visible in this photo) to disconnect the inner end of the lateral links from the rear crossmember

11.7 Remove the bolt (arrow) and nut (at rear end of bolt, not visible in this photo) to disconnect the outer end of the lateral links from the knuckle

idea to take the vehicle to a dealer or wheel alignment shop and have the rear wheel toe-in checked and, if necessary, adjusted after you're done.

Lateral links

Refer to illustrations 11.6a, 11.6b and 11.7

5   Raise the rear of the vehicle and support it securely on jackstands. Block the front wheels.

6   If you're replacing either left lateral link, support the rear crossmember with a floor jack, loosen the four rear crossmember-to-body nuts and bolts (two on each end of the crossmember) and lower the crossmember, then remove the bolts that attach the inner ends of the left lateral links to the rear crossmember **(see illustrations)**.

7   Remove the bolt and nut that attach the outer ends of the left lateral links to the knuckle **(see illustration)**. Remove the left lateral links.

8   Removal of the right lateral links is identical to the above procedure for the left links, except that it isn't necessary to lower the crossmember.

9   Installation is the reverse of removal. Be sure to tighten the fasteners to the torque listed in this Chapter's Specifications.

10   If you're replacing a rear lateral link, take the vehicle to a dealer or wheel alignment shop and have the rear wheel toe-in adjusted.

---

12   Rear hub and bearing assembly - removal and installation

---

Refer to illustration 12.3

Warning: *Dust created by the brake system may contain asbestos, which is harmful to your health. Never blow it out with compressed air and don't inhale any of it. Do not, under any circumstances, use petroleum-based solvents to clean brake parts. Use brake cleaner only.*

Note: *Due to the special tools required to replace the bearing, the hub and bearing assembly should not be disassembled by the home mechanic. The assembly can be removed, however, and taken to a dealer service department or other repair shop to have the bearing replaced.*

1   Loosen the wheel lug nuts, raise the vehicle and support it securely on jackstands. Remove the wheel.

2   Pull the brake drum from the hub (see Chapter 9).

3   Remove the four knuckle-to-hub bolts **(see illustration)**.

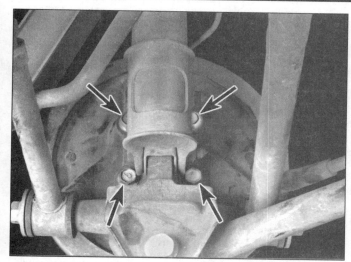

12.3 Remove the four knuckle-to-hub bolts (arrows)

15.2 Mark the position of the tie-rod end on the tie-rod threads with a paint mark; then when you install the new tie-rod end simply screw it on up to the paint mark

4   Remove the hub and bearing assembly.
5   Installation is the reverse of removal. Be sure to tighten the knuckle-to-hub bolts to the torque listed in this Chapter's Specifications.

13   Rear suspension knuckle - removal and installation

Warning: *Dust created by the brake system may contain asbestos, which is harmful to your health. Never blow it out with compressed air and don't inhale any of it. Do not, under any circumstances, use petroleum-based solvents to clean brake parts. Use brake cleaner only.*
1   Loosen the wheel lug nuts, raise the vehicle and support it on jackstands. Block the front wheels and remove the rear wheel.
2   Remove the rear brake drum (see Chapter 9).
3   Disconnect the brake line from the wheel cylinder (see Chapter 9). Use a flare nut wrench to prevent rounding off the tube nut corners.
4   Detach the rear brake assembly (see Chapter 9).
5   Remove the rear hub and bearing assembly (see Section 12).
6   Remove the backing plate and suspend it with a piece of wire from the coil spring. **Note:** *It isn't necessary to remove the parking brake cable from the backing plate.*
7   Disconnect the lower end of the strut from the knuckle (see Section 10).
8   Disconnect the rear end of the trailing link and the outer ends of both lateral links from the knuckle (see Section 11).
9   Remove the suspension knuckle.
10   Installation is the reverse of removal.
11   Bleed the wheel cylinder when you're done (see Chapter 9), then take the vehicle to a dealer or wheel alignment shop and have the rear wheel toe-in checked and, if necessary, adjusted.

14   Steering system - general information

All models are equipped with a power-assisted rack-and-pinion steering gear which operates the steering knuckles via a pair of tie-rods. The steering gear is bolted to the lower crossmember. The ends of the steering gear are protected by rubber boots which should be inspected periodically for secure attachment, tears and leaking lubricant.
The power assist system consists of a belt-driven pump and the lines and hoses between the pump and the steering gear. The fluid level in the power steering pump reservoir should be checked periodically (see Chapter 1).
The steering wheel operates the steering shaft, which actuates the steering gear rack through an intermediate shaft and a universal

joint. Looseness in the steering can be caused by wear in the universal joint, the steering gear rack-and-pinion or the tie-rod ends, or by loose retaining bolts.

15   Tie-rod ends - removal and installation

Refer to illustrations 15.2 and 15.4

Removal

1   Loosen the wheel lug nuts. Raise the front of the vehicle, support it securely on jackstands, block the rear wheels and set the parking brake. Remove the front wheel.
2   Hold the tie-rod with a pair of locking pliers or wrench and loosen the jam nut enough to mark the position of the tie-rod end in relation to the threads **(see illustration)**.
3   Loosen the nut on the tie-rod end balljoint stud.
4   Disconnect the tie-rod end stud from the steering knuckle arm with a puller **(see illustration)**. Remove the nut and separate the tie-rod from the knuckle.
5   Unscrew the tie-rod end from the tie-rod.

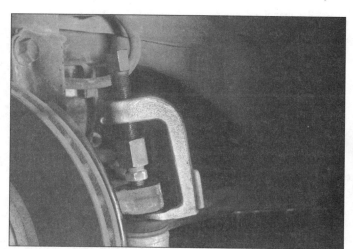

15.4 Disconnect the tie-rod end from steering knuckle with a puller or balljoint separator (note that the nut has been loosened, but not removed - this will prevent the components from separating violently)

10

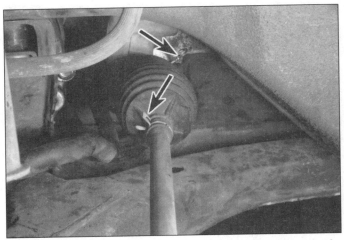

16.3 Remove the outer boot clamp (lower arrow) with a pair of pliers and cut the inner wire retaining ring (upper arrow) with a pair of diagonal cutters and remove the boot

17.2 Place a drain pan under the power steering pressure and return line fittings unscrew the fittings (arrows) and separate the lines from the steering gear

Installation

6   Screw the tie-rod end onto the tie-rod up to the marked position and tighten the jam nut securely.

7   Insert the tie-rod end stud into the steering knuckle, install a new nut and tighten it to the torque listed in this Chapter's Specifications.

8   Install the wheel and lug nuts. Lower the vehicle and tighten the lug nuts to the torque listed in the Chapter 1 Specifications.

9   Have the alignment checked by a dealer service department or an alignment shop.

16   Steering gear boots - replacement

Refer to illustration 16.3

1   Loosen the lug nuts, raise the vehicle and support it securely on jackstands. Remove the wheel.

2   Remove the tie-rod end and jam nut (see Section 15).

3   Remove the outer boot clamp, cut the inner boot retaining ring **(see illustration)** and slide the boot off.

4   Before installing the new boot, wrap the threads and
  on the tie-rod with a layer of tape so the small end of the new boot isn't damaged.

5   Slide the new boot into position on the steering gear until it seats in the groove in the steering rod and install new clamps.

6 . Remove the tape and install the tie-rod end (see Section 15).

7   Install the wheel and lug nuts. Lower the vehicle and tighten the lug nuts to the torque listed in the Chapter 1 Specifications.

17   Steering gear - removal and installation

Refer to illustrations 17.2, 17.3, 17.5 and 17.7

1   Loosen the front wheel lug nuts, raise the front of the vehicle and support it securely on jackstands. Apply the parking brake and remove the wheels. Remove the engine under covers on models so equipped.

2   Place a drain pan under the fittings for the power steering pressure and return lines, unscrew the fittings and detach both lines **(see illustration)**. Cap the ends of both lines to prevent excessive fluid loss and contamination.

3   From inside the vehicle, remove the plastic cover from the lower end of the steering column and mark the relationship of the lower end of the intermediate shaft with the upper end of the U-joint that connects it to the steering gear pinion shaft **(see illustration**. Loosen the upper U-joint pinch bolt.

4   Remove the nuts from the studs protruding through the firewall on either side of the hole for the U-joint and, working from underneath the vehicle, pull the dust boot down and peel it back.

5   Mark the relationship of the lower end of the U-joint to the steer-

17.3 Mark the relationship of the upper end of the U-joint to the lower end of the intermediate shaft, then loosen the upper pinch bolt (arrow)

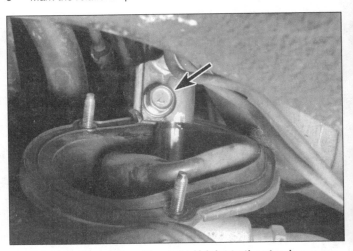

17.5 Mark the relationship of the U-joint to the steering gear pinion shaft then remove the lower U-joint pinch bolt (arrow)

17.7 Remove these bolts (arrows) from the steering gear retaining brackets (right side shown, left side similar)

18.3a Pinch the tangs on this wire harness clip together and separate the harness and clip from this bracket . . .

ing gear pinion shaft and loosen the lower U-joint pinch bolt **(see illustration)**.

6   Separate the tie-rod ends from the steering knuckle arms (see Section 15).

7   Remove the mounting bolts from the steering gear retaining brackets **(see illustration)** and remove the brackets.

8   Pull the steering gear out from the right side of the vehicle.

9   Installation is the reverse of removal. Be sure to align the marks on the U-joint with the marks on the shafts. Tighten the fastenerss to the torque listed in this Chapter's Specifications.

10   Lower the vehicle and bleed the steering system (see Section 19

---

18   Power steering pump - removal and installation

Removal

Refer to illustrations 18.3a, 18.3b, 18.3c, 18.4. 18.5a, 18.5b and 18.6

1   Using a large syringe or suction gun, suck as much fluid out of the power steering fluid reservoir as possible. Place a drain pan under the vehicle to catch any fluid that spills out when the hoses are disconnected.

2   Remove the drivebelt (see Chapter 1).

3   Disconnect the wire harness and unplug the electrical connector **(see illustrations)**.

4   Loosen the clamp and disconnect the fluid return hose from the pump; unscrew the threaded fitting and disconnect the fluid pressure line **(see illustration)**.

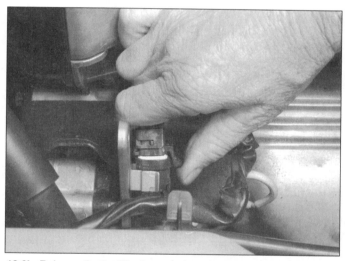

18.3b Release the locking tang and unplug this connector next to the power steering pump . . .

18.3c . . . then pry the lower half of the connector loose from its retaining bracket

18.4 Place a drain pan under the power steering pump then unscrew the pressure line fitting (upper arrow), remove the return hose clamp (lower arrow) and disconnect the line and the hose

18.5a Power steering pump upper through-bolt (left arrow) and nut (right arrow)

18.5b Use a deep socket to get at the the lower power steering pump adjuster bolt (serpentine belt removed for clarity)

5   Remove the pivot and adjusting bolts **(see illustrations)**.
6   Turn the pump over and disconnect the pressure switch wire from the bottom of the pump **(see illustration)**.
7   Remove the pump and bracket from the vehicle.
8   Separate the pulley from the pump with a GM J 25034-B power steering pump pulley remover or a similar tool.
9   Separate the pump from the bracket.

Installation

10   Installation is the reverse of removal. You'll need GM's J25033-B power steering pump puller installer or a similar tool to install the pulley. Be sure to tighten the adjusting and pivot bolts securely and the high pressure hose fitting to the torque listed in this Chapter's Specifications. Adjust the drivebelt tension following the procedure described in Chapter 1.
11   Top up the fluid level in the reservoir (see Chapter 1) and bleed the system (see Section 19).

remove all air and obtain proper steering performance.
2   With the front wheels in the straight ahead position, check the power steering fluid level and, if low, add fluid until it reaches the Cold mark on the dipstick.
3   Start the engine and allow it to run at fast idle. Recheck the fluid level and add more if necessary to reach the Cold mark on the dipstick.
4   Bleed the system by turning the wheels from side to side, without hitting the stops. This will work the air out of the system. Keep the reservoir full of fluid as this is done.
5   When the air is worked out of the system, return the wheels to the straight ahead position and leave the vehicle running for several more minutes before shutting it off.
6   Road test the vehicle to be sure the steering system is functioning normally and noise free.
7   Recheck the fluid level to be sure it is up to the Max mark on the side of the reservoir while the engine is at normal operating temperature. Add fluid if necessary (see Chapter 1).

19   Power steering system - bleeding

1   Following any operation in which the power steering fluid lines have been disconnected, the power steering system must be bled to

20   Steering wheel - removal and installation

Warning: *The following procedure is DANGEROUS! The steering wheel on every vehicle covered by this manual is equipped with an*

18.6 Turn the power steering pump over and disconnect the pressure switch wire

20.1a To disable the airbag system turn the ignition switch to Off, detach the cable from the negative battery terminal, remove fuses C-22 and C-23 (arrows) from the fuse box . . .

20.1b . . . and unplug the orange three-way connector (arrow) at the base of the steering column

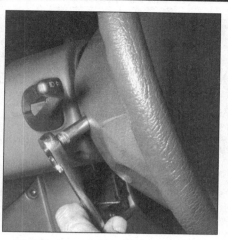

20.2 Remove the four inflator module retaining bolts from the backside of the steering wheel (two on each side)

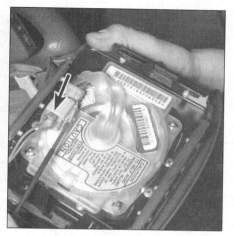

20.3 Turn the inflator module over, pry open the locking tangs on the electrical connector (arrow) and unplug the connector

airbag. DO NOT attempt to remove the steering wheel until you have read the Airbag Section in Chapter 12. Failure to observe all Warnings can result in accidental deployment of the airbag and serious physical injury.

Removal

Refer to illustrations 20.1a, 20.1b, 20.2, 20.3, 20.4 and 20.5

1   Disable the airbag system before removing it as follows:
 a) Turn the ignition switch to Off.
 b) Detach the cable from the negative battery terminal.
 c) Remove fuses C-22 and C-23 from the fuse box **(see illustration)**.
 d) Unplug the orange three-way connector at the base of the steering column **(see illustration)**.
2   Remove the four inflator module retaining bolts from the backside of the steering wheel **(see illustration)**.
3   Turn the inflator module over and unplug the electrical connector **(see illustration)**.
4   Remove the steering wheel retaining nut and mark the relationship between the steering wheel hub and the steering shaft **(see illustration)**. Unplug the electrical connector for the horn.
5   Use a puller to remove the steering wheel **(see illustration)**.

Installation

6   Before installing the steering wheel, MAKE SURE THE NEUTRAL ARROW ON THE CLEAR PLASTIC RING POINTS TOWARD THE MARK AT SIX O'CLOCK ON THE AIRBAG COIL (see the *Airbag* Section in Chapter 12).
7   To install the wheel, align the mark on the steering wheel hub with the mark on the shaft and slip the wheel onto the shaft. Install the nut and tighten it to the torque listed in this Chapter's Specifications. Plug in the electrical connector for the horn.
8   Plug in the electrical connector for the module. Place the airbag inflator module in position and install the four retaining screws.
9   To enable the airbag system:
 a) Turn the ignition switch to the Off position.
 b) Plug in the orange three-way connector at the base of the steering column.
 c) Install fuses C-22 and C-23.
 d) Connect the negative battery cable.

21   Wheels and tires - general information

Refer to illustration 21.1

1   All vehicles covered by this manual are equipped with metric-

20.4 After removing the steering wheel retaining nut mark the relationship between the steering wheel hub and the steering shaft then unplug the electrical connector (arrow) for the horn

20.5 Use a puller to remove the steering wheel

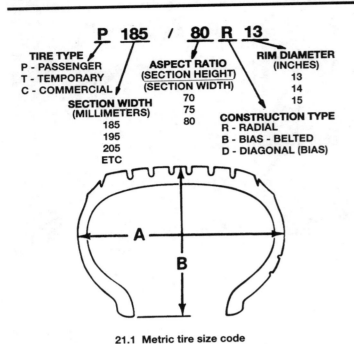

21.1 Metric tire size code

A = Section width   B = Section length

sized fiberglass or steel belted radial tires **(see illustration)**. Use of other size or type of tires may affect the ride and handling of the vehicle. Don't mix different types of tires, such as radials and bias belted, on the same vehicle as handling may be seriously affected. It's recommended that tires be replaced in pairs on the same axle, but if only one tire is being replaced, be sure it's the same size, structure and tread design as the other.

2   Because tire pressure has a substantial effect on handling and wear, the pressure on all tires should be checked at least once a month or before any extended trips (see Chapter 1).

3   Wheels must be replaced if they are bent, dented, leak air, have elongated bolt holes, are heavily rusted, out of vertical symmetry or if the lug nuts won't stay tight. Wheel repairs that use welding or peening are not recommended.

4   Tire and wheel balance is impor
tant in the overall handling, braking and performance of the vehicle. Unbalanced wheels can adversely affect handling and ride characteristics as well as tire life. Whenever a tire is installed on a wheel, the tire and wheel should be balanced by a shop with the proper equipment.

22   Wheel alignment - general information

Refer to illustration 22.1

A wheel alignment refers to the adjustments made to the wheels so they are in proper angular relationship to the suspension and the ground. Wheels that are out of proper alignment not only affect vehicle control, but also increase tire wear. Camber and caster can't be adjusted on the vehicles covered by this manual; if a dealer or wheel alignment shop discovers that the camber or caster is out of alignment, it's probably caused by dented or worn suspension parts or by body damage. Toe-in, however, is adjustable at all four wheels **(see illustration)**.

Getting the proper wheel alignment is a very exacting process, one which requires complicated and expensive machines. If you have removed and installed or replaced a suspension part that affects toe-in, have the toe-in checked and, if necessary, adjusted by a technician with the proper equipment to perform these tasks. The following information, however, will give you a basic idea of what a wheel alignment

involves so you communicate effectively with the shop that does the work.

Toe-in is the turning in of the wheels. The purpose of a toe specification is to ensure parallel rolling of the wheels. In a vehicle with zero toe-in, the distance between the front edges of the wheels will be the same as the distance between the rear edges of the wheels. The actual amount of toe-in is normally only a fraction of an inch. On the front end, toe-in is controlled by the position of the tie-rod end on the tie-rod. On the rear end, it's controlled by the position of the outer end of the rear lateral link in relation to the inner end of the link. Incorrect toe-in will cause the tires to wear improperly by making them scrub against the road surface.

Camber is the inclination of the wheels from vertical when viewed from one end of the vehicle. When the wheels tilt out at the top, the camber is said to be positive (+). When the wheels tilt in at the top, the camber is negative (-). The amount of tilt is measured in degrees from vertical and this measurement is called the camber angle. This angle affects the amount of tire tread which contacts the road and compensates for changes in the suspension geometry when the vehicle is cornering or traveling over an undulating surface.

Caster is the inclination of the front steering axis from the vertical. Positive caster is the inclination of the upper end of the steering axis to the rear; negative caster is the inclination of the upper end of the steering axis to the front.

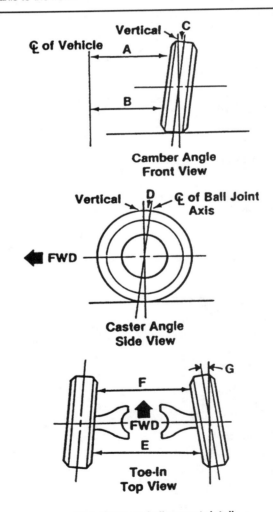

22.1 Front end alignment details

1   A minus B = C (degrees camber)
2   E minus F = toe-in (measured in inches)
3   G - toe-in (expressed in degrees)

Chapter 11 Body

Contents

1   General information

These models feature a "unibody" layout, using a floor pan with front and rear frame side rails which support the body components, front and rear suspension systems and other mechanical components. Certain components are particularly vulnerable to accident damage and can be unbolted and repaired or replaced. Among these parts are the body moldings, bumpers, hood and liftgates and all glass.

Only general body maintenance practices and body panel repair procedures within the scope of the do-it-yourselfer are included in this Chapter.

2   Body – maintenance

1   The condition of your vehicle's body is very important, because the resale value depends a great deal on it. It's much more difficult to repair a neglected or damaged body than it is to repair mechanical

components. The hidden areas of the body, such as the wheel wells, the frame and the engine compartment, are equally important, although they don't require as frequent attention as the rest of the body.
2   Once a year, or every 12,000 miles, it's a good idea to have the underside of the body steam cleaned. All traces of dirt and oil will be removed and the area can then be inspected carefully for rust, damaged brake lines, frayed electrical wires, damaged cables and other problems. The front suspension components should be greased after completion of this job.
3   At the same time, clean the engine and the engine compartment with a steam cleaner or water soluble degreaser.
4   The wheel wells should be given close attention, since undercoating can peel away and stones and dirt thrown up by the tires can cause the paint to chip and flake, allowing rust to set in. If rust is found, clean down to the bare metal and apply an anti-rust paint.
5   The body should be washed about once a week. Wet the vehicle thoroughly to soften the dirt, then wash it down with a soft sponge and plenty of clean soapy water. If the surplus dirt is not washed off very carefully, it can wear down the paint.

11

6   Spots of tar or asphalt thrown up from the road should be removed with a cloth soaked in solvent.

7   Once every six months, wax the body and chrome trim. If a chrome cleaner is used to remove rust from any of the vehicle's plated parts, remember that the cleaner also removes part of the chrome, so use it sparingly.

3   Vinyl trim – maintenance

Don't clean vinyl trim with detergents, caustic soap or petroleum-based cleaners. Plain soap and water works just fine, with a soft brush to clean dirt that may be ingrained. Wash the vinyl as frequently as the rest of the vehicle.

After cleaning, application of a high quality rubber and vinyl protectant will help prevent oxidation and cracks. The protectant can also be applied to weatherstripping, vacuum lines and rubber hoses, which often fail as a result of chemical degradation, and to the tires.

4   Upholstery and carpets – maintenance

1   Every three months remove the carpets or mats and clean the interior of the vehicle (more frequently if necessary). Vacuum the upholstery and carpets to remove loose dirt and dust.

2   Leather upholstery requires special care. Stains should be removed with warm water and a very mild soap solution. Use a clean, damp cloth to remove the soap, then wipe again with a dry cloth. Never use alcohol, gasoline, nail polish remover or thinner to clean leather upholstery.

3   After cleaning, regularly treat leather upholstery with a leather wax. Never use car wax on leather upholstery.

4   In areas where the interior of the vehicle is subject to bright sunlight, cover leather seats with a sheet if the vehicle is to be left out for any length of time.

5   Body repair – minor damage

See color photo sequence

Repair of minor scratches

1   If the scratch is superficial and does not penetrate to the metal of the body, repair is very simple. Lightly rub the scratched area with a fine rubbing compound to remove loose paint and built-up wax. Rinse the area with clean water.

2   Apply touch-up paint to the scratch, using a small brush. Continue to apply thin layers of paint until the surface of the paint in the scratch is level with the surrounding paint. Allow the new paint at least two weeks to harden, then blend it into the surrounding paint by rubbing with a very fine rubbing compound. Finally, apply a coat of wax to the scratch area.

3   If the scratch has penetrated the paint and exposed the metal of the body, causing the metal to rust, a different repair technique is required. Remove all loose rust from the bottom of the scratch with a pocket knife, then apply rust inhibiting paint to prevent the formation of rust in the future. Using a rubber or nylon applicator, coat the scratched area with glaze-type filler. If required, the filler can be mixed with thinner to provide a very thin paste, which is ideal for filling narrow scratches. Before the glaze filler in the scratch hardens, wrap a piece of smooth cotton cloth around the tip of a finger. Dip the cloth in thinner and then quickly wipe it along the surface of the scratch. This will ensure that the surface of the filler is slightly hollow. The scratch can now be painted over as described earlier in this section.

Repair of dents

4   When repairing dents, the first job is to pull the dent out until the affected area is as close as possible to its original shape. There is no point in trying to restore the original shape completely as the metal in the damaged area will have stretched on impact and cannot be restored to its original contours. It is better to bring the level of the dent up to a point which is about 1/8-inch below the level of the surrounding metal. In cases where the dent is very shallow, it is not worth trying to pull it out at all.

5   If the back side of the dent is accessible, it can be hammered out gently from behind using a soft-face hammer. While doing this, hold a block of wood firmly against the opposite side of the metal to absorb the hammer blows and prevent the metal from being stretched.

6   If the dent is in a section of the body which has double layers, or some other factor makes it inaccessible from behind, a different technique is required. Drill several small holes through the metal inside the damaged area, particularly in the deeper sections. Screw long, self-tapping screws into the holes just enough for them to get a good grip in the metal. Now the dent can be pulled out by pulling on the protruding heads of the screws with locking pliers.

7   The next stage of repair is the removal of paint from the damaged area and from an inch or so of the surrounding metal. This is done with a wire brush or sanding disk in a drill motor, although it can be done just as effectively by hand with sandpaper. To complete the preparation for filling, score the surface of the bare metal with a screwdriver or the tang of a file, or drill small holes in the affected area. This will provide a good grip for the filler material. To complete the repair, see the subsection on filling and painting later in this Section.

Repair of rust holes or gashes

8   Remove all paint from the affected area and from an inch or so of the surrounding metal using a sanding disk or wire brush mounted in a drill motor. If these are not available, a few sheets of sandpaper will do the job just as effectively.

9   With the paint removed, you will be able to determine the severity of the corrosion and decide whether to replace the whole panel, if possible, or repair the affected area. New body panels are not as expensive as most people think and it is often quicker to install a new panel than to repair large areas of rust.

10   Remove all trim pieces from the affected area except those which will act as a guide to the original shape of the damaged body, such as headlight shells, etc. Using metal snips or a hacksaw blade, remove all loose metal and any other metal that is badly affected by rust. Hammer the edges of the hole in to create a slight depression for the filler material.

11   Wire brush the affected area to remove the powdery rust from the surface of the metal. If the back of the rusted area is accessible, treat it with rust inhibiting paint.

12   Before filling is done, block the hole in some way. This can be done with sheet metal riveted or screwed into place, or by stuffing the hole with wire mesh.

13   Once the hole is blocked off, the affected area can be filled and painted. See the following subsection on filling and painting.

Filling and painting

14   Many types of body fillers are available, but generally speaking, body repair kits which contain filler paste and a tube of resin hardener are best for this type of repair work. A wide, flexible plastic or nylon applicator will be necessary for imparting a smooth and contoured finish to the surface of the filler material. Mix up a small amount of filler on a clean piece of wood or cardboard (use the hardener sparingly). Follow the manufacturer's instructions on the package, otherwise the filler will set incorrectly.

15   Using the applicator, apply the filler paste to the prepared area. Draw the applicator across the surface of the filler to achieve the desired contour and to level the filler surface. As soon as a contour that approximates the original one is achieved, stop working the paste. If you continue, the paste will begin to stick to the applicator. Continue to add thin layers of paste at 20-minute intervals until the level of the filler is just above the surrounding metal.

16   Once the filler has hardened, the excess can be removed with a body file. From then on, progressively finer grades of sandpaper should be used, starting with a 180-grit paper and finishing with a 600-

grit wet-or-dry paper. Always wrap the sandpaper around a flat rubber or wooden block, otherwise the surface of the filler will not be completely flat. During the sanding of the filler surface, the wet-or-dry paper should be periodically rinsed in water. This will ensure that a very smooth finish is produced in the final stage.

17   At this point, the repair area should be surrounded by a ring of bare metal, which in turn should be encircled by the finely feathered edge of good paint. Rinse the repair area with clean water until all of the dust produced by the sanding operation is gone.

18   Spray the entire area with a light coat of primer. This will reveal any imperfections in the surface of the filler. Repair the imperfections with fresh filler paste or glaze filler and once more smooth the surface with sandpaper. Repeat this spray-and-repair procedure until you are satisfied that the surface of the filler and the feathered edge of the paint are perfect. Rinse the area with clean water and allow it to dry completely.

19   The repair area is now ready for painting. Spray painting must be carried out in a warm, dry, windless and dust free atmosphere. These conditions can be created if you have access to a large indoor work area, but if you are forced to work in the open, you will have to pick the day very carefully. If you are working indoors, dousing the floor in the work area with water will help settle the dust which would otherwise be in the air. If the repair area is confined to one body panel, mask off the surrounding panels. This will help minimize the effects of a slight mismatch in paint color. Trim pieces such as chrome strips, door handles, etc., will also need to be masked off or removed. Use masking tape and several thicknesses of newspaper for the masking operations.

20   Before spraying, shake the paint can thoroughly, then spray a test area until the spray painting technique is mastered. Cover the repair area with a thick coat of primer. The thickness should be built up using several thin layers of primer rather than one thick one. Using 600-grit wet-or-dry sandpaper, rub down the surface of the primer until it is very smooth. While doing this, the work area should be thoroughly rinsed with water and the wet-or-dry sandpaper periodically rinsed as well. Allow the primer to dry before spraying additional coats.

21   Spray on the top coat, again building up the thickness by using several thin layers of paint. Begin spraying in the center of the repair area and then, using a circular motion, work out until the whole repair area and about two inches of the surrounding original paint is covered. Remove all masking material 10 to 15 minutes after spraying on the final coat of paint. Allow the new paint at least two weeks to harden, then use a very fine rubbing compound to blend the edges of the new paint into the existing paint. Finally, apply a coat of wax.

6   Body repair – major damage

1   Major damage must be repaired by an auto body shop specifically equipped to perform unibody repairs. These shops have the specialized equipment required to do the job properly.

2   If the damage is extensive, the body must be checked for proper alignment or the vehicle's handling characteristics may be adversely affected and other components may wear at an accelerated rate.

3   Due to the fact that all of the major body components (hood, fenders, etc.) are separate and replaceable units, any seriously damaged components should be replaced rather than repaired. Sometimes the components can be found in a wrecking yard that specializes in used vehicle components, often at considerable savings over the cost of new parts.

7   Hinges and locks – maintenance

Once every 3000 miles, or every three months, the hinges and latch assemblies on the doors, hood and trunk should be given a few drops of light oil or lock lubricant. The door latch strikers should also be lubricated with a thin coat of grease to reduce wear and ensure free movement. Lubricate the door and trunk locks with spray-on graphite lubricant.

8   Windshield and fix.ed glass – replacement

Replacement of the windshield and fixed glass requires the use of special fast-setting adhesive/caulk materials and some specialized tools. It is recommended that these operations be left to a dealer or a shop specializing in glass work.

9   Hood – removal, installation and adjustment

Refer to illustration 9.1

Note: *The hood is heavy and somewhat awkward to remove and install – at least two people should perform this procedure.*

Removal and installation

1   Make marks around the bolt heads to ensure proper alignment during installation **(see illustration)**.

2   Use blankets or pads to cover the cowl area of the body and fenders. This will protect the body and paint as the hood is lifted off.

3   Disconnect any cables or wires that will interfere with removal.

4   Have an assistant support the hood. Remove the hinge-to-hood screws or bolts.

5   Lift off the hood.

6   Installation is the reverse of removal.

Adjustment

7   Fore-and-aft and side-to-side adjustment of the hood is done by moving the hinge plate slot after loosening the bolts or nuts.

8   Scribe or draw a line around the bolt heads and the entire hinge plate so you can judge the amount of movement **(see illustration 9.1)**.

9   Loosen the bolts or nuts and move the hood into correct alignment. Move it only a little at a time. Tighten the hinge bolts or nuts and carefully lower the hood to check the position.

10   If necessary after installation, the entire hood latch assembly can be adjusted up-and-down as well as from side-to-side on the radiator support so the hood closes securely, flush with the fenders. To make the adjustment, scribe a line around the hood latch mounting bolts to provide a reference point, then loosen them and reposition the latch assembly, as necessary. Following adjustment, retighten the mounting bolts.

11   Finally, adjust the hood bumpers on the radiator support so the hood, when closed, is flush with the fenders.

12   The hood latch assembly, as well as the hinges, should be periodically lubricated with lithium-base grease to prevent binding and wear.

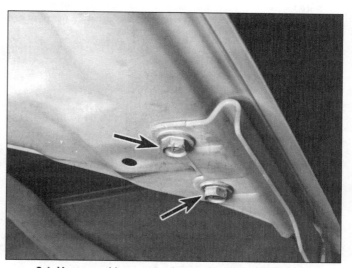

9.1 Use a marking pen to draw a line around the hood bolts (arrows)

These photos illustrate a method of repairing simple dents. They are intended to supplement *Body repair - minor damage* in this Chapter and should not be used as the sole instructions for body repair on these vehicles.

1   If you can't access the backside of the body panel to hammer out the dent, pull it out with a slide-hammer-type dent puller. In the deepest portion of the dent or along the crease line, drill or punch hole(s) at least one inch apart . . .

2   . . . then screw the slide-hammer into the hole and operate i Tap with a hammer near the edge of the dent to help 'pop' the metal back to its original shape. When you're finished, the den area should be close to its original contour and about 1/8-inch below the surface of the surrounding metal

3   Using coarse-grit sandpaper, remove the paint down to the bare metal. Hand sanding works fine, but the disc sander shown here makes the job faster. Use finer (about 320-grit) sandpaper to feather-edge the paint at least one inch around the dent area

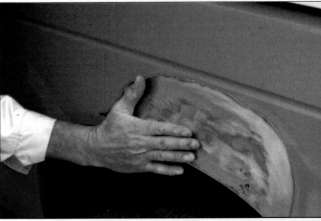

4   When the paint is removed, touch will probably be more helpful than sight for telling if the metal is straight. Hammer down the high spots or raise the low spots as necessary. Clean the repair area with wax/silicone remover

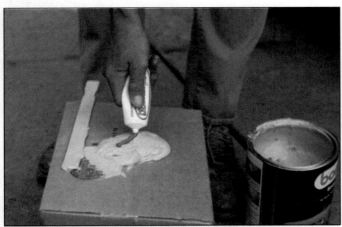

5   Following label instructions, mix up a batch of plastic filler and hardener. The ratio of filler to hardener is critical, and, if you mix it incorrectly, it will either not cure properly or cure too quickly (you won't have time to file and sand it into shape)

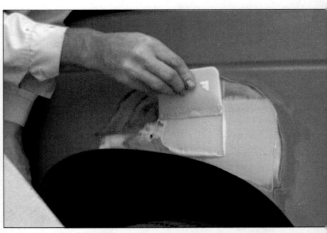

6   Working quickly so the filler doesn't harden, use a plastic applicator to press the body filler firmly into the metal, assuring bonds completely. Work the filler until it matches the original contour and is slightly above the surrounding metal

7   Let the filler harden until you can just dent it with your ngernail. Use a body file or Surform tool (shown here) to rough-shape the filler

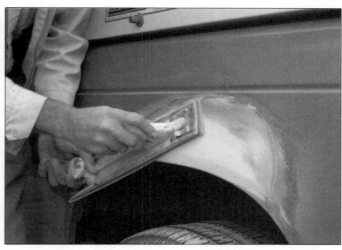

8   Use coarse-grit sandpaper and a sanding board or block to work the filler down until it's smooth and even. Work down to finer grits of sandpaper - always using a board or block - ending up with 360 or 400 grit

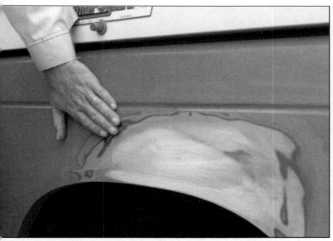

9   You shouldn't be able to feel any ridge at the transition from he filler to the bare metal or from the bare metal to the old paint. As soon as the repair is flat and uniform, remove the dust and mask off the adjacent panels or trim pieces

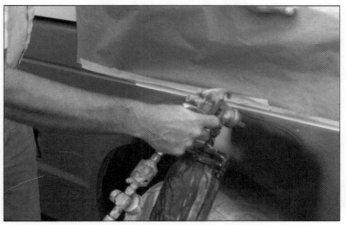

10   Apply several layers of primer to the area. Don't spray the primer on too heavy, so it sags or runs, and make sure each coat is dry before you spray on the next one. A professional-type spray gun is being used here, but aerosol spray primer is available inexpensively from auto parts stores

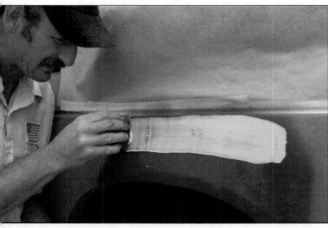

11   The primer will help reveal imperfections or scratches. Fill these with glazing compound. Follow the label instructions and sand it with 360 or 400-grit sandpaper until it's smooth. Repeat the glazing, sanding and respraying until the primer reveals a perfectly smooth surface

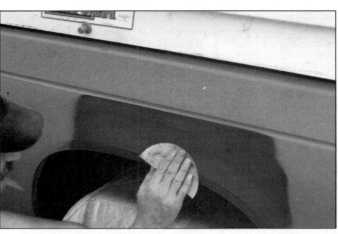

12   Finish sand the primer with very fine sandpaper (400 or 600-grit) to remove the primer overspray. Clean the area with water and allow it to dry. Use a tack rag to remove any dust, then apply the finish coat. Don't attempt to rub out or wax the repair area until the paint has dried completely (at least two weeks)

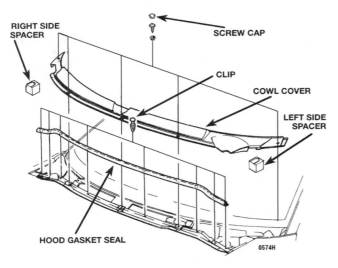

10.2 Cowl cover details

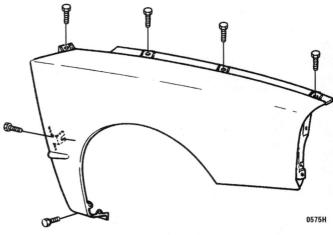

10.3 Front fender details

11.3 Scribe or draw a line around the hinge before loosening
the bolts

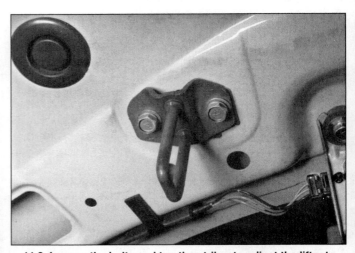

11.9 Loosen the bolts and tap the striker to adjust the liftgate
closed position

10   Fender – removal and installation

Refer to illustrations 10.2 and 10.3
1   Remove the front bumper (see Section 18).
2   Remove the screws and detach the cowl cover **(see illustration)**.
3   Remove the bolts and detach the fender **(see illustration)**.
4   Installation is the reverse of removal.

11   Liftgate – removal, installation and adjustment

Refer to illustrations 11.3 and 11.9
Note: *The liftgate is heavy and somewhat awkward to remove and in-stall – at least two people should perform this procedure.*
1   Open the liftgate and cover the edges of the rear compartment with pads or cloths to protect the painted surfaces when the lid is re-moved.
2   Disconnect any cables or wire harness connectors attached to the trunk lid that would interfere with removal.
3   Make alignment marks around the hinge bolt mounting flanges **(see illustration)**.
4   Have an assistant support the liftgate and detach the support struts (see Section 12).

5   While an assistant supports the liftgate, remove the lid-to-hinge bolts on both sides and lift it off.
6   Installation is the reverse of removal. **Note:** *When reinstalling the liftgate, align the lid-to-hinge bolts with the marks made during re-moval.*
7   After installation, close the liftgate and make sure it's in proper alignment with the surrounding body.
8   Forward-or-backward and side-to-side adjustments are made by loosening the hinge to liftgate bolts and gently moving the liftgate into correct alignment.
9   The lock striker can be adjusted by loosening the mounting bolts and gently tapping it with a plastic hammer **(see illustration)**.

12   Liftgate support strut – replacement

Refer to illustrations 12.1a, 12.1b and 12.1c
Warning: *The support strut is filled with pressurized gas – do not dis-sassemble this component (if it is faulty replace it with a new one).*
Note: *The trunk lid/rear liftgate is heavy and somewhat awkward to hold securely while replacing the struts – at least two people should perform this procedure.*
1   With the liftgate supported in the open position for the removal procedure, use an open end wrench to loosen the nuts and detach the ends of the struts **(see illustrations)**
2   Installation is the reverse of the removal procedure.

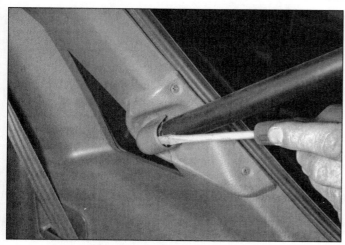

12.1a Use a screwdriver to pry the strut cover off

12.1b Unscrew the nut on the lower end of the strut

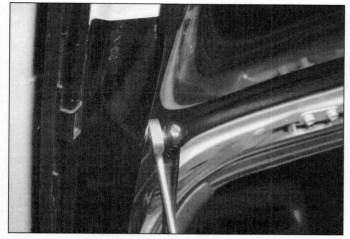

12.1c Use an open end wrench to loosen the nut, then detach the
upper end of the strut

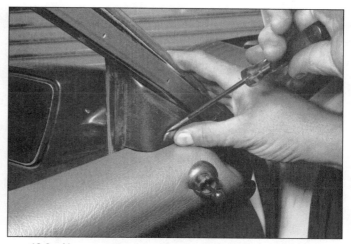

13.2a Use a small screwdriver to pry out the screw cover

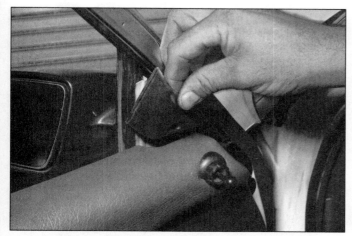

13.2b Remove the screw and detach the mirror cover

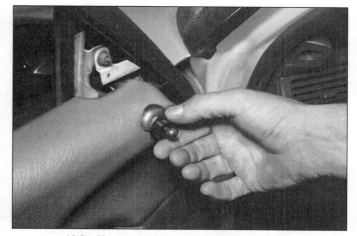

13.2c Unscrew the mirror control knob collar

11

13 Door trim panel – removal and installation

*Refer to illustrations 13.2a, 13.2b, 13.2c, 13.2d, 13.3, 13.4a, 13.4b,
13.4c, 13.6 and 13.7*

1   Disconnect the negative cable from the battery.

2   Remove the covers at each end of the window glass opening **(see
illustrations)**.

3   Remove the window crank by working a cloth back-and-forth behind the handle to dislodge the retainer **(see illustration)**. With the re-

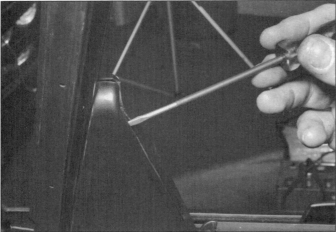

13.2d Use a small screwdriver to pry off the cover at the rear end of the door

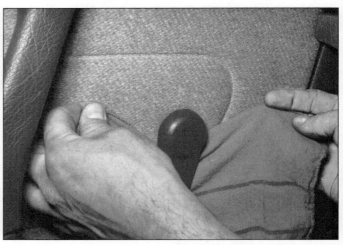

13.3 Work a cloth up behinde the window crank to detach the retaining clip, then pull the crank off

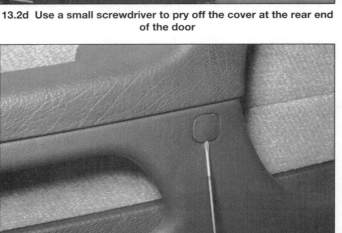

13.4a Some of the screws are hidden – pry their covers off with a small screwdriver . . .

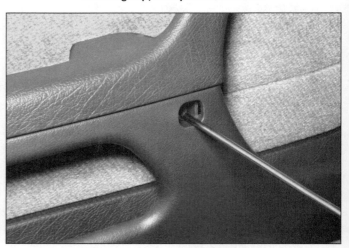

13.4b . . . then remove the screw

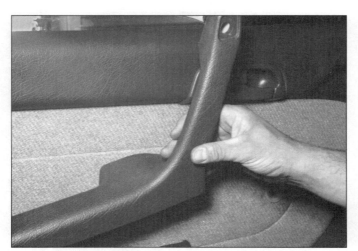

13.4c After removing the screws, detach the armrest

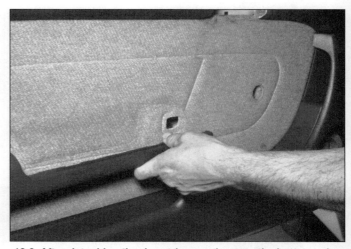

13.6 After detaching the door trim panel, rotate the bottom edge up and lift it out of the door window opening

tainer removed, pull off the handle.
4   Remove any door trim panel retaining screws and door pull/arm-rest assemblies **(see illustrations)**. Remove the speaker panels and the speaker assemblies (see Chapter 12).
5   Insert a wide putty knife or a thin prybar between the trim panel and door to disengage the retaining clips. Work around the outer edge until the panel is free.
6   Once all of the clips are disengaged, detach the trim panel, un-plug any electrical connectors and remove the trim panel from the ve-hicle by gently pulling it up and out **(see illustration)**.

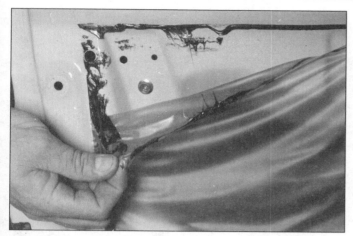

13.7 Peel the water deflector carefully away from the door, taking care not to tear or distort it

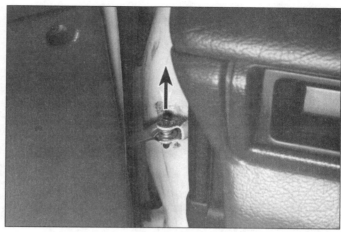

14.3 Detach the center pin by driving it up

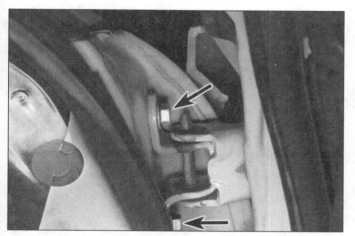

14.5 With the door supported, remove the bolts (arrows)

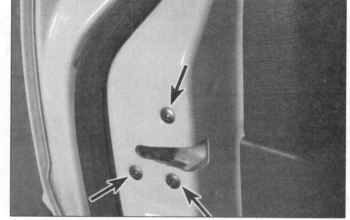

15.3 Remove the door latch screws in the end of the door (arrows)

7   For access to the inner door, peel back the plastic water deflector, taking care not to tear it **(see illustration)**. To install the trim panel, first press the water deflector into place.

8   Prior to installation of the door panel, be sure to reinstall any clips in the panel which may have come out during the removal procedure and stayed in the door.

9   Plug in any electrical connectors and place the panel in position. Press it into place until the clips are seated and install any retaining screws and armrest/door pulls. Install the manual regulator window crank.

---

14   Door – removal, installation and adjustment

Removal and installation

Refer to illustrations 14.3 and 14.5

1   Remove the door trim panel (see Section 13) and disconnect any electrical connectors and push them through the door opening so they won't interfere with removal.

2   Position a jack or jackstands under the door or have an assistant on hand to support the door when the hinge bolts are removed. **Note:** *If a jack or stand is used, place a rag between it and the door to protect the door's paint.*

3   Remove the center pin from the door stop strut **(see illustrations)**.

4   Scribe around the door bolts .

5   Remove the hinge-to-door bolts and carefully detach the door **(see illustration)**. Installation is the reverse of removal.

Adjustment

6   Following installation, make sure the door is aligned properly. Adjust it if necessary as follows:
  a) Up-and-down and forward-and-backward adjustments are made by loosening the hinge-to-body bolts and moving the door, as necessary. A special offset tool may be required to reach some of the bolts.
  b) In-and-out and up-and-down adjustments are made by loosening the door side hinge bolts and moving the door, as necessary.
  c) The door lock striker can also be adjusted both up-and-down and sideways to provide a positive engagement with the locking mechanism. This is done by loosening the screws and moving the striker, as necessary.

---

15   Door latch, lock cylinder and handle – removal and installation

11

Door lock

Refer to illustration 15.3

1   Remove the door trim panel and water deflector (see Section 13).

2   Reach behind the door panel and disconnect the links from the outside handle, the latch and the lock cylinder.

3   Remove the latch retaining screws from the end of the door **(see illustration)**.

4   Remove the door latch.

5   Installation is the reverse of removal.

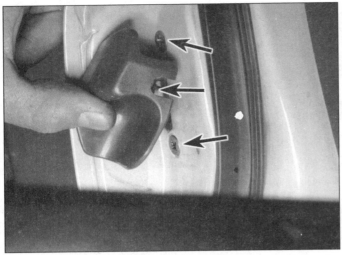

15.7 The door handle is held in place by three screws (arrows)

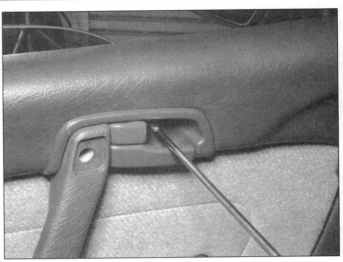

15.11 Remove the armrest and door handle screws

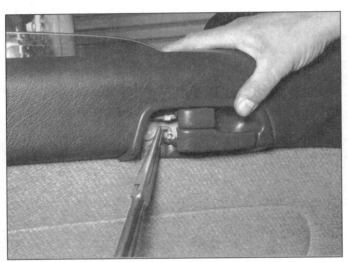

15.13a Detach the door handle rod clip with needle nose pliers

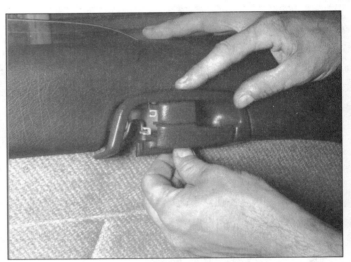

15.13b Pull the handle assembly straight out of the door

Lock cylinder and outside handle

Refer to illustration 15.7

6   Disconnect the control link and electrical connector (if equipped) from the lock cylinder and outside handle.

7   Remove the outside handle retention screws and detach the handle **(see illustration)** and lock cylinder from the door.

8   Use a screwdriver to pry the retaining clip off and remove the lock cylinder from the door.

9   Installation is the reverse of removal.

Inside handle

Refer to illustrations 15.11, 5.13a and 15.13b

10   The inside handle can be removed without removing the door trim panel.

11   Remove the armrest and handle-to-door screws **(see illustration)**.

12   Remove the remaining screws and detach the armrest (Section 13).

13   Use needle-nose pliers to disconnect the links from the inside handle control and pull the handle free **(see illustrations)**.

14   Installation is the reverse of removal.

16   Door window glass – removal and installation

Refer to illustration 16.3

1   Remove the door trim panel and water deflector (see Section 13).

2   Lower the window glass.

3   Remove the two glass guide bolts and one screw **(see illustration)**.

4   Remove the glass channel bolts and detach the guide rail.

5   Remove the glass by pulling it up.

6   Installation is the reverse of the removal procedure.

17   Window regulator – removal and installation

Refer to illustration 17.3

1   Remove the door trim panel and water deflector (see Section 13).

2   Remove the door window glass (see Section 16).

3   Remove the window crank and equalizer arm bracket mounting bolts, then detach the regulator **(see illustration)**

4   Pull the regulator through the service hole to remove it.

5   Installation is the reverse of removal.

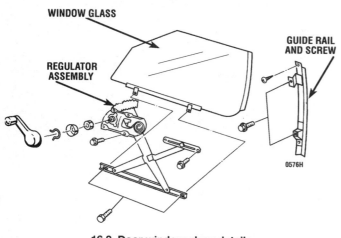

16.3 Door window glass details

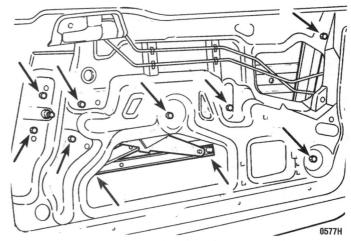

17.3 Regulator retaining bolts (arrows)

18 Bumpers – removal and installation

Refer to illustration 18.8

Front bumper

Warning: *These models are airbag-equipped. If the vehicle has been involved in a collision and the airbag discharged, the airbag and sensors should be checked and/or replaced by an authorized dealer. Also, always disconnect the negative battery cable, remove the airbag fuses and unplug the orange electrical connector under the steering column when working in the vicinity of the impact sensors or steering column to avoid the possibility of accidental deployment of the airbag, which could cause personal injury (see Chapter 12, Section 20).*

1   Apply the parking brake, block the rear wheels, lift the front of the vehicle and support it securely on jackstands.
2   Disconnect the negative battery cable from the battery and dis-connect any wiring that would interfere with bumper removal.
3   Remove the clips and detach the inner fender liner.
4   Remove the screws and clip and detach the cover under the left front corner of the bumper.
5   In the engine compartment, remove the battery and tray, relay box bolts (move the box out of the way with the wiring connected) and air cleaner assembly.
6   Remove the air cleaner assembly.
7   Remove the side support rod.
8   Disconnect any electrical connectors that would interfere with removal, then remove the bolts and detach the bumper assembly **(see illustration)**.
9   Pull the bumper assembly from the vehicle. To remove the bumper cover from the bumper unit remove the upper and lower cover nuts/bolts.
10   Installation is the reverse of removal.

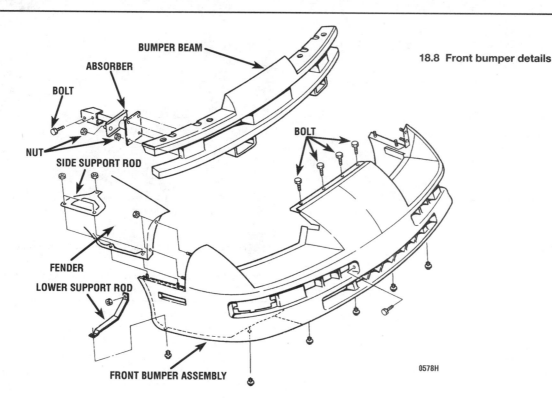

18.8 Front bumper details

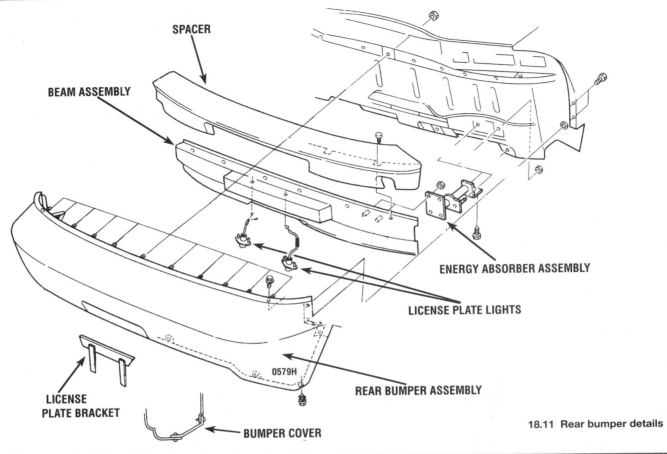

SPACER

BEAM ASSEMBLY

ENERGY ABSORBER ASSEMBLY

LICENSE PLATE LIGHTS

LICENSE PLATE BRACKET

BUMPER COVER

REAR BUMPER ASSEMBLY

0579H

18.11 Rear bumper details

19.2 Remove the nuts (arrows) and detach the mirror

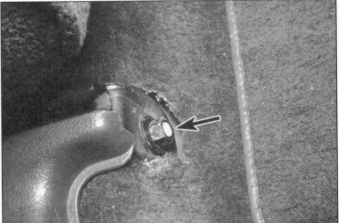

20.1 The seat is held in place at the front by two nuts (arrow)

Rear bumper

Refer to illustration 18.11

11   In the rear compartment, roll the carpet forward and remove the spare tire cover.

12   Remove the clips, nuts and bolts and detach the rear bumper assembly from the vehicle **(see illustration).**

13   Installation is the reverse of removal.

19   Outside mirror – removal and installation

Refer to illustrations 19.2

1   Remove the door trim panel (see Section 13).

2   Remove the retaining nuts and detach the mirror **(see illustration)**.

3   Installation is the reverse of removal.

20   Seats – removal and installation

Front seats

Refer to illustration 20.1

1   Remove the retaining nuts and bolts, unplug any electrical connectors and lift the seats from the vehicle **(see illustration)**.

2   Installation is the reverse of removal.

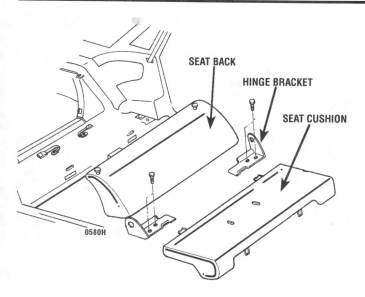

20.4 Rear seat details

21.3a Rotate the bezel forward, then pull it out of the dash

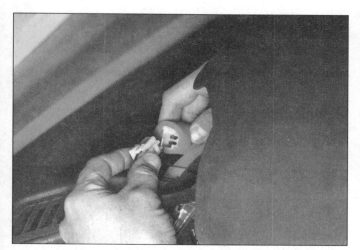

21.3b Press the tabs on the side of the connector and unplug it

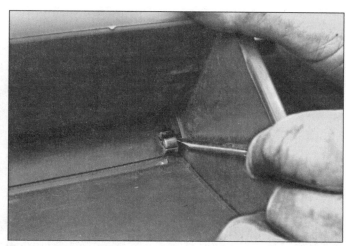

22.2 Use a long screwdriver to pry out the glovebox pin

Rear seats

Refer to illustration 20.4

3   Remove the lower seat cushion by pushing it back and then up, then release the clips at the front edge. Pull the seat belt buckle down to free it, then remove the cushion.

4   Remove the mounting bolts from the hinge bracket and lift the seat back assembly out of the vehicle **(see illustration)**.

5   Installation is the reverse of removal.

21   Instrument cluster bezel – removal and installation

Refer to illustrations 21.3a and 21.3b

Warning: *These models are airbag-equipped. Always disconnect the negative battery cable, remove the airbag fuses and unplug the orange electrical connector under the steering column when working in the vicinity of the impact sensors or steering column to avoid the possibility of accidental deployment of the airbag, which could cause personal injury.*

1   Disconnect the negative cable from the battery.

2   Remove the two screws along the bottom of the bezel, pry out the covers and remove the screws at the top forward edge.

3   Rotate the bezel forward, pull it back then unplug the electrical connectors and remove the bezel from the vehicle **(see illustrations)**.

4   Installation is the reverse of the removal procedure.

22   Glovebox – removal and installation

Refer to illustration 22.2

1   Rotate the two plastic hinge pivots at the bottom of the glovebox until they turn freely.

2   Use a screwdriver to pry the pivot pins out and lower the glovebox from the instrument panel **(see illustration)**.

3   Installation is the reverse of removal.

23   Steering column cover and knee bolster – removal and installation

Warning: *These models are airbag-equipped. Always disconnect the negative battery cable, remove the airbag fuses and unplug the orange electrical connector under the steering column when working in the vicinity of the impact sensors or steering column to avoid the possibility of accidental deployment of the airbag, which could cause personal injury.*

11

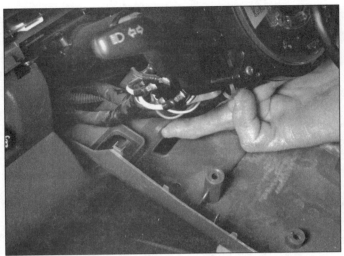

23.1 Lift up on the plastic release lever and withdraw the lower cover from the steering column

23.2 After removing the screws and detaching the lower cover, rotate the steering column upper cover off

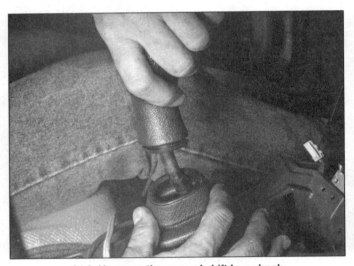

24.2 Unscrew the manual shift lever knob

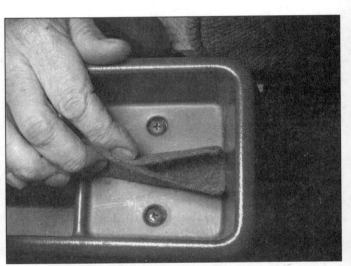

24.3 Pull up the carpet piece for access to the screws

Steering column cover

Refer to illustrations 23.1 and 23.2

1   Remove the lower steering cover retaining screws, then tilt the cover down and detach it by pressing the plastic tab **(see illustration)**.
2   Remove the steering wheel (see Chapter 10) and instrument cluster bezel (see Section 21). Rotate the upper cover up and remove it from the steering column **(see illustration)**.

Knee bolster

3   Remove the steering column cover.
4   Pry out the instrument panel switch bezel with a small screwdriver, then unplug the switches and remove the assembly.
5   Remove the retaining screws, detach the hood latch and move it out of the way.
6   Pry out the cigar lighter, unplug and remove it.
7   Remove the retaining screws and bolt detach the knee bolster and lower it from the instrument panel.
8   Installation is the reverse of the removal procedure.

24   Console and center trim panel – removal and installation

Refer to illustrations 24.2 24.3, 24.4a, 24.4b and 24.5
Warning: *These models are airbag-equipped. Always disconnect the negative battery cable, remove the airbag fuses and unplug the orange electrical connector under the steering column when working in the vicinity of the impact sensors or steering column to avoid the possibility of accidental deployment of the airbag, which could cause personal injury. The airbag discriminating sensor assembly is located under the center console on these models.*

Center console

1   Disconnect the negative cable from the battery.
2   Remove the shift knob by unscrewing it (manual) or removing the screw and detaching the handle (automatic) **(see illustration)**.
3   Remove the screws located in the bottom of the console compartment by pulling the cover up to gain access and the screws on the sides **(see illustration)**.
4   Remove the screws attaching the console to the center trim panel and rotate the console up and out of the vehicle **(see illustrations)**.

24.4a Remove the center trim panel screws (arrows)

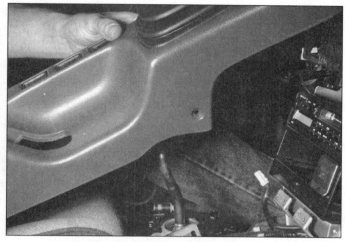

24.4b Lift the console straight up to remove it

Center trim panel

5   Remove the center trim panel side retention screws and detach the side panels **(see illustration)**.

6   Pull off the heating/air conditioning control knobs and remove the center trim panel.

7   Installation is the reverse of the removal procedure.

---

25   Seat belt check

---

1   Check the seat belts, buckles, latch plates and guide loops for any obvious damage or signs of wear.

2   Make sure the seat belt reminder light comes on when the key is turned on.

3   The seat belts are designed to lock up during a sudden stop or impact, yet allow free movement during normal driving. The retractors should hold the belt against your chest while driving and rewind the belt when the buckle is unlatched.

4   If any of the above checks reveal problems with the seat-belt system, replace parts as necessary.

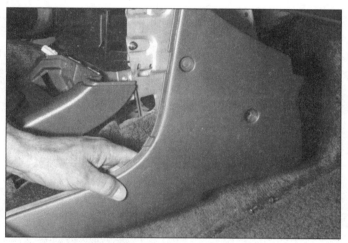

24.5 Detach the console/center panel sides

11

Notes

Chapter 12 Chassis electrical system

Contents

1 General information

The electrical system is a 12-volt, negative ground type. Power for the lights and all electrical accessories is supplied by a lead/acid-type battery which is charged by the alternator.

This Chapter covers repair and service procedures for the various electrical components not associated with the engine. Information on the battery, alternator, distributor and starter motor can be found in Chapter 5.

It should be noted that when portions of the electrical system are serviced, the cable should be disconnected from the negative battery terminal to prevent electrical shorts and/or fires.

2 Electrical troubleshooting - general information

A typical electrical circuit consists of an electrical component, any switches, relays, motors, fuses, fusible links or circuit breakers related to that component and the wiring and electrical connectors that link the component to both the battery and the chassis. To help you pinpoint an electrical circuit problem, wiring diagrams are included at the end of this book.

Before tackling any troublesome electrical circuit, first study the appropriate wiring diagrams to get a complete understanding of what makes up that individual circuit. Trouble spots, for instance, can often be narrowed down by noting if other components related to the circuit are operating properly. If several components or circuits fail at one time, chances are the problem is in a fuse or ground connection, because several circuits are often routed through the same fuse and ground connections.

Electrical problems usually stem from simple causes, such as loose or corroded connections, a blown fuse, a melted fusible link or a bad relay. Visually inspect the condition of all fuses, wires and connections in a problem circuit before troubleshooting it.

If testing instruments are going to be utilized, use the diagrams to plan ahead of time where you will make the necessary connections in order to accurately pinpoint the trouble spot.

The basic tools needed for electrical troubleshooting include a circuit tester or voltmeter (a 12-volt bulb with a set of test leads can also be used), a continuity tester, which includes a bulb, battery and set of test leads, and a jumper wire, preferably with a circuit breaker incorporated, which can be used to bypass electrical components. Before attempting to locate a problem with test instruments, use the wiring diagram(s) to decide where to make the connections.

3.1a The main fuse block is located on the drivers kick panel, under a cover

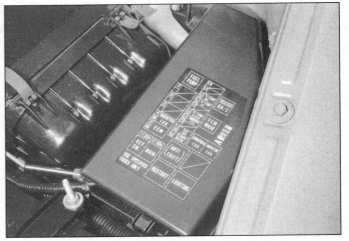

3.1b The engine compartment fuse block is located next to the battery

Voltage checks

Voltage checks should be performed if a circuit is not functioning properly. Connect one lead of a circuit tester to either the negative battery terminal or a known good ground. Connect the other lead to a electrical connector in the circuit being tested, preferably nearest to the battery or fuse. If the bulb of the tester lights, voltage is present, which means that the part of the circuit between the electrical connector and the battery is problem free. Continue checking the rest of the circuit in the same fashion. When you reach a point at which no voltage is present, the problem lies between that point and the last test point with voltage. Most of the time the problem can be traced to a loose connection. **Note:** *Keep in mind that some circuits receive voltage only when the ignition key is in the Accessory or Run position.*

Finding a short

One method of finding shorts in a circuit is to remove the fuse and connect a test light or voltmeter in its place to the fuse terminals. There should be no voltage present in the circuit. Move the wiring harness from side to side while watching the test light. If the bulb goes on, there is a short to ground somewhere in that area, probably where the insulation has rubbed through. The same test can be performed on each component in the circuit, even a switch.

Ground check

Perform a ground test to check whether a component is properly grounded. Disconnect the battery and connect one lead of a self-powered test light, known as a continuity tester, to a known good ground. Connect the other lead to the wire or ground connection being tested. If the bulb goes on, the ground is good. If the bulb does not go on, the ground is not good.

Continuity check

A continuity check is done to determine if there are any breaks in a circuit - if it is passing electricity properly. With the circuit off (no power in the circuit), a self-powered continuity tester can be used to check the circuit. Connect the test leads to both ends of the circuit (or to the "power" end and a good ground), and if the test light comes on the circuit is passing current properly. If the light doesn't come on, there is a break somewhere in the circuit. The same procedure can be used to test a switch, by connecting the continuity tester to the power in and power out sides of the switch. With the switch turned On, the test light should come on.

Finding an open circuit

When diagnosing for possible open circuits, it is often difficult to locate them by sight because oxidation or terminal misalignment are hidden by the electrical connectors. Merely wiggling an electrical connector on a sensor or in the wiring harness may correct the open cir-

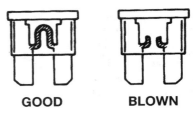

GOOD   BLOWN

3.3 The fuses used in these models can be checked visually to determine if they are blown

cuit condition. Remember this when an open circuit is indicated when troubleshooting a circuit. Intermittent problems may also be caused by oxidized or loose connections.

Electrical troubleshooting is simple if you keep in mind that all electrical circuits are basically electricity running from the battery, through the wires, switches, relays, fuses and fusible links to each electrical component (light bulb, motor, etc.) and to ground, from which it is passed back to the battery.

3   Fuses - general information

Refer to illustrations 3.1a, 3.1b and 3.3

The electrical circuits of the vehicle are protected by a combination of fuses, circuit breakers and fusible links. The fuse blocks are located on the kick panel below the left side of the instrument panel under a cover, and in the engine compartment next to the battery **(see illustrations)**.

Each of the fuses is designed to protect a specific circuit, and the various circuits are identified on the fuse panel itself.

Miniaturized fuses are employed in the fuse block. These compact fuses, with blade terminal design, allow fingertip removal and replacement. If an electrical component fails, always check the fuse first. A blown fuse is easily identified through the clear plastic body. Visually inspect the element for evidence of damage **(see illustration)**. If a continuity check is called for, the blade terminal tips are exposed in the fuse body.

Be sure to replace blown fuses with the correct type. Fuses of different ratings are physically interchangeable, but only fuses of the proper rating should be used. Replacing a fuse with one of a higher or lower value than specified is not recommended. Each electrical circuit needs a specific amount of protection. The amperage value of each fuse is molded into the fuse body.

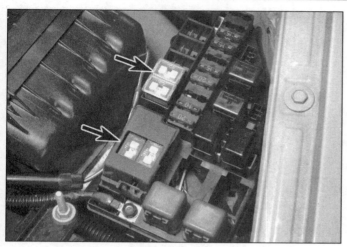

4.2 The fusible links (arrows) are located in the engine compartment fuse block

6.2 Several relays are located in the block in the right rear corner of the engine compartment

If the replacement fuse immediately fails, don't replace it again until the cause of the problem is isolated and corrected. In most cases, this will be a short circuit in the wiring caused by a broken or deteriorated wire.

4 Fusible links - general information

Refer to illustration 4.2

Some circuits are protected by fusible links. The links are used in circuits which are not ordinarily fused, such as the ignition circuit.

The fusible links on these models are similar to fuses in that they can be visually checked to determine if they are melted **(see illustration)**.

To replace a fusible link, first disconnect the negative cable from the battery. Unplug the burned-out link and replace it with a new one (available from your dealer or auto parts store). Always determine the cause for the overload which melted the fusible link before installing a new one.

5 Circuit breakers - general information

Circuit breakers protect components such as power windows, power door locks and headlights. Some circuit breakers are located in the fuse boxes **(see illustration 3.1a)**.

Because on some models the circuit breaker resets itself automatically, an electrical overload in a circuit breaker protected system will cause the circuit to fail momentarily, then come back on. If the circuit does not come back on, check it immediately. Once the condition is corrected, the circuit breaker will resume its normal function.

6 Relays - general information

Refer to illustration 6.2

Several electrical accessories in the vehicle use relays to transmit the electrical signal to the component. If the relay is defective, that component will not operate properly.

The various relays are mounted in several locations throughout the vehicle, although many key relays are located in the fuse/relay block next to the battery and in the relay block in the right rear corner of the engine compartment **(see illustration)**.

If a faulty relay is suspected, it can be removed and tested by a dealer or other qualified shop. Defective relays must be replaced as a unit.

7.1 The turn signal hazard flasher unit (arrow) is located at the top of the fuse block

7 Turn signal/hazard flashers - check and replacement

Refer to illustration 7.1

1 The turn signal/hazard flasher, a square module located behind the left kick panel at the top of the fuse block **(see illustration)**, flashes the turn signals and hazard flashers.

2 When the flasher unit is functioning properly, an audible click can be heard during its operation. If the turn signals fail on one side or the other and the flasher unit does not make its characteristic clicking sound, a faulty turn signal bulb is indicated.

3 If both turn signals fail to blink, the problem may be due to a blown fuse, a faulty flasher unit, a broken switch or a loose or open connection. If a quick check of the fuse box indicates that the turn signal fuse has blown, check the wiring for a short before installing a new fuse.

4 To replace the flasher, remove the kick panel, carefully pry back the clips and detach it from the fuse block.

5 Make sure the replacement unit is identical to the original. Compare the old one to the new one before installing it.

6 Installation is the reverse of removal.

12

8.5 Combination switch screw location (arrows) - the airbag coil has been removed for clarity

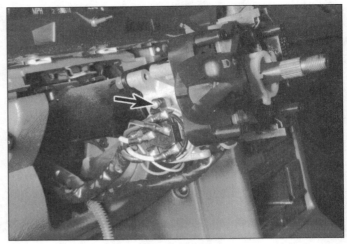

9.3 The ignition switch electrical harness is held in place by one screw (arrow)

8 Combination switch - removal and installation

Refer to illustration 8.5

Warning: *These models are airbag-equipped. Always disconnect the negative battery cable, remove the airbag fuses and unplug the orange electrical connector under the steering column when working in the vicinity of the impact sensors or steering column to avoid the possibility of accidental deployment of the airbag, which could cause personal injury (see Section 20).*

1   Disconnect the negative cable at the battery.
2   Remove the steering wheel (see Chapter 10).
3   Remove the knee bolster and steering column cover (see Chapter 11).
4   Remove the screws and move the airbag coil out of the way.
5   Remove the combination switch retaining screws **(see illustration)**.
6   Trace the wiring harness down the steering column to the connector. Release the wiring retainer clamps, if equipped, unplug the connector and slide the switch off the column.
7   Installation is the reverse of removal.

9 Ignition switch - removal and installation

Refer to illustrations 9.3 and 9.6

Warning: *These models are airbag-equipped. Always disconnect the negative battery cable, remove the airbag fuses and unplug the orange electrical connector under the steering column when working in the vicinity of the impact sensors or steering column to avoid the possibility of accidental deployment of the airbag, which could cause personal injury (see Section 20).*

1   Disconnect the negative cable at the battery.
2   Remove the steering wheel (see Chapter 10).
3   Remove the bolt and unplug the wires from the switch **(see illustration)**.
4   Remove the combination switch (see Section 8).
5   Remove the ignition lock cylinder (see Section 10).
6   Remove the snap-ring and bolts, then slide the switch assembly off the steering column **(see illustration)**.
7   Installation is the reverse of removal.

10 Ignition lock cylinder - removal and installation

Refer to illustration 10.5

Warning: *These models are airbag-equipped. Always disconnect the*

9.6 Remove the snap-ring and bolts (arrows) and slide the combination switch off the steering shaft

negative battery cable, remove the airbag fuses and unplug the orange electrical connector under the steering column when working in the vicinity of the impact sensors or steering column to avoid the possibility of accidental deployment of the airbag, which could cause personal injury (see Section 20).

1   Disconnect the negative cable at the battery.
2   Remove the steering wheel (see Chapter 10).
3   Remove the knee bolster and the steering column cover (see Chapter 11).
4   Remove the combination switch (see Section 8).
5   With the key in the Off position, insert a pin in the hole in the casting, pull the lock cylinder straight out and remove it from the steering column **(see illustration)**.
6   Installation is the reverse of removal.

11 Rear window defogger - check and repair

Refer to illustrations 11.4 and 11.14

1   The rear window defogger consists of a number of horizontal elements baked onto the glass surface.

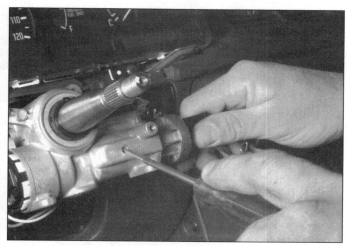

10.5 To remove the ignition lock cylinder, place the key in the "ON" position, push in on the release tab with a screwdriver and pull the cylinder straight out

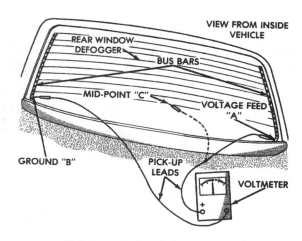

11.4 Rear window defogger test points

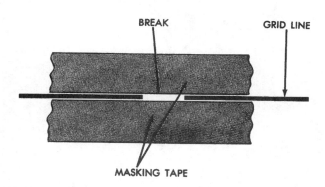

11.14 To repair the broken grid, first apply a strip of tape to either side of the grid to mask off the area

2   Small breaks in the element can be repaired without removing the rear window.

Check

3   Start the engine and turn the defogger switch On.
4   Ground the negative lead of a voltmeter to point B and the positive lead to point A **(see illustration)**.
5   The voltmeter should read between 10 and 15 volts. If the reading is lower there is a poor ground connection.
6   Connect the negative lead to a good body ground. The reading should stay the same.
7   Connect the negative lead to terminal B, then touch each grid line at the mid-point with the positive lead.
8   The reading should be approximately six volts. If the reading is 0, there is a break between the mid-point "C" and terminal "A".
9   A 10 to 14 volt reading is an indication of a break between mid-point "C" and ground B.
10   Move the lead toward the break; the voltage will change when the break is crossed.

Repair

11   Repair the break in the line using a repair kit specifically recommended for this purpose. Included in this kit is plastic conductive epoxy.
12   Prior to repairing a break, turn of the system and allow it to cool for a few minutes.
13   Lightly buff the element area with fine steel wool, then clean it thoroughly with rubbing alcohol.

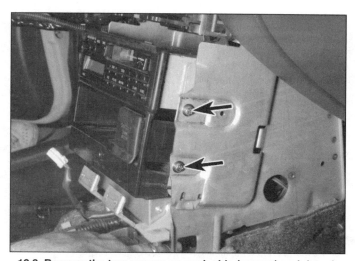

12.3 Remove the two screws on each side (arrows) and detach the radio

14   Use masking tape to mask off the area being repaired **(see illustration)**.
15   Mix the epoxy thoroughly, following the instructions provided with the repair kit.
16   Apply the epoxy material to the slit in the masking tape, overlapping the undamaged area about 3/4-inch on either end.
17   Allow the repair to cure for 24 hours before removing the tape and using the system.

---

12   Radio and speakers - removal and installation

Warning: *These models are airbag-equipped. Always disconnect the negative battery cable, remove the airbag fuses and unplug the orange electrical connector under the steering column when working in the vicinity of the impact sensors or steering column to avoid the possibility of accidental deployment of the airbag, which could cause personal injury (see Section 20).*
1   Disconnect the negative cable at the battery.

Radio

Refer to illustrations 12.3 and 12.4
2   Remove the console and center trim panel (see Chapter 11).
3   Remove the radio mounting screws **(see illustration)**.

12

12.4 Pull the radio out and unplug the antenna and electrical connectors (arrows)

12.6 Pry out the speaker cover with a small screwdriver

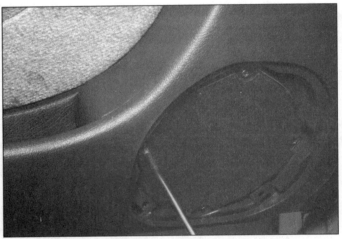

12.7a Use a Phillips head screwdriver to remove the speaker screws

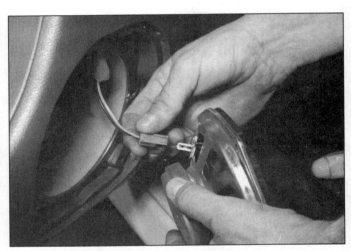

12.7b Support the speaker and unplug it

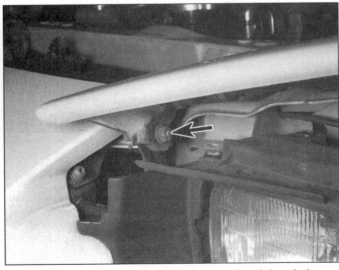

13.2 Remove the actuator arm nut (arrow) and detach the headlight cover

4   Pull the radio out, reach behind it, unplug the electrical connector and the antenna lead and lift the radio from the instrument panel **(see illustration)**.

5   Installation is the reverse of removal.

Speakers

Refer to illustrations 12.6, 12.7a and 12.7b

6   Remove the speaker covers **(see illustration)**.

7   Remove the speaker retaining screws, pull the speaker out and unplug the electrical connector **(see illustrations)**.

8   Installation is the reverse of removal.

---

13   Headlight - replacement

1   Disconnect the negative battery cable.

1991 and earlier models

Refer to illustrations 13.2, 13.3a, 13.3b, 13.4, 13.5a and 13.5b

2   Open the hood, remove the four bolts and the actuator rod nut, then lift off the headlight cover **(see illustration)**.

3   Remove the screws and lift off the upper headlight trim, then detach the headlight lower garnish **(see illustrations)**.

4   Remove the headlight retainer screws. Don't disturb the adjust-

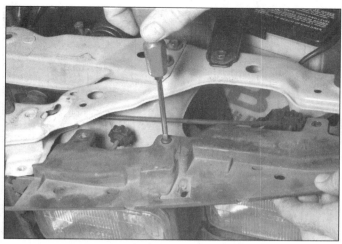

13.3a Remove the screws and lift off the trim cover

13.3b Grasp the lower garnish and detach it by pulling straight out

13.4 Remove the headlight retainer screws (arrows)

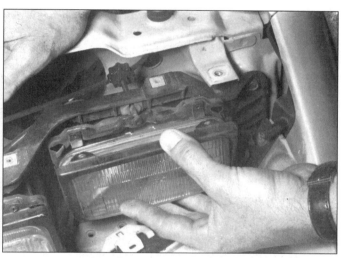

13.5a Pull the retainer and headlight out

ment screws **(see illustration)**.

5   Pull the headlight out, unplug the electrical connector and re-move the headlight assembly **(see illustrations)**.

6   Installation is the reverse of removal.

1992 and later models

7   Remove the two screws and lift off the lower headlight trim.

8   Remove the headlight retainer screws. Don't disturb the adjust-ment screws.

9   Pull the headlight out, unplug the electrical connector and re-move the headlight assembly.

10   Installation is the reverse of removal.

---

14   Headlights - adjustment

Refer to illustrations 14.1a, 14.1b, 14.10a and 14.10b

Note: *It is important that the headlights are aimed correctly. If adjusted incorrectly they could blind the driver of an oncoming vehicle and cause a serious accident or seriously reduce your ability to see the road. The headlights should be checked for proper aim every 12 months and any time a new headlight is installed or front end body work is performed. It should be emphasized that the following proce-dure is only an interim step which will provide temporary adjustment until the headlights can be adjusted by a properly equipped shop.*

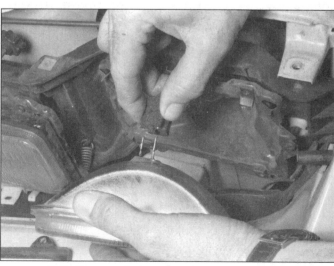

13.5b Support the headlight and detach the plug

12

14.1a   Adjust the headlight up-and-down movement with this knob (arrow)

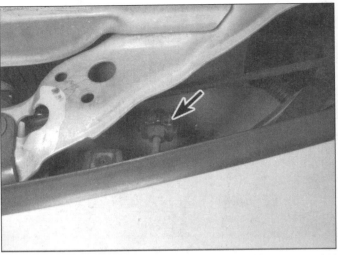

14.1b   This knob adjusts the headlight side-to-side movement

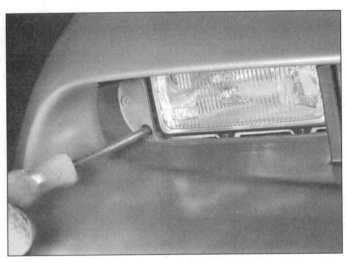

14.10a   On later models, adjust the up-and-down movement first, using a Torx-head screwdriver inserted from the front until the spirit level bubble is centered

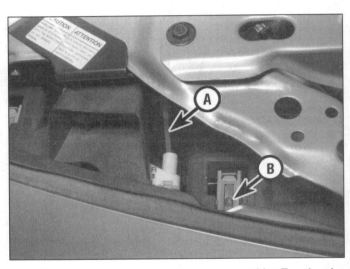

14.10b   Turn the side-to-side adjuster screw with a Torx-head screwdriver (A) until the bubble (B) is centered

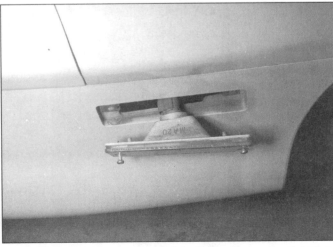

15.1a   Remove the screws and detach the side marker light for access to the bulb

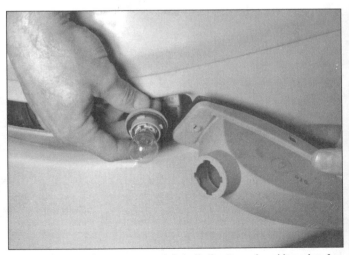

15.1b   Remove the screws and detach the turn signal housing for access to the bulb holder

15.2a Detach the rear compartment light for access

15.2b Detach the lens and pull the bulb out of the housing

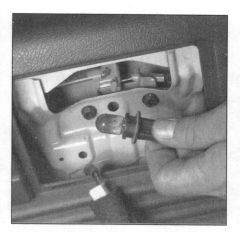

15.2c Reach into the opening, grasp the high mounted brake light bulb holder and turn it to detach it - pull the bulb out of the holder

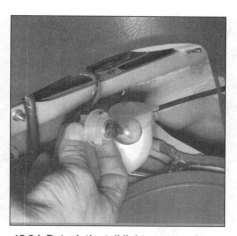

15.2d Detach the tail light cover and turn the bulb holder to remove it

15.3a Push the parking light bulb in and turn it counterclockwise to remove it

1991 and earlier models

1   On these models, the headlights have an adjusting screws with knobs on the top controlling up-and-down movement and one on the side controlling left-and-right movement **(see illustrations)**.

2   There are several methods of adjusting the headlights. The simplest method requires a blank wall 25 feet in front of the vehicle and a level floor.

3   Position masking tape vertically on the wall in reference to the vehicle centerline and the centerlines of both headlights.

4   Position a horizontal tape line in reference to the centerline of all the headlights. **Note:** *It may be easier to position the tape on the wall with the vehicle parked only a few inches away.*

5   Adjustment should be made with the vehicle sitting level, the gas tank half-full and no unusually heavy load in the vehicle.

6   Starting with the low beam adjustment, position the high intensity zone so it is two inches below the horizontal line and two inches to the right of the headlight vertical line. Twist the adjustment screws until the desired level has been achieved.

7   With the high beams on, the high intensity zone should be vertically centered with the exact center just below the horizontal line. **Note:** *It may not be possible to position the headlight aim exactly for both high and low beams. If a compromise must be made, keep in mind that the low beams are the most used and have the greatest effect on driver safety.*

8   Have the headlights adjusted by a dealer service department at the earliest opportunity.

1992 and later models

9   Later models also have two adjustment screws, one to the side controlling left-and-right movement and one below the light for up-and-down movement). The adjusters incorporate spirit levels that assure that the headlights are always level in relation to the chassis.

10   Adjusting the headlight is simply a matter of using a Torx head screwdriver to turn the adjustment screws until the spirit level bubble is centered for first the up-and-down, then the side-to-side adjustments **(see illustration)**.

---

15   Bulb replacement

Refer to illustrations 15.1a, 15.1b, 15.2a, 15.2b, 15.2c, 15.2d, 15.3a, 15.3b and 15.4

1   The lenses of many lights are held in place by screws. To gain access to the bulbs in these assemblies, simply remove the lenses **(see illustrations)**.

2   The lenses or covers of some light assemblies are held in place by clips. You can remove them by unsnapping them or by prying them off with a small screwdriver **(see illustrations)**.

3   Some bulbs can be removed simply by pushing them in and turning them counterclockwise while other can simply be pulled straight out of the socket **(see illustrations)**.

4   The instrument cluster bulbs are accessible after removing the cluster **(see illustration)**.

12

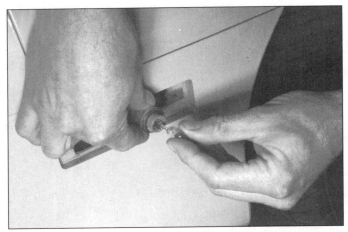

15.3b Pull the side marker bulb straight out of the holder

15.4 Turn the bulb holder counterclockwise and lift it out of the cluster

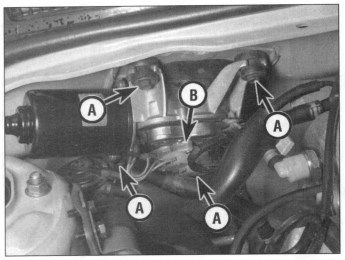

16.4 Unplug the electrical connector (B), remove the four bolts (A) and lower the windshield wiper motor from the firewall

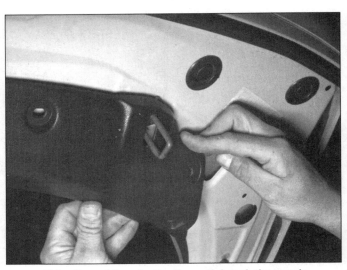

16.8a Pry out the plastic clips and detach the panels

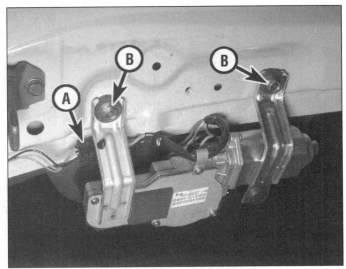

16.8b Unplug the electrical connector (A), remove the bolts (B) and lower the rear wiper motor from the liftgate

16   Wiper motor - removal and installation

Refer to illustration 16.4, 16.8 and 16.9

1   Disconnect the cable from the negative terminal of the battery.

Windshield wiper motor

2   Remove the cowl vent grille (see Chapter 11).
3   Remove the nut and disconnect the linkage from the wiper motor arm.
4   From inside the engine compartment, unplug the electrical connector and remove the mounting bolts **(see illustration)**. Remove the two bolts and disconnect the evaporative emission control system canister for access to the lower wiper mounting bolts. Lift the motor up and tilt it to allow the wiper motor arm to pass through the firewall.
5   Installation is the reverse of removal.

Rear window wiper motor

6   Lift up the cap, remove the nut and remove the rear wiper arm.
7   Remove the wiper shaft nut and washers.
8   Open the rear liftgate and detach liftgate inner trim panels **(see illustration)**. Unplug the electrical connector, then remove the two bolts and detach the wiper motor **(see illustration)**.

17.3a Remove the Phillips screws at the lower front edge of the
instrument cluster . . .

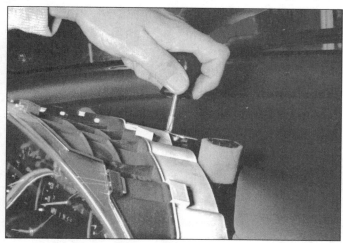

17.3b . . . and the bracket retainer screw at the rear of
the housing

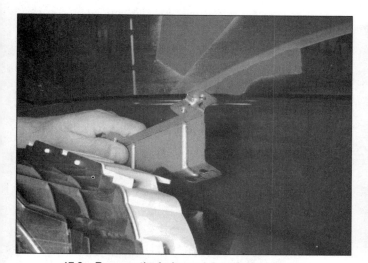

17.3c Remove the bolts and detach the bracket

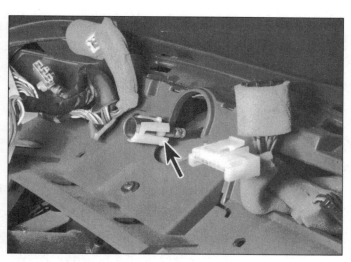

17.4 Reach behind the cluster and press the speedometer cable
release lever (arrow) (cluster removed for clarity)

17 Instrument cluster - removal and installation

Refer to illustrations 17.3a, 17.3b, 17.3c and 17.4

1   Disconnect the cable from the negative battery terminal.
2   Remove the instrument cluster trim panel (see Chapter 11).
3   Remove the retaining screws, detach the bracket and pull the
cluster forward **(see illustrations)**.
4   Reach behind the cluster, detach the speedometer cable by
pressing on the collar release lever and pull the cluster out **(see illustration)**.
5   Unplug the connectors and remove the cluster from the instrument panel.
6   Installation is the reverse of the removal procedure.

18 Instrument cluster switches- removal and installation

Refer to illustration 18.4

1   Disconnect the cable from the negative battery terminal.
2   Remove the instrument cluster trim panel (see Chapter 11).
3   Remove the four retaining screws and detach and detach the
bezel cover.
4   Remove the screws, release the wiring harness clips and detach
the switch from the bezel **(see illustration)**.
5   Installation is the reverse of the removal procedure.

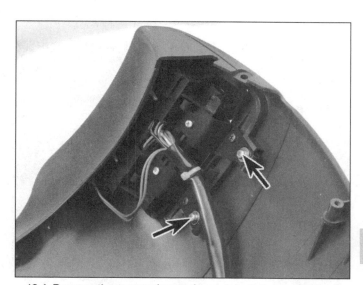

18.4 Remove the screws (arrows) and detach the switch from
the housing

12

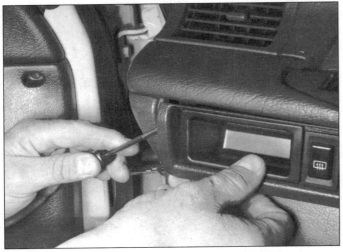

19.2a Use a small screwdriver to detach the panel and . . .

19.2b . . . pull it out for access to the switches

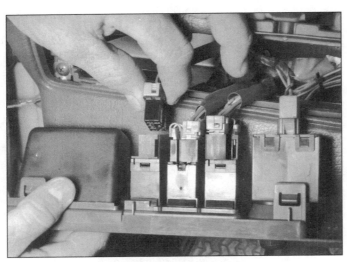

19.3a Unplug the switch and . . .

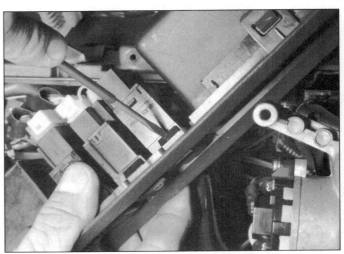

19.3b . . . use a small screwdriver to release the clip

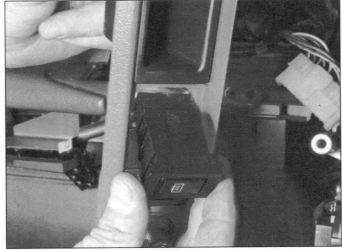

19.3c Push the switch out through the face of the panel

19   Instrument panel switches- removal and installation

Refer to illustrations 19.2a, 19.2b, 19.3a, 19.3b and 19.3c

1   Disconnect the cable from the negative battery terminal.
2   Use a small screwdriver to remove the instrument cluster trim panel **(see illustrations)**. (see Chapter 11).
3   Unplug the electrical connectors, detach the clips and push the switch out of the panel **(see illustrations)**.
4   Installation is the reverse of the removal procedure.

20   Airbag - general information

All models are equipped with a Supplemental Restraint System (SRS), more commonly known as an airbag. This system is designed to protect the driver from serious injury in the event of a head-on or frontal collision. It consists of an airbag module in the center of the steering wheel, two crash sensors mounted at the front and the interior of the vehicle and a diagnostic module which also contains an arming sensor located inside the passenger compartment.

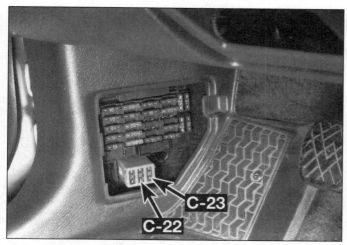

20.6a To disable the airbag system turn the ignition switch to Off, detach the cable from the negative battery terminal, remove fuses C-22 and C-23 (arrows) from the fuse box . . .

20.6b . . . and unplug the orange three-way connector (arrow) at the base of the steering column

Airbag module

The airbag inflator module contains a housing incorporating the cushion (airbag) and inflator unit, mounted in the center of the steering wheel. The inflator assembly is mounted on the back of the housing over a hole through which gas is expelled, inflating the bag almost instantaneously when an electrical signal is sent from the system. The airbag steering column coil assembly is mounted on the steering column under the module and carries this signal to the module. The coil assembly can transmit an electrical signal regardless of steering wheel position.

Sensors

The system has three sensors: a forward sensor at the front of the vehicle behind the bumper, a passenger compartment sensor and arming sensor under the front of the center console.

The forward and passenger compartment sensors are basically pressure sensitive switches that complete an electrical circuit during an impact of sufficient G force. The electrical signal from these sensors is sent to the arming sensor which then completes the circuit and inflates the airbag.

Diagnostic Energy Reserve Module (DERM)

The DERM supplies the current to the airbag system in the event of the collision, even if battery power is cut off. It checks this system every time the vehicle is started, causing the "INFL REST" light to go on then off, if the system is operating properly. If there is a fault in the system, the light will go on and stay on and the DERM will store fault codes indicating the nature of the fault. If the INFL REST light goes on and stays on, the vehicle should be taken to your dealer immediately for service.

Disabling the system

Refer to illustrations 20.6a and 20.6b

Whenever working in the vicinity of the steering wheel, steering column or near other components of the airbag system, the system should be disarmed. To do this, perform the following steps:
a) Turn the ignition switch to Off.
b) Detach the cable from the negative battery cable.
c) Remove fuses C-22 and C-23 from the fuse box **(see illustration)**.
d) Unplug the orange three-way connector at the base of the steering column **(see illustration)**.

Enabling the system

a) Turn the ignition switch to the Off position.
b) Plug in the orange three-way connector at the base of the steering column.
c) Install fuses C-22 and C-23.
d) Connect the negative battery cable.

21 Wiring diagrams - general information

Prior to troubleshooting any circuits, check the fuse and circuit breakers (if equipped) to make sure they are in good condition. Make sure the battery is properly charged and has clean, tight cable connections (see Chapter 1).

When checking the wiring system, make sure that all electrical connectors are clean, with no broken or loose pins. When unplugging an electrical connector, do not pull on the wires, only on the connector housings themselves.

1990-91 WIRING DIAGRAMS
Geo Storm

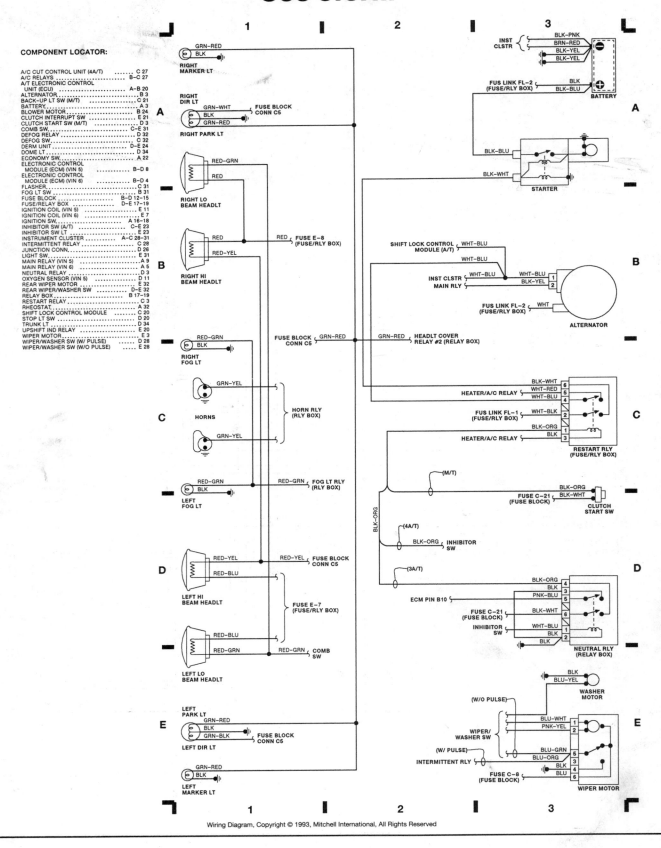

COMPONENT LOCATOR:

A/C CUT CONTROL UNIT (4A/T) .... C 27
A/C RELAYS .... B–C 27
A/T ELECTRONIC CONTROL
  UNIT (ECU) .... A–B 20
ALTERNATOR .... B 3
BACK-UP LT SW (M/T) .... C 21
BATTERY .... A 3
BLOWER MOTOR .... B 24
CLUTCH INTERRUPT SW .... E 21
CLUTCH START SW (M/T) .... D 3
COMB SW .... C–E 31
DEFOG RELAY .... D 32
DEFOG SW .... C 32
DERM UNIT .... D–E 24
DOME LT .... D 34
ECONOMY SW .... A 22
ELECTRONIC CONTROL
  MODULE (ECM) (VIN 5) .... B–D 8
ELECTRONIC CONTROL
  MODULE (ECM) (VIN 6) .... B–D 4
FLASHER .... C 31
FOG LT SW .... B 31
FUSE BLOCK .... B–D 12–15
FUSE/RELAY BOX .... D–E 17–19
IGNITION COIL (VIN 5) .... E 11
IGNITION COIL (VIN 6) .... E 7
IGNITION SW .... A 16–18
INHIBITOR SW (A/T) .... C–E 23
INHIBITOR SW LT .... E 23
INSTRUMENT CLUSTER .... A–C 28–31
INTERMITTENT RELAY .... C 28
JUNCTION CONN .... D 26
LIGHT SW .... E 31
MAIN RELAY (VIN 5) .... A 9
MAIN RELAY (VIN 6) .... A 5
NEUTRAL RELAY .... D 3
OXYGEN SENSOR (VIN 5) .... D 11
REAR WIPER MOTOR .... E 32
REAR WIPER/WASHER SW .... D–E 32
RELAY BOX .... B 17–19
RESTART RELAY .... C 3
RHEOSTAT .... A 32
SHIFT LOCK CONTROL MODULE .... A 20
STOP LT SW .... D 20
TRUNK LT .... D 34
UPSHIFT IND RELAY .... E 20
WIPER MOTOR .... E 3
WIPER/WASHER SW (W/ PULSE) .... D 28
WIPER/WASHER SW (W/O PULSE) .... E 28

1990-91 WIRING DIAGRAMS
Geo Storm (Cont.)

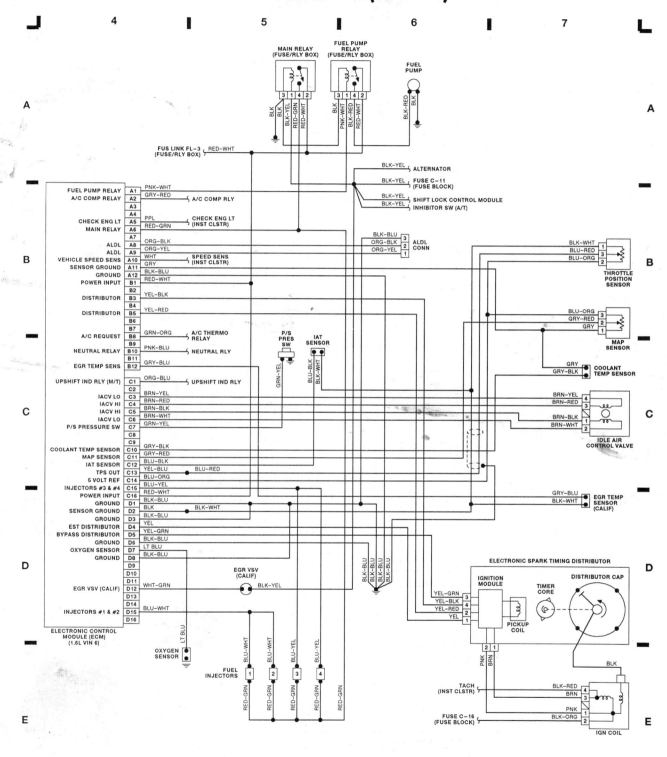

Wiring Diagram, Copyright © 1993, Mitchell International, All Rights Reserved

1990-91 WIRING DIAGRAMS
Geo Storm (Cont.)

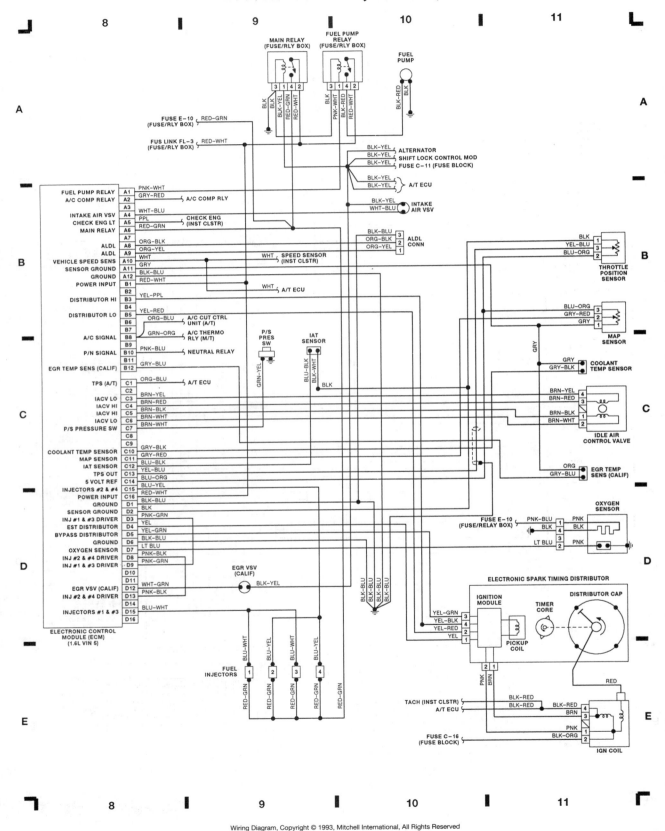

Wiring Diagram, Copyright © 1993, Mitchell International, All Rights Reserved

1990-91 WIRING DIAGRAMS
Geo Storm (Cont.)

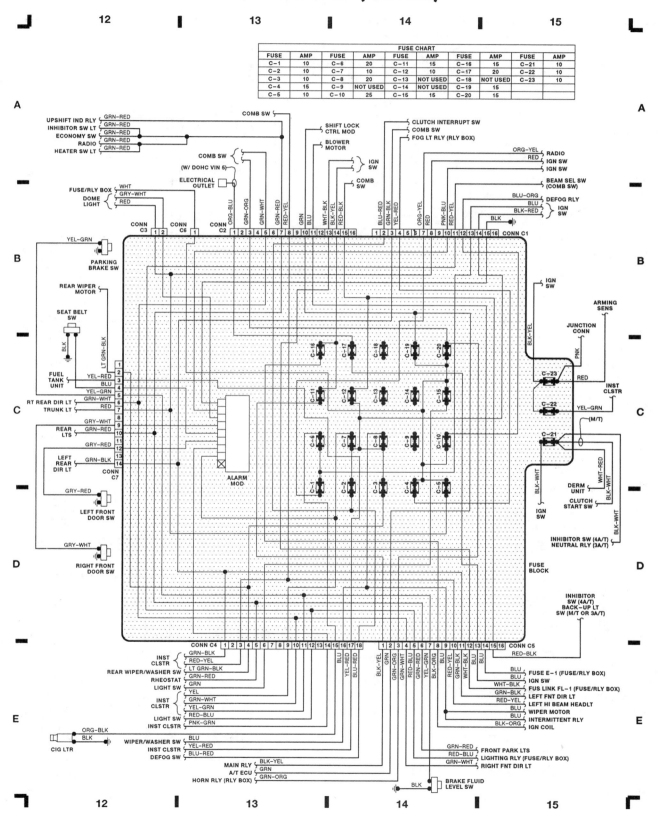

FUSE CHART									
FUSE	AMP	FUSE	AMP	FUSE	AMP	FUSE	AMP	FUSE	AMP
C-1	10	C-6	20	C-11	15	C-16	15	C-21	10
C-2	10	C-7	10	C-12	10	C-17	20	C-22	10
C-3	10	C-8	20	C-13	NOT USED	C-18	NOT USED	C-23	10
C-4	15	C-9	NOT USED	C-14	NOT USED	C-19	15		
C-5	10	C-10	25	C-15	15	C-20	15		

1990-91 WIRING DIAGRAMS
Geo Storm (Cont.)

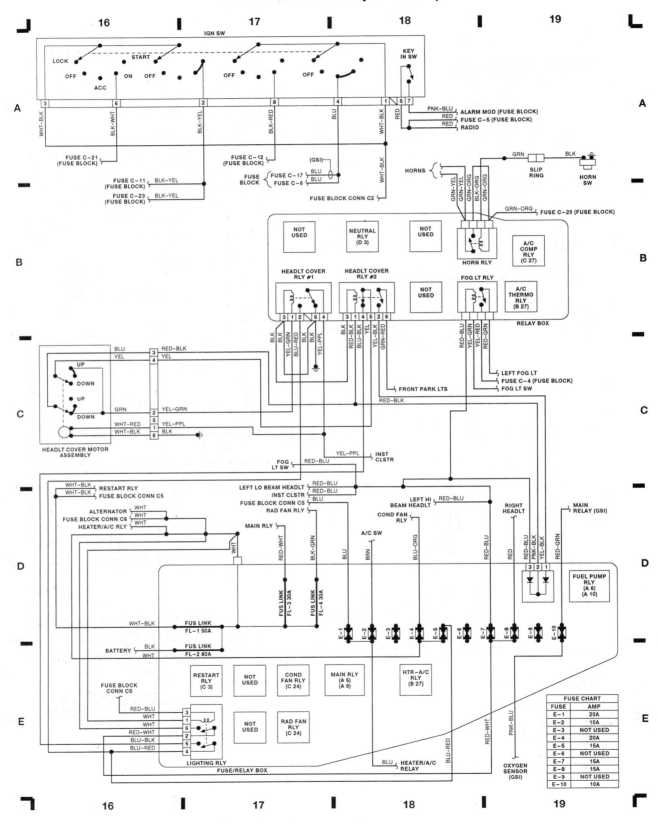

1990-91 WIRING DIAGRAMS
Geo Storm (Cont.)

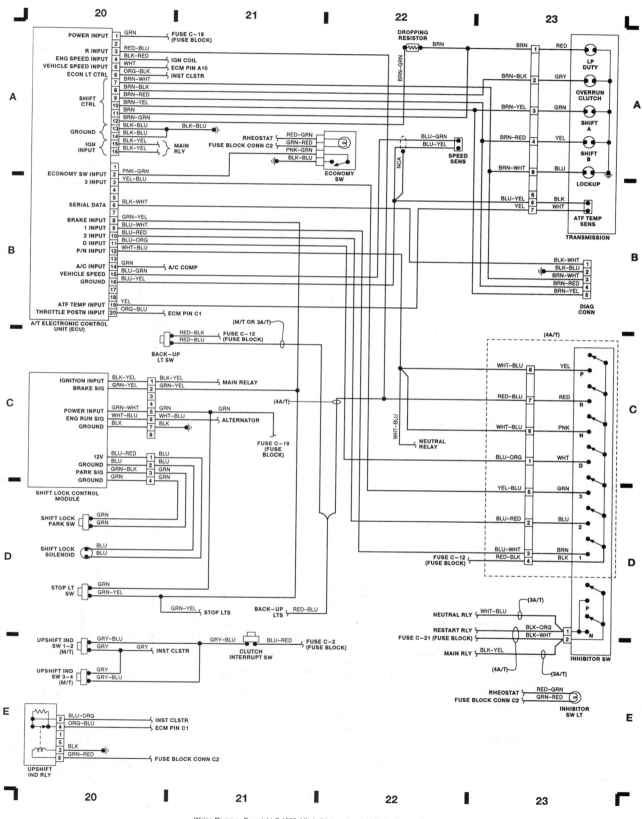

1990-91 WIRING DIAGRAMS
Geo Storm (Cont.)

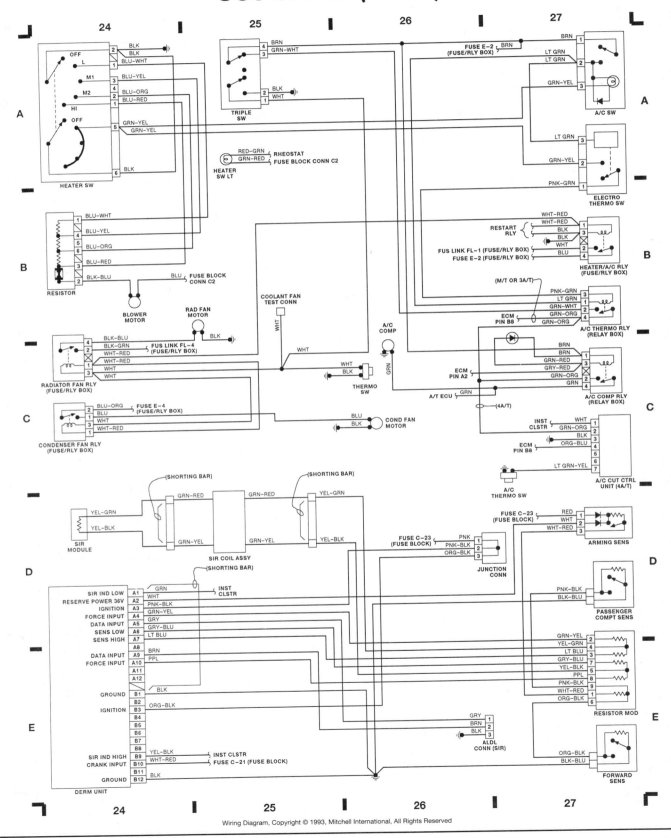

1990-91 WIRING DIAGRAMS
Geo Storm (Cont.)

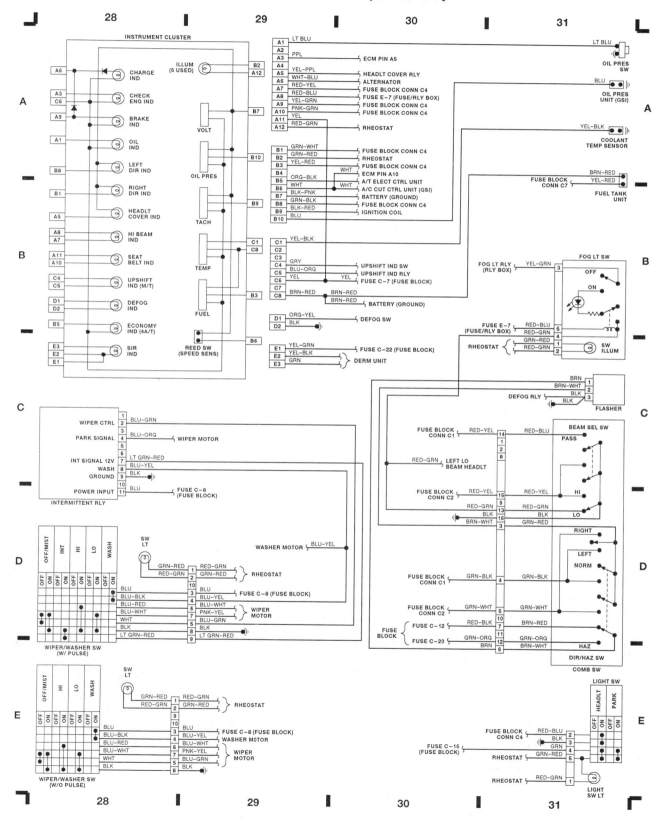

1990-91 WIRING DIAGRAMS
Geo Storm (Cont.)

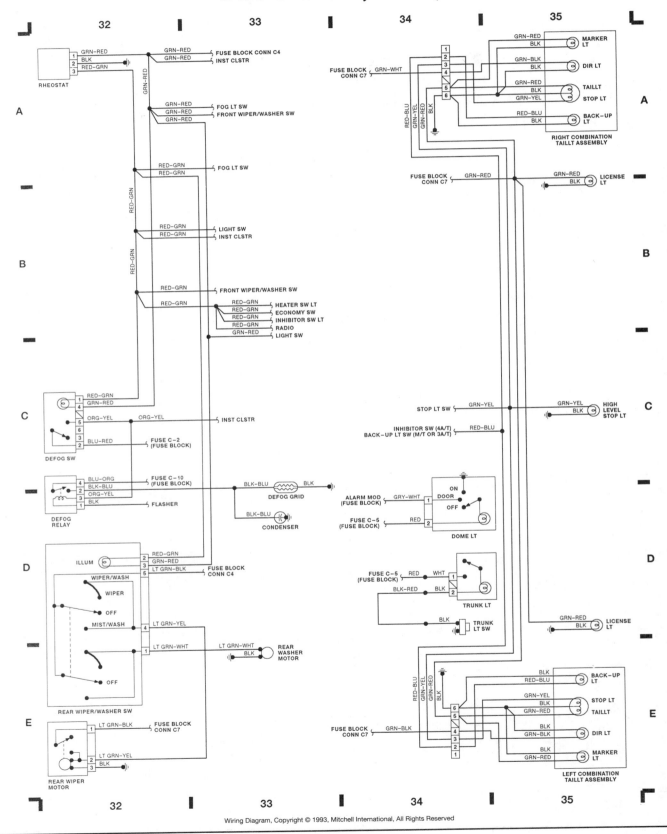

1992-93 WIRING DIAGRAMS
Geo Storm

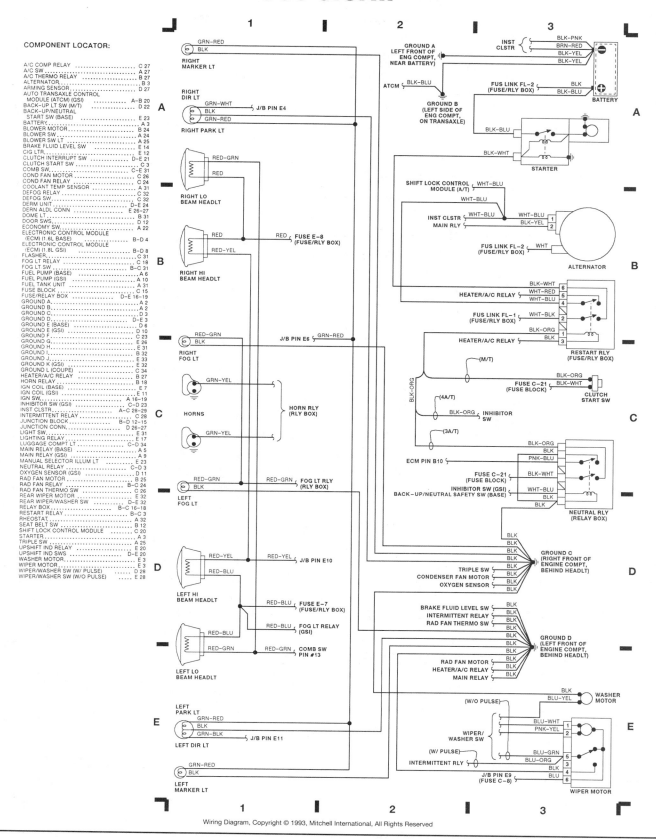

COMPONENT LOCATOR:

A/C COMP RELAY .... C 27
A/C SW .... A 27
A/C THERMO RELAY .... B 27
ALTERNATOR .... B 3
ARMING SENSOR .... D 27
AUTO TRANSAXLE CONTROL
  MODULE (ATCM) (GSI) .... A–B 20
BACK–UP LT SW (M/T) .... D 22
BACK–UP/NEUTRAL
  START SW (BASE) .... E 23
BATTERY .... A 3
BLOWER MOTOR .... B 24
BLOWER SW .... A 24
BLOWER SW LT .... A 25
BRAKE FLUID LEVEL SW .... E 14
CIG LTR. .... E 12
CLUTCH INTERRUPT SW .... D–E 21
CLUTCH START SW .... C 3
COMB SW. .... C–E 31
COND FAN MOTOR .... C 26
COND FAN RELAY .... C 24
COOLANT TEMP SENSOR .... A 31
DEFOG RELAY .... C 32
DEFOG SW .... C 32
DERM UNIT .... D–E 24
DERN ALDL CONN. .... E 26–27
DOME LT .... B 31
DOOR SWS. .... D 12
ECONOMY SW. .... A 22
ELECTRONIC CONTROL MODULE
  (ECM) (1.6L BASE) .... B–D 4
ELECTRONIC CONTROL MODULE
  (ECM) (1.8L GSI) .... B–D 8
FLASHER. .... C 31
FOG LT RELAY .... C 18
FOG LT SW .... B–C 31
FUEL PUMP (BASE) .... A 6
FUEL PUMP (GSI) .... A 10
FUEL TANK UNIT .... A 31
FUSE BLOCK .... C 15
FUSE/RELAY BOX .... D–E 16–19
GROUND A. .... A 2
GROUND B. .... A 2
GROUND C. .... D 3
GROUND D. .... D–E 3
GROUND E (BASE) .... D 6
GROUND E (GSI) .... D 10
GROUND F. .... C 23
GROUND G. .... E 26
GROUND H. .... E 31
GROUND I. .... B 32
GROUND J. .... E 33
GROUND K (GSI) .... E 32
GROUND L (COUPE) .... C 34
HEATER/A/C RELAY .... B 27
HORN RELAY .... B 18
IGN COIL (BASE) .... E 7
IGN COIL (GSI) .... E 11
IGN SW. .... A 16–19
INHIBITOR SW (GSI) .... C–D 23
INST CLSTR. .... A–C 28–29
INTERMITTENT RELAY .... C 28
JUNCTION BLOCK .... B–D 12–15
JUNCTION CONN. .... D 26–27
LIGHT SW. .... E 31
LIGHTING RELAY .... E 17
LUGGAGE COMPT LT .... C–D 34
MAIN RELAY (BASE) .... A 5
MAIN RELAY (GSI) .... A 9
MANUAL SELECTOR ILLUM LT ... E 23
NEUTRAL RELAY .... C–D 3
OXYGEN SENSOR (GSI) .... D 11
RAD FAN MOTOR .... B 25
RAD FAN RELAY .... B–C 24
RAD FAN THERMO SW .... C 26
REAR WIPER MOTOR .... E 32
REAR WIPER/WASHER SW ...... D–E 32
RELAY BOX .... B–C 16–18
RESTART RELAY .... B–C 3
RHEOSTAT. .... A 32
SEAT BELT SW .... B 12
SHIFT LOCK CONTROL MODULE ... C 20
STARTER .... A 3
TRIPLE SW .... A 25
UPSHIFT IND RELAY .... E 20
UPSHIFT IND SWS .... D–E 20
WASHER MOTOR .... E 3
WIPER MOTOR .... E 3
WIPER/WASHER SW (W/ PULSE) ... D 28
WIPER/WASHER SW (W/O PULSE) .. E 28

1992-93 WIRING DIAGRAMS
Geo Storm (Cont.)

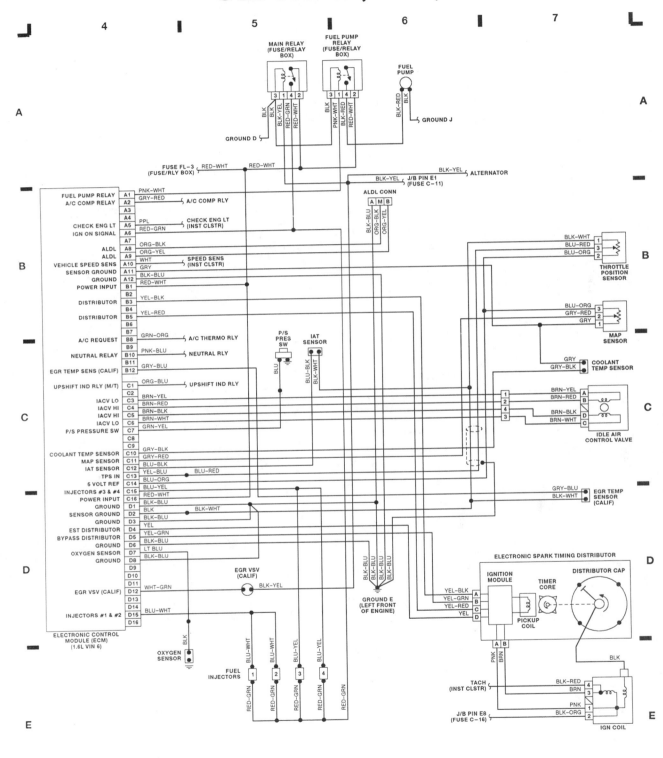

1992-93 WIRING DIAGRAMS
Geo Storm (Cont.)

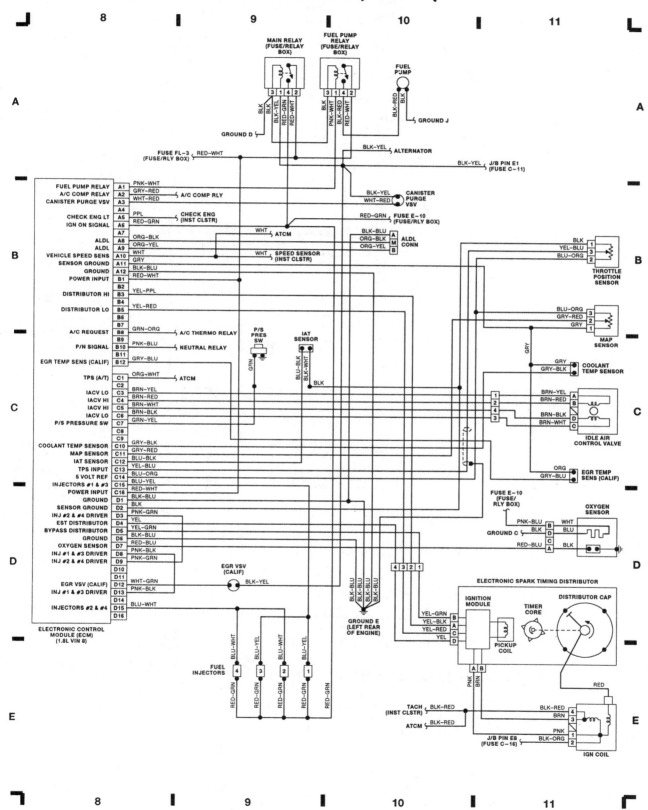

1992-93 WIRING DIAGRAMS
Geo Storm (Cont.)

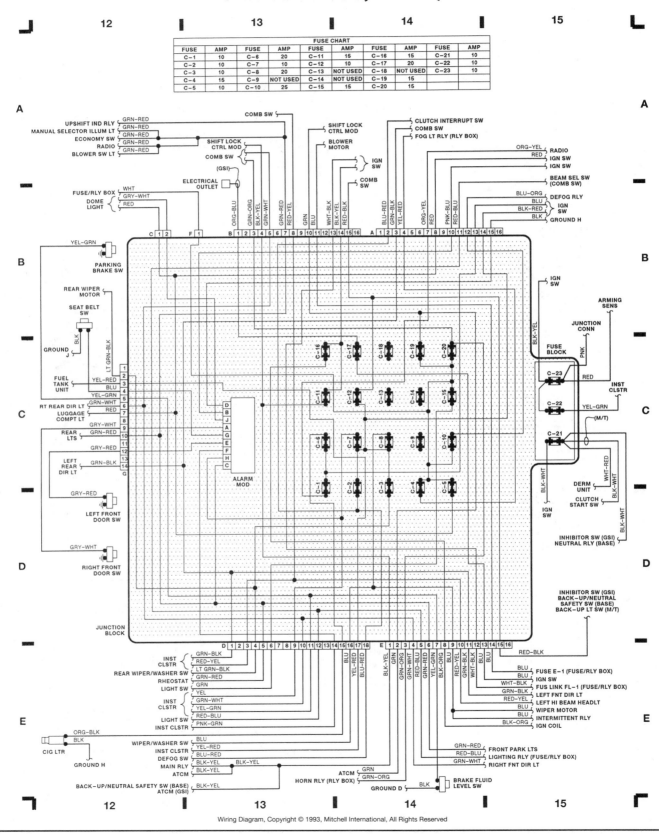

1992-93 WIRING DIAGRAMS
Geo Storm (Cont.)

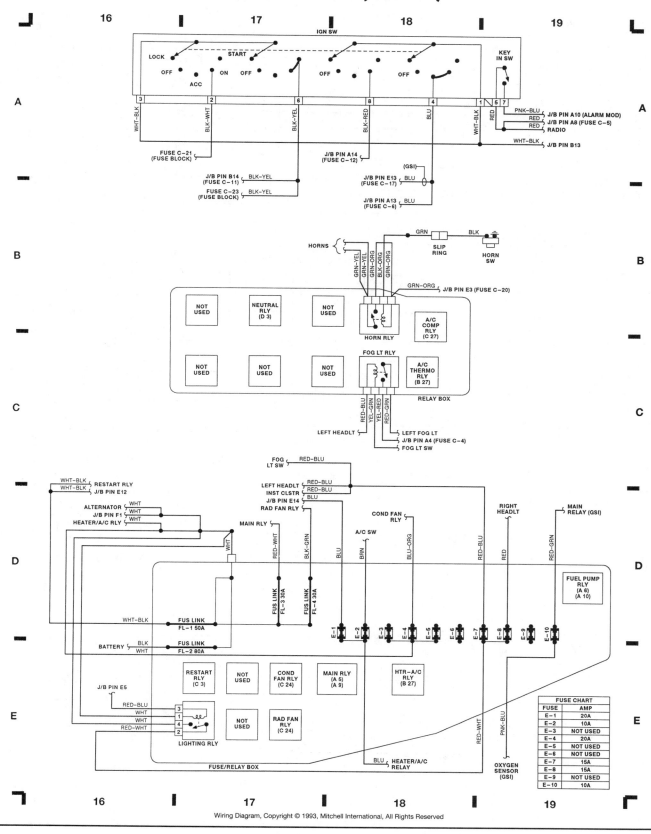

1992-93 WIRING DIAGRAMS
Geo Storm (Cont.)

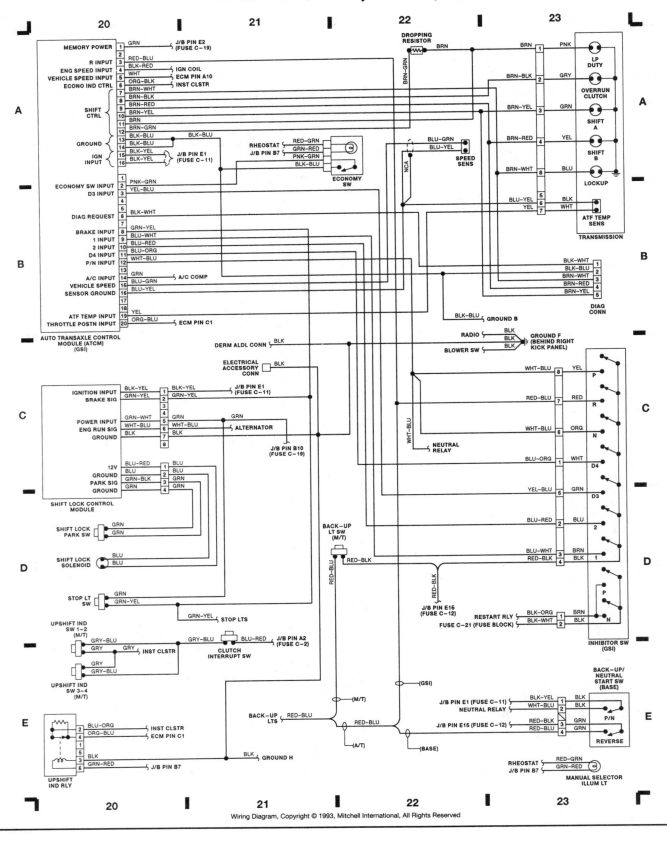

1992-93 WIRING DIAGRAMS
Geo Storm (Cont.)

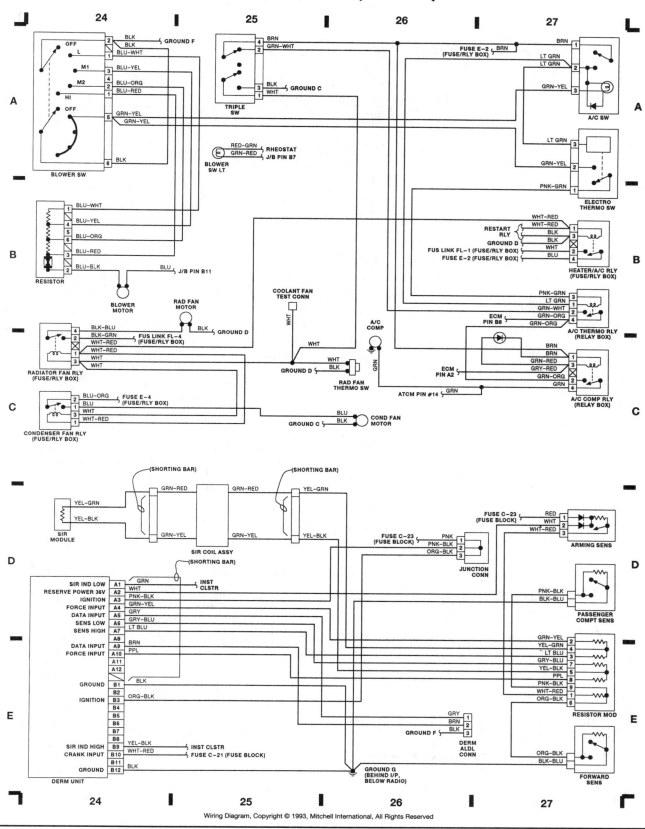

1992-93 WIRING DIAGRAMS
Geo Storm (Cont.)

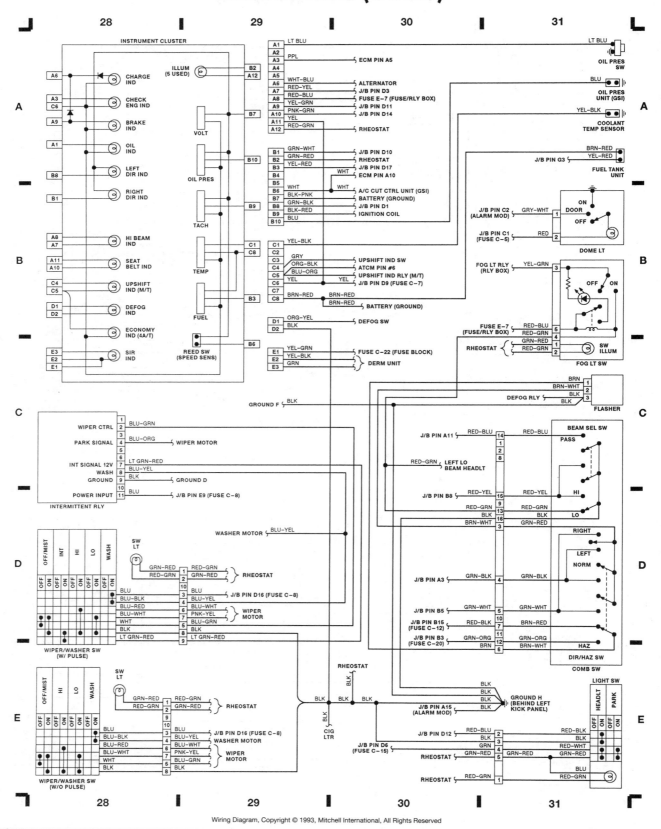

1992-93 WIRING DIAGRAMS
Geo Storm (Cont.)

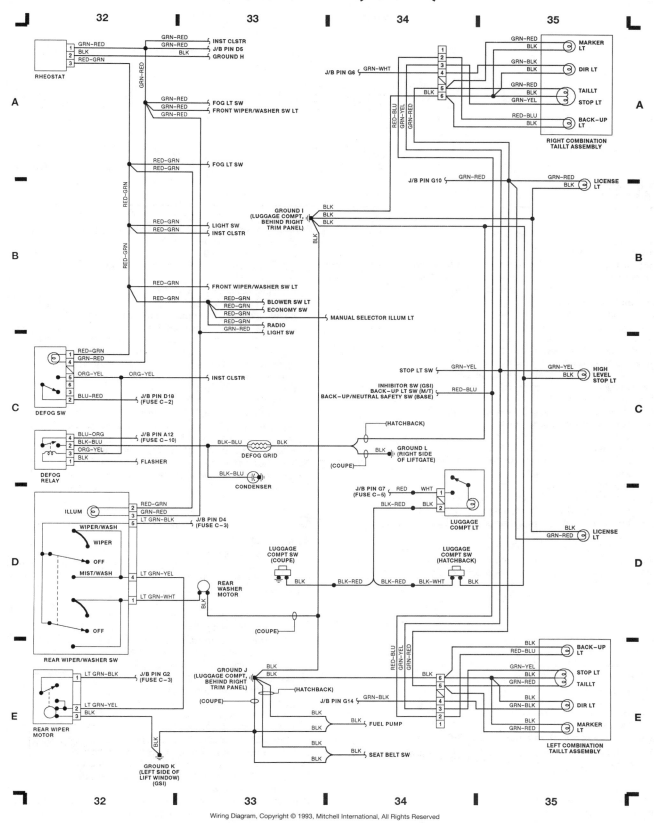

Index

Index

Index

Index

HAYNES AUTOMOTIVE MANUALS

NOTE: New manuals are added to this list on a periodic basis. If you do not see a listing for your vehicle, consult your local Haynes dealer for the latest product information.

ACURA
1776   **Integra & Legend** '86 thru '90

AMC
        Jeep CJ – see JEEP (412)
694   **Mid-size models,** Concord, Hornet, Gremlin & Spirit '70 thru '83
934   **(Renault) Alliance & Encore** all models '83 thru '87

AUDI
615   **4000** all models '80 thru '87
428   **5000** all models '77 thru '83
1117   **5000** all models '84 thru '88

AUSTIN
        Healey Sprite – see MG Midget Roadster (265)

BMW
276   **320i** all 4 cyl models '75 thru '83
632   **528i & 530i** all models '75 thru '80
240   **1500 thru 2002** all models except Turbo '59 thru '77
348   **2500, 2800, 3.0 & Bavaria** '69 thru '76

BUICK
        Century (front wheel drive) – see GENERAL MOTORS A-Cars (829)
*1627   **Buick, Oldsmobile & Pontiac Full-size** (Front wheel drive) all models '85 thru '93
        Buick Electra, LeSabre and Park Avenue; **Oldsmobile** Delta 88 Royale, Ninety Eight and Regency; **Pontiac** Bonneville
*1551   **Buick Oldsmobile & Pontiac Full-size (Rear wheel drive)**
        Buick Electra '70 thru '84, Estate '70 thru '90, LeSabre '70 thru '79
        Oldsmobile Custom Cruiser '70 thru '90, Delta 88 '70 thru '85, Ninety-eight '70 thru '84
        Pontiac Bonneville '70 thru '81, Catalina '70 thru '81, Grandville '70 thru '75, Parisienne '84 thru '86
627   **Mid-size** all rear-drive **Regal & Century** models with V6, V8 and Turbo '74 thru '87
        Regal – see GENERAL MOTORS (1671)
        Skyhawk – see GENERAL MOTORS J-Cars (766)
552   **Skylark** all X-car models '80 thru '85

CADILLAC
*751   **Cadillac Rear Wheel Drive** all gasoline models '70 thru '90
        Cimarron – see GENERAL MOTORS J-Cars (766)

CAPRI
296   **2000 MK I Coupe** all models '71 thru '75
205   **2600 & 2800 V6 Coupe** '71 thru '75
375   **2800 Mk II V6 Coupe** '75 thru '78
        Mercury Capri – see FORD Mustang (654)

CHEVROLET
*1477   **Astro & GMC Safari Mini-vans** all models '85 thru '91
554   **Camaro V8** all models '70 thru '81
*866   **Camaro** all models '82 thru '91
        Cavalier – see GENERAL MOTORS J-Cars (766)
        Celebrity – see GENERAL MOTORS A-Cars (829)
625   **Chevelle, Malibu & El Camino** all V6 & V8 models '69 thru '87
449   **Chevette & Pontiac T1000** all models '76 thru '87
550   **Citation** all models '80 thru '85
*1628   **Corsica/Beretta** all models '87 thru '92
274   **Corvette** all V8 models '68 thru '82
*1336   **Corvette** all models '84 thru '91

704   **Full-size Sedans** Caprice, Impala, Biscayne, Bel Air & Wagons, all V6 & V8 models '69 thru '90
        Lumina – see GENERAL MOTORS (1671)
        Lumina APV – see GENERAL MOTORS (2035)
319   **Luv Pick-up** all 2WD & 4WD models '72 thru '82
626   **Monte Carlo** all V6, V8 & Turbo models '70 thru '88
241   **Nova** all V8 models '69 thru '79
*1642   **Nova and Geo Prizm** all front wheel drive models, '85 thru '90
*420   **Pick-ups '67 thru '87** – Chevrolet & GMC, all full-size models '67 thru '87; Suburban, Blazer & Jimmy '67 thru '91
*1664   **Pick-ups '88 thru '92** – Chevrolet & GMC all full-size (C and K) models, '88 thru '92
*1727   **Sprint & Geo Metro** '85 thru '91
*831   **S-10 & GMC S-15 Pick-ups** all models '82 thru '92
*345   **Vans** – Chevrolet & GMC, V8 & in-line 6 cyl models '68 thru '92

CHRYSLER
*1337   **Chrysler & Plymouth Mid-size** front wheel drive '82 thru '89
        K-Cars – see DODGE Aries (723)
        Laser – see DODGE Daytona (1140)

DATSUN
402   **200SX** all models '77 thru '79
647   **200SX** all models '80 thru '83
228   **B-210** all models '73 thru '78
525   **210** all models '78 thru '82
206   **240Z, 260Z & 280Z** Coupe & 2+2 '70 thru '78
563   **280ZX** Coupe & 2+2 '79 thru '83
        300ZX – see NISSAN (1137)
679   **310** all models '78 thru '82
123   **510 & PL521 Pick-up** '68 thru '73
430   **510** all models '78 thru '81
372   **610** all models '72 thru '76
277   **620 Series Pick-up** all models '73 thru '79
        720 Series Pick-up – see NISSAN Pick-ups (771)
376   **810/Maxima** all gasoline models '77 thru '84
124   **1200** all models '70 thru '73
368   **F10** all models '76 thru '79
        Pulsar – see NISSAN (876)
        Sentra – see NISSAN (982)
        Stanza – see NISSAN (981)

DODGE
*723   **Aries & Plymouth Reliant** all models '81 thru '89
*1231   **Caravan & Plymouth Voyager Mini-Vans** all models '84 thru '91
699   **Challenger & Plymouth Saporro** all models '78 thru '83
236   **Colt** all models '71 thru '77
610   **Colt & Plymouth Champ (front wheel drive)** all models '78 thru '87
*556   **D50/Ram 50/Plymouth Arrow Pick-ups & Raider** '79 thru '91
*1668   **Dakota Pick-up** all models '87 thru '90
234   **Dart & Plymouth Valiant** all 6 cyl models '67 thru '76
*1140   **Daytona & Chrysler Laser** all models '84 thru '89
*545   **Omni & Plymouth Horizon** all models '78 thru '90
*912   **Pick-ups** all full-size models '74 thru '91
*1726   **Shadow & Plymouth Sundance** '87 thru '91
*1779   **Spirit & Plymouth Acclaim** '89 thru '92
*349   **Vans – Dodge & Plymouth** V8 & 6 cyl models '71 thru '91

FIAT
094   **124 Sport Coupe & Spider** '68 thru '78

479   **Strada** all models '79 thru '82
273   **X1/9** all models '74 thru '80

FORD
*1476   **Aerostar Mini-vans** all models '86 thru '92
788   **Bronco and Pick-ups** '73 thru '79
*880   **Bronco and Pick-ups** '80 thru '91
268   **Courier Pick-up** all models '72 thru '82
789   **Escort & Mercury Lynx** all models '81 thru '90
*2046   **Escort & Mercury Tracer** all models '91 thru '93
*2021   **Explorer & Mazda Navajo** '91 thru '92
560   **Fairmont & Mercury Zephyr** all in-line & V8 models '78 thru '83
334   **Fiesta** all models '77 thru '80
754   **Ford & Mercury Full-size,** Ford LTD & Mercury Marquis ('75 thru '82); Ford Custom 500, Country Squire, Crown Victoria & Mercury Colony Park ('75 thru '87); Ford LTD Crown Victoria & Mercury Gran Marquis ('83 thru '87)
359   **Granada & Mercury Monarch** all in-line, 6 cyl & V8 models '75 thru '80
773   **Ford & Mercury Mid-size,** Ford Thunderbird & Mercury Cougar ('75 thru '82); Ford LTD & Mercury Marquis ('83 thru '86); Ford Torino, Gran Torino, Elite, Ranchero pick-up, LTD II, Mercury Montego, Comet, XR-7 & Lincoln Versailles ('75 thru '86)
*654   **Mustang & Mercury Capri** all models including Turbo '79 thru '92
357   **Mustang V8** all models '64-1/2 thru '73
231   **Mustang II** all 4 cyl, V6 & V8 models '74 thru '78
649   **Pinto & Mercury Bobcat** all models '75 thru '80
*1670   **Probe** all models '89 thru '92
*1026   **Ranger & Bronco II** all gasoline models '83 thru '92
*1421   **Taurus & Mercury Sable** '86 thru '92
*1418   **Tempo & Mercury Topaz** all gasoline models '84 thru '91
1338   **Thunderbird & Mercury Cougar/XR7** '83 thru '88
*1725   **Thunderbird & Mercury Cougar** '89 and '90
*344   **Vans** all V8 Econoline models '69 thru '91

GENERAL MOTORS
*829   **A-Cars** – Chevrolet Celebrity, Buick Century, Pontiac 6000 & Oldsmobile Cutlass Ciera all models '82 thru '90
*766   **J-Cars** – Chevrolet Cavalier, Pontiac J-2000, Oldsmobile Firenza, Buick Skyhawk & Cadillac Cimarron all models '82 thru '92
*1420   **N-Cars** – Buick Somerset '85 thru '87; Pontiac Grand Am and Oldsmobile Calais '85 thru '91; Buick Skylark '86 thru '91
*1671   **GM: Buick** Regal, **Chevrolet** Lumina, **Oldsmobile** Cutlass Supreme, **Pontiac** Grand Prix, all front wheel drive models '88 thru '90
*2035   **GM: Chevrolet Lumina APV, Oldsmobile Silhouette, Pontiac Trans Sport** '90 thru '92

GEO
        Metro – see CHEVROLET Sprint (1727)
        Prizm – see CHEVROLET Nova (1642)
        Tracker – see SUZUKI Samurai (1626)

GMC
        Safari – see CHEVROLET ASTRO (1477)
        Vans & Pick-ups – see CHEVROLET (420, 831, 345, 1664)

(continued on next page)

---

* Listings shown with an asterisk (*) indicate model coverage as of this printing. These titles will be periodically updated to include later model years – consult your Haynes dealer for more information.

Haynes North America, Inc., 861 Lawrence Drive, Newbury Park, CA 91320 • (805) 498-6703

629.287 H GEO
Geo Storm automotive repair

als are added to this list on a periodic basis. If you do not see a listing for your vehicle,
consult your local Haynes dealer for the latest product information.

HONDA
351	**Accord CVCC** all models '76 thru '83
*1221	**Accord** all models '84 thru '89
160	**Civic 1200** all models '73 thru '79
633	**Civic 1300 & 1500 CVCC** all models '80 thru '83
297	**Civic 1500 CVCC** all models '75 thru '79
*1227	**Civic** all models '84 thru '91
*601	**Prelude CVCC** all models '79 thru '89

HYUNDAI
*1552	**Excel** all models '86 thru '91

ISUZU
*1641	**Trooper & Pick-up**, all gasoline models '81 thru '91

JAGUAR
*242	**XJ6** all 6 cyl models '68 thru '86
*478	**XJ12 & XJS** all 12 cyl models '72 thru '85

JEEP
*1553	**Cherokee, Comanche & Wagoneer Limited** all models '84 thru '91
412	**CJ** all models '49 thru '86
*1777	**Wrangler** all models '87 thru '92

LADA
*413	**1200, 1300. 1500 & 1600** all models including Riva '74 thru '86

MAZDA
648	**626** Sedan & Coupe (rear wheel drive) all models '79 thru '82
1082	**626 & MX-6 (front wheel drive)** all models '83 thru '91
370	**GLC Hatchback (rear wheel drive)** all models '77 thru '83
757	**GLC (front wheel drive)** all models '81 thru '86
*2047	**MPV** '89 thru '93
	Navajo – see FORD Explorer (2021)
*267	**Pick-ups** '72 thru '92
460	**RX-7** all models '79 thru '85
*1419	**RX-7** all models '86 thru '91

MERCEDES-BENZ
*1643	**190 Series** all four-cylinder gasoline models, '84 thru '88
346	**230, 250 & 280** Sedan, Coupe & Roadster all 6 cyl sohc models '68 thru '72
983	**280 123 Series** all gasoline models '77 thru '81
698	**350 & 450** Sedan, Coupe & Roadster all models '71 thru '80
697	**Diesel 123 Series** 200D, 220D, 240D, 240TD, 300D, 300CD, 300TD, 4- & 5-cyl incl. Turbo '76 thru '85

MERCURY
*For all PLYMOUTH titles
see FORD Listing*

MG
111	**MGB** Roadster & GT Coupe all models '62 thru '80
265	**MG Midget & Austin Healey Sprite** Roadster '58 thru '80

MITSUBISHI
*1669	**Cordia, Tredia, Galant, Precis & Mirage** '83 thru '90
*2022	**Pick-ups & Montero** '83 thru '91

MORRIS
074	**(Austin) Marina 1.8** all models '71 thru '80
024	**Minor 1000** sedan & wagon '56 thru '71

NISSAN
1137	**300ZX** all Turbo & non-Turbo models '84 thru '89
*1341	**Maxima** all models '85 thru '91
*771	**Pick-ups/Pathfinder** gas models '80 thru '91
*876	**Pulsar** all models '83 thru '86
*982	**Sentra** all models '82 thru '90
*981	**Stanza** all models '82 thru '90

OLDSMOBILE
	Custom Cruiser – see BUICK Full-size (1551)
658	**Cutlass** all standard gasoline V6 & V8 models '74 thru '88
	Cutlass Ciera – see GENERAL MOTORS A-Cars (829)
	Cutlass Supreme – see GENERAL MOTORS (1671)
	Firenza – see GENERAL MOTORS J-Cars (766)
	Ninety-eight – see BUICK Full-size (1551)
	Omega – see PONTIAC Phoenix & Omega (551)
	Silhouette – see GENERAL MOTORS (2035)

PEUGEOT
663	**504** all diesel models '74 thru '83

PLYMOUTH
*For all PLYMOUTH titles,
see DODGE listing.*

PONTIAC
	T1000 – see CHEVROLET Chevette (449)
	J-2000 – see GENERAL MOTORS J-Cars (766)
	6000 – see GENERAL MOTORS A-Cars (829)
1232	**Fiero** all models '84 thru '88
555	**Firebird** all V8 models except Turbo '70 thru '81
*867	**Firebird** all models '82 thru '91
	Full-size Rear Wheel Drive – see Buick, Oldsmobile, Pontiac Full-size (1551)
	Grand Prix – see GENERAL MOTORS (1671)
551	**Phoenix & Oldsmobile Omega** all X-car models '80 thru '84
	Trans Sport – see GENERAL MOTORS (2035)

PORSCHE
*264	**911** all Coupe & Targa models except Turbo & Carrera 4 '65 thru '89
239	**914** all 4 cyl models '69 thru '76
397	**924** all models including Turbo '76 thru '82
*1027	**944** all models including Turbo '83 thru '89

RENAULT
141	**5 Le Car** all models '76 thru '83
079	**8 & 10** all models with 58.4 cu in engines '62 thru '72
097	**12 Saloon & Estate** all models 1289 cc engines '70 thru '80
768	**15 & 17** all models '73 thru '79
081	**16** all models 89.7 cu in & 95.5 cu in engines '65 thru '72
	Alliance & Encore – see AMC (934)

SAAB
247	**99** all models including Turbo '69 thru '80
*980	**900** all models including Turbo '79 thru '88

SUBARU
237	**1100, 1300, 1400 & 1600** all models '71 thru '79
*681	**1600 & 1800** 2WD & 4WD all models '80 thru '89

SUZUKI
*1626	**Samurai/Sidekick and Geo Tracker** all models '86 thru '91

TOYOTA
*1023	**Camry** all models '83 thru '91
150	**Carina Sedan** all models '71 thru '74
*2038	**Celica** Front Wheel Drive '86 thru '92
935	**Celica** Rear Wheel Drive '71 thru '85
*1139	**Celica Supra** '79 thru '92
361	**Corolla** all models '75 thru '79
961	**Corolla** all models (rear wheel drive) '80 thru '87
*1025	**Corolla** all models (front wheel drive) '84 thru '91
*636	**Corolla Tercel** all models '80 thru '82
230	**Corona & MK II** all 4 cyl sohc models '69 thru '74
360	**Corona** all models '74 thru '82
*532	**Cressida** all models '78 thru '82
313	**Land Cruiser** all models '68 thru '82
200	**MK II** all 6 cyl models '72 thru '76
*1339	**MR2** all models '85 thru '87
304	**Pick-up** all models '69 thru '78
*656	**Pick-up** all models '79 thru '92

TRIUMPH
112	**GT6 & Vitesse** all models '62 thru '74
113	**Spitfire** all models '62 thru '81
322	**TR7** all models '75 thru '81

VW
159	**Beetle & Karmann Ghia** all models '54 thru '79
238	**Dasher** all gasoline models '74 thru '81
*884	**Rabbit, Jetta, Scirocco, & Pick-up** all gasoline models '74 thru '91 & Convertible '80 thru '91
451	**Rabbit, Jetta & Pick-up** all diesel models '77 thru '84
082	**Transporter 1600** all models '68 thru '79
226	**Transporter 1700, 1800 & 2000** all models '72 thru '79
084	**Type 3 1500 & 1600** all models '63 thru '73
1029	**Vanagon** all air-cooled models '80 thru '83

VOLVO
203	**120, 130 Series & 1800 Sports** '61 thru '73
129	**140 Series** all models '66 thru '74
*270	**240 Series** all models '74 thru '90
400	**260 Series** all models '75 thru '82
*1550	**740 & 760 Series** all models '82 thru '88

SPECIAL MANUALS
1479	**Automotive Body Repair & Painting Manual**
1654	**Automotive Electrical Manual**
1480	**Automotive Heating & Air Conditioning Manual**
1762	**Chevrolet Engine Overhaul Manual**
1736	**Diesel Engine Repair Manual**
1667	**Emission Control Manual**
1763	**Ford Engine Overhaul Manual**
482	**Fuel Injection Manual**
1666	**Small Engine Repair Manual**
299	**SU Carburetors** thru '88
393	**Weber Carburetors** thru '79
300	**Zenith/Stromberg CD Carburetors** thru '76

See your dealer for other available titles

* Listings shown with an asterisk (*) indicate model coverage as of this printing. These titles will be periodically updated to include later model years - consult your Haynes dealer for more information.

Over 100 Haynes
motorcycle manuals
also available

Haynes North America, Inc., 861 Lawrence Drive, Newbury Park, CA 91320 • (805) 498-6703